Transformative Role of Hypnotherapy for Business Professionals

Manjunath B.R.
https://orcid.org/0000-0002-5773-748X
Tecnologico de Monterrey, Mexico

Syed Mohammad Haider Rizvi
Shoolini University, India

Jeni Kakadiya
https://orcid.org/0009-0002-8143-1859
Shoolini University, India

IGI Global
Scientific Publishing
Publishing Tomorrow's Research Today

Vice President of Editorial	Melissa Wagner
Director of Acquisitions	Mikaela Felty
Director of Book Development	Jocelynn Hessler
Production Manager	Mike Brehm
Cover Design	Jose Rosado

Published in the United States of America by
IGI Global Scientific Publishing
701 East Chocolate Avenue
Hershey, PA, 17033, USA
Tel: 717-533-8845 | Fax: 717-533-7115
Website: https://www.igi-global.com E-mail: cust@igi-global.com

Library of Congress Cataloging-in-Publication Data

Names: Manjunath R., 1985- editor | Rizvi, Syed, 1971- editor | Kakadiya, Jeni, 2001- editor
Title: Transformative role of hypnotherapy for business professionals / [edited by] Manjunath B.R., Syed Rizvi, Jeni Kakadiya.
Description: Hershey, PA : IGI Global Scientific Publishing, [2026] | Includes bibliographical references and index. | Summary: "This book aims to explore how hypnotherapy can effectively manage workplace stress, enhance resilience, and improve overall mental well-being for business professionals"-- Provided by publisher.
Identifiers: LCCN 2025018892 (print) | LCCN 2025018893 (ebook) | ISBN 9798337323176 hardcover | ISBN 9798337323183 paperback | ISBN 9798337323190 ebook
Subjects: LCSH: Hypnotism--Therapeutic use | Job stress | Mental health
Classification: LCC RC495 .T735 2025 (print) | LCC RC495 (ebook) | DDC 615.8/512--dc23/eng/20250730
LC record available at https://lccn.loc.gov/2025018892
LC ebook record available at https://lccn.loc.gov/2025018893
British Cataloguing in Publication Data
A Cataloguing in Publication record for this book is available from the British Library.

Editorial Advisory Board

Table of Contents

Detailed Table of Contents

The hybrid work paradigm has transformed the traditional workplace, combining remote and in-office presence to provide greater freedom and flexibility without compromising efficiency. However, this shift has created substantial issues for business professionals. This chapter examines the psychological, emotional, and physiological impacts of prolonged job stress in the hybrid work culture. The chapter also covers ways for reducing stress and increasing long-term productivity. It emphasizes the value of self-regulation, boundary-setting, and mindfulness techniques in developing resilience in business workers. This chapter presents a system of knowledge for stress management in a hybrid workplace by combining empirical studies and real-world situations. The findings highlight the importance for organizations to take proactive steps to improve employee well-being while retaining operational efficiency. Finally, this chapter contributes to the area of workplace mental health by providing evidence-based recommendations for creating a productive hybrid work culture.

Mindfulness-based restorative practices—guided imagery, relaxation, and Yoga Nidra—are explored as integrative approaches to reduce work-related psychophysiological stress. The chapter conceptualizes stress through psychobiological and appraisal frameworks, emphasizing chronic allostatic load across healthcare, corporate, and gig sectors. Models like demand–control–support and effort–reward imbalance explain how digital, performance-driven environments sustain autonomic dysregulation. These practices promote nonjudgmental awareness and parasympathetic activation through breath regulation, imagery, and deep rest. Integrating contemplative traditions with neuroscientific findings on heart rate variability, cortisol, EEG, and emotion regulation, the chapter reviews mechanisms, outcomes, and design models. It concludes with recommendations for standardized, scalable, and sustainable workplace applications.

The contemporary information technology sector is dominated by substantial workloads, relentless pressure, incessant demands, rapid advancements, and swift innovations. In corporate information technology, professionals often endure prolonged stress, which can substantially affect their mental and physical well-being. This chapter examines the neurological, physiological, and behavioural effects of stress on individuals employed in the information technology sector. Despite the growing popularity of hypnosis and hypnotherapy in recent years, the impact of hypnosis on individuals' emotional responses to stress remains uncertain. This chapter, possess a comprehensive understanding of the neurological, physiological, and behavioural ramifications of stress on those employed in the information technology sector. It will significantly influence policy formulation, workplace interventions, and future research endeavours. Furthermore, it will elucidate the research deficiencies present in the field and demonstrate how hypnotherapy can enhance stress management and cognitive resilience.

This chapter explores hypnotherapy as an effective psychological intervention for addressing performance anxiety, perfectionism, and fear of failure among corporate professionals. These issues are common in competitive workplace environments and negatively impact productivity, emotional well-being, decision-making, and innovation, leading to burnout and reduced organizational effectiveness. Although cognitive-behavioral therapies have been widely used for such problems, they only address surface-level cognitions and miss the subconscious factors that sustain these patterns. Hypnotherapy focuses on modifying subconscious processes through guided relaxation, concentration, and suggestion. In corporate settings, hypnotherapy can enhance concentration, creativity, confidence, and adaptive coping, leading to higher job satisfaction, engagement, and productivity. This chapter synthesizes clinical research, psychological theory, and organizational applications, highlighting hypnotherapy's relevance for workplace mental health, leadership development, and sustainable performance outcomes.

Modern business settings demand sustained cognitive and emotional effort, often causing stress, burnout, and inconsistent results, even for skilled workers. Traditional organizational strategies mainly target conscious methods, which may provide only limited, short-term improvements. This chapter, informed by cognitive psychology, neuroscience, and clinical hypnotherapy, argues that much of professional performance is governed by subconscious processes, such as automatic stress reactions, implicit beliefs, and emotional conditioning. It introduces the Subconscious Performance Alignment Model, which suggests that lasting performance depends on aligning subconscious regulation with conscious task demands. Hypnotherapy is presented as an ethical, evidence-based approach to recalibrating subconscious mechanisms, thus enhancing executive functioning under pressure. Moving the focus from effort-based improvement to regulation aligned with subconscious processes, this chapter offers a fresh perspective to organizational psychology and sustainable performance at work.

This chapter explores how subconscious cognitive and emotional processes influence executive judgment and leadership effectiveness, especially in complex and uncertain conditions. It applies dual-process models of cognition and draws on research from cognitive psychology, neuroscience, and leadership studies. The chapter highlights hypnotherapy as a scientifically supported method for engaging and influencing subconscious processes that affect leadership performance. It covers the neurocognitive basis of hypnotherapy, reviews evidence on attention control, emotional regulation, stress management, and cognitive flexibility, and discusses its use in executive coaching and leadership development. Ethical and professional standards are also considered to ensure responsible application within organizations. Overall, hypnotherapy is presented as a credible, evidence-based tool for improving decision-making and leadership skills.

The purpose of this chapter is to explore, identify and explain various strategies that can be integrated into corporate wellness programs using self-hypnosis or hypnotherapy interventions. Also, how these strategies will take the organization as well as employees to the path of transformation by 'Being Self-aware', to resolve psychological and physiological issues and also act as preventive care. How self-awareness via practices of self-hypnosis or hypnotherapy can help evolve individuals as well as organizations to a better today and tomorrow.

This chapter aims to reframe gifted education not as identification and extraction but as ecological design. Instead of retrofitting rigid structures through differentiation or enrichment, we propose an alternative architecture that operates in parallel to traditional schooling. This architecture is fluid, permeable, and responsive to developmental variation. It builds environments. This chapter argues that the persistent challenges in educating gifted and twice-exceptional learners arise not from deficiencies in everyday instructional practice but from a fundamental misalignment embedded in the structure and design of educational systems.

This chapter examines the spiritual resilience and professional achievement, arguing that sustained performance in demanding environments depends on factors beyond effort, skills, and measurable outcomes. In high-pressure contexts marked by constant evaluation and emotional strain, stability often arises from intangible factors such as meaning, belonging, and intrinsic motivation. Spiritual resilience is thus conceptualized at the intersection of workplace spirituality and social belongingness. Grounded in existential theory and resilience research, the model draws on Frankl's view that meaning renders adversity bearable and Bandura's emphasis on agency

Foreword

In a time marked by rapid technological advances, high performance demands, and continuous digital connectivity, workplace stress has become a major challenge for modern workers. This is especially true in the information technology industry, where cognitive overload, long hours, fast-changing skills, and ongoing performance assessments are common. In this context, '*Hypnotherapy for IT Professionals: A Path to Stress-Free Work-Life Harmony*' offers an important and timely addition to discussions on workplace mental health and human performance.

Edited by Dr. Manjunath B. R., Dr. Syed Mohammad Haider Rizvi, and Ms. Jeni Kakadiya, this volume features a carefully selected mix of scholarly and practical chapters. It investigates hypnotherapy as a scientifically based and practically useful method for managing stress, burnout, and performance anxiety in high-pressure workplaces. The book views hypnotherapy not as a minor or alternative approach but as an integrative psychological tool that can complement current methods in organizational behavior, occupational health, and corporate wellness.

The initial chapters lay a solid conceptual and scientific groundwork by placing workplace stress in the context of the IT industry's specific challenges and explaining the core principles, mechanisms, and ethical aspects of hypnotherapy. By anchoring therapeutic techniques in well-established psychological theories and psychophysiological research, the book effectively links clinical insight with practical organizational use. This foundation helps readers understand hypnotherapy as both an evidence-based method and a scalable intervention suitable for professional environments.

Going beyond theory, the book provides a detailed examination of hypnotherapeutic techniques for combating stress, emotional fatigue, and burnout. Contributors demonstrate how methods such as guided imagery, subconscious reframing, relaxation exercises, and mindfulness-based restoration can be tailored to meet the cognitive and emotional needs of IT professionals. A key focus is the mind–body connection, illustrating how persistent psychological stress can lead to physical discomfort, reduced productivity, and diminished quality of life, and how specific hypnotherapeutic strategies can mitigate these effects.

This volume's key strength is its emphasis on resilience, work–life balance, and sustainable professional functioning. Instead of viewing stress management as a quick fix, it highlights long-term psychological adaptability, emotional intelligence, and self-awareness. Chapters on corporate wellness and leadership development expand the focus from personal well-being to organizational responsibility, providing practical insights for HR professionals, wellness designers, and leaders aiming to create healthier, more resilient workplaces.

The latter parts of the book deepen the discussion by exploring performance optimization, subconscious leadership conditioning, and overall human potential. Addressing topics like perfectionism, fear of failure, giftedness, and spiritual resilience, the text recognizes the intricate inner framework supporting professional success. These future-oriented debates present hypnotherapy as a useful method not just for stress relief, but also for boosting performance consciously and fostering career growth aligned with one's identity.

This edited collection stands out because of the editors' comprehensive perspective. By blending scientific rigor, therapeutic techniques, organizational insights, and forward-looking reflections, they create a work that appeals to academics, practitioners, and professionals dealing with modern work environments. The book does not promote hypnotherapy as a universal fix but presents it as a versatile, ethically responsible, and context-aware method for improving well-being in challenging workplace settings.

As organizations more often view mental health and resilience as key strategic priorities, this book offers valuable insights into how subconscious interventions can enhance structural and policy-based efforts. Hypnotherapy for IT Professionals: A Path to Stress-Free Work-Life Harmony aims to significantly advance research, practice, and professional development in psychology, organizational behavior, and workplace wellness.

Bhupendra Palan
Institute for Mind-Body Healing, India

Preface

The modern professional and organizational environment is experiencing significant change due to fast technological progress, increased competition, and shifting performance demands. Today, business professionals work in settings marked by cognitive overload, constant connectivity, shorter decision-making cycles, and greater accountability. Although digital tools and analytics have improved efficiency and expanded reach, they also contribute to higher stress levels, burnout, emotional exhaustion, and performance anxiety among workers. In this climate, psychological resilience and inner flexibility are now essential for maintaining long-term professional success.

For many years, organizations have primarily relied on cognitive, behavioral, and surface-level stress-management techniques to address workplace challenges. Although effective, these methods often neglect the deeper subconscious processes that shape habitual stress responses, emotional regulation, confidence, and decision-making. Hypnotherapy provides a complementary and increasingly vital approach by directly targeting subconscious conditioning, thereby opening new paths for stress relief, resilience building, leadership development, and enhanced performance. The book, *Transformative Role of Hypnotherapy for Business Professionals*, offers a structured and thorough examination of how hypnotherapy integrates into contemporary professional life.

Across global business ecosystems, organizations face a crucial turning point. Regulatory and institutional standards are increasingly emphasizing employee well-being and psychological safety, while leaders must manage uncertainty, complexity, and ethical responsibilities without sacrificing performance. At the same time, generational shifts, especially among millennials and zillennials, have increased demands for authenticity, work–life balance, purpose, and meaningful engagement. These combined trends underscore the need to adopt more robust, evidence-based interventions that extend beyond traditional wellness approaches.

This volume comes at an opportune time by presenting a cohesive view of hypnotherapy as a scientifically supported, ethically implemented, and practically significant intervention. By combining psychological theories, therapeutic models, and workplace uses, it offers readers a clear understanding of hypnotherapy's possibilities and limits in professional settings. The chapters together show how subconscious techniques can enhance traditional methods in areas like organizational behavior, leadership growth, and corporate health.

This book is written for a broad yet clearly defined audience:

- **Academics and Researchers** in psychology, organizational behavior, leadership studies, and workplace wellness seeking conceptual and applied insights into subconscious interventions.
- **Business Professionals and Executives** aiming to manage stress, enhance decision-making, and sustain high performance in demanding environments.
- **HR Professionals, Corporate Wellness Designers, and Executive Coaches** interested in integrating evidence-based hypnotherapeutic approaches into organizational development initiatives.
- **Postgraduate Students and Practitioners** in management, psychology, and human development seeking structured perspectives on emerging workplace interventions.

CHAPTER OVERVIEW

Chapter 1: Integration of Neurolinguistic Programming (NLP) and Hypnosis Tools for Well-being and Stress Reduction

This chapter explores the integration of NLP and hypnosis to enhance emotional regulation, cognitive flexibility, and professional well-being.

Chapter 2: Hypnotherapy for Stress Management for Working Professionals

Focusing on applied contexts, this chapter examines how hypnotherapy supports stress reduction across diverse professional roles.

Chapter 3: The Efficacy of Mindfulness-Based Restorative Practices in Reducing Work-Related Psychophysiological Stress

This chapter examines the complementary role of mindfulness and restorative practices in addressing psychophysiological stress at work.

Chapter 4: From Mental Pain to Physical Pain Addressing IT Stress Through Hypnotherapy: Psychological and Physical effects of stress in corporate IT roles

The contemporary information technology sector is dominated by substantial workloads, relentless pressure, incessant demands, rapid advancements, and swift innovations. In corporate information technology, professionals often endure prolonged stress, which can substantially affect their mental and physical well-being. This chapter examines the neurological, physiological, and behavioural effects of stress on individuals employed in the information technology sector. Despite the growing popularity of hypnosis and hypnotherapy in recent years, the impact of hypnosis on individuals' emotional responses to stress remains uncertain. This chapter, possess a comprehensive understanding of the neurological, physiological, and behavioural ramifications of stress on those employed in the information technology sector. It will significantly influence policy formulation, workplace interventions, and future research endeavours. Furthermore, it will elucidate the research deficiencies present in the field and demonstrate how hypnotherapy can enhance stress management and cognitive resilience.

Chapter 5: Hypnotherapy for Performance Anxiety, Perfectionism, and Fear of Failure in Corporate Professionals

Chapter 10 examines how hypnotherapy addresses subconscious barriers to confidence, execution, and professional performance.

Chapter 6: Enhancing Conscious Performance Through Subconscious Hypnotherapeutic Interventions in Business

This chapter analyzes the relationship between subconscious conditioning and conscious performance optimization.

Chapter 7: Subconscious Leadership Conditioning and Executive Decision-Making Through Hypnotherapy

Chapter 12 focuses on leadership development, executive cognition, and decision-making under complexity and uncertainty.

Chapter 8: Being Self-aware: Integrating Hypnotherapy in Corporate Wellness Programs

This chapter highlights self-awareness as a core professional competency and discusses integration within corporate wellness systems.

Chapter 9: Beyond the Bell Curve: Reimagining Gifted and High-Functioning Education

Chapter 14 explores giftedness, high-functioning individuals, and psychological intensity in professional and educational contexts.

Chapter 10: From Spiritual Resilience to Professional Achievement: Mapping the Inner Architecture of Excellence

This chapter integrates psychological, emotional, and inner resilience dimensions to map the architecture of professional excellence.

Chapter 11: Building Resilience in Zillennial-Hydrotherapeutic Strategies for Stress Management, Authenticity, and Workplace Relationships

The concluding chapter examines generational stress patterns, authenticity, and workplace relationships among zillennial professionals.

The chapters in *'Transformative Role of Hypnotherapy for Business Professionals'* collectively show how hypnotherapy goes beyond just stress relief to also impact resilience, leadership, performance, and professional identity. Combining scientific principles with workplace applications, this volume connects theory and practice and contributes valuable insights to the ongoing discussion of professional well-being and enduring excellence.

Acknowledgement

We sincerely thank the institutions and individuals whose support, encouragement, and academic environment made the development of this book, *The Transformative Role of Hypnotherapy for Business Professionals*, possible. This volume greatly benefited from the intellectual freedom, interdisciplinary culture, and commitment to scholarly excellence promoted by our affiliated institutions. We especially acknowledge Shoolini University in India and Tecnológico de Monterrey in Mexico for providing a supportive ecosystem that facilitated research, collaboration, and international academic engagement during this project.

We sincerely thank the chapter contributors and peer reviewers for their scholarly rigor, insights, and constructive feedback, which greatly improved the quality, coherence, and relevance of this volume. Their diverse perspectives from psychology, organizational studies, and professional practice enriched the book and bolstered its contribution to the ongoing discussion on workplace well-being and performance.

We also thank our colleagues, students, and professional networks for their valuable suggestions, encouragement, and logistical support throughout different stages of the editorial process. Their involvement exemplifies the collaborative spirit of academic inquiry and applied scholarship that underpins this book.

Finally, we acknowledge the broader academic and professional communities whose ongoing research, practice, and dialogue in hypnotherapy, mental health, and organizational development inspire continuous exploration at the intersection of human well-being and professional excellence.

Chapter 1
Integration of Neurolinguistic Programming (NLP) and Hypnosis Tools for Well-Being and Stress Reduction

María E. Raygoza-L.
https://orcid.org/0009-0000-5969-6602
Universidad Politécnica de Baja California, Mexico

Jesús Heriberto Orduño-Osuna
https://orcid.org/0009-0004-4850-7481
Universidad Politécnica de Baja California, Mexico

Fabian N. Murrieta-Rico
https://orcid.org/0000-0001-9829-3013
Universidad Politécnica de Baja California, Mexico

ABSTRACT

This chapter explores the integrative potential of Neurolinguistic Programming (NLP), hypnosis, and Gestalt therapy as complementary tools for well-being and stress reduction. By combining NLP's cognitive-behavioral techniques, hypnosis' access to subconscious resources, and Gestalt's present-moment awareness, the proposed model offers a holistic approach to addressing stress at emotional, mental, and physiological levels. The methodology includes practical strategies such as belief

DOI: 10.4018/979-8-3373-2317-6.ch001

restructuring and therapeutic anchoring, supported by interdisciplinary theoretical frameworks (e.g., Ericksonian hypnosis, NLP modeling, and Gestalt principles). Key applications focus on anxiety management, emotional self-regulation, and habit modification. The study concludes that this integration provides a versatile, client-centered toolkit for therapists and coaches, bridging conscious goal-setting with unconscious reprogramming.

INTRODUCTION

Human development and quality of life are central to the pursuit of personal and professional well-being. Today, stress has significantly increased, affecting the physical and mental health of millions of people worldwide. This phenomenon has become a determining factor in the onset of psychological disorders, reducing the quality of life and limiting performance in various areas. In this context, Neurolinguistic Programming (NLP) and hypnosis have emerged as complementary therapeutic tools that can significantly contribute to stress management and the improvement of well-being. NLP is based on the understanding of mental patterns and cognitive reprogramming to optimize communication and behavior (Higson-Sweeney et al., 2022), while hypnosis facilitates access to altered states of consciousness that can enhance emotional resilience and stress regulation. Hypnosis, considered an alternative therapy by some sectors and a complementary tool within clinical psychology by others, is situated in an interdisciplinary field that encompasses neuroscience, psychology (Kallio & Revonsuo, 2003), and medicine. Its application has been studied in various contexts, from pain management to behavior modification, making it a valuable resource in modern therapy. This article explores the synergy between NLP, hypnosis, and other psychological techniques, such as Gestalt therapy, analyzing their impact on stress reduction and overall well-being (Bundrant, 2024). The theoretical basis of each method will be discussed, along with their application in the therapeutic context and the benefits derived from their integration. A review of recent studies allows for a better understanding of how these tools can facilitate change and adaptation processes in an increasingly demanding world. Hypnosis, considered an alternative therapy by some sectors and a complementary tool within clinical psychology by others, is situated in an interdisciplinary field that spans neuroscience, psychology, and medicine. Its application has been studied in various contexts, from pain management to behavior modification, making it a valuable resource in modern therapy. One of the key texts in this field is *"Hypnotherapy: An Ericksonian Approach"* by Jeffrey Zeig and Michael L. Yapko, where clinical techniques based on the work of Milton H. Erickson, the pioneer of modern hypnosis, are detailed. Hypnosis has existed since ancient times, with historical records in *restructuring and therapeutic anchoring, supported by interdisciplinary theoretical frameworks (e.g., Ericksonian hypnosis, NLP modeling, and Gestalt principles). Key applications focus on anxiety management, emotional self-regulation, and habit modification. The study concludes that this integration provides a versatile, client-centered toolkit for therapists and coaches, bridging conscious goal-setting with unconscious reprogramming.*

INTRODUCTION

Human development and quality of life are central to the pursuit of personal and professional well-being. Today, stress has significantly increased, affecting the physical and mental health of millions of people worldwide. This phenomenon has become a determining factor in the onset of psychological disorders, reducing the quality of life and limiting performance in various areas. In this context, Neurolinguistic Programming (NLP) and hypnosis have emerged as complementary therapeutic tools that can significantly contribute to stress management and the improvement of well-being. NLP is based on the understanding of mental patterns and cognitive reprogramming to optimize communication and behavior (Higson-Sweeney et al., 2022), while hypnosis facilitates access to altered states of consciousness that can enhance emotional resilience and stress regulation. Hypnosis, considered an alternative therapy by some sectors and a complementary tool within clinical psychology by others, is situated in an interdisciplinary field that encompasses neuroscience, psychology (Kallio & Revonsuo, 2003), and medicine. Its application has been studied in various contexts, from pain management to behavior modification, making it a valuable resource in modern therapy. This article explores the synergy between NLP, hypnosis, and other psychological techniques, such as Gestalt therapy, analyzing their impact on stress reduction and overall well-being (Bundrant, 2024). The theoretical basis of each method will be discussed, along with their application in the therapeutic context and the benefits derived from their integration. A review of recent studies allows for a better understanding of how these tools can facilitate change and adaptation processes in an increasingly demanding world. Hypnosis, considered an alternative therapy by some sectors and a complementary tool within clinical psychology by others, is situated in an interdisciplinary field that spans neuroscience, psychology, and medicine. Its application has been studied in various contexts, from pain management to behavior modification, making it a valuable resource in modern therapy. One of the key texts in this field is *"Hypnotherapy: An Ericksonian Approach"* by Jeffrey Zeig and Michael L. Yapko, where clinical techniques based on the work of Milton H. Erickson, the pioneer of modern hypnosis, are detailed. Hypnosis has existed since ancient times, with historical records in

Chapter 1

Integration of Neurolinguistic Programming (NLP) and Hypnosis Tools for Well-Being and Stress Reduction

María E. Raygoza-L.
https://orcid.org/0009-0000-5969-6602
Universidad Politécnica de Baja California, Mexico

Jesús Heriberto Orduño-Osuna
https://orcid.org/0009-0004-4850-7481
Universidad Politécnica de Baja California, Mexico

Fabian N. Murrieta-Rico
https://orcid.org/0000-0001-9829-3013
Universidad Politécnica de Baja California, Mexico

ABSTRACT

This chapter explores the integrative potential of Neurolinguistic Programming (NLP), hypnosis, and Gestalt therapy as complementary tools for well-being and stress reduction. By combining NLP's cognitive-behavioral techniques, hypnosis' access to subconscious resources, and Gestalt's present-moment awareness, the proposed model offers a holistic approach to addressing stress at emotional, mental, and physiological levels. The methodology includes practical strategies such as belief

DOI: 10.4018/979-8-3373-2317-6.ch001

civilizations such as Egypt and Greece, but it was in the 18th century when Franz Anton Mesmer gave it a systematic approach that would evolve into contemporary hypnotherapy (dgoldenconlin, 2023).

Neurolinguistic Programming is an interdisciplinary approach to communication, personal development, and psychotherapy created in the 1970s by Richard Bandler and John Grinder. Its primary goal is to identify and model patterns of excellence in human behavior, allowing its application for personal change and the optimization of performance in various fields. Bandler and Grinder were inspired by the work of influential therapists such as Fritz Perls, creator of Gestalt therapy; Virginia Satir, pioneer of family therapy; and Milton H. Erickson (Grant, 2023), a key figure in clinical hypnosis. By observing and analyzing these experts, the founders of NLP designed replicable strategies that facilitate learning and personal transformation (Fitzpatrick et al., 2017). The term "Neurolinguistic Programming" reflects the interaction between neurological processes ("neuro"), language ("linguistics"), and learned behavioral patterns ("programming") (Dilts, 1983). According to Bandler and Grinder, these elements determine each person's subjective experience and can be modified using specific techniques to improve communication, emotional management, and decision-making (Bradley & Biedermann, 1985). One of the first books published by the creators of NLP (Grinder & Bandler, 1976), *"The Structure of Magic I"*, analyzed the impact of language on perception and behavior, establishing the foundation for many therapeutic techniques and personal development practices (Zaharia et al., 2015) . Over the years, NLP has been integrated with approaches like hypnosis and Gestalt therapy, strengthening its applicability in stress reduction, emotional regulation, and overall well-being improvement (Supriyono et al., 2024)

Among the most relevant concepts developed by Bandler and Grinder are rapport and calibration. Rapport refers to the ability to establish a deep connection based on empathy and trust with another person, which is essential in both therapeutic contexts and personal coaching processes (Raygoza-L. et al., 2024). This connection is achieved by synchronizing verbal and non-verbal language, including tone of voice, body movements, and posture. Calibration, on the other hand, involves the precise and systematic observation of the interlocutor's non-verbal signals to identify subtle changes in their emotional and mental state (Soler et al., 2013). These skills are fundamental in any therapeutic process as they allow for empathetic and effective intervention, creating a genuine supportive experience. In this framework, Gestalt therapy offers an experiential and humanistic approach that powerfully complements NLP and hypnosis. Gestalt therapy focuses on awareness of the present moment, the integration of thought, emotion, and action, and personal responsibility (Fromme, 2011).

BACKGROUND

The synergy between these disciplines enables an integrated approach to the human being, fostering deep transformation processes that address not only symptoms but also the underlying causes of distress. By integrating tools like rapport, calibration, hypnosis, and the principles of Gestalt therapy, the possibilities for intervention are expanded, allowing for effective stress reduction and sustained improvement in quality of life.

Rapport refers to the ability to establish a deep connection based on empathy and trust with another person, which is essential in both therapeutic contexts and personal coaching processes., connection is achieved by synchronizing verbal and non-verbal language, including tone of voice, body movements, and posture (Dash, 2023). In this context, Gestalt therapy offers an experiential and humanistic approach that powerfully complements NLP and hypnosis. Developed by Gestalt therapy focuses on awareness of the present moment, the integration of thought, emotion, action, and personal responsibility. Rather than over-analyzing or interpreting (Zahm & Gold, 2002), the Gestalt therapist facilitates the patient's exploration of their immediate experience, thus promoting an awareness that leads to change . This methodology emphasizes the "here and now" and lived experience as a way of self-knowledge and resolution of internal conflicts. The synergy between these disciplines allows for a comprehensive approach to the human being, fostering deep transformation processes that address not only the symptoms but also the underlying causes of distress. By integrating tools such as rapport, calibration, hypnosis, and the principles of Gestalt therapy, the possibilities for intervention are expanded, allowing for effective stress reduction and sustained improvement in quality of life (Spiegel et al., 2020).

Rapport, Calibration, and Gestalt Therapy as Transformational Tools

Hypnosis has come a long way from its ancient roots to become a therapeutic practice supported by numerous scientific studies. Today, it is successfully used in the treatment of phobias, anxiety, insomnia, chronic pain, smoking cessation, and psychosomatic disorders (Holroyd, 2003). The modern approach to hypnosis, based on the work of Milton H. Erickson, is distinguished by being indirect, flexible, and oriented toward the use of metaphorical language to induce therapeutic trance states (Holroyd, 2003). Ericksonian hypnotherapy promotes the activation of the patient's unconscious resources and their self-regulation capacity (*Ericksonian Hypnosis*, 2024). On the other hand, Gestalt therapy, developed in the mid-20th century, represents one of the most influential currents within humanistic psychology. Based on a phenomenological-existential philosophy, this therapy considers that human suffering originates from the lack of integration between thought, emotion, and action. The Gestalt therapist does not seek to interpret the patient but to accompany them in discovering their internal truth through awareness ("awareness") and genuine contact with themselves and their environment (Nevis, 2009). Both methodologies, hypnosis and Gestalt therapy, share the premise that therapeutic change does not occur solely through rational analysis, but through profound lived experience. Their joint application with NLP further enhances their effectiveness, offering an integrative framework that approaches the human being from a holistic perspective, promoting a sustainable, autonomous transformation focused on overall well-being.

The versatility of hypnosis and Gestalt therapy allows for their application in multiple professional contexts. In the clinical field, both techniques are used to treat conditions such as anxiety disorders, depression, phobias, addictions, sexual dysfunctions, and sleep disorders. Hypnosis is especially used to alleviate chronic pain (Jensen & Patterson, 2014), improve habit control, and facilitate brief and focused interventions Gestalt therapy, on the other hand, favors working with repressed emotions, unresolved conflicts, and dysfunctional behavior patterns. In the educational field, Gestalt therapy is applied to foster emotional self-regulation, improve self-esteem, and develop interpersonal skills in children, adolescents, and teachers (González-Ramírez et al., 2017). Similarly, hypnosis can be used to reinforce concentration, reduce academic stress, and enhance learning through positive suggestion techniques (Dillworth et al., 2012). In the organizational context, both hypnosis and Gestalt therapy are used in workplace wellness programs, stress management, conscious leadership, and conflict resolution. These tools help improve organizational climate and promote a work culture based on emotional awareness and individual responsibility. In the area of personal growth, both methodologies are widely used in therapeutic accompaniment processes and personal development workshops. Their experiential approach allows individuals to explore their inner world, connect with their personal resources, and make deep and sustainable changes in their daily lives. Clinical and experiential evidence has demonstrated that hypnosis is a highly effective tool for reducing stress, as it allows access to deep relaxation in which the body and mind can restore their natural balance. Through hypnotic trance, the hyperactivity of the sympathetic nervous system is deactivated, and the parasympathetic system is activated, favoring the reduction of muscle tension, normalization of heart rate and respiration, and a greater sense of calm and overall well-being. When integrated with Neurolinguistic Programming, the therapeutic power of hypnosis is amplified, as NLP allows for the identification, restructuring, and replacement of limiting beliefs, negative thought patterns, and dysfunctional behaviors. Together, hypnosis and NLP not only alleviate the symptoms of stress but also promote a state of self-awareness, emotional self-regulation, and personal empowerment, leading to an integral transformation of the individual (Tepe, 2025). With a focus on experience and the development of internal resources, these tools establish themselves as fundamental pillars in therapeutic accompaniment for human well-being in increasingly complex and demanding contexts. The connection is achieved by synchronizing verbal and non-verbal language, including tone of voice, body movements, and posture. Gestalt therapy offers an experiential and humanistic approach that powerfully complements NLP and hypnosis. Developed by Fritz Perls, Gestalt therapy focuses on awareness of the present moment, the integration of thought, emotion, and action, and personal responsibility(Watson et al., 2011) .

The synergy between these disciplines allows for a comprehensive approach to the human being, fostering deep transformation processes that address not only the symptoms but also the underlying causes of distress. By integrating tools such as rapport, calibration, hypnosis, and the principles of Gestalt therapy (Megha, 2024), the possibilities for intervention are expanded, allowing for effective stress reduction and sustained improvement in quality of life. Hypnosis has come a long way from its ancient roots to become a therapeutic practice supported by numerous scientific studies. Today, it is successfully used in the treatment of phobias, anxiety, insomnia, chronic pain, smoking cessation, and psychosomatic disorders (Weiner et al., 2012). The modern approach to hypnosis, based on the work of Milton H. Erickson, is distinguished by being indirect, flexible, and oriented toward the use of metaphorical language to induce therapeutic trance states (Sturt et al., 2012). Ericksonian hypnotherapy promotes the activation of the patient's unconscious resources and their self-regulation capacity. On the other hand, Gestalt therapy, developed in the mid-20th century, represents one of the most influential currents within humanistic psychology. Based on a phenomenological-existential philosophy, this therapy considers that human suffering originates from the lack of integration between thought, emotion, and action (Matthews, 2000). The Gestalt therapist does not seek to interpret the patient but to accompany them in discovering their internal truth through awareness ("awareness") and genuine contact with themselves and their environment. Both methodologies, hypnosis and Gestalt therapy, share the premise that therapeutic change does not occur solely through rational analysis, but through profound lived experience. Their joint application with NLP further enhances their effectiveness, offering an integrative framework that approaches the human being from a holistic perspective, promoting a sustainable, autonomous transformation focused on overall well-being (Higson-Sweeney et al., 2022).

The versatility of hypnosis and Gestalt therapy allows multiple professional contexts, in the clinical discipline are used to treat diverse disorders. Hypnosis is especially used to alleviate chronic pain, improve habit control, and facilitate brief and focused interventions. Gestalt therapy, on the other hand, favors working with repressed emotions, unresolved conflicts, and dysfunctional behavior patterns. In the educational field. Gestalt therapies are used in workplace wellness programs, stress management, conscious leadership, and conflict resolution. These tools help improve organizational climate and promote a work culture based on emotional awareness and individual responsibility. Clinical and experiential evidence has demonstrated that hypnosis is a highly effective tool for reducing stress, as it allows access to deep relaxation in which the body and mind can restore their natural balance. Through hypnotic trance, the hyperactivity of the sympathetic nervous system is deactivated, and the parasympathetic system is activated (De Benedittis, 2024), favoring the reduction of muscle tension, normalization of heart rate and respiration, and a greater sense of calm and overall well-being (Sevoz-Couche & Laborde, 2022).When integrated with Neurolinguistic Programming, the therapeutic power of hypnosis is amplified, as NLP allows for the identification, restructuring, and replacement of limiting beliefs, negative thought patterns, and dysfunctional behaviors. This synergy between both disciplines enables more precise, profound, and lasting interventions by connecting the unconscious dimension of the subject with their conscious capacity for change (Weissman & Mendes, 2021).

Support of Technology in NLP and Hypnosis Therapeutic Processes

When implemented ethically and consciously, technology can be a powerful ally for both therapists and coaches. Digital tools such as emotional tracking applications, teletherapy platforms, virtual journals, and video conferencing systems have expanded access to support services, overcoming geographical and time barriers (Olawade et al., 2024). In the therapeutic context, there are platforms that facilitate emotional self-management through breathing exercises, guided mindfulness, or personalized reminders, which strengthen the continuity of work done in sessions. For mental health professionals, the use of clinical management software, progress analysis, and digital resources for ongoing training helps improve organization, process evaluation, and constant professional updating. Specifically, technology has also begun to play a key role in the application of NLP and hypnosis. In the case of NLP, tools based on artificial intelligence and natural language processing can analyze users' linguistic patterns and provide personalized feedback, facilitating work with limiting beliefs, unprocessed emotions, and dysfunctional cognitive structures. This allows for quicker and more targeted interventions, tailored to the individual patient's profile. Hypnosis, on the other hand, has found a valuable application through audio or video recordings with guided hypnotic inductions, deep relaxation mobile apps, and digital hypnotherapy programs that allow users to access altered states of consciousness without the need for in-person sessions. These tools are professionally designed, providing support in managing stress, insomnia, chronic pain, and other conditions. Additionally, immersive virtual reality is being used as a medium to induce deep relaxation states, facilitating entry into the hypnotic trance and creating controlled sensory experiences that enhance the effectiveness of the intervention. Furthermore, emerging technologies such as biofeedback and virtual reality are beginning to integrate into therapeutic interventions focused on reducing stress and anxiety, facilitating the real-time connection between the body and mind. Figure 1 below shows an image of the integration of the NLP tool with hypnosis therapy.

Figure 1. Representation of the integration of the NLP tool with hypnosis therapy

In the coaching field, applications like goal-setting platforms, digital agendas, and habit tracking tools help maintain the motivation and focus of the client. In the case of Neurolinguistic Programming, technology has opened new possibilities to enhance its effectiveness. Mobile apps and interactive platforms allow users to perform NLP exercises, such as emotional anchoring, creative visualization, or belief reframing, from the comfort of their own environment. Similarly, programs that analyze linguistic patterns help identify limiting beliefs and emotional blockages, facilitating faster, more personalized, and effective interventions. Additionally, the use of immersive virtual reality has proven effective in inducing trance states, creating sensory scenarios that promote relaxation and mental retraining. Technology does not replace the human relationship or the therapeutic bond, but it does enhance it by providing means that optimize processes, improve accessibility, and strengthen the autonomy of the patient or client. When integrated with approaches such as hypnosis, NLP, coaching, or Gestalt therapy, it becomes an innovative resource that expands the positive impact of interventions on individual and collective well-being. This technological integration benefits not only patients but also professionals by providing tools that extend their intervention capacity, facilitate continuous monitoring, and improve treatment adherence. When applied responsibly, technology does not replace the human connection but rather acts as a catalyst that amplifies the positive impact of hypnosis, NLP, and Gestalt therapy on mental health, personal development, and overall well-being.

Applications of Hypnosis, NLP, and Gestalt Therapy in Well-being and Stress Reduction

Below are some of the most relevant applications of hypnosis, NPL and Gestalt therapy, focused on personal development, emotional self-regulation, and stress reduction:

1. Personal Development and Emotional Well-being

- **Hypnosis**: Induction of deep relaxation states that allow for the restructuring of limiting thoughts and the generation of new perspectives.
- **NLP**: Application of techniques such as anchoring and the timeline to improve self-esteem, motivation, and goal projection.
- **Gestalt Therapy**: Promotion of self-awareness and responsibility through contact with the present experience, which facilitates emotional integration and authenticity.

2. Stress and Anxiety Reduction

- **Hypnosis**: Use of therapeutic suggestions to decrease symptoms of anxiety, muscle tension, insomnia, and chronic stress.
- **NLP**: Reframing stressful experiences by changing sensory perception and linguistic patterns.
- **Gestalt Therapy**: Emotional processing of conflicting situations that generate tension, through awareness and the closure of unfinished gestalts.

3. Support in Individual Therapeutic Processes

- **Hypnosis**: Support in treatments for phobias, traumas, habit control, and pain management.
- **NLP**: Facilitation of rapid change processes, resolution of internal blockages, and transformation of dysfunctional beliefs.
- **Gestalt Therapy**: Exploration of internal polarities and work with internal dialogues to promote psycho-emotional integration.

4. Emotional Education and Development of Social Skills

- **Hypnosis**: Reinforcement of internal resources such as concentration, calm, and mental clarity in school or work contexts.
- **NLP**: Improvement of verbal and non-verbal communication, setting clear and effective goals.
- **Gestalt Therapy**: Strengthening of empathy, active listening, and authentic emotional expression.

5. Self-care and Personal Growth

- **Hypnosis**: Promotion of healthy habits and connection with the subconscious to achieve personal goals.
- **NLP**: Design of positive mental maps and construction of resilient coping strategies.
- **Gestalt Therapy**: Promotion of a lifestyle based on the present moment, emotional balance, and internal congruence.

6. Prevention and Maintenance of Overall Well-being

- **Hypnosis**: Regular application of guided relaxation sessions to maintain a state of mental and physical balance.
- **NLP**: Implementation of positive mental routines and creative visualizations to strengthen emotional resilience.
- **Gestalt Therapy**: Continuous practice of self-observation, emotional expression, and genuine contact with the environment.

These disciplines, when integrated, offer a powerful path to integral well-being, facilitating sustainable internal transformation and emotional recovery over time.

Integrated Proposal: Hypnosis, NLP, Gestalt Therapy, and Coaching for Health, Well-being, and Stress Reduction

Below is an integrated intervention model based on the combination of Hypnosis, Neurolinguistic Programming, Gestalt Therapy, and Coaching, with applications aimed at emotional health, well-being, and personal and organizational productivity:

Components of the Integrated Model

1. Comprehensive User Evaluation

- Diagnosis of stress and well-being levels.
- Identification of limiting beliefs, emotional patterns, and coping styles.
- Evaluation of awareness of the "here and now".

2. Personalized Intervention

- **Hypnosis**: Induction of deep relaxation and therapeutic suggestions to reduce stress and foster resilience.
- **NLP**: Application of positive anchoring, reframing beliefs, and visualizing desired states.
- **Gestalt Therapy**: Work with unresolved emotions, internal polarities, and contact with the present experience.
- **Coaching**: Reflective accompaniment oriented towards goals, follow-up, and strengthening self-management.

3. Continuous Learning and Development

- Workshops on emotional self-regulation and effective communication.
- Training in healthy habits and development of internal resources.
- Integration of self-care routines, mindfulness practices, and self-awareness.

Areas of Application and Benefits

• Mental Health and Personal Well-being:

- Reduction of anxiety, stress, and insomnia levels.
- Strengthening of self-esteem and self-confidence.
- Recovery of emotional balance and improvement in mood.

• Productivity and Work Performance:

- Increase in focus, creativity, and effective decision-making.
- Improvement in workplace climate and interpersonal relationships.
- Prevention of burnout and promotion of professional self-care.

• Education and Human Development:

- Development of social and leadership skills.
- Promotion of critical thinking, active listening, and empathy.
- Enhancement of personalized learning styles and intrinsic motivation.

This integrative approach allows for a holistic address of human well-being, combining experiential techniques and cognitive tools to achieve lasting balance between body, mind, and emotions.

Neurolinguistic Programming is a powerful tool that combines communication techniques, personal development, and behavioral change to facilitate internal transformation. Among its multiple applications, anchoring and visualization stand out, strategies that allow for voluntary access to desired emotional states, promote goal achievement, and strengthen emotional self-regulation. Anchoring involves associating specific stimuli physical, auditory, visual, or contextual with positive or productive emotions, while visualization is based on creating mental images that reinforce desired beliefs, motivations, and behaviors (Qureshi, 2024). These resources, when applied consciously and consistently, can become key allies for personal, professional, and emotional growth. Below, various types of anchoring and practical examples of visualization applied within the framework of NLP are described, along with recommendations to enhance their effectiveness.

Examples of NLP Application

Anchoring is the process of associating a stimulus with a specific emotional state, enabling its evocation in the future.

Types of Anchors

- **Physical Anchor**: Linking pressure on the body to a desired emotional state.
- **Auditory Anchor**: Repeating a key word with a positive tone.
- **Visual Anchor**: Connecting a color to an emotional state.
- **Sequential Anchor**: Gradually transitioning from one emotional state to another.

- **Spatial Anchor**: Using physical space to anchor emotions related to goals.
- **Temporal Anchor**: Associating a stimulus with the sensation of having achieved a goal.
- **Reward Anchor**: Connecting progress to a tangible or emotional reward.
- **Environmental Anchor**: Using objects as visual reminders of the goal.
- **Enhanced Visualization Anchor**: Combining visualization with a physical or auditory anchor.

Visualization

Visualization involves creating mental images to achieve desired emotional or behavioral states.

Examples of Visualization with NLP

- **Success Visualization**: Imagining in detail a desired future situation.
- **Stress Reduction Visualization**: Mentally recreating a calming environment.

Maximizing the Impact of Anchors

1. **Constant Repetition**: Reinforces the emotional connection.
2. **Define Specific Goals**: Ensures clarity and focus.
3. **Use a Progress Journal**: Track how anchors contribute to achieving goals.

METHODOLOGY

This chapter adopts a qualitative, experiential, and holistic approach based on psycho-emotional intervention models from three complementary fields: Neurolinguistic Programming, Gestalt Therapy, and Hypnotherapy. The main objective is to offer an integrated model of practices that support emotional self-regulation, reduce chronic stress, and activate empowering beliefs linked to personal and emotional abundance.

Methodological Structure

1. **Theoretical and Conceptual Framework**: Describing the foundations of each technique (NLP, Gestalt, Hypnotherapy) and their relationship to stress, limiting beliefs, and emotional transformation.

2. **Practical and Experiential Application**: Presenting strategies organized by phases, integrating specific tools for changing mental, emotional, and behavioral patterns.

Application Strategy

The methodology is designed in seven phases, each associated with activities from the three disciplines addressed. The techniques are presented in a functional sequence that facilitates recognition, reframing, release, and emotional integration.

RESULTS

In the path towards personal and professional growth, many individuals face internal blockages, limiting beliefs, high stress levels, and a lack of clarity on how to achieve their goals. The combination of Neurolinguistic Programming, coaching, and hypnosis represents a comprehensive and powerful strategy to transform these barriers into development opportunities while promoting a state of calm and emotional balance. These disciplines, when integrated, enable working with both the conscious and unconscious mind, reprogramming mental and emotional patterns, reducing accumulated stress, and creating new pathways to success. NLP focuses on how language, thoughts, and perception shape our internal experiences; coaching provides a structured space to set clear, sustainable, and meaningful goals; while hypnosis facilitates access to deep states of relaxation and awareness, where it is possible to install new beliefs, release emotional tension, and modify behaviors more effectively. Table 1 presents a synthesis of how to apply these tools together to achieve an overarching goal, including stress reduction as an essential component of overall well-being. Key concepts are described, their purpose, and how they can be implemented in personal transformation sessions. This guide can be adapted to various areas such as health, finances, self-esteem, relationships, productivity, or leadership, depending on the individual's needs (Raygoza Limón & Jiménez Sánchez, 2024).

Table 1. Integrated Strategies of NLP, Coaching, and Hypnosis for Achieving Personal and Professional Goals

Concept	Description	How to Apply it through NLP, Coaching, and Hypnosis
Clarification of the Goal	Define precisely what is desired (SMART goal).	In coaching, guide the client with key questions. In NLP, use the well-formed outcome model. In hypnosis, visualize the goal in detail
Identification of Obstacles	Detect limiting beliefs, fears, or automatic patterns that hinder progress.	Use inquiry techniques in coaching, language metamodel in NLP, and gentle hypnotic regression to uncover blockages.
Reformulation of Beliefs	Replace limiting thoughts with empowering ones.	Coaching: transformational dialogue. NLP: reframing beliefs. Hypnosis: positive suggestion in a trance state.
Installation of Anchors	Associate stimuli with positive emotions that help maintain motivation.	NLP: use physical or auditory anchors. Coaching: use symbols. Hypnosis: reinforce the anchor in a deep relaxation state.
Creative Visualization	Imagine the desired outcome with emotional intensity.	In coaching: guided visualization exercise. NLP: submodalities. Hypnosis: mental journey to the future with integrated emotions.
Structured Action Plan	Design concrete steps towards the goal.	Coaching: action map. NLP: anchor resources for each step. Hypnosis: visualize each step with success.
Reinforcement and Follow-up	Consolidate progress and make adjustments as necessary.	Coaching: follow-up sessions. NLP: update anchors. Hypnosis: record personalized reinforcement audios.

The use of integrated techniques such as NLP and hypnosis offers a profound and transformative approach. NLP allows for the modification of mental and emotional patterns that perpetuate stress, while hypnosis facilitates access to deep relaxation states where new internal resources and positive beliefs can be installed. The following table provides a structured guide for applying hypnosis and NLP with the goal of reducing stress. Table 2 outlines each phase, including hypnosis-based interventions, complementary NLP techniques, and their daily practical application. This combination promotes emotional balance, enhances mental clarity, and helps restore overall well-being.

Table 2. Strategies with Hypnosis and NLP to Reduce Stress

Phase	Hypnosis	NLP	Example Application
1. Definition of the goal	Brief induction to a calm state to visualize the desired state without stress.	Formulate a specific and positive goal (well-formed outcome model).	"I want to feel calm when I wake up and handle the day's challenges with serenity."
2. Identification of stress factors and associated beliefs	Light trance to explore memories or emotions that create tension.	Detect limiting beliefs: "I must do everything alone" / "I can't rest."	Identify automatic thoughts when stress appears in daily routines.
3. Restructuring of beliefs	Use of direct suggestions in trance: "Every time you breathe, you feel more calm".	Replace limiting beliefs with positive affirmations: "I am safe, I can let go."	Repeat affirmations like: "I trust that everything will be resolved in time."
4. Creation of a calming anchor	In a hypnotic state, link a gesture (e.g., touching the heart) to a sense of peace.	Create a physical or visual anchor to evoke calm states automatically.	Place the hand on the chest while taking deep breaths to reconnect with tranquility.
5. Practice of conscious breathing and physical relaxation	Induction based on guided breathing to calm the nervous system.	Observe breathing, use relaxing breathing patterns.	Breathe deeply for 3 minutes upon waking or before a stressful meeting.
6. Guided visualization of the desired state	Guide a hypnotic visualization of a safe and tension-free place.	Use submodalities to amplify the sensation of security (color, brightness, sound).	Imagine a forest or beach while feeling emotions of safety and control.
7. Weekly follow-up and self-evaluation	Reinforce progress through hypnosis: "You are achieving greater balance each day."	Evaluate changes, adjust affirmations and anchors according to evolution.	Review how the response to tense situations has changed.
8. Closure with gratitude or personal mantra	Final hypnotic suggestions that reinforce gratitude and well-being.	Daily repetition of phrases like "I am in harmony with life."	At the end of the day, express gratitude for moments of serenity and personal progress.

Stress is a natural response of the body, but when prolonged, it can severely affect physical, emotional, and mental health. For this reason, applying integrative approaches that act on different levels of consciousness is key to achieving deep transformation. Neurolinguistic Programming allows for reprogramming the mental patterns that generate tension; Gestalt Therapy promotes personal responsibility and being present. Hypnotherapy facilitates access to the unconscious to install resources of calm and resilience. The combination of these tools allows for identifying the emotional causes of stress, reframing painful experiences, releasing accumulated tension, and restoring inner balance. Through practices such as visualization, emotional anchoring, contact with one's own emotions, conscious breathing, and hypnotic suggestions, individuals can reach a state of greater clarity, well-being, and mental peace. The following table presents a practical approach to applying NLP, Gestalt, and Hypnotherapy in stress management, showing how each discipline contributes complementary techniques to achieve this goal (Rachmad, 2024).

THERAPEUTIC STRATEGIES FOR WELL-BEING AND STRESS REDUCTION BASED ON NLP, HYPNOSIS, AND GESTALT THERAPY

The techniques of Neurolinguistic Programming, hypnosis, and Gestalt therapy not only contribute to the treatment of psychological disorders but also have a profound impact on the development of a positive mindset and stress reduction. Below are strategies designed to create deep and sustainable changes toward well-being and overall health:

1. Cultivate Gratitude as the Foundation of Well-Being

- **How to apply it:** Record three things each day for which you are grateful.
- **NLP Approach:** Reprogram the mental focus toward the positive and strengthen internal patterns of satisfaction.
- **Hypnosis Approach:** Induce suggestions of abundance and gratitude in a trance state.
- **Gestalt Approach:** Contact with the present experience and valuing what is.

2. Conscious Visualization and Positive Reframing

- **How to apply it:** Visualize completed goals with intense sensory experience.
- **NLP Approach:** Anchoring and timeline techniques to consolidate positive emotions.
- **Hypnosis Approach:** Guided visuals inducing relaxation and self-confidence.
- **Gestalt Approach:** Recognition of genuine desires and acceptance of emotions.

3. Redefining Limiting Beliefs

- **How to apply it:** Replace scarcity beliefs with expansive affirmations.
- **NLP Approach:** Change of submodalities and internal language.
- **Hypnosis Approach:** Use of metaphors and indirect language to install new beliefs.
- **Gestalt Approach:** Dialogue between conflicting internal parts.

4. Breathing and Mindfulness Practices

- **How to apply it:** Pause your day to perform deep breaths with awareness.
- **NLP Approach:** Activation of the resource state.
- **Hypnosis Approach:** Induction of trance to calm the nervous system.
- **Gestalt Approach:** Focusing on the here and now.

5. Celebrating Personal Progress

- **How to apply it:** Reinforce each achievement, no matter how small, with emotional gratification.
- **NLP Approach:** Reinforcement of the motivational system using positive anchors.
- **Hypnosis Approach:** Suggestion of self-satisfaction and emotional integration.
- **Gestalt Approach:** Genuine contact with the achievement from both the body and emotions.

In Table 3, the information on the applications of NLP and hypnosis in stress reduction and overall well-being is reviewed, highlighting the impact areas and corresponding techniques utilized by both disciplines.

Table 3. Applications of NLP and Hypnosis for Stress Reduction and Well-Being

Technique / Strategy	NLP	Therapeutic Hypnosis	Gestalt Therapy
Belief Restructuring	Change in internal language and cognitive reframing.	Hypnotic suggestions and metaphors that penetrate the subconscious.	Exploration of internal polarities and integrative dialogue.
Visualization and Positive Anchoring	Activation of resource states and goal projection with anchors.	Guided imagery in trance to associate emotions with achievement.	Connection with desire from the present.
Stress and Anxiety Management	Techniques of dissociation, change of focus, and reframing.	Induction of deep relaxation states and physiological regulation.	Emotional recognition and authentic expression.
Formation of Positive Habits	Modeling and repetition of successful patterns.	Instilling habits through suggestive repetition.	Conscious experience of the process and taking responsibility.
Emotional Control and Resilience	Change in submodalities and emotional language.	Strengthening the inner self through trance.	Strengthening awareness and emotional acceptance.
Enhancing Personal Well-Being	Creation of internal states congruent with goals.	Mind-body integration in a harmonious state.	Fusion of thought, emotion, and action in the present.

These strategies, applied consciously and systematically, allow individuals to reconnect with their internal power, reduce the emotional burden of stress, and cultivate a fuller, more coherent, and healthier life. The integration of these disciplines enhances the therapeutic potential and provides practical tools to achieve holistic well-being. In Table 4, the integrated strategies of Neuro-Linguistic Programming (NLP), Gestalt Therapy, and Hypnotherapy for stress reduction are presented. This table outlines how each discipline contributes in different phases of the therapeutic process, from recognizing the stress state to the final emotional integration. The corresponding techniques from each therapeutic approach are described in relation to their practical application, providing a comprehensive framework to improve emotional well-being and facilitate stress self-regulation.

Table 4. Integrated Strategies of NLP, Gestalt, and Hypnotherapy for Stress Reduction

Phase or Need	Hypnotherapy	NLP	Gestalt	Example of Application
1. Recognizing the Stress State	Induction into a state of relaxation and self-observation.	Identify how stress is represented in mental images, sounds, or sensations.	Techniques of body and emotional awareness (contacting what is felt without judgment).	Notice tension in the chest upon waking; write it down and bring it to the therapeutic session.
2. Identifying Internal Beliefs or Messages	Regression search in a hypnotic state to detect unconscious messages.	Use the language metamodel to question beliefs like "I don't have time for myself."	Authentic expression: verbalizing what is thought/feeling without filters, from the present.	"I feel like I have to be strong all the time"; work with that belief.
3. Reframing Stressful Thoughts	Installation of new beliefs in deep trance: "I deserve peace."	Reframe content: transform the meaning of a challenging situation.	Explore internal polarities (e.g., demand vs. rest) through internal dialogue.	Change "I have too many responsibilities" to "I can prioritize without guilt."
4. Anchoring Calm and Security States	Hypnotic anchoring with guided visualization of a safe place.	Associate a gesture or word with a feeling of tranquility.	Full attention to the body while performing that gesture (Gestalt self-support).	Touch the chest and breathe deeply whenever anxiety is felt.
5. Releasing Contained Emotions	Allow emotional catharsis in a safe and contained trance.	Collapse anchors technique to transform negative emotions.	Empty chair technique or dialogue with internal parts.	Crying or expressing anger without judgment to release accumulated emotional burden.

continued on following page

Table 4. Continued

Phase or Need	Hypnotherapy	NLP	Gestalt	Example of Application
6. Reinforcing Relaxing Habits	Post-hypnotic suggestions: "You will feel more relaxed when walking in the mornings."	Visualizing a daily routine without stress and with regulatory actions.	Incorporating self-care rituals (baths, walks, breathing, boundaries).	Listen to an audio every night to reinforce calmness and practice conscious breathing.
7. Integrating the Emotional Experience	Close the trance with an integration affirmation: "You are at peace with yourself."	"As if" technique: act as if you were already a calm person.	Becoming aware of how the body feels after releasing or expressing what hasn't been said.	"Today I feel lighter, more present. I choose to continue on this path."

Table 5 shows outline the potential advantages of these tools, including expanding access to wellness processes and enhancing personalization through tailored techniques. It also highlights the challenges involved, such as the need for professional quality across different cultural contexts and the risk of reductive approaches without in-depth training. The table further addresses the importance of integrating these tools effectively and ensuring professional training to prevent unethical practices.

Table 5. Opportunities and Challenges in the Use of NLP, Hypnosis, and Coaching for Stress Reduction

Aspect	Opportunities	Challenges
Access and Reach	- Expanding access to wellness processes through in-person or remote sessions. - Application of accessible and adaptable techniques.	- Need to ensure professional quality across different cultural contexts.
Personalization	- Visualizations, anchors, and affirmations tailored to the client's objectives. - Individualized action plans.	- Difficulty in ensuring coherence between tools without ethical guidance.
Efficiency and Scalability	- Structured coaching programs complemented by NLP or hypnosis sessions.	- Risk of reductive approaches without deep training.
Progress Evaluation	- Continuous review of progress through coaching. - Observation of emotional and cognitive changes.	- Subjectivity in measuring results if clear indicators are not used.
Integration of Tools	- Synergy between hypnosis, coaching, and NLP to address stress at various levels (cognitive, emotional, and behavioral).	- Requires specific training for ethical and effective integration.
Professional Training	- Formal training in coaching, hypnosis, and NLP as the foundation for comprehensive intervention.	- Risk of unethical practices if therapeutic roles are not respected.
Impact on Mental Health	- Strengthening self-awareness, emotional self-regulation, and resilience.	- Excessive techniques without guidance may cause confusion in some clients.

It is essential to understand how both disciplines contribute to key areas such as emotional regulation, stress management, sleep improvement, motivation, and overall health. Table 6 presents the applications of NLP and hypnosis in stress reduction and the promotion of well-being.

Table 6. Applications of NLP and Hypnosis in Stress Reduction and Promoting Well-Being

Impact Area	NLP Application	Hypnosis Application
Emotional Regulation	Reframing, positive visualization, and anchors to neutralize anxiety.	Induction of deep relaxation and therapeutic suggestion.
Stress Management	Dissociation techniques, belief reformulation, and positive self-talk.	Short trances aimed at physiological and emotional balance.
Improvement of Sleep	Reprogramming nightly habits and reducing intrusive thoughts.	Guided hypnosis to induce sleepiness and deep rest.
Motivation and Well-Being	Activation of resource states and construction of positive mental maps.	Reinforcement of pleasant emotions and self-confidence during trance.
Health and Quality of Life	Increase in perception of control and personal self-efficacy.	Mind-body integration with a focus on overall well-being.

Ethical Considerations in the Application of NLP, Hypnosis, and Coaching in Therapeutic Processes

Although these tools offer numerous benefits, it is essential to apply rigorous ethical standards to protect the well-being of the user:

- **Privacy and Confidentiality**: All information gathered during therapeutic processes must be handled with full professional responsibility.
- **Authenticity of the Therapeutic Bond**: The human bond is fundamental; no technique should replace the empathetic relationship between professional and client.
- **Ethical Training of the Professional**: Professionals must have formal and ethical training in each tool they integrate.
- **Professional Boundaries**: It is crucial to respect the boundaries between coaching and clinical therapy and refer when necessary.

This well-implemented integrative approach allows NLP, hypnosis, and coaching to be valuable tools for supporting emotional health and reducing stress, fostering overall well-being from an ethical and conscious perspective.

PROPOSALS FOR FUTURE RESEARCH

Given the growing interest in the interdisciplinary approach to stress, well-being, and quality of life, it becomes essential to foster research lines that strengthen clinical and scientific evidence about the benefits of hypnosis, Neuro-Linguistic Programming (NLP), and Gestalt therapy. These disciplines have shown promising results in emotional self-regulation, mental health, and the development of more conscious and balanced lifestyles. The following key areas of future research are proposed:

1. Hypnosis and Neuroscience Applied to Emotional Well-Being

- Delve into the neurophysiological effects of hypnosis on the autonomic nervous system using neuroimaging techniques (fMRI, EEG), evaluating its relation to states of calm, relaxation, and emotional balance.
- Explore the role of hypnosis in modulating the hypothalamic-pituitary-adrenal (HPA) axis, particularly in patients with chronic stress, insomnia, or anxiety-related disorders.

2. Empirical Validation of NLP and Contemporary Applications of Gestalt Therapy

- Design controlled clinical trials to assess the effectiveness of specific NLP techniques (such as anchoring, reframing, timeline) for reducing stress, anxiety, and psychosomatic symptoms.
- Analyze the relationship between the systematic use of NLP and variables such as subjective well-being, self-esteem, emotional resilience, and perceived quality of life.
- Investigate the effectiveness of Gestalt therapy in contemporary contexts (educational, clinical, and organizational) and its impact on stress management, emotional expression, and personal empowerment.

3. Integrative Models Focused on Well-Being and Emotional Health

- Develop therapeutic protocols that integrate hypnosis, NLP, and Gestalt therapy into structured programs for stress reduction, emotional self-care, and strengthening healthy habits.
- Compare the effectiveness of these models with conventional interventions, both in terms of clinical outcomes and user satisfaction.

- Explore factors that promote adherence to integrative therapeutic practices, their everyday application, and their impact on preventing emotional relapses or crises.

These research lines will not only scientifically validate the clinical applications of hypnosis, NLP, and Gestalt therapy but also provide essential evidence to design preventive, educational, and therapeutic programs aimed at strengthening individual and collective well-being, emotional resilience, and promoting a better quality of life in societies increasingly affected by stress.

CONCLUSION

In a global context where stress levels are rising daily and profoundly affecting the quality of life of millions, the design of effective therapeutic approaches that integrate different disciplines to address the cognitive, emotional, and somatic dimensions of the human being is urgent. The combination of hypnosis, Neuro-Linguistic Programming (NLP), and Gestalt therapy represents a powerful, ethical, and humanistic response to this need. These tools allow access to deep relaxation states, reframe painful experiences, transform limiting beliefs, and reconnect with internal resources.

Hypnosis offers a path to induce expanded states of consciousness, favoring emotional self-regulation and the integration of new perspectives. NLP provides effective techniques for mental reprogramming and the development of healthier coping strategies, while Gestalt therapy promotes full awareness of the present moment and personal responsibility in the change process. When integrated, these disciplines enable a more comprehensive, profound therapeutic intervention centered on the individual's overall well-being.

Furthermore, the incorporation of coaching as a complementary tool strengthens the practical implementation of therapeutic learning, promotes active client engagement, and enhances their autonomy in the transformation process. This integrative approach not only relieves stress but also fosters the development of a more coherent, conscious, and fulfilling life. The synergy between hypnosis, NLP, Gestalt, and coaching, applied with ethical sensitivity and professionalism, represents a solid and hopeful alternative for those seeking to heal, grow, and build a life with greater balance, meaning, and well-being. The responsible implementation of these methodologies can significantly contribute not only to individual mental health but also generate a positive impact in communities, educational institutions, and workplaces. In this way, a culture of self-care, resilience, and transformation is strengthened, responding to the demands of an increasingly complex and demanding world.

REFERENCES

Bradley, E. J., & Biedermann, H.-J. (1985). Bandler and Grinder's neurolinguistic programming: Its historical context and contribution. *Psychotherapy (Chicago, Ill.)*, *22*(1), 59–62. DOI: 10.1037/h0088527

Bundrant, H. (2024, March 4). *NLP and Hypnosis: Similarities, Differences, and Synergies*. iNLP Center. https://inlpcenter.org/whats-the-connection-between-nlp-and-hypnosis/

Dash, B. (2023). *Significance of Nonverbal Communication and Paralinguistic Features in Communication: A Critical Analysis*. https://doi.org/DOI: 10.2015/IJIRMF/202204029

De Benedittis, G. (2024). Hypnotic Modulation of Autonomic Nervous System (ANS) Activity. *Brain Sciences*, *14*(3), 249. DOI: 10.3390/brainsci14030249 PMID: 38539637

dgoldenconlin. (2023, August 15). *Writing Across Ancient History and Civilizations*. Mysite. https://www.dgoldenconlin.com/post/writing-across-ancient-history-and-civilizations

Dillworth, T., Mendoza, M. E., & Jensen, M. P. (2012). Neurophysiology of pain and hypnosis for chronic pain. *Translational Behavioral Medicine*, *2*(1), 65–72. DOI: 10.1007/s13142-011-0084-5 PMID: 24073099

Dilts, R. B. (1983). *Roots of neuro-linguistic programming*. Meta Publications.

Ericksonian Hypnosis: What it is and How it is Used in Therapy | 2025. (2024, March 15). https://psychologyfor.com/ericksonian-hypnosis-what-it-is-and-how-it-is-used-in-therapy/

Fitzpatrick, K. K., Darcy, A., & Vierhile, M. (2017). Delivering Cognitive Behavior Therapy to Young Adults With Symptoms of Depression and Anxiety Using a Fully Automated Conversational Agent (Woebot): A Randomized Controlled Trial. *JMIR Mental Health*, *4*(2), e19. DOI: 10.2196/mental.7785 PMID: 28588005

Fromme, D. K. (2011). Humanism: Experiential Approaches. In D. K. Fromme, *Systems of Psychotherapy* (pp. 223–261). Springer New York. https://doi.org/DOI: 10.1007/978-1-4419-7308-5_8

González-Ramírez, E., Carrillo-Montoya, T., García-Vega, M. L., Hart, C. E., Zavala-Norzagaray, A. A., & Ley-Quiñónez, C. P. (2017). Effectiveness of hypnosis therapy and Gestalt therapy as depression treatments. *Clinica y Salud*, *28*(1), 33–37. DOI: 10.1016/j.clysa.2016.11.001

Grant, S. (2023, November 15). NLP Hypnosis Reading vs. Traditional Hypnosis: What Sets Them Apart? *Medium*. https://medium.com/@samanthagrant2024/nlp-hypnosis-reading-vs-traditional-hypnosis-what-sets-them-apart-5b57e3ab6e04

Grinder, J., & Bandler, R. (with Internet Archive). (1976). *The structure of magic*. Palo Alto, Ca.: Science and Behavior Books. http://archive.org/details/structureofmagic00grin

Higson-Sweeney, N., Mikkola, A., Smith, L., Shafique, J., Draper, L., Cooper, K., Dunn, B. D., & Loades, M. E. (2022). Nonpharmacological interventions for treating fatigue in adolescents: A systematic review and narrative synthesis of randomised controlled trials. *Journal of Psychosomatic Research*, *163*, 111070. DOI: 10.1016/j.jpsychores.2022.111070 PMID: 36327529

Holroyd, J. (2003). The science of meditation and the state of hypnosis. *The American Journal of Clinical Hypnosis*, *46*(2), 109–128. DOI: 10.1080/00029157.2003.10403582 PMID: 14609297

Jensen, M. P., & Patterson, D. R. (2014). Hypnotic Approaches for Chronic Pain Management. *The American Psychologist*, *69*(2), 167–177. DOI: 10.1037/a0035644 PMID: 24547802

Kallio, S., & Revonsuo, A. (2003). Hypnotic phenomena and altered states of consciousness: A multilevel framework of description and explanation. *Contemporary Hypnosis*, *20*(3), 111–164. DOI: 10.1002/ch.273

Matthews, W. J. (2000). Ericksonian approaches to hypnosis and therapy: Where are we now? *The International Journal of Clinical and Experimental Hypnosis*, *48*(4), 418–426. DOI: 10.1080/00207140008410370 PMID: 11011501

Megha. (2024, February 15). *Gestalt Therapy: The Power of the Present Moment in Healing*. Careme.Health. https://careme.health/blog/gestalt-therapy-the-power-of-the-present-moment-in-healing

Nevis, E. C. (2009). *Gestalt therapy: Perspectives and applications* (1st paperback ed). Routledge.

Olawade, D. B., Wada, O. Z., Odetayo, A., David-Olawade, A. C., Asaolu, F., & Eberhardt, J. (2024). Enhancing mental health with Artificial Intelligence: Current trends and future prospects. *Journal of Medicine, Surgery, and Public Health, 3*, 100099. DOI: 10.1016/j.glmedi.2024.100099

Qureshi, D. A. (2024, July 23). *NLP Therapy Explained: Discover the Benefits and Techniques.* Therapy Helpers. https://therapyhelpers.com/therapy-types/what-is-neuro-linguistic-programming-therapy/

Rachmad, Y. E. (2024). *Stress Management Theory.* https://doi.org/DOI: 10.17605/OSF.IO/5UT3K

Raygoza-L, M. E., Orduño-Osuna, J. H., Jimenez-Sanchez, R., Mercado-Herrera, A., Ling, J. C., & Rico, F. N. M. (2024). Leadership and Coaching Management as a Governance Instrument for Sociocultural Development. In Wefald, A. J. (Ed.), (pp. 37–57). Advances in Logistics, Operations, and Management Science. IGI Global., DOI: 10.4018/979-8-3693-5242-7.ch003

Raygoza Limón, M. E., & Jiménez Sánchez, R. (2024). Perspectives and challenges for the development of leadership in Latin American women. *Entretextos, 16*(40), 1–19. DOI: 10.59057/iberoleon.20075316.202440738

Sevoz-Couche, C., & Laborde, S. (2022). Heart rate variability and slow-paced breathing:when coherence meets resonance. *Neuroscience and Biobehavioral Reviews, 135*, 104576. DOI: 10.1016/j.neubiorev.2022.104576 PMID: 35167847

Soler, L., Wieber, F., Allamel-Raffin, C., Gangloff, J.-L., Dufour, C., & Trizio, E. (2013). Calibration: A Conceptual Framework Applied to Scientific Practices Which Investigate Natural Phenomena by Means of Standardized Instruments. *Journal for General Philosophy of Science, 44*(2), 263–317. DOI: 10.1007/s10838-013-9231-7

Spiegel, E. B., Baker, E. L., Daitch, C., Diamond, M. J., & Phillips, M. (2020). Hypnosis and The Therapeutic Relationship: Relational Factors of Hypnosis in Psychotherapy. *The American Journal of Clinical Hypnosis, 62*(1–2), 118–137. DOI: 10.1080/00029157.2019.1599319 PMID: 31265368

Sturt, J., Ali, S., Robertson, W., Metcalfe, D., Grove, A., Bourne, C., & Bridle, C. (2012). Neurolinguistic programming: A systematic review of the effects on health outcomes. *The British Journal of General Practice, 62*(604), e757–e764. DOI: 10.3399/bjgp12X658287 PMID: 23211179

Wibawa, , A. P., Bihari Dash, & Kurniawan, F. (2024). Advancements in natural language processing: Implications, challenges, and future directions. *Telematics and Informatics Reports, 16*, 100173. DOI: 10.1016/j.teler.2024.100173

Tepe, J. (2025, January 7). *Unlocking the Power of NLP, Hypnosis, and Applied Neuroscience*. John Tepe. https://www.johntepe.com/post/unlocking-the-power-of-nlp-hypnosis-and-applied-neuroscience

Watson, J. C., Goldman, R. N., & Greenberg, L. S. (2011). Humanistic and experiential theories of psychotherapy. In *History of psychotherapy: Continuity and change* (2nd ed., pp. 141–172). American Psychological Association., DOI: 10.1037/12353-005

Weiner, I. B., Stricker, G., & Widiger, T. A. (2012). *Clinical Psychology*. Handbook of Psychology. John Wiley & Sons.

Weissman, D. G., & Mendes, W. B. (2021). Correlation of sympathetic and parasympathetic nervous system activity during rest and acute stress tasks. *International Journal of Psychophysiology : Official Journal of the International Organization of Psychophysiology, 162*, 60–68. DOI: 10.1016/j.ijpsycho.2021.01.015 PMID: 33561515

Zaharia, C., Reiner, M., & Schütz, P. (2015). Evidence-based Neuro Linguistic Psychotherapy: A meta-analysis. *Psychiatria Danubina, 27*(4), 355–363. PMID: 26609647

Zahm, S. G., & Gold, E. K. (2002). Gestalt Therapy. In Hersen, M., & Sledge, W. (Eds.), *Encyclopedia of Psychotherapy* (pp. 863–872). Academic Press., DOI: 10.1016/B0-12-343010-0/00105-7

KEY TERMS AND DEFINITIONS

Belief Transformation: A therapeutic process that identifies challenges, and replaces limiting beliefs with empowering beliefs, facilitating change and self-realization.

Calibration (NLP): A process of careful observation of non-verbal signals (facial expressions, body language) to detect emotional changes and adjust the therapeutic intervention precisely.

Contact (Gestalt): The ability to be fully present in the immediate experience, favoring authenticity and emotional integration.

Creative Visualization: A tool used in NLP, hypnosis, and coaching to vividly imagine desired states, goals, or scenarios that reinforce positive emotions and guide behavior.

Emotional Anchors: An NLP technique that associates a specific stimulus (visual, auditory, or kinesthetic) with a desired emotional state, allowing it to be evoked in the future as a resource.

Emotional Self-Regulation: The ability to manage one's emotions adaptively. It is strengthened through practices such as hypnosis, NLP, and mindfulness.

Hypnotic Trance: A modified state of consciousness induced in hypnosis, characterized by deep relaxation, focused concentration, and high receptivity to therapeutic suggestions.

Rapport (NLP): The ability to establish a connection of trust and empathy with another person by synchronizing verbal and non-verbal language (tone of voice, gestures, posture). It is essential in effective communication and therapy processes.

Reframing (NLP): A technique that involves changing the perspective on a situation to give it a new, functional, and positive meaning.

Somatic Self-Regulation: Regulation of the body's physiological state as a pathway to calm, through techniques such as breathing, visualization, and emotional anchoring.

Therapeutic Suggestion: A verbal, symbolic, or sensory proposal introduced during a hypnotic trance to promote changes in behavior, thought, or emotions.

Well-Formed Outcome Model (NLP): A strategy for defining objectives clearly, specifically, measurably, ecologically, and oriented towards the desired results.

Chapter 2

Hypnotherapy as a Workplace Intervention for Business Professionals: Addressing Stress, Burnout, and Productivity in Hybrid Organizations

Sangeeta Kakkar
https://orcid.org/0009-0007-9139-8040
Shoolini University of Biotechnology and Management Sciences, India

S. M. Haider Rizvi
Shoolini University of Biotechnology and Management Sciences, India

ABSTRACT

The hybrid work paradigm has transformed the traditional workplace, combining remote and in-office presence to provide greater freedom and flexibility without compromising efficiency. However, this shift has created substantial issues for business professionals. This chapter examines the psychological, emotional, and physiological impacts of prolonged job stress in the hybrid work culture. The chapter also covers ways for reducing stress and increasing long-term productivity. It emphasizes the value of self-regulation, boundary-setting, and mindfulness techniques in developing resilience in business workers. This chapter presents a system of knowledge for stress management in a hybrid workplace by combining empirical studies and real-world situations. The findings highlight the importance for organizations to

DOI: 10.4018/979-8-3373-2317-6.ch002

take proactive steps to improve employee well-being while retaining operational efficiency. Finally, this chapter contributes to the area of workplace mental health by providing evidence-based recommendations for creating a productive hybrid work culture.

I. INTRODUCTION

The hybrid work model is a flexible work arrangement that allows employees to split their time between working remotely (such as from home) and working on-site (such as in an office) (Krajčík, 2023). This model provides a balance between the benefits of remote work—such as flexibility, reduced commuting time, and improved work-life balance—and the advantages of in-office collaboration, including team bonding, brainstorming, and access to resources (Dexter, 2024). The COVID-19 pandemic significantly accelerated the adoption of remote work (Amankwah-Amoah et al.,2021). With lockdowns and social distancing measures, companies had to transition to remote work quickly (Bhattacharyya & Thakre, 2021). However, as restrictions eased, organizations recognized the need for a more sustainable and flexible approach rather than a full return to office-based work (Barath & Schmidt, 2022). The hybrid work model has become a long-term trend rather than a temporary post-pandemic adjustment (Hopkins & Bardoel, 2023). While each organization tailors its hybrid strategy based on industry needs, employee preferences, and technological capabilities. The model is proving to be an effective middle ground between fully remote and fully in-office work (Ayoko & Ashkanasy, 2020).

Although the system of hybrid work has its advantages and seems effective out there are certain challenges as well. There is a significant impact on the work-life balance that leads to stress, burnout and productivity. So, it is essential to understand the intricate relationship between stress, burnout, and workplace productivity. Ther is a need to explore the causes, consequences, and coping strategies related to stress to provide valuable insights for organizations, business leaders, and employees. Addressing stress effectively can lead to improved employee well-being, increased productivity, and a healthier work environment. Furthermore, as workplaces continue to evolve, understanding stress in different work settings—onsite, online, and hybrid—becomes imperative for designing effective interventions and policies.

II. NATURE AND DEFINITION OF STRESS

Stress is a complex phenomenon characterized by emotional, cognitive, behavioral, and physiological reactions to perceived threats or challenges (Biggs et al., 2017).

The body's response to stress, commonly known as the 'fight-or-flight' response, is regulated by the autonomic nervous system and the hypothalamic-pituitary-adrenal (HPA) axis (Thiel & Dretsch, 2011). While moderate levels of stress can improve performance and alertness, chronic or excessive stress can result in serious health issues, including cardiovascular diseases, anxiety disorders, and diminished cognitive function (Esch et al., 2002). Previous studies indicate that prolonged stress exposure can modify brain function, particularly in regions associated with memory, emotional regulation, and decision-making, leading to enduring psychological consequences (McEwen, 1998). Additionally, stress can present itself through various physical symptoms such as headaches, gastrointestinal issues, and muscle tension (Kabat-Zinn, 1990). It is also linked to detrimental coping strategies, including smoking, overeating, and alcohol use, which further intensify the adverse effects on both physical and mental well-being (Wagner et al., 2015). Furthermore, coping techniques such as mindfulness, cognitive restructuring, and relaxation methods have been demonstrated to mitigate the negative effects of stress (Zeidner et al., 2017). In conclusion, while stress serves as a natural and essential physiological response to challenges, it becomes problematic when it is excessive or chronic. Gaining insight into the mechanisms of stress and its impact on various health dimensions is crucial.

III. TYPES OF STRESS

1. **Acute Stress:** Acute stress is a temporary form of stress that arises from immediate challenges or events. It represents the body's instinctive response to specific situations requiring attention, such as meeting deadlines, public speaking, or narrowly escaping an accident (Lazarus & Folkman, 1984). This type of stress is marked by a rapid onset of physiological reactions, including increased heart rate, accelerated breathing, and heightened alertness, all of which prepare the individual to effectively confront the perceived threat (Thiel & Dretsch, 2011). Generally, acute stress dissipates quickly once the stressor is eliminated, or the situation is resolved. While occasional acute stress is manageable and can even improve focus and performance (Biggs et al., 2017), frequent or excessively intense acute stress may result in adverse psychological and physiological consequences if not adequately addressed (Esch et al., 2002).
2. **Chronic Stress:** Chronic stress is a prolonged state of stress that endures for an extended duration, often stemming from persistent issues such as job dissatisfaction, relationship difficulties, or financial worries (McEwen, 2007). It can last for weeks, months, or even years, gradually depleting the body's resources. This form of stress has been demonstrated to have a more harmful effect on health, contributing to conditions such as hypertension, cardiovascu-

lar disease, depression, and anxiety (Esch et al., 2002). Additionally, chronic stress can hinder cognitive functioning, impacting the memory, concentration, and decision-making skills (Lupien et al., 2009). The continuous activation of the body's stress response, particularly the HPA axis, exhausts energy reserves, and over time, this can lead to a condition referred to as 'allostatic load,' which undermines the immune system and overall health.

3. **Episodic Stress:** Episodic stress is characterized by the repeated occurrence of acute stress episodes, where individuals undergo successive periods of stress over time. This condition is commonly observed in those who are susceptible to anxiety or frequently encounter high-pressure environments, such as professionals in demanding roles, caregivers, or individuals facing persistent life challenges (Kabat-Zinn, 1990). In contrast to acute stress, which is generally short-lived, episodic stress is ongoing and can have a profound impact on an individual's mental and physical well-being over time. Prolonged exposure to episodic stress may result in burnout, leading to feelings of physical and emotional exhaustion, and can also contribute to chronic health issues like hypertension and gastrointestinal disorders (Maslach & Leiter, 2016). Effective strategies for managing this type of stress include stress-reduction techniques, cognitive-behavioral therapy, and lifestyle modifications that assist individuals in better handling stressors (Zeidner et al., 2017).
4. **Eustress vs. Distress:** Stress can be classified into two categories: eustress, which is positive stress, and distress, which is negative stress, depending on the nature of the stressor and the individual's reaction to it. Eustress is characterized as a motivating and advantageous form of stress that often results in favorable outcomes, such as enhanced performance, concentration, and personal development (Selye, 1976). Conversely, distress represents the detrimental type of stress that arises when an individual feels overwhelmed, powerless, or incapable of managing the demands imposed upon them (Lazarus & Folkman, 1984). Distress frequently results in various physical and psychological health issues, including anxiety, depression, insomnia, and cardiovascular problems (Esch et al., 2002). The primary distinction between these two types of stress lies in the individual's perception and respon``se to the stressor—eustress is seen as a challenge that can be overcome, whereas distress is perceived as a threat that surpasses one's coping abilities (Cohen & Wills, 1985).

IV. STRESS IN PROFESSIONAL AND OCCUPATIONAL SETTINGS

Professional stress, or occupational stress, refers to work-related stressors that arise due to job demands, work environment, or interpersonal conflicts (Cooper & Quick, 2017). It is a significant concern in organizational psychology and human resource management, affecting employee's well-being and performance. Workplace stress has emerged as a critical issue in contemporary society, posing significant risks to both employees and organizations. Factors such as excessive workloads, stringent deadlines, limited control over job duties, poor interpersonal dynamics, and job insecurity contribute to heightened stress levels among workers (Leka et al., 2004). Prolonged stress in the workplace is associated with increased absenteeism, reduced job satisfaction, and diminished productivity (Kabat-Zinn, 1990). Furthermore, it can result in burnout, which is characterized by emotional fatigue, depersonalization, and a reduced sense of personal achievement (Maslach & Leiter, 2016). Acknowledging and addressing workplace stress not only improves employee performance but also enhances the overall success of the organization.

V. SOURCES OF PROFESSIONAL STRESS

1. **Workload and Job Demands:** The demands of workload and job responsibilities significantly contribute to workplace stress. An excessive workload, stringent deadlines, and unrealistic expectations can result in chronic stress and employee burnout. According to Karasek's Demand-Control Model (1979), a combination of high job demands, and low decision-making authority can foster a stressful work atmosphere, leading to adverse health effects for employees. When individuals are tasked with managing an overwhelming number of responsibilities in a limited timeframe, they may feel helpless and lack control, which can heighten stress levels (Karasek, 1979). Moreover, when job demands do not correspond with available resources—such as time, support, or skills—employees are more susceptible to experiencing fatigue, anxiety, and even depression (Cohen & Wills, 1985). The urgency to fulfil tight deadlines, often with scarce resources, can lead to extended working hours, a decline in quality of life, and lower job satisfaction (Leka et al., 2004). Furthermore, employees might resort to maladaptive coping mechanisms, such as neglecting self-care or social connections, in their efforts to meet elevated expectations (Kabat-Zinn, 1990). Over time, these ongoing job demands can adversely affect both mental and physical health, increasing the likelihood of cardiovascular diseases, burnout, and other stress-related conditions (Esch et al., 2002). Organizations can mitigate these challenges by

establishing more attainable expectations, enhancing workload distribution, and cultivating a supportive environment that promotes open communication and employee well-being (Karasek, 1979).

2. **Role Ambiguity and Conflict:** Ambiguous job responsibilities and conflicting demands significantly contribute to workplace stress, as they generate confusion and heighten the cognitive and emotional load on employees. When job roles and expectations lack clarity, employees frequently find it challenging to comprehend their specific responsibilities, prioritize tasks, and manage their time effectively (Katz & Kahn, 1978). This uncertainty can foster feelings of doubt and frustration, as employees are unclear about how to meet performance expectations or align their efforts with the organization's objectives (Katz & Kahn, 1978). Furthermore, conflicting demands, where employees are tasked with competing priorities or receive inconsistent guidance from supervisors or colleagues, can intensify stress levels. For instance, an employee might be instructed to complete a project under a tight deadline while simultaneously being told to focus on another task that requires greater time and attention (Katz & Kahn, 1978). This situation creates internal conflict, as employees feel torn between competing expectations, potentially leading to inefficiencies, frustration, and diminished morale. The role conflict that emerges from such circumstances can culminate in burnout, as employees feel overwhelmed by their inability to meet all demands at once (Rizzo et al., 1970). In the absence of clear communication and defined roles, employees may lack confidence in their capacity to perform effectively, which can lead to job dissatisfaction and mental strain (Katz & Kahn, 1978). To alleviate these stressors, organizations should aim to clearly delineate job roles, set realistic expectations, and promote open communication between employees and supervisors to minimize ambiguity and conflicting demands.
3. **Job Insecurity:** The apprehension regarding potential job loss constitutes a major contributor to stress within the workplace, especially during economic recessions or organizational changes. In situations where companies encounter financial difficulties or implement downsizing measures, employees frequently experience increased anxiety concerning their job security (Greenhalgh & Rosenblatt, 1984). This state of uncertainty can result in feelings of helplessness and stress, as individuals worry about their capacity to sustain their livelihoods and provide for their families. The persistent fear of layoffs can adversely affect job performance, elevate absenteeism rates, and lead to emotional fatigue (Greenhalgh & Rosenblatt, 1984). Furthermore, employees may witness a decrease in morale and dedication to the organization, as the absence of job security erodes their sense of stability and control (Marmot et al., 1991). Organizations can alleviate this stress by ensuring effective communication, providing support services, and

establishing transparent procedures to assist employees in navigating times of economic instability.

4. **Workplace Relationships:** Interpersonal conflicts, insufficient social support, and workplace harassment are significant sources of stress that can profoundly impact an employee's well-being. Conflicts among colleagues or supervisors create a hostile and uncomfortable atmosphere, contributing to stress and dissatisfaction (Einarsen et al., 2003). Such disputes often hinder collaboration and communication, resulting in frustration and emotional distress. Moreover, the absence of social support—whether from peers, supervisors, or family—can intensify stress, as employees lacking robust support networks may feel isolated and ill-equipped to tackle workplace challenges (Cohen & Wills, 1985).

This deficiency in support can heighten feelings of vulnerability and helplessness. Additionally, workplace bullying, characterized by repeated mistreatment such as verbal abuse, intimidation, or social exclusion, can lead to severe psychological and physical repercussions for the victim. Employees subjected to bullying frequently experience anxiety, depression, and diminished self-esteem, along with challenges in concentration and task performance (Einarsen et al., 2003). Bullying fosters a toxic work environment, resulting in high turnover rates and reduced productivity. To alleviate these stressors, organizations should cultivate a culture of respect and inclusion, implement conflict resolution strategies, and ensure that employees have access to sufficient social support systems.

VI. STRESS IN AN INDUSTRIAL SETUP AND ITS CONTRIBUTING FACTORS

Industrial workplaces present distinct stressors due to their physical requirements, hazardous conditions, and repetitive tasks. Workers in industries such as manufacturing, logistics, and heavy engineering frequently endure physical strain from manual labor, exposure to dangerous machinery, toxic substances, and extreme temperatures, which heightens the risk of injuries and chronic health problems like musculoskeletal disorders (Karasek & Theorell, 1990). Furthermore, the repetitive nature of tasks and high-pressure settings with stringent production deadlines can contribute to mental exhaustion, job dissatisfaction, and burnout (Maslach & Leiter, 2016). The interplay of these elements results in a demanding work environment where employees may face both physical and psychological stress, highlighting the need for effective safety measures, ergonomic interventions, and mental health resources to alleviate the effects on worker well-being (Leka et al., 2004).

VII. FACTORS OF STRESS IN INDUSTRIAL SETTINGS

1. **Physical Demands: Long working hours, repetitive tasks, and exposure to harmful substances** are significant sources of stress in industrial and high-risk work environments. Working extended hours, especially without adequate breaks, leads to physical exhaustion and increased vulnerability to errors, accidents, and long-term health issues like cardiovascular diseases and sleep disturbances (Sauter et al., 1999). Repetitive tasks, often required in manufacturing and assembly line jobs, can result in mental fatigue, reduced job satisfaction, and musculoskeletal disorders due to constant strain on the same muscle groups (Karasek & Theorell, 1990). Additionally, workers who are exposed to harmful substances such as chemicals, dust, or fumes face an elevated risk of respiratory problems, skin conditions, and chronic illnesses over time (Sauter et al., 1999). Together, these factors create a physically and mentally demanding environment, underscoring the importance of workplace safety measures and strategies to reduce exposure to these stressors.
2. **Job Autonomy:** Prolonged working hours, monotonous tasks, and contact with hazardous materials are major contributors to stress in industrial and high-risk occupational settings. Extended work hours, particularly without sufficient breaks, result in physical fatigue and heightened susceptibility to mistakes, accidents, and chronic health conditions such as cardiovascular diseases and sleep disorders (Sauter et al., 1999). Monotonous tasks, frequently found in manufacturing and assembly line roles, can lead to cognitive fatigue, diminished job satisfaction, and musculoskeletal issues due to the continuous strain on specific muscle groups (Karasek & Theorell, 1990). Furthermore, employees exposed to harmful substances like chemicals, dust, or fumes are at an increased risk of respiratory ailments, skin disorders, and long-term health issues (Sauter et al., 1999). Collectively, these elements contribute to a physically and mentally challenging work environment, highlighting the necessity for workplace safety protocols and initiatives aimed at minimizing exposure to these stressors.
3. **Shift Work and Circadian Disruptions:** Working in shifts, particularly during the night, interferes with the natural sleep patterns of employees, causing disturbances in their circadian rhythms (Åkerstedt, 2003). The inconsistency between work hours and the body's internal clock may lead to persistent fatigue, reduced cognitive abilities, and long-term health complications, including insomnia, gastrointestinal issues, and a heightened risk of cardiovascular diseases. This disruption has a profound effect on both physical and mental well-being, rendering shift workers more susceptible to stress.
4. **Organizational Culture:** Strict hierarchies, autocratic leadership, and insufficient employee engagement can foster a workplace culture that suppresses

innovation and impedes productivity. In such settings, decision-making tends to be centralized, leaving little opportunity for employees to express their views or contribute creatively. The lack of open communication and collaboration may result in disengagement, diminishing motivation and overall job satisfaction. Autocratic leadership further intensifies these challenges by promoting a culture of control rather than empowerment, causing employees to feel undervalued and reluctant to take initiative. As Edgar Schein (2010) highlights, organizational culture is pivotal in influencing behavior, and a rigid, top-down structure can restrict adaptability, hindering companies' ability to succeed in dynamic and competitive markets. To overcome these obstacles, organizations should emphasize inclusivity, promote participative leadership, and cultivate an environment that encourages employee engagement and collaborative decision-making.

5. **Workplace Safety Concerns:** Workplace safety and employee well-being are profoundly affected by accidents, injuries, and the fear of potential hazards. When employees are in a constant state of concern regarding possible dangers, it can result in increased stress, reduced productivity, and general dissatisfaction. Physical injuries and accidents not only present immediate threats but also lead to long-term psychological consequences, causing workers to be reluctant to engage in tasks perceived as risky. As noted by Cooper and Marshall (1976), creating a safe work environment necessitates proactive risk management, well-defined safety protocols, and the cultivation of a culture in which employees feel secure and supported. Organizations that emphasize workplace safety can minimize accidents, mitigate fears, and foster a healthier, more engaged workforce.

VIII. STRESS AND BURNOUT – THE INTERCONNECTION

Burnout is a prolonged response to chronic stress, characterized by emotional exhaustion, depersonalization, and reduced personal accomplishment (Maslach & Jackson, 1981). When employees experience persistent workplace stress without effective coping strategies, they are at high risk of burnout.

Stress Leading to Burnout

1. **Emotional Exhaustion:** Experiencing fatigue and an inability to fulfill professional obligations is frequently attributed to burnout, a psychological condition stemming from extended workplace stress. According to Maslach et al. (2001), burnout encompasses emotional exhaustion, depersonalization, and a reduced sense of personal achievement, all of which can adversely affect an individual's performance and overall well-being. When employees encounter excessive

workloads, insufficient support, or a disparity between effort and reward, they may find it challenging to sustain motivation and engagement. Over time, this state of exhaustion can result in diminished job satisfaction, lower productivity, and even health complications. Organizations that emphasize employee well-being through effective workload management, transparent communication, and robust support systems can alleviate burnout, promoting a healthier and more sustainable work environment.

2. **Cynicism and Depersonalization:** Hostile attitudes towards work and colleagues can foster a detrimental workplace atmosphere, diminishing morale and overall efficiency. Leiter and Maslach (1988) indicate that these attitudes frequently arise from burnout, dissatisfaction, or unresolved conflicts within the workplace, resulting in disengagement and strained relationships among staff members. When employees feel undervalued, unsupported, or overwhelmed, they may develop animosity towards their roles or coworkers, which further intensifies stress and reduces productivity. To tackle these challenges, it is essential to nurture a positive organizational culture, promote open communication, and enhance feelings of belonging and recognition. By emphasizing employee well-being and teamwork, organizations can alleviate negativity and develop a more engaged and motivated workforce.
3. **Inefficacy:** A diminished sense of competence and productivity can profoundly affect an individual's motivation and overall job performance. Schaufeli et al. (2009) identify this issue as a fundamental element of burnout, where employees perceive themselves as less effective and find it difficult to fulfill professional obligations. Prolonged stress, lack of acknowledgment, or inadequate support can erode individuals' confidence in their capabilities, resulting in disengagement and decreased output. This reduction in productivity not only hampers personal career advancement but also impacts workplace morale and efficiency. To address these issues, organizations should cultivate a supportive atmosphere, promote skill enhancement, and offer meaningful recognition to assist employees in restoring their sense of competence and motivation.

IX. STRESS AND BURNOUT IMPACTING PRODUCTIVITY IN BUSINESS PROFESSIONALS

Burnout significantly affects workplace productivity, leading to absenteeism, reduced job satisfaction, and higher turnover rates (Schaufeli & Bakker, 2004).

Consequences of Burnout on Business Productivity

1. **Decreased Efficiency:** Cognitive overload and diminished focus can greatly impede productivity and overall well-being, especially in high-pressure work settings. Maslach and Leiter (2016) emphasize that when individuals are inundated with excessive information, tasks, or responsibilities, their capacity to concentrate and process information effectively declines. This mental burden frequently results in stress, exhaustion, and challenges in decision-making, further diminishing workplace efficiency. Extended exposure to cognitive overload may also lead to burnout, making it crucial for organizations to adopt strategies that encourage manageable workloads, clear task prioritization, and opportunities for mental recuperation. By cultivating a balanced and supportive work atmosphere, individuals can improve their focus, alleviate stress, and sustain performance levels.
2. **Increased Absenteeism:** Frequent absenteeism due to mental and physical health challenges can serve as a significant indicator of workplace stress and burnout, as noted by Schaufeli et al. (2009). Prolonged exposure to excessive workloads, high-pressure environments, or insufficient support can adversely affect employees' well-being, resulting in psychological distress and physical health problems. Stress-related conditions such as anxiety, depression, fatigue, and even chronic illnesses may compel individuals to take leave, ultimately impacting productivity and team cohesion. Organizations that neglect to address these issues may experience elevated absenteeism rates, reduced engagement, and long-term health complications among their workforce. To mitigate these challenges, companies should advocate for work-life balance, promote mental health resources, and cultivate a culture of care and well-being, ensuring that employees feel appreciated and supported in both their professional and personal endeavors.
3. **Employee Turnover:** Elevated turnover rates can significantly undermine organizational stability, resulting in operational inefficiencies, heightened expenses, and reduced employee morale. According to Maslach and Leiter (2016), factors such as burnout, disengagement, and dissatisfaction are primary contributors to employee turnover, often arising from overwhelming workloads, inadequate support, and detrimental work environments. Frequent employee departures pose challenges for organizations in preserving institutional knowledge, maintaining team unity, and ensuring steady productivity. Furthermore, high turnover rates can adversely affect an employer's reputation, complicating the recruitment of new talent. To mitigate these issues, organizations should cultivate a supportive and inclusive culture, emphasize employee well-being, and adopt retention strategies that promote long-term commitment and engagement.

4. **Workplace Errors:** Cognitive impairments caused by stress can result in a higher frequency of errors, adversely impacting both individual performance and the overall efficiency of the workplace. Cooper and Quick (2017) emphasize that excessive stress interferes with cognitive functions such as memory, attention, and decision-making, making it increasingly challenging for employees to accurately process information and respond appropriately. When employees feel overwhelmed, they may encounter obstacles in problem-solving, misremember critical details, or find it difficult to concentrate, thereby raising the risk of mistakes. These errors can have significant repercussions, particularly in high-stakes sectors where precision and accuracy are essential. It is imperative for organizations to prioritize stress management initiatives, foster mental health support, and cultivate a balanced work environment to alleviate cognitive overload and improve employees' capacity to perform at their best.

X. DIFFERENTIAL IMPACT IN ONSITE, ONLINE, AND HYBRID CONTEXTS

The mode of work influences how stress and burnout manifest among employees.

1. **Onsite Work:** High social interaction but physical and mental fatigue (Bailey & Kurland, 2002).
2. **Online Work:** Flexibility but isolation and digital fatigue (Golden & Veiga, 2005).
3. **Hybrid Work:** Balanced approach but challenges in maintaining consistency (Allen et al., 2015).

a. Role of AI and Technology in Managing Workloads

Artificial intelligence (AI) and digital tools are transforming the way professionals handle workloads, offering solutions to optimize time management, automate repetitive tasks, and enhance decision-making efficiency. AI-driven analytics can predict burnout risks by assessing work patterns and suggesting preventive measures, such as workload redistribution and task prioritization. Additionally, AI chatbots and virtual assistants help employees manage stress by providing immediate support and mental health resources (Torous et al., 2020).

b. Redesigning Workplaces for Better Hybrid Work Experiences

The shift toward hybrid work requires organizations to rethink workspace design. Flexible office layouts, ergonomic home office setups, and technology-driven collaboration tools are essential for maintaining productivity and reducing stress. Companies are increasingly adopting smart scheduling systems to balance in-office and remote work, ensuring employees can collaborate effectively while maintaining a healthy work-life balance (Allen et al., 2015).

c. Shifting Organizational Focus to Holistic Employee Well-Being

Modern organizations are expanding their employee well-being initiatives beyond traditional health benefits. Workplace wellness programs now emphasize mental health support, mindfulness training, and resilience-building workshops. Companies are investing in initiatives such as employee assistance programs (EAPs), mental health counseling, and wellness apps to address stress proactively. A culture of well-being fosters higher engagement, reduced burnout, and improved job satisfaction (Cooper & Quick, 2017).

d. Stress Management through Hypnotherapeutic Interventions:

In the hybrid work era, business professionals are required to continuously adapt to fluctuating work demands, shifting role expectations, and persistent digital engagement. These conditions intensify cognitive load and emotional strain, making effective stress management a critical determinant of both individual well-being and organizational productivity. Hypnotherapeutic interventions represent a psychologically grounded and increasingly evidence-based approach to managing occupational stress by engaging subconscious cognitive, emotional, and physiological processes that shape stress perception and response.

From a theoretical standpoint, hypnotherapy operates by inducing a state of focused attention and deep relaxation, allowing individuals to access and modify maladaptive cognitive schemas, emotional reactions, and automatic stress responses. This altered state of consciousness facilitates enhanced suggestibility, enabling therapeutic reframing of stressors, reduction of anticipatory anxiety, and restoration of autonomic balance. In occupational contexts, particularly hybrid work settings, such mechanisms are highly relevant as employees must self-regulate in environments characterized by blurred boundaries, reduced supervisory cues, and continuous performance monitoring.

Empirical research increasingly supports the efficacy of hypnotherapy in stress reduction and resilience building. A multicenter randomized controlled trial by Peter et al. (2020) demonstrated that structured group hypnosis significantly reduced perceived stress while improving mental quality of life, emotional regulation, and self-efficacy among working professionals. Notably, participants reported sustained benefits beyond the intervention period, indicating hypnotherapy's potential for long-term stress regulation rather than short-term symptom relief. Such outcomes are particularly valuable in hybrid organizations where chronic, low-grade stress is prevalent.

Further strengthening this evidence base, Zucker et al. (2020) introduced mindful hypnotherapy, an integrative model combining hypnotic induction with mindfulness-based awareness and acceptance practices. Their eight-week randomized controlled trial revealed significant reductions in perceived distress alongside improvements in mindfulness, attentional control, and emotional clarity. This hybridized therapeutic approach is especially well suited to contemporary workplaces, as it enhances employees' capacity to remain present, cognitively flexible, and emotionally grounded amid digital distractions and competing role demands.

Meta-analytic findings also reinforce the clinical and organizational relevance of hypnotherapy. Kirsch et al. (2011) reported medium to large effect sizes for hypnotherapy as both a standalone and adjunct intervention for managing psychosomatic and stress-related symptoms. Modern and integrative hypnotherapeutic approaches—incorporating cognitive-behavioral, mindfulness-based, and psychodynamic elements—were found to yield superior outcomes compared to traditional directive hypnosis. Although systematic reviews by Hammond (2017) and Cardeña et al. (2017) acknowledge methodological variability across studies, the overall convergence of evidence consistently indicates meaningful reductions in stress, anxiety, and emotional exhaustion following hypnotherapeutic interventions.

From a managerial and organizational perspective, hypnotherapy aligns well with contemporary workplace mental health strategies that emphasize preventive care, self-regulation, and psychological resilience. Hypnotherapeutic programs can be delivered through individual sessions, group-based workshops, or digitally mediated platforms, making them adaptable to hybrid organizational structures. Group hypnosis formats, in particular, offer cost-effective scalability while fostering collective stress normalization and shared coping narratives among employees.

Importantly, hypnotherapy contributes not only to stress reduction but also to enhanced productivity-related outcomes. By improving attentional focus, emotional stability, and cognitive clarity, hypnotherapeutic interventions support better decision-making, creativity, and task engagement. Employees who develop greater awareness and control over their internal stress responses are better equipped to manage workload pressures, navigate interpersonal challenges, and sustain performance across both remote and in-office contexts.

In sum, hypnotherapeutic interventions represent a valuable yet underutilized component of organizational well-being frameworks. When integrated with broader managerial initiatives—such as supportive leadership, workload optimization, and digital boundary management—hypnotherapy offers a holistic and evidence-informed pathway for mitigating stress and promoting sustainable productivity in hybrid work environments.

XI. CONCLUSION

This chapter has examined the complex interplay between stress, burnout, and productivity within hybrid organizational contexts, highlighting the psychological and managerial implications of evolving work arrangements. Hybrid work, while offering flexibility and autonomy, introduces unique stressors that demand integrative and evidence-based responses. The chapter underscores the importance of addressing occupational stress through multi-level interventions encompassing organizational design, leadership practices, technological support, and individual coping mechanisms.

Notably, hypnotherapeutic interventions emerge as a promising and underutilized approach within workplace mental health frameworks. By targeting subconscious stress responses and enhancing self-regulatory capacity, hypnotherapy offers a valuable complement to traditional stress management strategies. As organizations continue to navigate the future of work, integrating psychological interventions such as hypnotherapy into holistic well-being programs may prove critical for sustaining both employee health and organizational performance.

XII. CALL FOR ACTION: CREATING A SUSTAINABLE WORK CULTURE

As hybrid work arrangements become embedded within organizational structures, there is a pressing need for a shift from reactive stress management to proactive, systemic cultivation of sustainable work cultures. Organizations must intentionally integrate flexibility, transparency, and psychological safety into both policy frameworks and everyday managerial practices. When flexibility is thoughtfully designed and equitably implemented, it enables employees to better navigate competing professional and personal demands, thereby reducing chronic stress and mitigating burnout risk.

Equally critical is the creation of psychologically safe environments in which employees feel empowered to express concerns, seek support, and engage in open dialogue without fear of stigma or negative consequences. Organizations should embed stress management initiatives within broader employee well-being strategies, incorporating evidence-based interventions such as counseling services, mindfulness programs, and hypnotherapeutic approaches. Ensuring realistic performance expectations and equitable workload distribution is essential for sustaining motivation and engagement. Leadership development initiatives must explicitly prepare managers to recognize early indicators of stress and burnout, respond with empathy, and foster supportive team climates that prioritize well-being alongside performance (Maslach & Leiter, 2016).

XIII. FINAL THOUGHTS ON MAINTAINING PRODUCTIVITY AND WELL-BEING IN A HYBRID ERA

The ongoing evolution of hybrid work models demands a holistic and integrative approach to managing stress, burnout, and productivity. Organizations must strategically align technological innovation, workplace design, and human-centered management practices to create environments that support both operational efficiency and psychological health. AI-driven tools can assist in workload optimization and early identification of burnout risks, while thoughtfully designed physical and virtual workspaces can reduce cognitive overload and enhance collaboration.

Sustainable productivity in hybrid organizations ultimately depends on cultivating cultures that recognize employee well-being as a strategic organizational asset, rather than a peripheral concern. By embedding well-being into organizational values, leadership practices, and governance structures, organizations can foster resilient, engaged, and high-performing workforces. The future of work will increasingly favor institutions that successfully balance efficiency with empathy, innovation with inclusion, and performance with care.

XIV. POLICY DEVELOPMENT

Robust policy development is foundational to institutionalizing work–life balance and mental health support within hybrid organizations. Policies should clearly articulate expectations regarding working hours, digital availability, and boundary management to prevent role overload and technostress. Initiatives such as paid mental health days, flexible scheduling arrangements, and formalized remote or hybrid work options can normalize self-care and reduce stigma associated with help-seeking behaviors.

Employee Assistance Programs (EAPs) offering confidential counseling and psychological support should be positioned as core components of organizational well-being strategies rather than ancillary benefits. Transparent communication regarding policy intent, accessibility, and confidentiality is essential to foster employee trust and utilization. By embedding mental health considerations into organizational policy frameworks, employers can proactively support psychological sustainability and long-term engagement.

XV. WORKPLACE DESIGN

The physical and psychological design of workplaces plays a pivotal role in shaping employee stress experiences, particularly in hybrid contexts where individuals alternate between home and office environments. Organizations should prioritize ergonomic, inclusive, and sensory-friendly workspaces that support concentration, comfort, and emotional regulation. Design strategies may include access to natural lighting, quiet zones for focused work, collaborative spaces for social interaction, and biophilic elements such as indoor plants and outdoor access.

Equally important is the design of digital work environments. Clear communication protocols, streamlined task management systems, and well-integrated collaboration platforms can significantly reduce informational overload and role ambiguity. Flexible scheduling arrangements—such as customizable start times or compressed workweeks—further enable employees to align work demands with personal responsibilities, thereby reducing stress and enhancing overall well-being.

XVI. LEADERSHIP TRAINING

Leadership behavior is a central determinant of employee well-being in hybrid organizations. Managers function as both cultural role models and primary points of support, making leadership training a critical lever for stress prevention and burnout mitigation. Training programs should emphasize emotional intelligence, active listening, and empathetic communication, enabling leaders to identify early signs of distress and respond constructively.

Additionally, leaders should be equipped with skills in conflict resolution, workload calibration, and strengths-based feedback to foster trust and psychological safety within teams. Importantly, leaders must model healthy work behaviors—such as setting boundaries around after-hours communication, taking restorative breaks, and openly valuing well-being—to legitimize these practices across organizational levels.

XVII. FUTURE RESEARCH

Although significant advances have been made in understanding workplace stress and burnout, further research is needed to address the evolving challenges associated with hybrid work. Future studies should investigate industry-specific stressors, examining how job demands, technological intensity, and organizational culture interact across sectors. Longitudinal research designs would be particularly valuable in assessing the sustained psychological and productivity-related impacts of hybrid work arrangements.

Moreover, empirical investigations into the comparative effectiveness of stress mitigation strategies—including hypnotherapy, mindfulness-based interventions, digital well-being tools, and organizational policy reforms—are warranted. Such research will support evidence-based decision-making and enable organizations to develop tailored interventions that respond to the diverse and dynamic needs of contemporary workforces.

REFERENCES

Åkerstedt, T. (2003). Shift work and disturbed sleep/wakefulness. *Occupational Medicine, 53*(2), 89–94. DOI: 10.1093/occmed/kqg046

Allen, T. D., Golden, T. D., & Shockley, K. M. (2015). How effective is telecommuting? Assessing the status of our scientific findings. *Psychological Science in the Public Interest, 16*(2), 40–68. DOI: 10.1177/1529100615593273

Amankwah-Amoah, J., Khan, Z., Wood, G., & Knight, G. (2021). COVID-19 and digitalization: The great acceleration. *Journal of Business Research, 136*, 602–611.

Ayoko, O. B., & Ashkanasy, N. M. (2020). The physical environment of office work: Future open plan offices. *Australian Journal of Management, 45*(3), 488–506.

Bailey, D. E., & Kurland, N. B. (2002). A review of telework research: Findings, new directions, and lessons for the study of modern work. *Journal of Organizational Behavior, 23*(4), 383–400. DOI: 10.1002/job.144

Barath, M., & Schmidt, D. A. (2022). Offices after the COVID-19 pandemic and changes in perception of flexible office space. *Sustainability, 14*(18), 11158.

Bhattacharyya, S. S., & Thakre, S. (2021). Coronavirus pandemic and economic lockdown; study of strategic initiatives and tactical responses of firms. *The International Journal of Organizational Analysis, 29*(5), 1240–1268.

Biggs, A., Brough, P., & Drummond, S. (2017). Lazarus and Folkman's psychological stress and coping theory. *The handbook of stress and health: A guide to research and practice*, 349-364.

Cardeña, E., Cardeña-Buelna, D., & Spiegel, D. (2017). Hypnosis for the treatment of anxiety, stress-related disorders, and chronic pain. *Current Psychiatry Reports, 19*(6), 40. DOI: 10.1007/s11920-017-0791-8

Cooper, C. L., & Marshall, J. (1976). Occupational sources of stress: A review of the literature relating to coronary heart disease and mental ill health. *Journal of Occupational Psychology, 49*(1), 11–28. DOI: 10.1111/j.2044-8325.1976.tb00325.x

Cooper, C. L., & Quick, J. C. (2017). *The handbook of stress and health: A guide to research and practice*. Wiley Blackwell.

Dexter, Á. (2024). The Impact of Remote Work on Interdisciplinary Collaboration in Game Development Projects.

Einarsen, S., Hoel, H., Zapf, D., & Cooper, C. L. (2003). *Bullying and emotional abuse in the workplace: International perspectives in research and practice*. CRC Press.

Esch, T., Stefano, G. B., Fricchione, G. L., & Benson, H. (2002). Stress in cardiovascular diseases. *Signature (Ramsey, N.J.)*, *8*(5), 101.

Golden, T. D., & Veiga, J. F. (2005). The impact of extent of telecommuting on job satisfaction: Resolving inconsistent findings. *Journal of Management*, *31*(2), 301–318. DOI: 10.1177/0149206304271768

Greenhalgh, L., & Rosenblatt, Z. (1984). Job insecurity: Toward conceptual clarity. *Academy of Management Review*, *9*(3), 438–448. DOI: 10.5465/amr.1984.4279673

Hammond, D. C. (2017). Hypnosis in the treatment of stress-related disorders. *The American Journal of Clinical Hypnosis*, *59*(4), 343–350. DOI: 10.1080/00029157.2016.1223593

Hopkins, J., & Bardoel, A. (2023). The future is hybrid: How organisations are designing and supporting sustainable hybrid work models in post-pandemic Australia. *Sustainability*, *15*(4), 3086.

Kabat-Zinn, J. (1990). *Full catastrophe living: Using the wisdom of your body and mind to face stress, pain, and illness*. Delta.

Karasek, R. A. (1979). Job demands, job decision latitude, and mental strain: Implications for job redesign. *Administrative Science Quarterly*, *24*(2), 285–308. DOI: 10.2307/2392498

Katz, D., & Kahn, R. L. (1978). *The social psychology of organizations* (2nd ed.). Wiley.

Kirsch, I., Montgomery, G., & Sapirstein, G. (2011). Hypnosis as an adjunct to cognitive-behavioral psychotherapy: A meta-analysis. *Journal of Consulting and Clinical Psychology*, *63*(2), 214–220. https://www.ncbi.nlm.nih.gov/books/NBK73898/

Krajčík, M., Schmidt, D. A., & Baráth, M. (2023). Hybrid work model: An approach to work–life flexibility in a changing environment. *Administrative Sciences*, *13*(6), 150.

Lazarus, R. S., & Folkman, S. (1984). *Stress, appraisal, and coping*. Springer.

Leiter, M. P., & Maslach, C. (1988). The impact of interpersonal environment on burnout and organizational commitment. *Journal of Organizational Behavior*, *9*(4), 297–308. DOI: 10.1002/job.4030090402

Maslach, C., & Jackson, S. E. (1981). The measurement of experienced burnout. *Journal of Occupational Behaviour*, *2*(2), 99–113. DOI: 10.1002/job.4030020205

Maslach, C., Jackson, S. E., & Leiter, M. P. (2001). *Maslach burnout inventory manual* (3rd ed.). Consulting Psychologists Press.

Maslach, C., & Leiter, M. P. (2016). *Burnout: The cost of caring*. Malor Books.

McEwen, B. S. (1998). Protective and damaging effects of stress mediators. *The New England Journal of Medicine*, *338*(3), 171–179. DOI: 10.1056/NEJM199801153380307

Peter, B., Schedlowski, M., Warth, M., & Hölzel, L. P. (2020). Stress reduction through group hypnosis in professional settings: A randomized controlled trial. *The International Journal of Clinical and Experimental Hypnosis*, *68*(4), 485–503. DOI: 10.1080/00207144.2020.1780651

Sauter, S. L., Murphy, L. R., & Hurrell, J. J. (1999). Prevention of work-related psychological disorders: A national strategy proposed by the National Institute for Occupational Safety and Health (NIOSH). *The American Psychologist*, *45*(10), 1146–1158. DOI: 10.1037/0003-066X.45.10.1146

Schaufeli, W. B., & Bakker, A. B. (2004). Job demands, job resources, and their relationship with burnout and engagement: A multi-sample study. *Journal of Organizational Behavior*, *25*(3), 293–315. DOI: 10.1002/job.248

Schaufeli, W. B., Leiter, M. P., & Maslach, C. (2009). Burnout: 35 years of research and practice. *Career Development International*, *14*(3), 204–220. DOI: 10.1108/13620430910966406

Schein, E. H. (2010). *Organizational culture and leadership* (4th ed.). Jossey-Bass.

Selye, H. (1976). *The stress of life* (Rev. ed.). McGraw-Hill.

Thiel, K. J., & Dretsch, M. N. (2011). The basics of the stress response: A historical context and introduction. *The handbook of stress: Neuropsychological effects on the brain*, 1-28.

Zucker, T. L., Samuelson, K. W., Muench, F., Greenberg, M. A., & Gevirtz, R. N. (2020). Mindful hypnotherapy to reduce stress and increase mindfulness: A randomized controlled pilot study. *The International Journal of Clinical and Experimental Hypnosis*, *68*(2), 169–186. DOI: 10.1080/00207144.2020.1690494

Chapter 3
The Efficacy of Mindfulness-Based Restorative Practices in Reducing Work-Related Psychophysiological Stress

Bhawna Singh
https://orcid.org/0009-0003-6258-8671
Shoolini University, India

S. M. Haider Rizvi
Shoolini University, India

Aditya Sharma
Mental Health Hospital and Rehabilitation, Shimla, India

ABSTRACT

Mindfulness-based restorative practices—guided imagery, relaxation, and Yoga Nidra—are explored as integrative approaches to reduce work-related psychophysiological stress. The chapter conceptualizes stress through psychobiological and appraisal frameworks, emphasizing chronic allostatic load across healthcare, corporate, and gig sectors. Models like demand–control–support and effort–reward imbalance explain how digital, performance-driven environments sustain autonomic dysregulation. These practices promote nonjudgmental awareness and parasympathetic activation through breath regulation, imagery, and deep rest. Integrating

DOI: 10.4018/979-8-3373-2317-6.ch003

contemplative traditions with neuroscientific findings on heart rate variability, cortisol, EEG, and emotion regulation, the chapter reviews mechanisms, outcomes, and design models. It concludes with recommendations for standardized, scalable, and sustainable workplace applications.

1. INTRODUCTION

In today's fast-paced world, job-related stress occurs when constant work pressure keeps the body's fight-or-flight response active and leaves no room for rest. Work-related psychophysiological stress has become a defining feature of contemporary occupational life, cutting across sectors such as healthcare, IT, education, finance, and the gig economy (Uchida & Kawakami, 2010; McEwen, 2017; Rugulies et al., 2022; World Health Organization, 2024). Prolonged exposure to high cognitive load, emotional labor, and organizational pressures activates stress-response systems in a chronic, dysregulated manner, contributing to burnout, somatic complaints, sleep disturbance, and heightened cardiovascular risk. Within this context, non-pharmacological interventions that simultaneously address mental, emotional, and bodily dimensions of stress are of growing importance in occupational health research and practice.

Mindfulness-based restorative practices like guided imagery, relaxation techniques, and Yoga Nidra occupy a distinctive position because they combine attentional training with intentional physiological down-regulation. Spiritual and contemplative traditions (e.g., Om Swami's writings on OS.me, teachings popularized by Art of Living) have long described these methods as ways of repossessing scattered attention and restoring subtle "life energy," whereas contemporary clinical and neuroscientific work links them to measurable changes in autonomic balance, endocrine activity, and neural oscillations (Brown & Ryan, 2003; Creswell, 2017; Khusid & Vythilingam, 2016; Om Swami, n.d.).

The purpose of this chapter is to (a) conceptualize work-related psychophysiological stress, (b) define mindfulness-based restorative practices and their spiritual and scientific underpinnings, (c) synthesize empirical evidence on guided imagery, relaxation, and Yoga Nidra in occupational populations, and (d) propose directions for integrating these practices into evidence-informed workplace interventions.

2. CONCEPTUAL DEFINITIONS

2.1 Stress – Nature and Definitions

From a psychobiological standpoint, stress can be described as a coordinated pattern of neural, endocrine, and autonomic responses that emerges when internal or external demands are evaluated as potentially harmful or overwhelming (StatPearls, 2024; McEwen, 2017). These responses involve activation of the hypothalamic–pituitary–adrenal axis and the autonomic nervous system, with consequent changes in cardiovascular activity, cortisol release, and conscious experience of tension or threat.

Psychologically, stress is often conceptualized as arising when individuals judge that environmental demands outstrip their perceived resources or coping abilities (Lazarus & Folkman, 1984; Uchida & Kawakami, 2010). This appraisal process explains why the same situation can be experienced as a manageable challenge by one person and an overwhelming threat by another.

Types of stress

The stress response can be categorized into several broad types, which differ in duration, intensity, and impact (Explorable, 2012; Herald Open Access, 2018; Talkspace, 2022; NeuronUP, 2020).

- **Acute stress**: Acute stress refers to short-lived responses to immediate demands—such as an unexpected presentation, a disruptive meeting, or a tight deadline—that resolve once the situation passes.
- **Episodic acute stress**: Episodic stress describes frequent or recurrent acute episodes in individuals who habitually face crises or maintain overloaded schedules, often associated with time urgency and perfectionistic tendencies.
- **Chronic stress**: Chronic stress denotes prolonged exposure to persistent difficulties—such as ongoing job insecurity, long-term work–family conflict, or structurally high workload—that are not easily resolved and carry substantial health risk.

In the workplace, employees often cycle between acute episodes (e.g., product launches) and longer-term, chronic strains (e.g., understaffing, continuous monitoring, precarious contracts), with episodic patterns in between.

2.2 From Stress to Psychophysiological Stress

A busy-life scenario: an illustrative case

Consider Dipika, a 35-year-old project manager in a multinational IT firm in a metropolitan city.

- She manages multiple international teams, attends late-night video calls due to time-zone differences, and is expected to respond to work messages on her smartphone almost 24/7.
- Her company is undergoing restructuring, so she worries about job security, while simultaneously caring for young children and aging parents at home.
- Over months, she begins to experience insomnia, persistent headaches, irritability, gastrointestinal discomfort, and a racing heart whenever a new email marked "urgent" appears on her screen.

Dipika's experience captures how chronic work pressure, role overload, and blurred work–home boundaries translate into both psychological strain and physiological arousal, creating a classic picture of psychophysiological stress.

Psychophysiological stress is a tightly integrated pattern of cognitive–emotional reactions including worry, rumination, and threat interpretation that is coupled with physiological changes such as elevated heart rate, increased blood pressure, and altered endocrine activity (Climate Sustainability Directory, 2023). This concept emphasizes that psychological experiences cannot be separated from bodily reactions, particularly when stress activation is frequent or sustained over time.

2.3 Work-related Psychophysiological Stress

In work contexts, psychophysiological stress is seen when:

- Persistent job demands and role conflicts lead to sustained activation of the sympathetic nervous system, manifesting as tachycardia, muscle tension, gastrointestinal problems, and sleep disturbances (Study.com, 2024).
- Cognitive factors such as perfectionism, fear of evaluation, or job insecurity maintain chronic rumination, which keeps stress systems activated even outside working hours (Uchida & Kawakami, 2010).

Over time, such chronic activation contributes to allostatic load, increasing risks for cardiovascular disease, metabolic dysregulation, depression, and burnout (Arasek & Theorell, 1990; Rugulies et al., 2022).

Work-related psychophysiological stress is a blend of psychological and bodily reactions that emerge when job demands are appraised as exceeding available resources or coping capacity. These reactions typically involve worry, irritability, and emotional exhaustion, alongside autonomic changes (e.g., elevated heart rate, reduced heart rate variability, increased blood pressure), altered cortisol secretion, and muscular tension. Chronic exposure to such stress states accelerates allostatic load and predisposes individuals to cardiovascular disease, metabolic vulnerabilities, and mental health problems such as depression and burnout (McEwen, 2017; Uchida & Kawakami, 2010).

2.4 Mechanisms and Models of Work-Related Stress

There are several occupational/work related stress models are relevant:

- **The demand–control–support model** proposes that combinations of high job demand, low decision latitude, and limited social support generate high strain, expressed in both psychological and physiological symptoms (Arasek & Theorell, 1990; Rugulies et al., 2022).
- **The effort–reward imbalance model** argues that a mismatch between high work effort and inadequate rewards—such as salary, esteem, or career prospects—elicits sustained stress responses and elevates risk for stress-related disease (Siegrist, 1996; Rugulies et al., 2022).
- **The allostatic load framework** describes how chronic exposure to stressors produces cumulative "wear and tear" across cardiovascular, metabolic, immune, and neural systems, increasing vulnerability to illness (McEwen, 2017).

2.5 Stress in Contemporary Occupational Settings

Contemporary occupational settings refer to the current, rapidly evolving world of work shaped by globalization, digitalization, flexible and precarious employment, and hybrid or remote work arrangements (Park University, 2023; Rugulies et al., 2022). These settings extend beyond traditional, stable employer–employee relationships to include:

- Knowledge-intensive, technology-driven roles with constant connectivity and information overload (Spill, 2024).
- Gig and freelance work organized through digital platforms, characterized by short-term contracts, variable hours, and performance ratings (Science Direct, 2024).

- Hybrid and remote work arrangements that blur spatial and temporal boundaries between work and home, often increasing expectations of availability (Park University, 2023).

Such environments often combine high cognitive and emotional demands with uncertainty, surveillance, and boundarylessness—conditions that are fertile ground for psychophysiological stress.

There is stress in different work settings though in varied degrees and magnitude, but in the contemporary work setting few sectors are potentially more stressful than others. Few examples from workplace contexts are as below.

i. Healthcare Professionals

During and after the COVID-19 pandemic, high levels of occupational stress were observed among healthcare personnel. One study reported that 46.7% of staff in primary health units had high levels of occupational stress (Uchida & Kawakami, 2010). Staff reported stressors such as heavy workload, lack of resources, emotional demands of patient care, and limited control over schedules. Psycho-physiologically, these stressors were associated with fatigue, insomnia, headaches, elevated blood pressure, and emotional exhaustion.

ii. Corporate Knowledge Workers

In high-pressure corporate environments, employees face continuous performance monitoring, tight deadlines, and "always on" digital communication (Spill, 2024). Surveys from developed economies suggest that close to 79% of employees commonly experience work-related stress, with a marked increase in recent years. Psychophysiological manifestations include chronic muscle tension, eye strain, gastrointestinal issues, and disrupted circadian rhythms due to late-night work and screen exposure.

iii. Gig and Platform Workers

The growth of the gig economy and digital platform work has created new forms of occupational stress, characterized by job insecurity, unstable income, client ratings, and algorithmic surveillance (Park University, 2023). Gig workers—such as ride-share drivers or delivery personnel—may experience long hours, unsafe conditions, and lack of occupational health protections, leading to chronic activation of stress systems and increased risk of cardiovascular and mental health problems.

iv. Case Vignette: Call Centre Employee

A call centre employee in a large urban hub works rotating night shifts to handle international clients. She must adhere to strict scripts and performance metrics, with her calls continuously monitored. Over time, she develops chronic neck and shoulder pain, gastric acidity, sleep inversion, irritability, and feelings of depersonalization during interactions. This vignette illustrates work-related psychophysiological stress, where organizational demands, lack of control, disrupted circadian rhythms, and emotional labor combine to produce both somatic and psychological symptoms (Uchida & Kawakami, 2010).

2.6 Psychophysiological Stress in Contemporary Occupational Settings

Psychophysiological stress is particularly salient in contemporary work because modern stressors are often chronic, ambiguous, and psychologically mediated rather than purely physical (Karasek & Theorell, 1990). Workers may not face immediate physical danger, but they encounter:

- Persistent performance pressure, complex multitasking, and information overload, which keep the cognitive–emotional system in a near-constant state of arousal (Spill, 2024).
- Digital monitoring, algorithmic management, and customer rating systems that heighten vigilance and social-evaluative threat (Park University, 2023).
- Precarious contracts, gig work, and restructuring that create enduring job insecurity and financial strain (Park University, 2023).

Empirical studies link these conditions to increased prevalence of insomnia, cardiovascular problems, depression, and burnout among employees and professionals across sectors (Study.com, 2024). In addition, a substantial proportion of workers report high levels of occupational stress—for instance, nearly half of staff in some health settings and large majorities in corporate surveys—indicating that work-related psychophysiological stress is not an exception but a widespread occupational health issue (Spill, 2024).

In sum, work-related psychophysiological stress can be defined as the constellation of cognitive–emotional and bodily reactions that arise when contemporary work demands chronically exceed an individual's coping resources, leading to sustained activation of stress-response systems and associated health, performance, and well-being consequences (Science Direct, 2024). This makes it a central construct for understanding and intervening in occupational health within today's complex, digitally mediated, and often precarious labor markets.

3.MINDFULNESS IN REDUCING WORK RELATED STRESS

Within contemporary psychology, mindfulness is understood as a trainable capacity to sustain deliberate, nonjudgmental awareness of present-moment experiences—including thoughts, emotions, bodily sensations, and environmental stimuli—while maintaining an orientation of curiosity and acceptance (American Psychological Association, 2024; Brown & Ryan, 2003; Creswell, 2017). Empirical research distinguishes between dispositional mindfulness, a relatively stable individual tendency toward awareness, and state mindfulness, which refers to momentary modes of conscious experience often cultivated through structured practice such as Mindfulness-Based Stress Reduction (MBSR).

3.1 Mindfulness-based Restorative Practices

Mindfulness-based restorative practices can be described as structured interventions that explicitly cultivate mindfulness while targeting recovery of depleted cognitive, emotional, and physiological resources. These practices integrate core mindfulness components—present-moment awareness, nonjudgmental observation, and acceptance—with techniques explicitly designed to down-regulate autonomic arousal and promote parasympathetic activation, such as slow breathing, body scanning, guided visualization, and deep relaxation (StatPearls, 2024; Brown & Ryan, 2003).

In occupational health contexts, such practices are considered "restorative" because they support recovery from job-related demands, reduce allostatic load, and facilitate psychophysiological restoration (improved heart rate variability, sleep, and subjective vitality) between and during work episodes (Hartfiel et al., 2011).

In a research chapter, this category would be positioned as a broader umbrella, under which guided imagery, relaxation training, and Yoga Nidra are three distinct but overlapping modalities, each with specific techniques and hypothesized mechanisms of action.

3.1.1 Guided Imagery as a Mindfulness-based Restorative Practice

Guided imagery refers to attentional guidance toward vivid, multisensory mental images that evoke safety, calmness, and positive affect. Guided imagery involves focusing attention on detailed, multi-sensory mental images (e.g., a safe, calming place) under verbal guidance, while maintaining awareness of bodily sensations and emotional responses. From a mindfulness perspective, guided imagery cultivates sustained, intentional attention and noticing of internal experiences (sensations, emotions, thoughts) as they arise in response to imagery (Kallesøe et al., 2014).

As a restorative practice, it has been shown in occupational samples to reduce perceived stress, improve mood, and lower physiological stress indices such as cortisol and somatic distress, particularly among workers with long-term stress-related sick leave (Kallesøe et al., 2014). Guided imagery can be framed as a cognitively oriented, imagery-based pathway to restoration, especially relevant for knowledge workers who are prone to worry and mental rehearsal of work problems.

3.1.2 Relaxation Techniques as Mindfulness-based Restorative Practices

Relaxation techniques (e.g., progressive muscle relaxation, diaphragmatic breathing, autogenic training) are not inherently mindfulness-based, but they become mindfulness-based when paired with intentional, nonjudgmental awareness of bodily sensations and breath. When individuals systematically tense and release muscles or observe slow, diaphragmatic breathing while attending to sensations with acceptance, they practice both attentional regulation and somatic awareness, core components of mindfulness (Brown & Ryan, 2003).

Empirical work shows that such practices reduce heart rate, blood pressure, and muscle tension, and improve perceived stress and sleep, indicating genuine psychophysiological restoration in occupational populations (e.g., healthcare workers, office staff) (Herald Open Access, 2018; Talkspace, 2022). Relaxation techniques can be conceptualized as primarily somatic restorative tools that become mindfulness-based when they explicitly incorporate present-focused, nonjudgmental awareness of bodily states.

3.1.3 Yoga Nidra as a Mindfulness-based Restorative Practice

Yoga Nidra ("yogic sleep") is a structured, guided practice typically performed lying down, moving through stages such as body scanning, breath awareness, awareness of opposite sensations, imagery, and affirmation (sankalpa). It involves sustained, open monitoring of bodily sensations, breath, and mental contents while remaining consciously aware, aligning closely with mindfulness as present-centered, nonreactive awareness (Science Direct, 2024).

Physiologically, Yoga Nidra promotes deep relaxation and parasympathetic dominance; worksite-based yoga and related practices have demonstrated improvements in heart rate variability, anxiety, musculoskeletal discomfort, and job satisfaction among office workers, indicating robust restorative effects (Hartfiel et al., 2011). Yoga Nidra can be presented as the most "deep-state" form of mindfulness-based restoration, integrating attentional regulation, imagery, and somatic relaxation in a single protocol with promising evidence for mitigating work-related psychophysiological stress.

Taken together, mindfulness and mindfulness-based restorative practices provide the conceptual and empirical backbone of the chapter's argument: that cultivating nonjudgmental present-moment awareness through guided imagery, relaxation, and Yoga Nidra can systematically attenuate work-related psychophysiological stress responses and support sustainable occupational functioning.

Although not all relaxation-based methods are inherently "mindfulness-based," in this chapter they are considered such when they explicitly incorporate present-centered, nonjudgmental awareness of bodily sensations, breath, and mental states (Brown & Ryan, 2003; Herald Open Access, 2018).

4. DIFFERENT APPROACHES AND FRAMEWORKS ON WORK-RELATED STRESS

4.1 Spiritual and Contemplative Framework in Mindfulness Based Restorative Practices

4.1.1 Om Swami, OS.me, and Contemporary Contemplative Accounts

In contemplative writings shared on OS.me, Om Swami portrays stress as a fragmentation of awareness: attention is dispersed across worries, regrets, and anticipatory anxieties, leading to what he describes as "leakage" of inner energy and clarity (Om Swami, n.d.). Relaxation, from this perspective, is not mere idleness but a conscious withdrawal of attention from incessant mental noise into the immediacy of breath, bodily feeling, or a chosen focal point. Yoga Nidra is presented as a disciplined descent into stillness wherein the practitioner learns to remain lucid while the body sinks into profound rest, thereby accessing deeper layers of conditioning and emotion without becoming overwhelmed.

Art of Living teachings carry a similar ethos, especially in their emphasis on rhythmic breathing (Sudarshan Kriya) as a doorway to releasing emotional residues stored in the body and quietening the mind (Art of Living Foundation, n.d.). Though distinct in method, these spiritual approaches converge on key claims: (a) chronic stress is fundamentally a disturbance of internal rhythm and attention, and (b) practices that harmonize breath, body, and attention allow this inner rhythm to re-emerge, fostering resilience and equanimity (Om Swami, n.d.; Art of Living Foundation, n.d.).

4.2 Convergence with Classical Yogic Psychology

Classical yogic texts describe the stressed mind as a fluctuation (vritti) of consciousness, continually pulled outward by sensory impressions and mental narratives. Practices analogous to guided imagery (bhavana), relaxation (shavasana, pratyahara), and Yoga Nidra aim to still these fluctuations, enabling the practitioner to experience deeper calm and insight. Contemporary spiritual teachers draw upon this heritage to interpret modern occupational stress as a manifestation of unceasing mental engagement, arguing that deliberate inner withdrawal and mindful rest are prerequisites for sustainable outer activity (Creswell, 2017; Om Swami, n.d.).

5. SCIENTIFIC AND NEUROPHYSIOLOGICAL FRAMEWORK IN REDUCING WORK RELATED STRESS

5.1 Stress Physiology and Allostatic Load

Biologically, stress involves activation of the sympathetic–adrenomedullary system and the hypothalamic–pituitary–adrenal (HPA) axis, leading to the release of catecholamines and glucocorticoids such as cortisol (McEwen, 2017). In acute situations, these responses are adaptive, mobilizing energy and sharpening attention; however, in persistent occupational stress, repeated activation without adequate recovery contributes to "allostatic load," a cumulative burden on cardiovascular, metabolic, immune, and neural systems (Lazarus & Folkman, 1984; StatPearls, 2024; McEwen, 2017).

5.2 Mindfulness-based Practices and Autonomic Regulation

Meta-analytic findings indicate that mindfulness-based interventions can reduce perceived stress and anxiety and enhance well-being, with moderate effect sizes, across a range of populations including workers (Creswell, 2017; Hartfiel et al., 2011). Physiologically, such practices are associated with:

- Increased high-frequency heart rate variability (HF-HRV), reflecting enhanced parasympathetic (vagal) modulation.
- Decreases in resting heart rate and blood pressure.
- Normalization of dysregulated cortisol patterns in some studies.

Yoga- and meditation-based practices, including Yoga Nidra and related protocols, have been shown to foster alpha and theta oscillations on EEG, which are associated with relaxed wakefulness and internalized attention (Pascoe et al., 2017; StatPearls, 2024).

5.3 Mechanisms of Mindfulness-based Restorative Practices

Table 1. Mechanisms and Outcomes of Mindfulness-based Restorative Practices

Practice	Primary Mechanisms	Psychophysiological Outcomes
Guided Imagery	Focused sensory–cognitive visualization; reappraisal of threat cues; activation of positive affect networks (Kallesøe et al., 2014).	Reduced perceived stress and anxiety; lower cortisol; improved mood; decreased muscle tension.
Relaxation Techniques (PMR, breathing, body scan)	Parasympathetic activation via slow breathing and muscle release; interoceptive awareness; interruption of worry–tension cycles (Herald Open Access, 2018; Talkspace, 2022).	Reduced heart rate and blood pressure; improved HRV; better sleep; fewer somatic complaints.
Yoga Nidra	Systematic withdrawal of sensory engagement (pratyahara); body–breath awareness; meta-awareness of thoughts; deep EEG slowing (Pascoe et al., 2017; StatPearls, 2024).	Marked reductions in stress, anxiety, and insomnia; improved HRV and subjective vitality; enhanced emotional regulation.

5. GUIDED IMAGERY

5.1 Concept and Clinical Usage

Guided imagery is a mind–body intervention in which individuals receive structured guidance through vivid, multisensory mental visualizations designed to evoke soothing, motivational, or empowering experiences (Kallesøe et al., 2014). Scripts typically engage multiple sensory modalities—sight, sound, touch, smell—to create immersive mental scenes that redirect attention away from threat-focused cognition toward restorative experiences. In clinical and occupational settings, guided imagery has been applied to anxiety management, pain reduction, surgical preparation, and rehabilitation from work-related stress and burnout.

5.2 Empirical Evidence in Occupational Contexts

A randomized controlled trial examining Guided Imagery and Music (GIM) for employees on long-term stress-related sick leave found that participants in the

GIM condition demonstrated significantly greater improvements in general well-being, mood disturbance, physical distress, and salivary cortisol compared with a wait-list control group (Kallesøe et al., 2014). Importantly, a large proportion of the intervention group had returned to work by the end of the study, suggesting that guided imagery can support both psychophysiological recovery and occupational functioning.

Other workplace studies and online-delivered imagery-based programs have documented reductions in perceived stress, improvements in sleep quality, and decreases in somatic symptoms, particularly when imagery is combined with relaxation and breathing techniques (Kallesøe et al., 2014; Pascoe et al., 2017).

5.3 Case Vignette

Consider an employee in a high-pressure call centre environment who experiences palpitations and tension headaches before performance-monitoring calls. Implementing a 10-minute guided imagery protocol before shifts—visualizing a safe, expansive natural landscape while focusing on slow breathing—can, over several weeks, reduce anticipatory anxiety, normalize heart rate responses, and enhance perceived self-efficacy, paralleling outcomes seen in empirical GIM studies (Kallesøe et al., 2014; Pascoe et al., 2017; Om Swami, n.d.).

6. RELAXATION TECHNIQUES

6.1 Types and Procedures

Relaxation techniques comprise a family of practices designed to reduce neuromuscular and autonomic arousal (Herald Open Access, 2018; Talkspace, 2022). These include:

- **Progressive Muscle Relaxation (PMR)**: A method involving the systematic contraction and release of various muscle sets to help the individual distinguish between physical stress and a state of rest.
- **Diaphragmatic Breathing**: The practice of deep, abdominal breathing and extended exhales, which helps activate the vagus nerve to promote calmness.
- **Autogenic Training**: A relaxation practice using mental affirmations—such as imagining the limbs feeling weighted or heated—to trigger a relaxation response.
- **Body Scanning**: A mindful exercise where one mentally surveys the body to identify and consciously ease areas of physical tightness.

When practiced with mindful awareness, these methods not only reduce muscular and autonomic arousal but also cultivate a refined sensitivity to early stress cues, enabling more timely self-regulation (Brown & Ryan, 2003; Herald Open Access, 2018).

6.2 Evidence in Workplace Populations

Systematic reviews of relaxation-based interventions have found significant reductions in occupational stress, anxiety, and musculoskeletal pain among nurses, office workers, and other occupational groups (Hartfiel et al., 2011; Pascoe et al., 2017; Creswell, 2017). Online-delivered guided relaxation and breathing programs have been shown to decrease stress and improve sleep and emotional states, illustrating the feasibility of scalable digital formats (Talkspace, 2022).

Worksite programs that integrate relaxation with psychoeducation and organizational support show particularly robust benefits, including reductions in sick days and improvements in self-rated health and job satisfaction (Cambridge Core, 2019; Science Direct, 2024).

7. YOGA NIDRA

7.1 Structure and Experiential Features

Yoga Nidra is often described as a state between wakefulness and sleep, characterized by profound bodily relaxation while awareness remains intact. Standard protocols involve:

1. Settling in a supine posture (usually shavasana).
2. Systematic rotation of awareness through body parts.
3. Breath awareness and sensing of natural rhythms.
4. Experiencing opposite sensations (e.g., heaviness/lightness, heat/cold).
5. Visualization of symbolic images or scenarios.
6. Affirmation or sankalpa, a concise intention planted in the receptive mind.

Spiritual teachers such as Om Swami describe Yoga Nidra as a direct method for untying knots of subconscious tension and conditioning, allowing vital energy to "recollect and stabilize" at deeper levels (Om Swami, n.d.).

7.2 Empirical Research

Controlled trials have documented that Yoga Nidra practice sustained over 6–8 weeks produces significant reductions in self-reported stress, anxiety, and insomnia in adult samples, with several investigations demonstrating improvements in heart rate variability and other autonomic indices (Pascoe et al., 2017). Research conducted across clinical and non-clinical populations has identified beneficial effects on depressive symptoms, sleep quality, and subjective well-being (StatPearls, 2024; Pascoe et al., 2017).

In an office-based yoga program that included relaxation and meditative components, participants showed improvements in HRV, state anxiety, musculoskeletal fitness, and job satisfaction relative to controls, supporting the idea that yoga-based protocols can ameliorate work-related psychophysiological stress (Hartfiel et al., 2011). Although not all such interventions explicitly label their relaxation component as Yoga Nidra, the underlying mechanisms of deep parasympathetic engagement and meta-awareness are highly convergent.

8. INTEGRATING SPIRITUAL AND SCIENTIFIC PERSPECTIVES

8.1 Complementarity Rather than Conflict

Spiritual and contemplative teachings from sources such as Om Swami and the Art of Living Foundation emphasize experiential transformation—that sustained practice fundamentally shifts one's relationship to thoughts, emotions, and bodily discomfort, cultivating greater equanimity and compassion (Om Swami, n.d.; Art of Living Foundation, n.d.; Brown & Ryan, 2003). Scientific accounts, by contrast, operationalize outcomes in terms of cortisol levels, heart rate variability, EEG patterns, or validated psychometric scales. Rather than conflicting, these perspectives are complementary: spiritual traditions articulate the qualitative texture of inner transformation, while empirical research quantifies its physiological and psychological correlates (Creswell, 2017; Pascoe et al., 2017).

8.2 Table: Spiritual Insights and Empirical Parallels

Table 2. Convergence of Spiritual Teachings and Empirical Findings

Spiritual Theme (Om Swami / Art of Living)	Empirical Parallel
"Scattered attention drains prana (life energy)" (Om Swami, n.d.).	Chronic stress associated with allostatic load and reduced HRV (McEwen, 2017; Uchida & Kawakami, 2010).
"Conscious relaxation is active, not passive idleness" (Om Swami, n.d.).	Mindfulness-based relaxation increases parasympathetic tone and improves cognitive performance (Hartfiel et al., 2011; Pascoe et al., 2017).
"Yoga Nidra opens access to deeper layers of mind without being overwhelmed" (Om Swami, n.d.).	Yoga Nidra linked to alpha/theta activity, improved sleep, and reduced anxiety (Pascoe et al., 2017; StatPearls, 2024).
"Breath regulation purifies emotional residues" (Art of Living Foundation, n.d.).	Slow breathing protocols reduce anxiety, cortisol, and blood pressure in clinical and occupational samples (Herald Open Access, 2018; Talkspace, 2022).

9. PRACTICAL APPLICATIONS IN WORKPLACE SETTINGS

9.1 Program Design Considerations

Effective workplace implementation requires sensitivity to organizational culture, time constraints, and employee readiness. Short, modular practices are more feasible than lengthy retreats. Evidence suggests that:

- Sessions of 10–20 minutes, delivered 2–3 times per week, can yield measurable benefits in perceived stress and physiological markers (Hartfiel et al., 2011; Pascoe et al., 2017).
- Digital delivery (apps, recorded sessions) increases accessibility, especially in hybrid or remote work contexts (Talkspace, 2022).
- Combining individual practices with organizational-level changes (e.g., protected micro-breaks, supportive leadership) enhances sustainability and impact (Cambridge Core, 2019; Science Direct, 2024).

9.2 Illustrative Multi-component Program

A workplace intervention might incorporate:

- 5-minute guided imagery breaks mid-shift.
- 10-minute progressive muscle relaxation at the end of the workday.
- Weekly 30-minute Yoga Nidra sessions, onsite or online.

Outcome evaluation could include self-report scales (e.g., perceived stress, burnout, sleep quality), physiological measures (HRV, blood pressure), and occupational indices (absenteeism, presenteeism, job satisfaction) (Hartfiel et al., 2011; Pascoe et al., 2017).

10. DISCUSSION

10.1 Synthesis of Evidence

The converging evidence base indicates that guided imagery, relaxation techniques, and Yoga Nidra collectively form a robust toolkit for mitigating work-related psychophysiological stress. Guided imagery primarily targets cognitive–emotional appraisal and affective tone; relaxation techniques emphasize somatic and autonomic release; Yoga Nidra appears to offer the deepest level of systemic restoration, with multi-layered effects on mood, sleep, and autonomic regulation (Pascoe et al., 2017; Kallesøe et al., 2014; Om Swami, n.d.).

Across occupational groups, these practices reduce subjective stress and distress and show promising effects on physiological indices such as HRV, blood pressure, and cortisol, although effect sizes and methodological rigor vary. The alignment between contemplative descriptions and empirical outcomes enhances the plausibility of underlying mechanisms and supports the integration of these practices into mainstream occupational health frameworks (Hartfiel et al., 2011; Creswell, 2017).

11. CONCLUSION

Mindfulness-based restorative practices—guided imagery, relaxation techniques, and Yoga Nidra—represent accessible, low-cost, and culturally adaptable interventions for addressing work-related psychophysiological stress in contemporary organizational settings. These practices require minimal infrastructure, can be easily embedded into daily work routines, and are adaptable across diverse occupational and cultural contexts, making them particularly relevant in environments characterized by increasing workload pressures and psychosocial demands.

Rooted in long-standing spiritual and contemplative traditions, these approaches are portrayed as pathways to reclaiming inner stillness, self-awareness, and personal integrity. Such traditions emphasize the restoration of balance between the mind and body as a foundation for resilience and purposeful engagement. Complementing these perspectives, a growing body of scientific literature documents the capacity of mindfulness-based restorative practices to modulate autonomic and endocrine functioning, enhance emotional regulation, and improve overall psychological well-being (Art of Living Foundation, n.d.; Brown & Ryan, 2003; Om Swami, n.d.). Together, these spiritual and empirical viewpoints offer a holistic understanding of stress management that transcends purely symptom-focused interventions.

Importantly, the effectiveness of these practices is maximized when they are thoughtfully integrated into organizational policies and wellness frameworks rather than offered as isolated or short-term initiatives. Supportive leadership, organizational commitment to employee well-being, and alignment with broader occupational health strategies are essential for ensuring sustained engagement and meaningful outcomes. Furthermore, the adoption of rigorous research designs—including longitudinal and mixed-method approaches—can strengthen the evidence base by clarifying mechanisms of action, identifying moderating factors, and establishing long-term benefits for both individuals and organizations.

In conclusion, mindfulness-based restorative practices hold significant promise for fostering healthier, more sustainable workplaces by addressing the psychophysiological dimensions of work-related stress. Their integrative nature, combining experiential wisdom with scientific validation, positions them as valuable components of comprehensive occupational stress management strategies. As organizations continue to seek humane and effective responses to workplace stress, these practices offer a viable pathway toward enhancing employee well-being, organizational resilience, and overall work-life quality.

12. LIMITATIONS AND FUTURE DIRECTIONS

Despite the growing interest in mindfulness-based restorative practices, including Yoga Nidra and guided imagery, the existing body of research is characterized by several methodological and conceptual limitations that warrant careful consideration. One of the primary challenges lies in the substantial heterogeneity of intervention protocols across studies. Variations in session frequency, duration, instructional content, and delivery modes (in-person versus digital formats) limit the comparability of findings and hinder meaningful meta-analytic synthesis. This lack of standardization makes it difficult to isolate active components of the interventions and to draw robust conclusions regarding optimal dosage and implementation strategies.

Another significant limitation concerns sample characteristics and study design. Many empirical investigations rely on relatively modest sample sizes, often drawn from single organizations or occupational groups, which restricts the generalizability of results.

Measurement approaches further constrain the strength of existing evidence. A substantial proportion of studies rely predominantly on self-report instruments to assess stress, well-being, and related psychological outcomes. While such measures provide valuable subjective insights, they are vulnerable to response biases and may not fully capture underlying psychophysiological processes.

In light of these limitations, future research should adopt more rigorous and integrative methodological frameworks. Priority should be given to the development and testing of standardized Yoga Nidra and guided imagery protocols that clearly specify intervention components, duration, and delivery mechanisms. Cross-industry and multi-site comparative trials are needed to examine the applicability and effectiveness of these practices across diverse occupational contexts and organizational cultures. Furthermore, mixed-methods research designs that combine quantitative outcome measures with qualitative exploration of employee's lived experiences can provide richer insights into mechanisms of change, contextual influences, and subjective meaning-making in workplace settings (Creswell, 2017; Hartfiel et al., 2011; Om Swami, n.d.).

By addressing these methodological gaps, future studies can strengthen the empirical foundation of mindfulness-based restorative practices and enhance their credibility, scalability, and integration within evidence-informed organizational stress management and employee well-being initiatives.

REFERENCES

American Psychological Association. (2024). *Dictionary of psychology*. Retrieved from https://dictionary.apa.org

Arasek, R. A., & Theorell, T. (1990). *Healthy work: Stress, productivity, and the reconstruction of working life*. Basic Books.

Art of Living Foundation. (n.d.). *Breathing techniques and stress management*. Retrieved from https://www.artofliving.org

Brown, K. W., & Ryan, R. M. (2003). The benefits of being present: Mindfulness and psychological well-being. *Journal of Personality and Social Psychology*, *84*(4), 822–848. DOI: 10.1037/0022-3514.84.4.822 PMID: 12703651

Cambridge Core. (2019). *Be Well: A systems-based wellness intervention using mindfulness in the workplace: A case study*. Retrieved from https://www.cambridge.org/core/journals/journal-of-management-and-organization/article/

Climate Sustainability Directory. (2023). *Psychophysiological stress*. Retrieved from https://climate.sustainability-directory.com/term/psychophysiological-stress

Creswell, J. D. (2017). Mindfulness interventions. *Annual Review of Psychology*, *68*, 491–516. DOI: 10.1146/annurev-psych-042716-051139 PMID: 27687118

Explorable. (2012). *Three different kinds of stress*. Retrieved from https://explorable.com/three-different-kinds-of-stress

Hartfiel, N., Hetherington, S. H., Darzi, A., Goodman, N., & Spencer, A. (2011). The effectiveness of yoga for the improvement of well-being and resilience to stress in the workplace. *Scandinavian Journal of Work, Environment & Health*, *37*(1), 70–76. DOI: 10.5271/sjweh.3137 PMID: 20369218

Herald Open Access. (2018). *Physiology of stress and its management*. https://www.heraldopenaccess.us/openaccess/physiology-of-stress-and-its-management

Kallesøe, K. H., Andersen, R. R., & Vinther, M. (2014). Coping with work-related stress through Guided Imagery and Music (GIM). *Journal of Music Therapy*, *51*(4), 348–365. DOI: 10.1093/jmt/51.4.348

Khusid, M. A., & Vythilingam, M. (2016). The emerging role of mindfulness meditation as an effective self-management strategy, part 1: Clinical implications for depression, anxiety, and stress. *Military Medicine*, *181*(9), 961–968. DOI: 10.7205/MILMED-D-15-00412 PMID: 27612338

Lazarus, R. S., & Folkman, S. (1984). *Stress, appraisal, and coping*. Springer.

McEwen, B. S. (2017). Neurobiological and systemic effects of chronic stress. *Chronic Stress (Thousand Oaks, Calif.)*, *1*, 2470547017692328. DOI: 10.1177/2470547017692328 PMID: 28856337

Neuron, U. P. (2020). *Work stress: Definition, types, causes and consequences for health*. Retrieved from https://neuronup.us/psychology/work-stress-definition-types-causes-and-consequences-for-health/

Om Swami. (n.d.). *Reflections on meditation, awareness, and health*. OS.me. Retrieved from https://www.os.me

Park University. (2023). *The gig economy: Shaping the future of work and business*. Retrieved from https://www.park.edu/blog/the-gig-economy-shaping-the-future-of-work-and-business/

Pascoe, M. C., Thompson, D. R., & Ski, C. F. (2017). Yoga, mindfulness-based stress reduction and stress-related physiological measures: A meta-analysis. *Psychoneuroendocrinology*, *86*, 152–168. DOI: 10.1016/j.psyneuen.2017.08.008 PMID: 28963884

Rugulies, R., Madsen, I. E., & Hjarsbech, P. U.. (2022). Work-related stress and risk of mental disorders: A prospective cohort study. *Frontiers in Public Health*, *10*, 849310. DOI: 10.3389/fpubh.2022.849310

ScienceDirect. (2024). *Mindfulness and mental health: Contemporary applications*. https://www.sciencedirect.com

Siegrist, J. (1996). Adverse health effects of high-effort/low-reward conditions. *Journal of Occupational Health Psychology*, *1*(1), 27–41. DOI: 10.1037/1076-8998.1.1.27 PMID: 9547031

Spill. (2024). *Mental health and workplace stress statistics*. Retrieved from https://www.spill.chat/mental-health-statistics/workplace-stress-statistics

StatPearls. (2024). *Physiology, stress*. In StatPearls [Internet]. National Center for Biotechnology Information. https://www.ncbi.nlm.nih.gov/books/NBK541120/

Study.com. (2024). *Consequences of stress at work: Physiological, psychological and behavioral symptoms*. Retrieved from https://study.com/academy/lesson/consequences-of-stress-at-work-physiological-psychological-behavioral-symptoms.html

Talkspace. (2022). *What is stress? Types of stress and stress management techniques*. Retrieved from https://www.talkspace.com/blog/types-of-stress/

Uchida, M., & Kawakami, N. (2010). Work-related stress and psychosomatic medicine. *Industrial Health*, *48*(6), 503–516. DOI: 10.2486/indhealth.48.503

World Health Organization. (2024). *Mental health at work.* https://www.who.int/news-room/fact-sheets/detail/mental-health-at-work

Chapter 4
From Mental Strain to Physical Pain: Addressing IT Stress Through Hypnotherapy

Debasrita Das
https://orcid.org/0009-0003-3468-907X
Shoolini University, India

Azhar Shahab
https://orcid.org/0009-0008-6524-3130
Shoolini University, India

ABSTRACT

The contemporary information technology sector is dominated by substantial workloads, relentless pressure, incessant demands, rapid advancements, and swift innovations. In corporate information technology, professionals often endure prolonged stress, which can substantially affect their mental and physical well-being. This chapter examines the neurological, physiological, and behavioural effects of stress on individuals employed in the information technology sector. Despite the growing popularity of hypnosis and hypnotherapy in recent years, the impact of hypnosis on individuals' emotional responses to stress remains uncertain. This chapter, possess a comprehensive understanding of the neurological, physiological, and behavioural ramifications of stress on those employed in the information technology sector. It will significantly influence policy formulation, workplace interventions, and future research endeavours. Furthermore, it will elucidate the research deficiencies present in the field and demonstrate how hypnotherapy can enhance stress management and cognitive resilience.

DOI: 10.4018/979-8-3373-2317-6.ch004

1. INTRODUCTION

Burnout and workplace stress have grown major problems in the fast-paced, competitive, and very demanding work world of today. These issues not only compromise personal welfare but also significantly impact corporate performance, productivity, and employee retention (Ahmad et al. (2025). Often referred to as the "Einstein of Medicine, Hans Selye changed our understanding of stress with his theory of General Adaptation Syndrome (GAS), a three-phase physiological response to prolonged stress. In this model, stress is not simply a psychological burden but a biological necessity—the body's overall response to any demand, be it physical, emotional, or environmental. To Selye, stress was not an adversary but the core of life itself—"the spice of life"—a power that can either fortify or undermine us, depending on our capability to adapt. Job stress refers to a detrimental physical and emotional response that an employee may experience when the demands of their position surpass their capabilities, available resources, or personal requirements. If not addressed appropriately, this condition can result in various health problems (National Institute for Occupational Safety and Health, NIOSH). Additionally, the IT sector is always changing as new trends and technologies appear on a regular basis (El Kadiriet al. 2016). It is one of the most fascinating and dynamic industries, and in the upcoming years, it is anticipated to develop rapidly. Every year, hundreds of workers join the IT business due to its promising future. Even though working in the IT industry seems like a promising career path, IT positions are extremely demanding and fast-paced. In a rapidly evolving technical environment, IT workers must put in lengthy hours to achieve deadlines (Franken et al. 2021). Stress is one of the most prevalent issues among IT workers as a result of all these variables. According to a Spacelift research, 73% of IT workers said they have experienced stress, with strict deadlines and a hefty workload ranking as the main stressors. Unrealistic customer expectations, a lack of appreciation and acknowledgment, and a poor work-life balance are additional pressures in the IT industry (Hytry, 2022). Numerous physical, emotional, and behavioral health problems can result from the stress that IT workers endure at work. Furthermore, as they are in charge of upholding the company's vision, mission, and objectives, workers are its most valuable resource. Stress, however, can affect a company's performance and general efficiency. Employees in the information technology sector are more susceptible to a range of health issues due to the perpetually demanding nature of their roles, both physically and emotionally. Stress can cause, worsen, or prolong illness. Stress can trigger urticaria, pruritus, lichen planus, psoriasis, and neurodermatitis. Acid reflux, alcoholism, diabetes, lethargy, tension headaches, hypertension, insomnia, IBS, psychoneurosis, and sexual dysfunction are all made worse by stress. Stress is caused by job insecurity, unstable working conditions, and skill obsolescence. Globalization and privatization changed workplace relationships.

Job stress is not only an individual issue, but also an organizational challenge that impacts employee productivity and workforce stability (Antwi et al., 2019). According to research, working under too much pressure can result in mental and physical exhaustion (burnout) as well as decreased performance. In the midst of these dynamics, developing efficient strategies for stress management becomes increasingly important. These methods not only help employees feel better, but they also make an effort to keep the company's operations sustainable (Ahmed et al., 2020) These days, stress management strategies are crucial to therapeutic practice. Hypnotherapy and contemporary therapeutic hypnosis have gained popularity and attention globally in recent years (Fisch et al., 2017). A 2017 definition characterizes hypnosis as "a state of consciousness distinguished by an augmented ability to respond to suggestion," accompanied by concentrated focus and diminished peripheral awareness. It is the utilization of hypnosis for the therapy of a medical or psychological ailment or condition. Systemic language and resource-activating, solution-oriented hypnotherapy are used.". (Elkins et al. (2015). Clinical hypnosis works on the physiological, attentional, and integrative levels as an integrative therapy and help one develop coping skills to manage their inner health in terms of their thoughts, feelings, attention, and performance. The effectiveness of hypnosis as a therapy is supported by a substantial body of a component of the integrative approach to treating a variety of conditions that traditional medicine has discovered difficult to treat (Elkins, Jensen, & Patterson, 2007). Along with a decrease in stress and anxiety, it may also result in certain changes to physiological markers (Poddar et al., 2021).

Physiological and psychological effects of stress

Due to their physically and emotionally taxing jobs, IT workers are more likely to develop health difficulties. Stress can cause, worsen, or maintain illness Psoriasis, lichen planus, urticaria, pruritus, and neurodermatitis all can be brought on by stress. Stress can aggravate acid reflux, alcohol abuse, asthma, diabetes, lethargy, tension headaches, hypertension, insomnia, IBS, psychoneurosis, and sexual dysfunction. Professional relationship changes owing to globalization and privatization, job insecurity, concern about future work prospects, and skill obsolescence all cause stress. (Padma et al., 2015)

Physiological Effects of Stress

1. The musculoskeletal system

During periods of stress, the muscles exhibit increased contraction. To safeguard itself from pain and injury, the body utilizes muscle tension as a defensive strategy, which is almost a reflexive response to stress. The muscles abruptly stiffen when exposed to acute tension and subsequently relax after the stress subsides. Chronic stress often keeps muscles tense, Muscles maintained in a condition of tension and tautness for prolonged durations may elicit numerous physiological responses and potentially facilitate the onset of stress-related illnesses. (APA,2024).

2. The Respiratory System

Apart from removing waste carbon dioxide from the body, the respiratory system helps the oxygen to reach the cells. An individual breaths through the nose, then passes through the larynx, the trachea, and finally the lungs via the bronchi. For systemic circulation, bronchioles help red blood cells to receive oxygen. Respiratory problems could arise when the airway linking the nose and lungs gets restricted. The symptoms consist in dyspnea and tachypnea. Strong emotions and stress can cause these symptoms to show themselves. Those without respiratory issues usually have no trouble since the body can control the extra effort required for comfortable breathing. Psychological stress can worsen asthma and COPD, which combines emphysema and chronic bronchitis (APA,2024).

3. Cardiovascular system

The organs of the body get food and oxygen from the heart and blood arteries. Under stress, the body coordinates these two elements. Adrenaline, noradrenaline, and cortisol signal acute stress—that is, that which results from meeting deadlines, getting caught in traffic, or heavy braking to get away from an accident. For instance, achieving deadlines. Dilation of blood vessels supplying the heart and important muscles increases blood pressure and blood flow. This is the response for fight-or-flight. The body comes back to normal once extreme stress passes.

Over time, chronic stress could compromise blood arteries and the heart. Constant rise in blood pressure, stress hormones, and heart rate could be detrimental. Stress over long terms can lead to stroke, heart attacks, and hypertension.(APA,2024).

4. The hypothalamic-pituitary-adrenal (HPA)

The main control of the endocrine stress response, the hypothalamic-pituitary-adrenal (HPA) axis starts a series of actions when a person finds a situation difficult, dangerous, or unmanageable according to APA. Produced as a glucocorticoid, a class of steroid hormones, cortisol, sometimes referred to as the "stress hormone," is

The HPA axis:

Comprising a cluster of nuclei connecting the brain and endocrine system, the hypothalamus stimulates the pituitary gland to produce a hormone. The pituitary gland then sends a message to the adrenal glands above the kidneys to synthesis more cortisol.Cortisol facilitates the mobilization of glucose and fatty acids from the liver, hence augmenting the availability of energy substrates. The production of cortisol frequently fluctuates during the day. Upon awakening, your concentration levels rise, then diminishing as the day advances, thereby supplying you with energy throughout the day. An elevation in cortisol levels can furnish the requisite energy to confront a prolonged or intense challenge during a stressful situation.

The correlation between stress and health Glucocorticoids, particularly cortisol, play essential roles in regulating the immune system and mitigating inflammation. In stressful or perilous conditions, where an injury may provoke heightened immune system activation, this is advantageous. Extended stress can compromise the relationship between the immune system and the HPA axis, therefore influencing immunological response. This reduced future communication has linked to a spectrum of medical and psychological issues. Conditions include immunological problems, metabolic ailments (including diabetes and obesity), and depression as well as chronic tiredness.

5. Gastrointestinal system

The sensation of "butterflies" in the stomach can be elucidated by the presence of hundreds of millions of neurons in the gastrointestinal tract. These neurons maintain constant connectivity with the brain and possess the ability to operate with considerable autonomy. Stress can influence the communication between the brain and the gastrointestinal system, potentially leading to discomfort in the gut, including pain, bloating, and other symptoms. Numerous bacteria inhabit the gut, and their existence can influence both gastrointestinal and neurological health. This can subsequently influence cognitive function and the feelings one experiences.

Stress affects gut microbes, which may affect mood. Thus, stomach neurons and bacteria greatly impact the brain and vice versa.

Early life stress can affect both nervous system development and physical reaction to stress. These modifications raise the likelihood of subsequent gastrointestinal illnesses or dysfunctioning.

6. Esophagus & Stomach:

During periods of stress, individuals may consume considerably more or considerably less food than their usual intake. An individual may experience heartburn or acid reflux if they ingest a larger number or diverse range of foods, consume alcohol or tobacco more frequently, or engage in all of these behaviors. The frequency of heartburn discomfort might be intensified by variables such as stress or fatigue. Severe stress can induce a rare occurrence of esophageal spasms, which may be readily misidentified as a myocardial infarction. This condition is exceedingly rare. Additional signs of stress encompass dysphagia and an elevated intake of air, perhaps resulting in heightened belching, flatulence, and bloating issues.

Stress may facilitate the experience of pain, bloating, nausea, and other gastrointestinal discomforts. Extreme tension may induce vomiting. Moreover, stress may induce an unjustified increase or decrease in appetite, contingent upon the individual. Consequently, bad meals might exacerbate one's mood.

Contrary to popular belief, stress does not precipitate stomach ulcers nor does it elevate stomach acid production. The aforementioned symptoms are, in fact, induced by a disease caused by pathogens. In periods of stress, ulcers may induce heightened discomfort. A segment of the intestine

Another consequence of stress is that it may facilitate the sense of intestinal discomfort, along with pain and bloating. Constipation or diarrhea may occur as a consequence of this, as it impedes the transit of food through the body, potentially leading to these symptoms. Moreover, stress may induce muscle spasms in the gastrointestinal tract, leading to pain for the individual.

A association exists between stress and the digestive process, as well as nutrient absorption by the intestines. The augmentation of gas production may result from food intake. The intestines include a robust barrier that safeguards the body from most microorganisms linked to food. Stress can break the intestinal barrier, letting gut germs in. Most of these germs are quickly eliminated by the immune system, but the modest inflammatory reaction may cause minor symptoms.

People with chronic gastrointestinal illnesses like IBS or IBD, are predisposed to experiencing the adverse consequences of stress. This may be attributable to heightened sensitivity of the stomach nerves, alterations in gut bacteria, changes in the transit speed of food through the gastrointestinal tract, or modifications in the gut's immune responses.

PSYCHOLOGICAL EFFECT OF STRESS

A association exists between stress and heightened anxiety, exacerbated depressive symptoms, increased irritability, and diminished cognitive performance. While transient stress is a typical and adaptive reaction to difficulties, chronic stress, which endures over an extended duration, can harm mental and physical health. Chronic stress can cause dysthymia or celiac disease. Psychoneuroimmunology (PNI) examines the interplay between the neurological and immunological systems and its impact on mental and emotional well-being. Despite the field's nascence, Research on the effects of stress on the brain and immunological systems abound. According to the PNI, extended stress can aggravate mood disorders including depression, anxiety, bipolar illness, cognitive impairments, personality changes, and maladaptive behaviours including drug use and impulsive gambling (Erin L. George,2024).

1.1. IT Role Stress: Mental Strain & Decision Drain

Stress is a silent killer in the contemporary era. Stress is the priceless toxin for human life in the planet. It can disturb any one's mental, emotional, behavioral and physical balance. The human body's muscles, tissues, organs, and blood vessels can all be harmed by stress. It elevates breathing and heart rate. It elevates blood pressure and body temperature. Furthermore, it may interfere with sexuality, hunger, digestion, metabolism, sleep, and even fertility (Deekshitulu P.V. 2017)

- Emotional exhaustion, depression, and anxiety Career stagnation and workplace dissatisfaction are both caused by chronic stress:

The phrase "burnout" is a widely used term that refers to overall sensations of tiredness and emotional exhaustion. Following a tough day at work or managing unruly kids at home, for instance, someone might say, "I am simply so burned out." Remarks like these enter into everyday language and essentially serve as personal accounts of tiredness arising from involvement in a demanding or a draining task. The "solution" for these emotions is to cease participation in the activity and perhaps to pursue relaxation or involvement in a fun or diverting activity. This common understanding of burnout differs from the clinical psychology definition of the same term. In this context, the word refers to a much more serious ailment that is difficult to ease by diverting activities. In severe burnout situations, the only way to stop the activity linked to burnout. (Jacobs, C.2024). Burnout is influenced by a number of factors, such as an overwhelming workload, anxiety, and a lack of professional assistance. According to a recent World Health Organization classification, burnout is a symptom associated with ongoing professional stress that can lead to depression, inactivity, discontent, and a lack of purpose in one's work.

- Physical Effects of IT Stress in the Workplace Chronic stress's somatic manifestations include high blood pressure, migraines, and gastrointestinal issues. musculoskeletal issues and cardiovascular dangers from sedentary living Sleep deprivation and its cascading effects on cognitive performance:

Prolonged exposure to work-related stress has been linked to a number of detrimental health effects, according to studies. It has been discovered that job stress raises the chance of physical health issues including cardiovascular disease, musculoskeletal disorders, and gastrointestinal disorders and other neurobiological issues (European Agency for Safety and Health at Work, 2019).

Source: Hasin, H., Johari, Y. C., Jamil, A., Nordin, E., & Hussein, W. S., 2023, *The Harmful Impact of Job Stress on Mental and Physical Health*, International Journal of Academic Research in Business and Social Sciences, 13(4), https://doi .org/10.6007/IJARBSS/v13-i4/16655

THE STRESSED MIND

Research conducted by Lagraauw et al. (2015) demonstrates that chronic stress negatively impacts the immunological and endocrine systems, as well as the metabolic response of individuals. Ziegler (2012) and Herman et al. (2016) believe the HPA axis and autonomic nervous system regulate stress. Leistner and Menke (2020) found that HPA axis dysfunctions increase stress susceptibility and stress-related mental illnesses. Experience-dependent stress responses vary due to genetics in animal models. The source is Terenina et al. (2019). Additionally, chronic stress adapts the hypothalamic-pituitary-adrenal (HPA) axis (Herman and Tasker, 2016). Acute psychological stress may be reduced by this adaptation (Matthews et al., 2001). Chronic stress, such as in severe depressive disorders, can cause sympathetic nervous system hyperactivity and a pro-inflammatory immunological response (Won and Kim, 2016).Hereing et al. (2015) assert that acute cardiovascular events, including myocardial infarctions, may stem from an autonomic imbalance induced by chronic stress. This imbalance results in heightened sympathetic tone and diminished vagal tone.

Occupational stress is an escalating issue impacting enterprises globally. It impacts both employee health and well-being, as well as global corporate productivity. Individuals encounter job-related stress when the demands of their positions, which may manifest in various forms and combinations, surpass their abilities to manage them. Musculoskeletal disorders are the most prominent category of compensated diseases or injuries in Australia, while work-related stress ranks as the second most common type.

Numerous events can contribute to stress at work. For instance, if a person's job demands If the demands (such as hours or duties) exceed their capacity, people may encounter emotions of strain. Additional forms of occupational stress encompass interpersonal conflicts with colleagues or superiors, persistent changes, and concerns regarding job security, including the possibility of redundancy. The National Health and Safety Commission states that prolonged absenteeism is primarily attributed to workplace stress. What one individual may perceive as challenging, another may regard as stressful. The occupation, the individual's psychological disposition, and additional factors (including personal circumstances and overall health) all contribute to the likelihood of experiencing workplace stress.

What are the signs of stress?

During stressful situations, relaxation becomes challenging, resulting in various emotions such as annoyance and anxiety. We may encounter difficulties in maintaining concentration when subjected to significant pressure. Symptoms we may encounter include headaches, bodily discomfort, gastrointestinal disturbances, or sleep difficulties. We may consume either a lesser or greater quantity than usual. Chronic stress may increase the likelihood of utilizing substances such as alcohol and smoke, exacerbating pre-existing health issues.

Stressful events can lead to mental health disorders, namely anxiety and depression, and can also aggravate pre-existing illnesses, necessitating medical intervention. The challenges we have regarding our mental health may stem from the escalating severity of stress-related symptoms, which have started to disrupt our daily activities, including employment. (WHO, 2023)

CAUSES OF WORK-RELATED STRESS

At work, stress can be caused by a variety of factors, some of which are listed below:

1. Long hours and loads of work to be done
2. Changes made within the company under the organization's strict deadlines
3 Changes in responsibilities
4. A lack of job stability

The lack of independence, the monotony of the work, the deficiencies in the qualifications required for the position, the excessive supervision, and the inadequate working environment

Lack of resources; lack of equipment; little opportunities for promotion; harassment; poor relationships with bosses or colleagues; crisis events such an armed hold-up or workplace death.

1.2. IT Stress Blind Spots: The Hidden Long-Term Toll:

- Professionals are poorly studied in longitudinal studies. Lack of research on coping strategies specific to the industry. The lack of research into alternative treatments for stress management, such as hypnotherapy still needs to be explored.

Despite extensive global research on workplace stress, stigma, and attitudes toward employees experiencing stress or mental illness, as well as interventions to mitigate these issues (Hanisch et al. 2016; Joyce et al., 2016), numerous industries and countries, including India, continue to overlook these concerns, with only a minimal fraction of the insights gained being implemented. Articles 23 of the Universal UNGA, 1948 Declaration of Human Rights; UNGA, 1976 International Covenant on Economic, Social, and Cultural Rights; UN Convention on the Rights of Persons with Disabilities (UNGA, 2007) have long been implemented to safeguard .Nevertheless, the execution of policies is not always at its best and might vary greatly. Furthermore, countries with low and intermediate incomes that have the biggest populations of people of working age are lagging behind in adopting or developing viable solutions of the problem.; hence, there is a hidden long term toll and usually lack sufficient laws to stop discrimination against workers with mental diseases (Nardodkar et al., 2016).

Surviving the IT Storm:

Renowned as India's top IT talents, they find their workspace to be a pressure cooker. The reasons behind this stress are far from black and white.

The Story of Overwork:

The objective of managers is to cultivate personnel who are prepared to work extended hours, respond to emails at any time, and offer their personal time, including weekends, vacations, and evenings, without expressing any grievances. Overwork initiates a domino effect that commences at the apex of the organizational hierarchy and descends to the base. The subordinates in this equation possess minimal authority. That constitutes one view of excessive labor. This edition necessitates extensive work hours as mandated by our managers. This edition is prominently highlighted in the latest book released by the New York Times and available on Amazon. Consequently, the more pertinent inquiry regarding excessive work is not merely, "Who is culpable?" but rather, the more essential question is, "Is it effective?" Does undertaking more labor than anticipated yield superior quality and increased quantity of output? Is it possible that we are genuinely attaining greater accomplishments? A significant amount of research has shown that working extended hours is not advantageous, irrespective of the motivations for such prolonged labor. Firstly, it does not seem to lead to an enhancement in capacity. Erin Reid, a professor at the Questrom School of Business at Boston University, did a study on consultants. The researchers discovered that managers could not distinguish between individuals who authentically worked 80 hours per week and those who only seemed to do so. Reid found no evidence that employees who were candid about working fewer hours achieved less, nor was there any indication that those who underperformed achieved more. This occurred despite supervisors penalizing employees who were candid about reduced work hours. (Sarah Green Carmichael, Harvard Business Review, 2015).

Fear of being obsolete (FOBO):

The fear of becoming obsolete, or FOBO, is spreading worldwide. Many workers fear that their skills will soon be out of date as a result of AI and automation's reshaping of the employment market across a variety of industries. As a result, they risk losing their jobs. However, India has a different perspective. According to the ETS Human Progress Report 2025, as the job market becomes more competitive, the value placed on 'Evidential Currency' -- credentials and real-time assessments of skills -- continues to rise, with 60% of all employees experiencing FOBO (India Today, 2025).

Burnout:

The syndrome known as "workplace burnout" is connected to a particular field and caused by unaddressed prolonged stress in the workplace. Methodically verified techniques allow one to assess burnout scientifically. It is typified by persistent emotional tiredness, psychological detachment or pessimism, and ineffectiveness, which taken together prevent conventional rest during breaks, weekends, and time off from effectively managing job-related stressors (World Health Organization, 2019). Burnout affects people as well as organizational performance, said P. Dennis Stolle, JD, senior director of applied psychology at the American Psychological Association. Burnout among employees results in lower output, less creativity, and more inclination for mistakes. Moreover, people could have less drive to work. Should this problem be present in a company, it could seriously affect profitability, service quality, and output.

Poor Work life balance:

The survey was conducted in 2016 by the European Foundation for Improving Living and Working Conditions. Survey of the Quality of Life in Europe. shows that modern society changes have made the problem of work-life balance ever more important. Many negative effects can result from a poor work-life balance, most importantly a decline in mental and physical health.(Davis & Tuttle, 2017).

Anxiety and Depression:

Among the three most common work-related disorders individuals in the information technology industry report having, Studies conducted by Pinto et al. (2004), Rocha and Debert-Ribeiro (2004), and Sharma (2006) indicate a correlation between stress and psychological illnesses. Software engineers are increasingly reporting, according to Rashidi and Jalbani (2009) and Das (2012), and Nayak (2014) claim that job profiles determine the degree and type of problems experienced. 66% of respondents to a 2019 poll taken in the United Kingdom reported feeling stressed about their jobs. This level of tension was like what medical professionals go through. Although stress is not usually considered a medical condition, persistent or too high stress can lead to mental health problems including anxiety and depression (HSE, 2020).

Stress can cause depression, substance misuse, and anxiety. Severe cases may cause depression and self-harm. Corporate women face mental health issues as well as physical issues like cardiovascular disease, cancer, endocrine, sexual, and reproductive health, according to Dr. Dhanya Chandran, a clinical psychologist at Amrita Hospital in Kochi. She said women in these occupations are more likely to have mental health difficulties include depression, anxiety, stress, addictive behaviors, eating disorders, emotional disorders, self-harm, emotional abuse, and relationship problems.

Daunting commutes

Since it takes a good chunk of the day to get to and from the office, this is a waste of critical energy. It gives daily activities more weight and often turns an ordinary trip into a hated experience that can lead to mental exhaustion to develop more rapidly than it would otherwise. Encouragement of employees to utilize public transportation wherever it is practical, carpool, or use ride-sharing applications will help to both lower environmental effect and costs.

Job insecurity:

Within the context of employment, the term "job insecurity" describes circumstances whereby workers lack assurances that their jobs would remain constant from one day to the next, week to week, or year to year. Under these circumstances, employees sometimes find themselves in contingent, unstable, and insecure employment configurations. Fixed-term contracts, on-demand labor, seasonal employment, casual work, freelancing, and gig job employment are a few instances of these kinds of work arrangements.

"Experiencing job loss due to layoffs, downsizing, premature retirement, or a decline in contract opportunities is among the most stressful life events." stated one participant. "It makes no difference what happened that resulted in your employment loss." Apart from negatively impacting your income, the stress of losing a job can affect your attitude, relationships, mental and emotional state, and general health. (Harvard Business Review, 2022)

Job insecure people want to achieve, but the chance of losing their jobs and the stress, annoyance, resentment, and tiredness of working more or hunting for new work negate any potential gains. Participant: "My workplace problems make me less productive, not more successful." This makes me more distracted and anxious. Despite working harder and advocating for himself, the prospect of getting laid off creates "a walking ball of anxiety," which inhibits his ability to impress management. Concerned about losing your job makes it harder to work well. Therefore, even if you are more motivated to grow your profession, your extra effort is unlikely to provide greater results. (Harvard Business Review).

Cultural Shift:

An individual's well-being may suffer in the job if their culture is weak. Moreover, it might significantly affect the company's bottom line, which would result in low production rates and a large staff turnover. In contrast, employees in positive organizational cultures exhibit greater health, happiness, productivity, and reduced turnover intentions. Studies show that companies with pleasant workplace cultures have higher average annual returns. "The role may correspond with your career, the travel may be beneficial, or the remuneration may satisfy or exceed your expectations — yet that is inadequate," says Harvard DCE Professional & Executive Development instructor and "Happy at Work" podcast host Michael McCarthy. To enhance your career, the company must share your values and provide a good work environment with good leadership.

Lack of Mental Health Support:

Over fifty percent of the world's population is employed, despite the fact that fifteen percent of persons of working age have a mental disorder. In addition to having an impact on work confidence, productivity, absenteeism, and job search, mental diseases and other mental health concerns can also have an impact. Anxiety and depression are responsible for 12 billion lost workdays. However, significant mental health patients rarely work, despite the fact that work is essential to treatment. Family members, caregivers, coworkers, communities, and society as a whole are all impacted by mental illness. The unhappiness and stress cost of the global economy, which is measured in trillions of dollars, is driven by productivity loss. Every employee has the right to get a job and to work in an environment that is both safe and healthy. Work can either improve or worsen one's mental health. It could compromise one's mental health. Preventing mental health challenges in the workplace necessitates vigilance. Numerous measures can be used to safeguard and enhance mental health in the workplace and assist individuals with mental health disorders. The WHO provides guidelines for occupational mental health. This page contains the ILO's Policy Brief about Workplace Mental Health. Applications improve workplace mental health standards grounded in facts. Helping persons with mental health challenges achieve success in the workplace is one of the goals, along with promoting mental health and preventing difficulties related to mental health.

1.3. A paradigm shift in stress management (Revolutionizing Workplace Mental Health Support):

- A new approach to hypnotherapy as an intervention:

Over the last several decades, hypnosis has evolved into both an intriguing area for scientific research and a powerful therapeutic instrument. This remarkable history signifies and symbolizes its unparalleled adaptability and evolutionary strength (De Benedittis 2020). A social interaction known as hypnosis occurs when one individual, known as the subject, complies with recommendations made by another, known as the hypnotist, for creative experiences including changes in conscious perception and memory as well as the voluntary control of behavior. Subjective certainty that verges on hallucination and emotions of involuntariness that verges on compulsion accompany these experiences in the typical case (Kihlstrom, 2008). Hypnotherapy is defined as "the application of hypnosis for the treatment of a medical or psychological disorder or issue" (Elkins et al. (2015)). Clinical hypnosis works on the physiological, attentional, and integrative levels as an integrative therapy and help one develop coping skills to manage their inner health in terms of their thoughts, feelings, attention, and performance. The effectiveness of hypnosis as a therapy is supported by a substantial body of a component of the integrative approach to treating a variety of conditions that traditional medicine has discovered difficult to treat (Elkins, Jensen, & Patterson, 2007). Along with a decrease in stress and anxiety, it may also result in certain changes to physiological markers (Poddar et al., 2021).

Hypnotherapy for Stress – Case Study: (Alix Needham, Hypnotherapist)

Eric Whitfield, a 54-year-old architect, * My wife forced me to seek help with stress management because my mood swings were making my home life unbearable for her and my kids. Due to the fact that 30% of my coworkers were laid off, work stress was the cause worked too much because I was afraid of losing my job. I overworked too.

As a result of my job life taking over, my home life faded away to a significant degree. I was either too exhausted to go out and do anything fun on the weekends, so I didn't have time for the family. My libido and vitality diminished, resulting in a complete disinterest in sexual encounters. Despite my family's complaints regarding my behavior, I was too apprehensive to acknowledge that I had an issue. I endeavored to maintain my family's happiness. I presumed that my anxiousness and hostility stemmed from the detrimental working environment, an aspect beyond my control. All aspects were altered as a direct result of one's work with Alix. Alix effectively alleviated my apprehensions and first guided me through what to expect from our meetings, despite my initial reluctance to engage in this "therapy" approach, which my wife had planned for me. A valuable lesson I received was the understanding that, while I could not alter the outward conditions I faced, I could modify my responses to them. Throughout my employment, I cultivated increased self-confidence and became less apprehensive about exerting my utmost effort. I exerted my utmost effort, which therefore led to an immediate improvement in my self-esteem and performance perception.

Acquiring stress management skills has profoundly influenced my energy levels, enabling me to regain control over my personal life and markedly enhance the productivity and satisfaction of my work endeavors. Upon recognizing that stress management could facilitate a more effective approach to a hard situation, I saw a significant improvement in my well-being. I was entirely oblivious to the significant influence that stress could have on my family life. Comments made by Alix concerning stress management

If stress is inadequately managed, it can adversely affect both the individual experiencing it and their immediate associates. Despite working extended hours without respite, Eric remained oblivious to his stress levels. This is a frequent phenomenon for individuals engaged in extended work hours without respite. Eric was exerting excessive pressure on himself, resulting in a loss of perspective due to his anxiety around the potential loss of his work. Over time, he experienced escalating stress, nearing exhaustion or a nervous breakdown. At this juncture, the body will psychologically and physiologically cease functioning to avert any additional harm. Recovery from this circumstance may require only a little period. Hypnotherapy enabled Eric to discuss his concerns in a tranquil and confidential environment. He was able to reflect and acknowledge how his job habits had become counterproductive, adversely affecting both his health and his familial ties.

Through the application of hypnosis, he discerned the elements contributing to his insomnia and elevated stress levels. During his childhood, he was subjected to bullying by his father, and the present situation was eliciting a stress response akin to that experience.

Eric began to better manage his stress after three sessions. He had been avoiding having a conversation with his boss, but he overcame his fear of appearing weak. As a result, his workload was reduced to make it easier to manage. Eric was able to modify his lifestyle with the assistance of stress counseling and hypnosis, incorporating healthier eating habits and exercise, both of which are essential for stress management. Eric has developed a heightened self-appreciation and respect, and although he remains highly occupied, he has accumulated a repertoire of effective tactics that he use often. He is evidently having significant enjoyment at work, and the quality of his familial relationships has markedly improved.

Psychological and physiological impacts of the hypnotic state include the following:

Consciousness is environmental awareness and responsiveness, defined by its state—wakefulness—and content—awareness. 2019 Zhao and colleagues' findings. Demertzi et al. (2013) and Calabr (2015) studied awareness's neural correlates. These studies aim to identify consciousness-related brain areas and neuronal mechanisms needed for certain conscious experiences. Herbert et al. (2016), Crone et al. (2015), Qin, Ren, Pal, Medford and Critchley (2010), and Zhang (2018) studied the prefrontal cortex. According to Goll et al. (2015), the prefrontal cortex is connected to motor, visual, auditory, and sensory regions. This implies that it regulates these processes to allow selective concentration and stop distraction. Comprising an altered state of consciousness, the "hypnotic state" is able to influence subjective experience as well as physiological reactions (Rainville and Price, 2003). Under hypnosis, the individual enters a different state of awareness that helps them to absorb ideas: According Karle and Boys (1987) and Rhue et al. (1993), a hypnosis session consists in four separate phases: (i) An induction phase in which the client is instructed to listen to the hypnotherapist's voice and either close their eyes or concentrate on little items, such pen. Starting with deep relaxation indoctrination, the client goes through three separate phases of treatment: intently listening to the hypnotherapist's voice then performing eye closure or pen-targeting exercises (Rainville and Price 2003; Vanhaudenhuyse et al. 2014). The degree of subject hypnotizability determines their reaction to hypno-suggestions. Hypnotic responses can seem within reach of any population demographic since heap et al. (2004) estimate two-thirds of all individuals are susceptible to this controlled state. Studies indicate that stronger hypnotizability levels show direct connections between the dorsal anterior cingulate cortex and the left dorsolateral prefrontal cortex (Faerman et al., 2024). Research by Vanhaudenhuyse et al. (2014) and Jensen et al. (2015) demonstrates that a hypnotic state elevates theta band frequencies, associated with fatigue, while concurrently diminishing gamma band activity, linked to problem-solving and concentration. This was shown through an analysis of brain oscillations employing electroencephalography (EEG). Hypnosis reduced dorsal anterior cingulate brain activity in academic fMRI studies. The dorsolateral prefrontal cortex, executive control network, and salience network insula were also studied. Jiang et al. (2016) found decreased posterior cingulate cortex and functional connection between executive control and default mode networks. Compared to waking states, hypnosis lowered brainstem, right main somatosensory cortex, and insular area fMRI activity. A 2009 study by Vanhaudenhuyse and colleagues noted this. Hypnosis reduces sympathetic nervous system activity, as shown by autonomic nervous system changes, according to Aubert et al. (2009), Yuksel et al. (2013), Kekecs et al. (2016), and Fernandez et al. (2021). Hypnosis alters HPA axis mediators, including cortisol, according to limited evidence. A crucial element of hypnosis requires users to achieve mental relaxation. Hypnosis typically includes progressive muscle relaxation as an induction method while relaxation serves effectively in reducing anxiety according to Kim and Kim (2018). According to the findings of a quasi-experimental study conducted by Garvin et al. in 2001, which involved 45 healthy volunteers, both hypnosis and deep relaxation were beneficial in reducing levels of state anxiety and tension experienced by the participants. Hypnosis is similar to meditation in a number of ways, including the fact that it can successfully produce relaxation and lessen anxiety symptoms (Bamber and Morpeth, 2019; Lemay et al., 2019). Yoga and mindfulness are two examples of meditation exercises that have these similarities. According to Rhue et al. (1993), the effects of hypnosis on relaxation are greatly boosted by the use of guided imagery, which educates patients in various types of deep breathing. The practice of deep breathing exercises proves successful in minimizing anxiety while simultaneously reducing sympathetic activity while boosting parasympathetic activity according to Cho et al. (2016) and Chen Y. F. et al. (2017) and Zaccaro et al. (2018).

Background Investigation:

Hypnotherapy focuses on the restoration of nervous sleep, as hypnosis equates to nervous sleep. Hypnosis was employed in ancient religious ceremonies, a tradition that has persisted for millennia. In the 1700s and 1800s, many individuals believed that hypnosis was conducted by supernatural creatures and spirits. Franz Mesmer, a physician born in Australia in the late 18th century, is renowned as the "father of hypnotism." To complete the procedure of conventional hypnosis, a lightweight object, such as a pocket watch, was suspended before the subjects' eyes, and they were directed to focus on the object until they entered a profound state of sleep. The fundamental hypnotic techniques employed in modern hypnotherapy include a reclining posture, muscle relaxation, and visual fixation. Prior to closing one's eyes, the individual must also relax their musculature. The patient, being in a trance state, has increased receptivity compared to their awake state; hence, the hypnotherapist provides suggestions to facilitate behavioral modification. The patient is more accessible in the trance state. In 1958, the American Medical Association endorsed hypnotherapy as a form of treatment. (Kenzy Gilsdorf)

Understanding Hypnotherapy:

"At its foundation, hypnotherapy works by modifying our state of mind. In this relaxed condition, folks are more open to recommendations. Hypnotherapists assist clients in visualizing and starting a journey toward their desired changes, such as reducing stress or conquering phobias, by using positive affirmations and guided imagery" (Steph Peltier).

Dispelling Myths: (Steph Peltier)

Myth: Mind control is hypnotherapy.

Truth: Customers have complete autonomy over their lives and cannot be forced to do anything against their will.

Myth: You can divulge secrets when under hypnosis.

Truth: Clients only discuss what they feel comfortable discussing during hypnotherapy, which is a collaborative procedure.

Myth: It is only a form of pseudo-science.

Truth: Hypnotherapy has been shown in several studies to be beneficial for a number of ailments, including pain and anxiety.

Steps of Hypnosis:

Self-hypnosis can help with bodily relaxation, anxiety relief, the reduction of stress hormones like adrenalines. Negative thoughts alter one's perspective on life and help one become more focused on positive vision and objectives. Because you don't have to see your hypnotherapist every time, self-hypnosis is far less expensive. The benefits of doing fewer than ten steps a day, or at least three to four days a week, for fifteen to twenty minutes are as follows: (Deekshitulu PV, 2017)

Step 1: Find a peaceful, comfortable spot to sit.

Step 2: Shut your eyes, inhale deeply, and exhale fully, all the way to the bottom of your lung. To bring in fresh, pure air, take another breath. After five seconds of holding it in, relcasc the breath once more.

Do this two or three times until your entire body feels relaxed. In addition to cleaning and reviving the lungs, this also helps them relax.

Step 3: Pay close attention to and first relax your knees. Relax your calf, ankle, foot, and toes in the same manner. Everything below your knee will be loose and flexible.

Step 4: Slowly relax your waist and thighs in the same manner. Your thigh must feel relaxed and heavy in your chair.

Step 5: After that, let your chest relax. When you relax your chest, you're also relaxing your heart, lungs, stomach, and other internal organs. Give yourself permission to breathe more easily, deeply, regularly, and comfortably.

Step 6: Same way, relax your shoulder, arm, forearm, hand, fingers, neck, and throat. . As all the muscles in your neck relax, let your head to sag.

Step 7: After that, fully relax your facial muscles until they are loose and smooth. Allow your jaw to relax and your teeth to remain apart. The muscles around the eye should be relaxed.

Step 8: You feel your pressures, anxieties, and concerns spreading from head to toe through your shoulder, chest, hip, thigh, knee, calf, ankle, and foot.

Step 9: Think more deeply. Calmly recite the positive phrase or affirmation you have prepared for the day. Eight to ten times, repeat the affirmations and relaxation techniques at the same time.

Step 10: Feel the difference as you open your eyes. You will now feel as though you have just awoken from an extended period of profound slumber. Your body and mind are very clear, and you feel more rested, energized, and renewed than before.

HYPNOTHERAPY AND STRESS REDUCTION IN WORKPLACE

A model of the mind used in hypnotherapy includes parts of the conscious and subconscious.1 These two parts work together to come up with problems and come up with solutions, which is a good metaphor for helping people make the changes they want. Generally speaking, the conscious mind is very focused, like a laser pointer. For instance, driving a car in a new neighborhood while ignoring all other sensory input is an example of intense focus by the conscious mind. On the other hand, the subconscious mind constantly receives, processes, and stores information, whether we are aware of it or not. Sleep disorders, anxiety disorders, and unnecessary stress are just a few of the conditions brought on by the persistence in the subconscious of erroneous beliefs and habits. Under hypnosis, when the subconscious mind is more active and accessible, the hypnotherapist guides the client toward resolution of problems. With relaxation, guided imagery, and positive hypnotic suggestions, hypnotherapists can change attitudes, behaviours, and stressful patterns.

Workplace stress is significantly reduced through hypnotherapy, resulting in a more tranquil and focused workforce. This deep relaxation technique improves concentration and opens the mind to creative problem-solving, encouraging innovative thinking. The end result is a team that is more nimble and able to change, ready to take on challenging problems. Employee Happiness and Job Satisfaction

Mental health initiatives like hypnotherapy are linked to higher levels of job satisfaction and happiness among employees. A positive workplace culture is created and employee loyalty to the company is strengthened when employees feel supported and valued. Organizational Advantages Reduced Absenteeism: Hypnotherapy's stress-reducing effects may reduce absenteeism rates, as stress is a leading cause of sick leave. Decreased Turnover: Enhanced job satisfaction and workplace happiness contribute to reduced turnover, saving costs related to recruitment and training.

The benefits of preventing stress in the workplace include:

- A decrease in the number of mental and physical health symptoms
- A decrease in the number of injuries, illnesses, and lost time
- A decrease in the number of sick leave days taken, absences, and employee attrition

Work engagement boosts productivity, job happiness, work engagement, business savings, employee health, and community wellness.

Hypnotic Techniques for Stress

In the management of stress, hypnotherapeutic methods often incorporate relaxation techniques that enable individuals to release worry. The individual may receive assistance from a hypnotherapist to acquire mindfulness skills that promote relaxation.

Hypnotic strategies for managing stress encompass:

Relaxation

To attain a state of calm conducive to entering hypnosis, the therapist will lead the subject through a systematic focus on each bodily region. By employing mindfulness, concentrated awareness, and calming concepts, one can alleviate tension and stress. Once physical relaxation is attained, mental relaxation becomes significantly easier to achieve. This strategy often considerably alleviates stress symptoms, facilitating the initiation of the therapeutic process.

Right-Sizing

Obsessive and fearful thoughts on the future are a prevalent source of stress and can exacerbate the disease. Catastrophizing, information suppression, and exaggeration are all strategies employed to achieve this. A therapist will assist the individual in "right-sizing" their anxieties and concerns to align more closely with the reality of their situation while the individual is in a hypnotic state.

Reframing

The utilization of imagination and guided imagery is crucial for reframing. A person can imagine experiencing unsettling conditions while in a hypnotic state, akin to a dreaming condition. They can introduce fresh resources, perspectives, and attitudes to those situations, facilitating the development of healthy responses from multiple viewpoints.

Numerous hypnotherapists advocate for an array of self-management strategies alongside these treatments to assist their customers in managing stress. Self-hypnosis instructions, deep breathing exercises, and self-directed relaxation meditations exemplify activities that belong to this group.

How to use Hypnosis to treat Stress?

An initial evaluation, several hypnosis sessions, and support are typically included in a typical stress hypnosis treatment plan. A person's past and present experiences might be brought up. Chronic stress can create major medical and mental health issues, therefore a therapist may ask about past or present treatments. The therapist can collaborate with other practitioners as needed. The person and therapist will then design hypnotic recommendations and a stress-reduction plan using all this knowledge.

Then come real hypnotherapy treatments. Individuals need different numbers of sessions. Some people see results after one or two sessions, while others need ongoing treatment.

The therapist will induce a hypnotic trance in the first session and help the patient relax and focus. In addition to the above methods, a therapist may employ other methods to treat stress and anxiety.

The Benefits and Drawbacks of Stress Hypnosis:

It is entirely natural: Hypnosis is a state of mental and physical relaxation that does not require the administration of any pharmacological substances. Medications prescribed for stress and anxiety may have many undesirable effects, including dependency, sexual dysfunction, and sleep disturbances. It functions rapidly. Many folks claim immediate relief from stress symptoms while utilizing hypnotherapy. The body and mind can be tranquilized and relaxed, leading to a natural decrease in sensations of tension. Hypnotic techniques such as focused breathing, progressive relaxation, and anchoring can be employed to address residual issues following the completion of a session. It can address basic issues: It has been previously asserted that stress may originate from past occurrences. Regardless of their magnitude, these experiences can be traumatic as they result from abuse, accidents, or injuries. Individuals may discover a psychological resolution to the root causes of stress through hypnosis, either independently or in combination with other therapies, contingent upon their specific conditions. The subsequent are few disadvantages of employing hypnosis for stress treatment:

Results may differ: It is essential to recognize that treatment outcomes may vary among individuals. Although the person-centered approach linked to hypnotherapy can significantly aid many individuals, the treatment may not consistently yield positive outcomes. If an individual is disappointed with the initial result, they may need to consult multiple hypnotherapists.

Absence of universal criteria: Hypnotherapy is not regulated by a standardized framework. Consequently, the services and treatments provided by hypnotists may vary significantly. The majority of practitioners, conversely, are dedicated to maintaining professional and ethical standards. Your hypnotherapist ought to be affiliated with a reputable professional organization, such as the National Guild of Hypnotists, to guarantee their professionalism.

Hypnosis treatment is sometimes not reimbursed by insurance, necessitating out-of-pocket expenses for individuals. Before pursuing hypnotherapy for stress management, it is essential to consult your insurance provider.

THE NEUROCHEMISTRY OF HYPNOSIS

Signals can be transmitted from one neuron to another via synapses, which are minute brain connections, through the utilization of chemical molecules called neurotransmitters. The three most critical neurotransmitters in hypnotherapy are serotonin (C10H12N2O), dopamine (C8H11NO2), and GABA (C4H9NO2). Dopamine facilitates the acquisition of new concepts by mediating information flow between different brain regions, and its release engenders sensations of pleasure and satisfaction. Serotonin, GABA, and dopamine are the three principal neurotransmitters linked to hypnosis. Furthermore, neuropeptides, composed of amino acid sequences, play a role in this process. Moreover, they possess the capacity to inhibit unpleasant sensations and activate brain receptors, leading to emotional detachment from traumatic memories and experiences. New York Health Hypnosis & Integrative Therapy states that hypnosis promotes the release of endorphins, hence diminishing pain perception and facilitating stress alleviation.

The Roles of Chemistry Brain waves, neurotransmitters, and neuropeptides are chemicals naturally created by the human body. Hypnotherapy is successful as it decreases brain wave frequency, hence enhancing the subconscious's receptivity to suggestion. During hypnotherapy, neuropeptides are activated and novel brain networks are formed. This transpires when outdated cognitive patterns, such as habits, are relinquished and new cognitive patterns are cultivated. Examples of these cognitive processes encompass habits. Subsequently, chemicals are released into the body, enabling adherence to the instructions provided by the hypnotist to address all previously addressed problems. Hypnotherapy is typically employed to alleviate pain and address detrimental habits such as smoking. The somatosensory cortex, responsible for the perception of touch and pain, is utilized for pain control. Chemicals can reduce pain by blocking pain sensations. In the nervous system, neuropeptides regulate the transmission and inhibition of sensations at numerous gates. Consequently, specific unpleasant sensations are obstructed from reaching the brain, and the ability to manage them is employed in hypnotherapy treatment. Upon reaching the brain, emotions traverse the emotional centre, where they are transformed into pain by the element of fear. Another facet of hypnotherapy involves the dissociation of emotional attachment linked to pain. This process, akin to the effects of morphine, leads individuals to feel detached from their bodies and to disregard the sensations they are experiencing. Moreover, hypnotherapy effectively manages pain by stimulating the brain to release a substantial number of endorphins. The prefrontal cortex, the brain region responsible for decision-making, is engaged while breaking habits. Upon the release of neuropeptides, they bind to receptors, thus initiating a cascade of actions within the cell or neuron. These processes ultimately lead to the activation of the cell or neuron. A single molecule, when release from a neuron, stimulates another neuron, so activating a circuit. Circuits govern the alteration of emotions and behaviours. A hypnotist can alter an individual's pain or detrimental habit by "rewiring" neural pathways through the power of suggestion and hypnosis. (Kenzy Gilsdorf, The Chemistry of Hypnothderapy).

Dopamine is the most studied molecule in relation to hypnosis and plays a major role among the neurotransmitters in the human body. Dopamine and suggestion are closely related, as summed up by Acunzo and colleagues (2021). Landry's neuroimaging research (Landry et al., 2017) highlighted dopamine's prominent function in ACC (Anterior Cingular Cortex in the mesocortical dopamine system) activation during hypnosis.

1.4. Neurobiological constructs around hypnosis:

Neuroplasticity and hypnotherapy are related because the brain may create new neural connections in response to therapeutic recommendations. Through the use of hypnotherapy, the therapist can assist the patient in forming new brain connections that support constructive thinking and behavior patterns.

Take a person who is afraid of flying, for instance. Hypnotherapy can immediately assist to change a person's reaction to flying, whereas more conventional treatment techniques may include exposing the patient to the frightening stimuli gradually. The brain may develop new neural connections that link flight to safety and tranquillity rather than anxiety and dread through repeated hypnotherapy sessions. The notion that hypnotherapy may use neuroplasticity to effect positive transformation is supported by a large body of scientific research. For example, hypnosis may change patterns of brain connection, improving communication across various brain areas, according to research published in the journal Cerebral Cortex. This enhanced connection is a sign of neuroplastic alterations that may facilitate novel thought and behaviour patterns. The use of hypnosis for pain relief was the subject of another research that was published in The American Journal of Clinical Hypnosis. The researchers discovered that hypnotherapy significantly altered brain activity linked to pain processing and decreased pain perception. These results imply that hypnotherapy can help people with chronic pain by rewiring the brain networks involved in pain perception.

1.5. Implementing hypnotherapy into corporate wellness programs:

It takes careful policy-making to integrate hypnotherapy into corporate wellness initiatives in a way that is morally sound, practical, and easily accessible. Organizations have to set explicit policies regarding the incorporation of hypnotherapy, guaranteeing that it is led by qualified experts and provided as a voluntary service. Confidentiality, inclusion, and connection with larger mental health programs should all be covered by policies. In order to promote a culture that values employee well-being.

Steps for Integration:

Assessment: Hypnotherapy can fill gaps in the current wellness landscape by evaluating it. Choose certified hypnotherapists with corporate experience as your provider. Pilot Program: Start with a pilot to gauge effectiveness and gather feedback.

Tailoring Sessions:

Offer a range of sessions catering to different needs: stress reduction, smoking cessation, and improving focus.

Take into consideration individual sessions for specific issues and group sessions for gcncral wcllncss. Facilitating Acccssibility Offcr scssions during work hours, remotely, or in a designated quiet space to address logistical issues. Communicate clearly about the nature of hypnotherapy, debunking myths and highlighting benefits to encourage participation.

This strategy makes sure that hypnotherapy is easily integrated into workplace wellness, tailored to meet a variety of needs, and available to all employees, resulting in a workplace that is healthier and more productive. (Steph Peltier)

Gaining Leadership Support: Secure commitment from all management levels by demonstrating the benefits with data-driven insights.

Employee Involvement: Engage employees early to tailor the program to their needs and foster enthusiasm.

Selecting the Best Providers Qualifications and Expertise: Select certified providers with a strong track record in corporate wellness.

Cultural Fit: Ensure the provider's methods align with your company's values and work environment.

Measuring Effectiveness

Employee Feedback: Conduct regular surveys to gather insights and refine the program.

Key Performance Indicators: Monitor absenteeism, productivity, and employee morale before and after implementation to assess impact.

Strategic planning, implementation, and ongoing evaluation are all required to put a hypnotherapy wellness program into action. However, it is a worthwhile investment for modern workplaces because of its potential to improve employee well-being and organizational performance.

CONCLUSION:

As final observations for the current investigation, the effective management of stress within the Information Technology sector is of paramount significance for maintaining both employee satisfaction and productivity levels. The current study has meticulously elucidated how the IT sector represents one of the most rapidly expanding domains globally, as well as the challenges that accompany advancing technologies and novel methodologies of work. The various factors contributing to workplace stress have been systematically examined in the research, along with the repercussions that such stress inflicts on both the physical and mental well-being of employees. The chapter has provided results from several publications and journals to demonstrate how Stress may have a negative influence on workers, thus steps to lessen stress and improve performance are necessary. The chapter has also carefully examined the measures that must be implemented to lessen stress, such as hypnotherapy. Despite the many myths surrounding hypnotherapy, it is a potent practice that has been utilized for generations. It is used to encourage healing and transformation in addition to traditional therapy. It's critical to realize that hypnosis may be a useful tool for helping IT Professionals overcome a range of obstacles and manage physiological and psychological stress when administered by qualified and moral practitioners. By addressing both psychological and physiological stress, hypnotherapy promotes mental health holistically, making it a valuable addition to workplace wellness programs.

In conclusion, this chapter focus on the critical importance of stress management in the IT sector and the necessity of adopting comprehensive strategies to support employees' well-being. While conventional stress-relief methods remain essential, hypnotherapy emerges as a compelling complementary approach that can help IT professionals navigate their careers with greater ease and resilience. Hypnotherapy's inclusion in corporate wellness programs may significantly contribute to fostering a workforce that is healthier and more productive as awareness of its benefits continues to rise.

SIGNIFICANCE OF THE CHAPTER

By providing hypnotherapy as a novel, scientifically supported solution and providing a comprehensive synthesis of stress-related issues among IT professionals, this chapter fills a critical gap in the literature. This work will have profound effects on policymaking, workplace interventions, and future research because of the growing concerns about mental health in high-pressure corporate roles.

REFERENCES

Ahmad, N. R., Ullah, I., Aziz, M. U., & Iqbal, F. (2025). Investigating stress, burnout, and organizational factors contributing to psychological well-being at work. Review of Education. *Administration & Law*, *8*(1), 29–40. DOI: 10.47067/real.v8i1.401

Ahmed, M., Zehou, S., Raza, S. A., Qureshi, M. A., & Yousufi, S. Q. (2020). Impact of CSR and environmental triggers on employee green behavior: The mediating effect of employee well-being. *Corporate Social Responsibility and Environmental Management*, *27*(5), 2225–2239. DOI: 10.1002/csr.1960

Antwi, C. O., Fan, C.-J., Aboagye, M. O., Brobbey, P., Jababu, Y., Affum-Osei, E., & Avornyo, P. (2019). Job demand stressors and employees' creativity: A within-person approach to dealing with hindrance and challenge stressors at the airport environment. *Service Industries Journal*, *39*(3–4), 250–278. DOI: 10.1080/02642069.2018.1520220

BIMA. (2019). The voices of our industry: BIMA Tech Inclusion & Diversity Report 2019. Retrieved from https://bima.co.uk/wp-content/uploads/2020/01/BIMA-Tech -Inclusion-and-Diversity-Report-2019

Carmichael, S. G. (2015, August 19). The research is clear: Long hours backfire for people and for companies. Harvard Business Review. https://hbr.org

Das, R. (2012). Occupational health concerns of software professionals and their coping strategies. *International Journal of Management Research and Business Strategy*, *1*, 81–85.

Davis, S. N., & Tuttle, J. D. (2017). Context, opportunity, and demands: Satisfaction with work-life balance in 26 countries. *Journal of Comparative Family Studies*, *48*(4), 329–347. DOI: 10.3138/jcfs.48.4.329

. De Benedittis, G. (2020). Hypnosis: From neural mechanisms to clinical practice. OBM Integrative and Complementary Medicine, 5(3), 039. https://doi.org/DOI: 10.21926/obm.icm.2003039

El Kadiri, S., Grabot, B., Thoben, K. D., Hribernik, K., Emmanouilidis, C., Von Cieminski, G., & Kiritsis, D. (2016). Current trends on ICT technologies for enterprise information systems. *Computers in Industry*, *79*, 14–33. DOI: 10.1016/j.compind.2015.06.008

Elkins, G. R., Barabasz, A. F., Council, J. R., & Spiegel, D. (2015). Advancing research and practice: The revised APA Division 30 definition of hypnosis. *The American Journal of Clinical Hypnosis*, *57*(4), 378–385. DOI: 10.1080/00029157.2015.1011465 PMID: 25928776

European Foundation for the Improvement of Living and Working Conditions. (2016). European Quality of Life Survey. Retrieved October 24, 2022, from https://www.eurofound.europa.eu/data/european-quality-of-life-survey

Fisch, S., Brinkhaus, B., & Teut, M. (2017). Hypnosis in patients with perceived stress – A systematic review. *BMC Complementary and Alternative Medicine*, *17*, 323. DOI: 10.1186/s12906-017-1806-0 PMID: 28629342

Franken, E., Bentley, T., Shafaei, A., Farr-Wharton, B., Onnis, L., & Omari, M. (2021). Forced flexibility and remote working: Opportunities and challenges in the new normal. *Journal of Management & Organization*, *27*(6), 1131–1149. DOI: 10.1017/jmo.2021.40

Hanisch, S. E., Twomey, C. D., Szeto, A. C., Birner, U. W., Nowak, D., & Sabariego, C. (2016). The effectiveness of interventions targeting the stigma of mental illness at the workplace: A systematic review. *BMC Psychiatry*, *16*, 1. DOI: 10.1186/s12888-015-0706-4 PMID: 26739960

Hasin, H., Johari, Y. C., Jamil, A., Nordin, E., & Hussein, W. S. (2023). The harmful impact of job stress on mental and physical health. *International Journal of Academic Research in Business & Social Sciences*, *13*(4), 1–XX. DOI: 10.6007/IJARBSS/v13-i4/16655

Health & Safety Executive. UK. (2020). Mental health conditions, work and the workplace. Retrieved February 25, 2022, from https://www.hse.gov.uk/stress/mental-health.htm

Joyce, S., Modini, M., Christensen, H., Mykletun, A., Bryant, R., & Mitchell, P. B. (2016). Workplace interventions for common mental disorders: A systematic meta-review. *Psychological Medicine*, *46*, 683–697. DOI: 10.1017/S0033291715002408 PMID: 26620157

Kihlstrom, J. F. (2008). The domain of hypnosis, revisited. In Nash, M. R., & Barnier, A. J. (Eds.), *The Oxford handbook of hypnosis* (pp. 21–52). Oxford University Press.

Nardodkar, R., Pathare, S., Ventriglio, A., Castaldelli-Maia, J., Javate, K. R., & Torales, J.. (2016). Legal protection of the right to work and employment for persons with mental health problems: A review of legislation across the world. *International Review of Psychiatry (Abingdon, England)*, *28*, 375–384. DOI: 10.1080/09540261.2016.1210575 PMID: 27499197

Padma, V., Anand, N. N., Gurukul, S. M., Javid, S. M., Prasad, A., & Arun, S. (2015). Health problems and stress in Information Technology and Business Process Outsourcing employees. *Journal of Pharmacy & Bioallied Sciences*, *7*(Suppl 1), S9–S13. DOI: 10.4103/0975-7406.15576 PMID: 26015763

Poddar, S., Kar, B., Samanta, S., & Bhaumi, A. (Eds.). (2021). *Human resource management and mental health: A psychosocial aspect*. KIIT University., DOI: 10.46977/book.2021.hrmmh

Rashidi, Z., & Jalbani, A. A. (2009). Job stress among software professionals in Pakistan: A factor analytic study. [MSSE]. *Journal of Independent Studies and Research*, *7*(1), 1–1.

Rocha, L. E., & Debert-Ribeiro, M. (2004). Working conditions, visual fatigue, and mental health among systems analysts in São Paulo, Brazil. *Occupational and Environmental Medicine*, *61*(1), 24–32. DOI: 10.1136/oem.61.1.24 PMID: 14691269

Chapter 5
Hypnotherapy for Performance Anxiety, Perfectionism, and Fear of Failure in Corporate Professionals

Manish Sahu
https://orcid.org/0009-0002-7944-9435
Shoolini University, India

Arun Jyoti
Shoolini University, India

ABSTRACT

This chapter explores hypnotherapy as an effective psychological intervention for addressing performance anxiety, perfectionism, and fear of failure among corporate professionals. These issues are common in competitive workplace environments and negatively impact productivity, emotional well-being, decision-making, and innovation, leading to burnout and reduced organizational effectiveness. Although cognitive-behavioral therapies have been widely used for such problems, they only address surface-level cognitions and miss the subconscious factors that sustain these patterns. Hypnotherapy focuses on modifying subconscious processes through guided relaxation, concentration, and suggestion. In corporate settings, hypnotherapy can enhance concentration, creativity, confidence, and adaptive coping, leading to higher job satisfaction, engagement, and productivity. This chapter synthesizes

DOI: 10.4018/979-8-3373-2317-6.ch005

clinical research, psychological theory, and organizational applications, highlighting hypnotherapy's relevance for workplace mental health, leadership development, and sustainable performance outcomes.

1.INTRODUCTION

In the competitive landscape of corporate work, professionals face high performance demands, rapid changes, and frequent evaluation cycles. These pressures lead to performance anxiety, which comprises emotional, cognitive, and physiological reactions that can impair job functions, like presentations, negotiations, and decision-making.

In addition to anxiety, many professionals struggle with perfectionism, a drive for unrealistic high standards and a fear of failure, which frequently leads to procrastination, self-doubt, and avoidance behaviors. Although cognitive-behavioral strategies are widely implemented in organizational coaching and therapy, but subconscious beliefs often remain and shape automatic reactions to stress, evaluation, and threats.

Hypnotherapy, uses hypnosis as a therapeutic tool to accesses the subconscious mind by promoting focused attention and increased suggestibility. This process helps individuals change maladaptive thoughts and behaviors. The American Psychological Association describes hypnosis as a state of consciousness where people respond more readily to suggestions (Elkins et al., 2015a) This capacity enables professionals to explore underlying beliefs associated with performance stress and to implement adaptive cognitive-emotional strategies.

This chapter combines research from psychology, neuroscience, and business to show how hypnotherapy can support corporate professionals in reducing performance anxiety, managing perfectionism, and overcoming fear of failure, ultimately enhancing workplace effectiveness, and well-being.

2.CONCEPTUAL FOUNDATIONS: HYPNOTHERAPY, SUBCONSCIOUS MECHANISMS, AND CORPORATE STRESS

Hypnotherapy is based on using hypnosis as a clinical and psychological tool, where a trained professional guides a client to enter into a state of heightened focus and suggestibility along with deep relaxation, which facilitates access to subconscious processes that affect their thoughts and feelings. A systematic umbrella review of meta-analyses from diverse clinical fields has indicated that hypnosis interventions can have positive effects on both mental and physical outcomes. Many studies found medium to large improvements compared to control groups, with very few showing no effect. These findings suggests that hypnosis may facilitate significant improvements in psychological functioning across different contexts and populations. (Rosendahl et al., 2023)

Specifically for anxiety reduction, hypnotherapy integrate techniques such as guided imagery, relaxation, and suggestion to disrupt maladaptive thought patterns and reduce physiological arousal, both of which are important factors in performance anxiety. Evidence from various meta-analytic research show that hypnosis, especially when combined with other therapeutic interventions, is highly effective in reducing anxiety. It often leads to greater emotional regulation and improved stress management compared to control groups.(Valentine et al., 2019a)

Research on the neural mechanisms of hypnosis shows that when a person enters a hypnotic state, there are measurable changes in cognitive processing and neural activity. Notable, modifications occur in areas associated with attention, imagery, and perception, including higher-order visual networks. Hypnosis also affects the brain's top-down regulatory processes that influence how sensations and emotions are experienced. These neural dynamics are fundamental to hypnotherapy's ability to modify the subconscious framing of thoughts and emotional responses.(Landry et al., 2017)

In addition to psychological perspectives, the physiological mechanisms influenced by hypnotic states have been documented as well. Studies demonstrate that hypnosis can modulate the autonomic nervous system (ANS), enhancing parasympathetic activity associated with relaxation while reducing sympathetic responses linked to stress. This modulation leads to measurable reduction in heart rate, blood pressure, and overall stress responses, which are particularly significant for professionals facing chronic workplace stress and performance anxiety. Impact of Hypnosis on the ANS provides a biological pathway for stress reduction and emotional regulation that complements cognitive reframing.(De Benedittis, 2025)

Clinical studies also support hypnosis as an effective evidence-based method for reducing anxiety. A meta-analysis of randomized controlled trials found that combining hypnosis with other psychological treatments significantly reduce anxiety symptoms, with lasting effects at follow-up. This finding supports using hypnotherapy for stress and performance anxiety in corporate professionals through clinical adaptation.(Valentine et al., 2019a)

Collectively, these findings illustrate that hypnotherapy operates through a complex interaction of cognitive, neural, and physiological mechanisms that influence subconscious processing. By inducing a state of concentrated attention and reduced emotional reactivity, hypnotherapy enables individuals to modify limiting beliefs, reduce stress responses, and alter automatic emotional habits, all of which are essential for corporate professionals facing performance-related stress and psychological challenges. These underlying mechanisms form the basis for targeted interventions addressing issues such as performance anxiety, perfectionism, and fear of failure.

3.PERFORMANCE ANXIETY IN CORPORATE PROFESSIONALS

Performance anxiety refers to the intense feelings of nervousness, worry, and physiological arousal that individuals experience when they believe they're being evaluated or judged—such as during presentations, leadership meetings, negotiations, or important tasks. While earlier research on performance anxiety mainly focused on contexts like public speaking or sporting performance, studies on hypnotherapy now cover a wider range of situations and show that hypnosis can help lower anxiety and improve performance. For example, studies focusing on performance stress in sports and educational settings has found that hypnosis, using guided imagery and cognitive reframing, can significantly reduce performance anxiety by changing subconscious associations with threat. (Stanton, 1993)

Professionals experiencing performance anxiety often show the following:

- Catastrophic self-talk, where mistakes are interpreted as a sign of personal failure.
- Emotional responses such as tension, dread, or anticipatory panic.
- Physiological symptoms, such as a racing heart, shallow breathing, and muscle tightness, all of which can intensify feelings of anxiety.
- Behavioral patterns including either avoiding situations altogether or over-preparing in an effort to prevent perceived negative outcomes.

The mechanisms by which hypnotherapy alleviates performance anxiety involves enhancing emotional regulation, minimizing fear-based cognitive processing, and fostering adaptive patterns of thought and physiological calm. By guiding individuals into a state of focused relaxation and embedding positive suggestions related to performance confidence and competence, hypnotherapy helps individuals to modify their internal responses to evaluative cues that typically provoke anxiety. As a result, the conditioned nervous system response to performance triggers can be adjusted not only at a cognitive level but also at the level where emotional reactions are generated.

Performance anxiety frequently overlaps with perfectionism and fear of failure, as high evaluative pressure feeds a cycle of unrealistic standards, self-criticism, and avoidant behaviors. If unaddressed, these patterns can reduce productivity and hinder career progression by diverting cognitive resources toward anxiety management instead of effective task completion. Hypnotherapy addresses performance anxiety by reducing the automatic threat associations between performance cues and anxiety responses, while enhancing calm concentration through therapeutic suggestion and visualization techniques.

In practice, structured hypnotherapeutic sessions typically incorporate success imagery, in which professionals mentally rehearse confident performance outcomes in a calm subconscious state, reducing the emotional intensity associated with real life performance situations. By consistently repeating these positive subconscious scripts, the professionals begin to respond to performance cues with confidence and composure rather than threat and tension.

4.PERFECTIONISM IN HIGH-PERFORMANCE WORK CULTURES

Perfectionism is a personality trait characterized by striving for flawlessness, adherence to exceptionally high performance standards, and being overly critical of oneself when those standards are not achieved. Perfectionists often define success in absolute terms — where any deviation is perceived as failure. This mindset is often influenced by a desire to avoid criticism, fear of negative evaluation, and worry over not meeting external standards.(Koutra et al., 2023)

Clinical and psychological studies distinguish between adaptive and maladaptive perfectionism. Adaptive perfectionism, sometimes referred as "perfectionistic strivings," is characterized by having high personal standards and a careful pursuit of excellence that can correlate with persistence and strong performance. Maladaptive perfectionism, or "perfectionistic concerns," is characterized by fear of making mistakes, intense self-criticism, and preoccupation with avoiding failure, and is closely associated with negative emotional outcomes such as anxiety and distress. (Koutra et al., 2023)

Extensive research shows that when perfectionism becomes maladaptive, it can significantly impact mental health. High levels of perfectionistic concern are associated with increased psychological distress, mistake rumination, and excessive worry, which in turn can lead to anxiety, depressive symptoms, and burnout. In academic or performance settings, individuals with elevated maladaptive perfectionism feel more stressed and enjoy less well-being when facing tasks that challenge their high expectations.(Philpot & Donachie, 2025)

Within professional settings, especially in competitive corporate cultures, maladaptive perfectionism can amplify stress associated with performance evaluations, leadership responsibilities, and career progression. When perfectionists equate self-worth exclusively with error-free performance, they are more likely to experience procrastination (fear of making mistakes), excessive focus on minor details, and avoidance of risk. Collectively, these tendencies may hinder adaptability, creativity, and overall strategic productivity.(Frost et al., 1990)

According to Hewitt and Flett's model, perfectionism includes self-oriented, other-oriented, and socially prescribed dimensions:

- Self-oriented perfectionism involves setting unrealistic high standards for yourself.
- Other-oriented perfectionism involves demanding perfection from others.
- Socially prescribed perfectionism involves the belief that others expect one to be perfect. This last type is especially linked to psychological distress and anxiety because it connects self-worth to external expectations rather than internal mastery.(Hewitt et al., 1991)

In corporate environments, these characteristics frequently appear as:

- Delaying tasks from fear of mistakes.
- Micromanaging or struggling to delegate tasks to others.
- Persistent burnout from overwork and heightened self-criticism.
- Avoiding new situations where perfection cannot be guaranteed.

The psychological mechanism underlying perfectionism is characterized by self-worth contingencies, where achievement becomes the primary source of self-validation. When perfectionists fail to meet high standards, they often engage in harsh self-criticism, which can lead to performance anxiety, fear of negative judgment, and avoidance of risk. These internal obstacles are among those that hypnotherapy seeks to address at the subconscious level.

5.FEAR OF FAILURE AND IDENTITY IN CORPORATE CONTEXTS

Fear of failure is a widely recognized psychological construct defined as a tendency to avoid situations where failure may occur, due to anticipatory emotional responses such as embarrassment, shame, social judgment, and loss of status. These responses can create significant emotional and cognitive obstacles to optimal performance. Research rooted in achievement motivation theory describes fear of failure as more than mere anxiety, it is a motivation to avoid outcomes perceived as threatening to one's identity or self-worth.(Sunkarapalli & Agarwal, n.d.)

In corporate setting, fear of failure often leads to:

- Avoiding risks, which hinders innovation.
- Delaying tasks because of anxiety over outcomes.
- Lower emotional resilience when performance expectations are high and uncertainty is unavoidable.

Research examining the relationship between perfectionism and fear of failure indicates that:

- Individuals who equate their self-worth with flawless performance are more likely to experience intense fear of failure.
- This fear in turn reinforces rigid perfectionistic standards and leads to increased emotional self-criticism following any performance errors.
- Fear of failure can result in an avoidance of challenging or uncertain tasks, which is a liability in adaptive corporate environments where innovation and strategic agility are expected.(Sagar & Stoeber, 2009)

Although fear of failure has mainly been studied in the fields of education and sports psychology, the same motivational factors are relevant for professionals in the corporate world:

- Fear of being judged unfavorably by peers or leaders.
- Fear of damaging one's professional reputation.
- Fear of reduced future career opportunities because of mistakes.

These fears can contribute to perfectionism, forming a cycle that hinders performance, creativity, and well-being.(Sagar & Stoeber, 2009)

Perfectionism and fear of failure are closely intertwined constructs as evidenced by both empirical research and theoretical frameworks. Research utilizing validated psychological assessments show that maladaptive perfectionistic concerns such as excessive worry about mistakes and perceived external pressures are strong predictors of fear of failure. This means that individuals who evaluate their performance harshly and fear negative evaluation are more likely to perceive failure as a substantial personal threat. As a result, they may exhibit behaviours such as avoidance, procrastination, or risk aversion.(Sagar & Stoeber, 2009)

6.SUBCONSCIOUS MECHANISMS UNDERLYING PERFORMANCE ANXIETY, PERFECTIONISM, AND FEAR OF FAILURE

Performance anxiety, perfectionism, and fear of failure are not merely conscious thought patterns; they are embedded in subconscious emotional mechanisms that shape how individuals interpret performance situations, attach meaning to success and failure, and automatically respond to evaluation, uncertainty, and perceived risk.

One of the most influential explanations for subconscious influence comes from schema theory. According to Aaron T. Beck, individuals develop core beliefs (schemas) during early life through interactions with authority figures, experiences of success and failure, and evaluative feedback. These core beliefs operate automatically and influence perception without requiring conscious effort. When activated, they shape emotional responses and behavior.(Beck & Clark, 1997)

In performance settings, common maladaptive schemas include beliefs such as:

- "My worth depends on my success"
- "Mistakes mean incompetence"
- "Failure leads to rejection"

These underlying beliefs are often subconscious, so individuals may not be consciously aware that such assumptions are influencing their anxiety or perfectionistic behavior. Beck highlighted that anxiety persists when such schemas are not effectively addressed, even if individuals attempt conscious challenges.(Beck & Clark, 1997)

Subconscious anxiety responses typically develop through classical and operant conditioning, where emotional reactions become associated with specific cues. when evaluative situations such as presentations, exams, performance reviews are repeatedly paired with criticism, embarrassment, or punishment, anxiety becomes automatically triggered in similar contexts later.

Joseph LeDoux's research on emotional learning indicate that once fear associations are formed, they can be triggered independently without conscious cognitive processing. This explains why individuals experience significant anxiety in performance situations even when they are rationally aware of their own competence. (LeDoux, 1996)

Achievement motivation research describes fear of failure not as a deliberate choice, but as a learned tendency to avoid certain situations. Conroy and colleagues explain that fear of failure is fueled by subconscious anticipatory beliefs that failing will result in feelings of shame, embarrassment, or social rejection. Their research suggest that these beliefs can unconsciously drive people to avoid risks, procrastinate, or shy away from difficult goals at work, even if they consciously deny fearing failure. This process helps explain why some individuals hesitate to tackle professional challenges.(Conroy et al., 2007)

Perfectionism is often linked to conditional self-worth, where individuals subconsciously tie their sense of value to always performing flawlessly. Hewitt and Flett describe perfectionism as a personality trait in which self-esteem depends on meeting extremely high standards. These standards become internalized and operate automatically, resulting in chronic self-criticism, fear of making mistakes, and emotional distress—especially in settings characterized by frequent evaluation and comparison.(Hewitt et al., 1991)

David H. Barlow's model of anxiety highlights that anxiety is maintained by automatic threat appraisals, where individuals subconsciously overestimate potential danger while underestimating their coping capabilities. These appraisals occur rapidly and beyond conscious awareness, leading to anticipatory anxiety well before performance situations arise. This mechanism explains why professionals often experience heightened anxiety days or weeks before presentations, evaluations, or significant decision-making events, even when objectively prepared.(Barlow, 2004)

7.HYPNOTHERAPEUTIC INTERVENTIONS FOR PERFORMANCE ANXIETY, PERFECTIONISM, AND FEAR OF FAILURE

Hypnotherapeutic interventions are designed to address psychological challenges by accessing subconscious cognitive and emotional processes through methods such as focused attention, relaxation, and therapeutic suggestion. The American Psychological Association defines hypnosis as a state involving focused attention and diminished peripheral awareness, thereby facilitating an increased capacity to respond to suggestion.(Elkins et al., 2015b) Within clinical contexts, hypnotherapy uses this state to modify maladaptive beliefs, emotional responses, and behavioral patterns that contribute to anxiety and performance related issues.

7.1.Anxiety Reduction Through Hypnotic Relaxation and Suggestion

Hypnotherapy is strongly supported by empirical evidence for its effectiveness in anxiety reduction. Hypnosis facilitates deep physical relaxation while simultaneously altering cognitive-emotional processing through therapeutic suggestion. This dual mechanism is important because anxiety persists not only by cognitive worry but also by physiological arousal.

A meta-analysis of randomized controlled trials investigating hypnosis as an intervention for anxiety found that hypnosis led to significant reductions in anxiety symptoms, especially when combined with other psychological interventions. The authors concluded that hypnosis contributes to improved treatment outcomes by reducing subconscious threat appraisal and promoting emotional regulation.(Valentine et al., 2019b)

This is highly relevant to performance anxiety among corporate professionals, where anxiety is often triggered automatically in response to evaluative situations such as presentations, meetings, or performance reviews. Through hypnotherapy, individuals may be exposed to these situations while maintaining physiological composure, which helps to reduce learned association between evaluation and fear.

7.2.Ego-Strengthening and Subconscious Confidence Development

Ego-strengthening is a well-established hypnotherapeutic technique aimed at enhancing self-efficacy, promoting emotional stability, and fostering internal validation. Clinical hypnosis literature describes ego-strengthening as a method of strengthening adaptive self-beliefs and reducing vulnerability to external evaluation.

Heap, Brown, and Oakley explain that ego-strengthening suggestions are commonly used in cases of anxiety, low confidence, or stress, especially when individuals struggle with self-doubt and excessive dependence on approval. These suggestions work at a subconscious level to foster a more stable sense of self-worth and resilience during difficulties.(Heap et al., 2004)

Ego-strengthening is highly relevant for corporate professionals, as performance anxiety and perfectionism often stem from contingent self-worth, where confidence depends on flawless outcomes. Through hypnotherapy, individuals can separate their sense of self-worth from performance outcomes by reinforcing beliefs such as competence, adaptability, and emotional regulation. These qualities remain stable regardless of individual successes or failures.

7.3.Guided Imagery and Performance Rehearsal

Another fundamental hypnotherapeutic intervention is guided imagery, also referred to as mental rehearsal. In this approach, individuals are guided to visualize successful performance scenarios while under hypnosis. Imagery practiced during hypnosis is considered effective because emotional learning is enhanced when focused attention is maintained and physiological arousal is minimized.

A randomized controlled trial comparing hypnosis with progressive muscle relaxation found that hypnosis significantly reduced anxiety and attentional bias toward perceived threat. Participants who underwent hypnosis showed improved emotional regulation and reduced fear responses to evaluative stimuli, suggesting that hypnotic imagery may effectively influence subconscious emotional conditioning. (Zhang et al., 2022)

Although this research was conducted in an academic performance context, the underlying mechanisms, anticipatory anxiety, evaluation, and fear of negative outcomes—are directly comparable to corporate performance environments.

8.ORGANIZATIONAL IMPLICATIONS AND PERFORMANCE OUTCOMES

The World Health Organization reports that mental health interventions at workplace can boost productivity and cut down on health-related expenses. Organizations that prioritize psychological safety and e encourage motional resilience are more likely to foster innovation and adaptability among their employees

8.1.Workplace Mental Health Interventions Yield Measurable Organizational Benefits

An increasing volume of global research indicates that workplace mental health interventions producc mcasurablc and quantifiablc organizational bcncfits. Thc WHO reports that for every $1 invested in the treatment of common mental health conditions such as anxiety and depression, there is an estimated $4 return in improved health and productivity. These gains occur through decreased absenteeism, improved employee engagement, and enhanced functional capacity.(*Investing in Treatment for Depression and Anxiety Leads to Fourfold Return*, n.d.)

This evidence highlights that addressing psychological challenges, such as performance anxiety and fear of failure is not only a well-being initiative but a strategic business investment.

8.2 Impact on Productivity, Absenteeism, and Presenteeism

Organizational research identifies two distinct phenomena:

- Absenteeism which refers time away from work due to illness.

- Presenteeism which refers being physically present but psychologically impaired.

Anxiety and stress-related conditions are particularly associated with presenteeism, where employees continue working but with diminished concentration, decision making ability, and overall efficiency. Research show that presenteeism often generates greater productivity losses than absenteeism.

The Harvard Business Review emphasizes that untreated mental health concerns can compromise focus, creativity, and strategic thinking, all of which are key competencies required in modern corporate roles.(*It's a New Era for Mental Health at Work*, n.d.)

8.3.Reduction in Burnout and Turnover Risk

Performance anxiety and maladaptive perfectionism significantly increase the risk of burnout, which is marked by feelings of emotional exhaustion, cynicism, and a decline in professional effectiveness. Burnout is strongly associated with higher turnover intentions and less engagement at work.

Organizations that take active steps to address stress and mental health proactively experience:

- Lower employee turnover
- Boosted morale and employee participation
- Greater organizational commitment

By targeting underlying causes of stress such as fear of failure and excessive self-criticism hypnotherapy can help prevent burnout as part of broader mental health strategies.

8.4.Decision-Making, Risk-Taking, and Innovation

Psychological safety and effective emotional regulation are critical for innovation and adaptive decision-making. When workplace culture is dominated by a fear of failure, employees are more likely to avoid risk, suppress ideas, and strictly adhere to existing processes.

Amy Edmondson's research on psychological safety demonstrates that environments in which individuals feel safe to make mistakes and learn from failure show higher levels of innovation, collaboration, and overall performance. Conversely, Fear-based cultures restrict learning and adaptability.(Edmondson, 2018)

Addressing subconscious fear responses at the individual level through hypnotherapy can supports broader organizational goals related to agility, creativity, and effective leadership.

8.5 Leadership Effectiveness and Emotional Regulation

Leaders affected by unmanaged performance anxiety or perfectionism may struggle with delegation, decision-making under uncertainty, and maintaining emotional availability. Strong emotional regulation and internal confidence are essential for effective leadership, especially in volatile and complex environments.

The APA notes that leaders who manage stress successfully contribute to healthier team climates and promote employee trust and engagement. Interventions that enhance emotional self-regulation at a subconscious level can create positive, far-reaching impacts across organizational systems.(*Learn How to Manage Your Workplace Stress*, n.d.)

9.CONCLUSION

Performance anxiety, perfectionism, and fear of failure are prevalent yet often overlooked psychological challenges faced by corporate professionals. While these experiences are often framed as individual weaknesses or motivational deficits, the literature examined in this chapter clearly demonstrates that these issues are rooted in subconscious belief systems, learned emotional responses, and automatic threat appraisals shaped by past experiences and reinforced by contemporary organizational cultures. As a result, purely rational or skills based interventions are frequently insufficient to produce sustained change.

This chapter has demonstrated that hypnotherapy offers a unique and complementary approach by working directly with subconscious mechanisms that maintain anxiety, rigid self-assessment, and fear-based avoidance. Drawing on established psychological theories, clinical research, and organizational evidence, hypnotherapy has been shown to enhance emotional regulation, cognitive flexibility, and internal confidence through mechanisms such as focused attention, therapeutic suggestion, ego-strengthening, and guided imagery. These interventions enable professionals to disengage self-worth from performance outcomes, reinterpret failure as constructive feedback, and respond to evaluative situations with greater composure and resilience.

Importantly, the impact of addressing these challenges extend beyond individual well-being. Organizational studies consistently demonstrate that unmanaged performance anxiety and maladaptive perfectionism are linked to increased burnout, reduced engagement, and higher employee turnover, while interventions that support mental health and foster emotional regulation have been shown to enhance productivity, improve retention rates, strengthen leadership capabilities, and encourage innovation. By reducing subconscious fear-based responses, hypnotherapeutic approaches contribute meaningfully to organizational objectives such as advancing psychological safety, promoting sustainable performance, and cultivating adaptive leadership within complex and dynamic business contexts.

In an era where professional success increasingly depends on emotional intelligence, adaptability, and resilience, hypnotherapy provides a valuable framework converting subconscious barriers into constructive psychological assets. By addressing the underlying psychological factors that influence performance, both organizations and professionals can pursue excellence in a manner that is healthier and more sustainable, rather than being motivated solely by fear or pressure.

REFERENCES

Barlow, D. H. . (2004). *Anxiety and its disorders : the nature and treatment of anxiety and panic*. 704.

Beck, A. T., & Clark, D. A. (1997). An information processing model of anxiety: Automatic and strategic processes. *Behaviour Research and Therapy, 35*(1), 49–58. DOI: 10.1016/S0005-7967(96)00069-1 PMID: 9009043

Conroy, D. E., Kaye, M. P., & Fifer, A. M. (2007). Cognitive Links Between Fear Of Failure And Perfectionism. *Journal of Rational-Emotive & Cognitive-Behavior Therapy 2007 25:4, 25*(4), 237–253. https://doi.org/DOI: 10.1007/S10942-007-0052-7

De Benedittis, G. (2025). Brain Mechanisms of Hypnosis. *Brain Sciences, 15*(2), 142. DOI: 10.3390/BRAINSCI15020142 PMID: 40002475

Edmondson, A. C. (2018). *The Fearless Orginization*. 21–22. https://learning.oreilly.com/library/view/the-fearless-organization/9781119477242/c04.xhtml

Elkins, G. R., Barabasz, A. F., Council, J. R., & Spiegel, D. (2015a). Advancing research and practice: The revised APA division 30 definition of hypnosis. *The International Journal of Clinical and Experimental Hypnosis, 63*(1), 1–9. DOI: 10.1080/00207144.2014.961870 PMID: 25365125

Elkins, G. R., Barabasz, A. F., Council, J. R., & Spiegel, D. (2015b). Advancing research and practice: The revised APA division 30 definition of hypnosis. *The International Journal of Clinical and Experimental Hypnosis, 63*(1), 1–9. DOI: 10.1080/00207144.2014.961870 PMID: 25365125

Frost, R. O., Marten, P., Lahart, C., & Rosenblate, R. (1990). The dimensions of perfectionism. *Cognitive Therapy and Research, 14*(5), 449–468. DOI: 10.1007/BF01172967

Heap, M. Heap, M. R. J., & Oakley, D. A. (2004). *The Highly Hypnotizable Person*. https://books.google.com/books/about/The_Highly_Hypnotizable_Person.html?id=vvmOAgAAQBAJ

Hewitt, P. L., Flett, G. L., & York, N. (1991).. . *Perfectionism in the Self and Social Contexts: Conceptualization, Assessment, and Association With Psychopathology.*, *60*(3), 456–470.

Investing in treatment for depression and anxiety leads to fourfold return. (n.d.). Retrieved December 21, 2025, from https://www.who.int/news/item/13-04-2016-investing-in-treatment-for-depression-and-anxiety-leads-to-fourfold-return

It's a New Era for Mental Health at Work. (n.d.). Retrieved December 21, 2025, from https://hbr.org/2021/10/its-a-new-era-for-mental-health-at-work

Koutra, K., Mouatsou, C., & Psoma, S. (2023). The Influence of Positive and Negative Aspects of Perfectionism on Psychological Distress in Emerging Adulthood: Exploring the Mediating Role of Self-Compassion. *Behavioral Sciences (Basel, Switzerland)*, *13*(11), 932. DOI: 10.3390/BS13110932 PMID: 37998679

Landry, M., Lifshitz, M., & Raz, A. (2017). Brain correlates of hypnosis: A systematic review and meta-analytic exploration. *Neuroscience and Biobehavioral Reviews*, *81*, 75–98. DOI: 10.1016/J.NEUBIOREV.2017.02.020 PMID: 28238944

Learn how to manage your workplace stress. (n.d.). Retrieved December 21, 2025, from https://www.apa.org/topics/healthy-workplaces/workplace-stress

LeDoux, J. (1996). *Cognitive and emotional interactions in the brain: The mysterious underpinnings of emotional life*. 384. https://books.google.com/books/about/The_Emotional_Brain.html?id=7EJN5I8sk2wC

Philpot, N., & Donachie, T. C. (2025). Perfectionism and psychological distress in university students: The role of mistake rumination. *Personality and Individual Differences*, *246*, 113368. DOI: 10.1016/J.PAID.2025.113368

Rosendahl, J., Alldredge, C. T., & Haddenhorst, A. (2023). Meta-analytic evidence on the efficacy of hypnosis for mental and somatic health issues: A 20-year perspective. *Frontiers in Psychology*, *14*, 1330238. DOI: 10.3389/FPSYG.2023.1330238/BIBTEX PMID: 38268815

Sagar, S. S., & Stoeber, J. (2009). Perfectionism, fear of failure, and affective responses to success and failure: The central role of fear of experiencing shame and embarrassment. *Journal of Sport & Exercise Psychology*, *31*(5), 602–627. DOI: 10.1123/JSEP.31.5.602 PMID: 20016111

Stanton, H. E. (1993). Research Note: Alleviation of Performance Anxiety through Hypnotherapy. *Psychology of Music*, *21*(1), 78–82. DOI: 10.1177/030573569302100106

Sunkarapalli, G., & Agarwal, T. (n.d.).. . *Fear of Failure and Perfectionism in Young Adults.*, *4*. Advance online publication. DOI: 10.25215/0403.131

Valentine, K. E., Milling, L. S., Clark, L. J., & Moriarty, C. L. (2019a). THE EFFICACY OF HYPNOSIS AS A TREATMENT FOR ANXIETY: A META-ANALYSIS. *The International Journal of Clinical and Experimental Hypnosis*, *67*(3), 336–363. DOI: 10.1080/00207144.2019.1613863 PMID: 31251710

Valentine, K. E., Milling, L. S., Clark, L. J., & Moriarty, C. L. (2019b). THE EFFICACY OF HYPNOSIS AS A TREATMENT FOR ANXIETY: A META-ANALYSIS. *The International Journal of Clinical and Experimental Hypnosis*, *67*(3), 336–363. DOI: 10.1080/00207144.2019.1613863 PMID: 31251710

Zhang, Y., Yang, X.-X., Luo, J.-Y., Liang, M., Li, N., Tao, Q., Ma, L.-J., & Li, X.-M. (2022). Randomized trial estimating effects of hypnosis versus progressive muscle relaxation on medical students' test anxiety and attentional bias. *World Journal of Psychiatry*, *12*(6), 801. DOI: 10.5498/WJP.V12.I6.801 PMID: 35978973

Chapter 6
Enhancing Conscious Performance Through Subconscious Hypnotherapeutic Interventions in Business

Jeni Kakadiya
https://orcid.org/0009-0002-8143-1859
Shoolini University, India

Sangeeta Kakkar
https://orcid.org/0009-0007-9139-8040
Shoolini University, India

ABSTRACT

Modern business settings demand sustained cognitive and emotional effort, often causing stress, burnout, and inconsistent results, even for skilled workers. Traditional organizational strategies mainly target conscious methods, which may provide only limited, short-term improvements. This chapter, informed by cognitive psychology, neuroscience, and clinical hypnotherapy, argues that much of professional performance is governed by subconscious processes, such as automatic stress reactions, implicit beliefs, and emotional conditioning. It introduces the Subconscious Performance Alignment Model, which suggests that lasting performance depends on aligning subconscious regulation with conscious task demands. Hypnotherapy is presented as an ethical, evidence-based approach to recalibrating subconscious mechanisms, thus enhancing executive functioning under pressure. Moving the focus

DOI: 10.4018/979-8-3373-2317-6.ch006

from effort-based improvement to regulation aligned with subconscious processes, this chapter offers a fresh perspective to organizational psychology and sustainable performance at work.

1. INTRODUCTION

The modern business environment is characterized by ongoing psychological stress, rapid decision-making demands, emotional labor, and constant performance assessments. Technological advancements, globalization, and competitive organizational cultures have increased cognitive demands and shortened recovery times for professionals in various fields. Consequently, many business professionals experience chronic stress, decision fatigue, emotional burnout, and changing performance levels, even when they have the necessary skills and expertise (Burn-out an "Occupational Phenomenon": International Classification of Diseases, n.d.; Maslach & Leiter, 2016).

To address these challenges, organizations primarily use conscious interventions such as time-management training, cognitive-behavioral stress management, mindfulness, and resilience workshops. Although these methods offer short-term gains, their capacity to sustain long-term performance and mental well-being varies. New research from cognitive psychology and neuroscience suggests that a substantial portion of human behavior, emotion regulation, and decision-making is governed by automatic, subconscious processes rather than conscious effort (Bargh & Chartrand, 1999; Evans & Stanovich, 2013). As a result, interventions focused solely on the conscious level might not tackle the underlying mechanisms that affect professional performance under stress.

Stress-related performance issues in workplaces often continue even when people are highly motivated and skillful. This paradox indicates that these problems are not solely due to lack of effort or talent but are often caused by subconscious factors such as conditioned emotional reactions, unhealthy belief systems, and automatic perceptions of threat. Neuroscientific studies show that chronic stress changes how the prefrontal cortex functions, reducing attention control, cognitive flexibility, and decision-making abilities—key aspects of professional performance (Arnsten, 2009a; McEwen & Morrison, 2013). These changes mostly occur outside of conscious awareness, strengthening harmful patterns that conscious effort alone finds hard to change.

In this context, hypnotherapy stands out as a scientifically supported but underused method for tackling subconscious factors affecting performance. It involves a state of focused attention and increased openness, making cognitive and emotional patterns more receptive to change. Studies in clinical and cognitive neuroscience indicate that hypnotic techniques can impact attention, emotional regulation, stress response, and cognitive control processes (Landry et al., 2017a; Oakley & Halligan, 2013). Meta-analytic and empirical studies further confirm that hypnotherapy effectively alleviates stress, anxiety, and psychosomatic symptoms, resulting in better functional outcomes (Lynn et al., 2000a).

Although there is increasing evidence supporting hypnotherapy, it has mostly been studied in clinical and health contexts, with little focus on organizational and performance psychology. Its role in enhancing conscious performance in business settings is still largely unexplored. This is especially important because many common workplace issues—like burnout, performance anxiety, concentration problems, and emotional dysregulation—are often driven by subconscious processes rather than conscious goals.

This chapter emphasizes that conscious performance is governed by subconscious regulation rather than initiation. Emotional conditioning, automatic stress responses, and internalized beliefs formed through repeated professional experiences deeply influence how individuals handle pressure. When these subconscious factors do not align with conscious role expectations and goals, professionals may face ongoing stress, cognitive overload, and lower effectiveness. Conversely, aligning subconscious processes with conscious aims can enhance psychological resilience, maintain focus, and improve adaptive performance.

This chapter presents the Subconscious Performance Alignment Model (SPAM) to illustrate this relationship. The model suggests that peak professional performance results from aligning subconscious emotional and cognitive processes with conscious task demands. Hypnotherapy is seen as a systematic method within this framework that helps recalibrate subconscious stress responses, beliefs, and emotional conditioning, ultimately aiding conscious performance with less mental effort.

Drawing on insights from cognitive psychology, neuroscience, and clinical hypnotherapy, this chapter redefines hypnotherapy as a credible, ethical, and evidence-based method for improving performance in business. Instead of viewing stress and burnout just as issues to control, it emphasizes subconscious alignment as essential to lasting productivity and workplace health.

This chapter has three main objectives:

(1) to reconceptualize challenges in workplace performance by examining subconscious regulation;
(2) to introduce the Subconscious Performance Alignment Model as a new theoretical framework; and
(3) to analyze the practical and ethical considerations of using hypnotherapy-based interventions for business professionals and organizations.

This chapter advances ongoing academic discussions on sustainable performance, organizational mental health, and the psychological foundation of current work settings by transitioning the emphasis from effort-driven improvement to alignment-centered performance regulation.

2. CONSCIOUS PERFORMANCE IN BUSINESS SETTINGS

Conscious performance in business settings involves intentionally using cognitive, emotional, and behavioral skills in professional environments. It includes the ability to focus selectively, regulate emotions, make thoughtful decisions, communicate clearly, and stay engaged with tasks despite challenges, evaluations, and uncertainties. Unlike in controlled or repetitive tasks, business performance occurs within complex systems that involve time constraints, interpersonal interactions, and ongoing mental effort.

At a neuropsychological level, conscious performance mainly relies on executive functions linked to the prefrontal cortex. These include working memory, attentional control, planning, inhibiting irrelevant impulses, and cognitive flexibility. Collectively, they allow professionals to prioritize information, stay focused, evaluate options, and coordinate actions with long-term objectives (Diamond, 2012). In organizational environments, these abilities are constantly engaged, often at the same time, exerting ongoing pressure on conscious cognitive resources.

Modern business environments have heightened these challenges. Digital acceleration, continuous connectivity, performance indicators, and multitasking cultures demand sustained alertness and quick transitions between tasks. Organizational psychology research shows that these conditions substantially raise cognitive load, causing attentional splitting and decision fatigue (Baumeister et al., 2007). Consequently, conscious performance tends to become less consistent over time, even in highly skilled and motivated professionals.

A key aspect of conscious performance relies on internal regulation rather than mere effort. Conventional performance models tend to believe that boosting motivation, discipline, or skills will directly improve results. Nevertheless, evidence shows that conscious effort has limited capacity and is greatly affected by emotional and physiological conditions. When people try to sustain high performance through continuous conscious control without proper internal regulation, their performance usually worsens instead of getting better (Hockey, 2014).

Stress significantly influences conscious performance. While short-term stress can boost alertness temporarily, ongoing stress hampers executive functions by impairing prefrontal cortex regulation. Over time, neural processing moves away from reflective and adaptable thinking, favoring rigid, habitual, and emotion-driven responses controlled by subcortical systems (Arnsten, 2009). In business settings, this change appears as impulsive decisions, less creativity, focus narrowing, and challenges in handling complex information.

Importantly, professionals often realize their performance is waning but feel powerless to fix it consciously. This highlights a core limitation of conscious regulation: being aware doesn't ensure control. Cognitive neuroscience shows that when stress-related neural patterns take over, conscious efforts alone can't reliably override them (McEwen & Morrison, 2013). This results in a paradox where people put in more effort exactly when that effort is least effective.

A key aspect of conscious performance is how it interacts with self-evaluation and identity. Business performance is seldom neutral; it is deeply connected to self-worth, professional identity, and perceived competence. Performance reviews, feedback systems, and competitive environments enhance self-monitoring, which can strain executive resources. Excessive self-monitoring due to evaluative pressure has been found to hinder task execution by raising cognitive interference and anxiety (Beilock & Carr, 2001).

From a practical standpoint, conscious performance isn't just about knowledge or technical skills. Instead, it results from the interplay of cognitive load, emotional control, stress response, and internal standards. When these elements are in harmony, performance tends to be smooth, confident, and sustainable. If they are out of sync, performance can feel strained, inconsistent, and prone to failure under pressure.

This insight has important consequences for organizational interventions. Traditional methods—like time management training, motivational programs, or performance incentives—mainly focus on conscious behavior and rational planning. Although useful, these strategies often overlook the deeper regulatory systems that influence whether conscious abilities can be accessed consistently under stress. As a result, improvements tend to be temporary and dependent on context.

An increasing amount of occupational health psychology research highlights that sustainable performance depends on interventions that lower internal cognitive and emotional burdens, rather than just enhancing conscious control (Sonnentag & Fritz, 2015a). In this perspective, conscious performance is seen primarily as a result of underlying regulatory mechanisms rather than a standalone skill that can be endlessly improved through effort.

This reconceptualization provides the basis for incorporating subconscious interventions into business environments. Since conscious performance represents outward expressions of deeper psychological regulation, enhancing performance effectively requires engaging the underlying systems that function below conscious awareness. As discussed in later sections, hypnotherapy offers a structured and ethical way to influence these foundational processes, supporting conscious performance while minimizing cognitive load.

3. SUBCONSCIOUS PROCESSES INFLUENCE PROFESSIONAL PERFORMANCE

Subconscious processes serve as the core mechanisms by which people perceive, interpret, and react to workplace demands. These processes work automatically and persistently, influencing emotional responses, behavior, and performance without conscious thought. In work environments, subconscious functioning guides how individuals evaluate situations, manage stress, and access their conscious abilities during pressure.

Cognitive psychology separates controlled, conscious processing from automatic, subconscious processing. While deliberate and requiring effort, conscious processing is slow, whereas subconscious processing is fast, efficient, and mostly hidden from introspection (Bargh & Chartrand, 1999). In business settings, where quick and repeated responses to complex stimuli are needed, subconscious systems play a dominant role in real-time functioning. Consequently, professional performance relies less on rational goals and more on deeply rooted cognitive-emotional habits.

Implicit appraisal is a key subconscious factor influencing performance. Before we consciously evaluate, our brain automatically assesses situations for threat, relevance, and emotional importance. Neurobiological studies show that limbic areas, especially the amygdala, drive these assessments, triggering physiological and emotional reactions before we're even aware of them. (LeDoux & Pine, 2016). In organizational environments, elements such as presentations, evaluations, deadlines, and conflicts with others can be subconsciously perceived as threats. This triggers stress responses even when people consciously believe they can handle the situation.

These automatic stress reactions directly affect performance by redirecting neural resources from executive control to survival-driven processing when threat systems activate. This transfer hampers attention regulation, working memory, and cognitive flexibility, which are critical for complex professional tasks. (Arnsten, 2009c). As a result, people might find it hard to concentrate, make decisions, or manage emotions, even if they are highly skilled and well-prepared.

Subconscious learning strengthens these patterns over time. Repeated exposure to performance stressors conditions emotional responses. Failures, criticism, or excessive pressure become linked with physiological arousal, forming associative learning loops. Once formed, these loops trigger automatically in similar situations, causing anticipatory anxiety or avoidance without conscious effort. (Phelps & LeDoux, 2005). This mechanism clarifies why performance issues often continue even when external conditions get better.

Implicit beliefs are a key subconscious factor affecting professional performance. They consist of deeply held assumptions regarding competence, responsibility, control, and self-worth. Unlike explicit beliefs, which can be consciously expressed and examined, implicit beliefs function as fundamental principles shaping perception and actions. Studies show that implicit beliefs about ability and failure play a crucial role in stress response, resilience, and persistence in achievement settings (Dweck, 2006). In business environments, maladaptive beliefs like excessive perfectionism or fear of evaluation increase internal pressure and can impair performance stability.

Emotional regulation strategies are mostly controlled by subconscious processes. Many professionals habitually suppress their emotional responses to meet perceived performance standards. Although suppression can help maintain short-term functionality, it also raises physiological stress and cognitive load, which can negatively affect performance and overall well-being (Gross & John, 2003). Since these regulatory patterns develop slowly and function subconsciously, people often do not realize their overall effect until their performance declines or burnout occurs.

Burnout illustrates the long-term effects of subconscious deregulation. Modern models see burnout as stemming from a persistent mismatch between demands and internal regulation, not just workload. Unconscious habits of overcommitment, excessive responsibility, and emotional suppression drive sustained high effort, even as returns decrease, gradually draining cognitive and emotional resources (Maslach & Leiter, 2016). Importantly, people suffering from burnout frequently describe a decline in their sense of effectiveness and motivation that cannot be fixed by conscious effort alone.

These findings question the idea that performance can be reliably improved by deliberate strategies like motivation boosting, skills development, or behavioral oversight. Although these approaches target observable actions, they do not alter the subconscious processes that control stress reactions and emotional management. As a result, any performance gains are often fragile and influenced by context.

Viewing professional performance through the lens of subconscious regulation reshapes the approach to psychological intervention in business. If subconscious processes influence whether conscious abilities are accessible under stress, then improving performance requires directly working with these deeper systems. Hypnotherapy provides a structured way to access and adjust subconscious patterns, helping to align internal regulation with external performance requirements.

This perspective provides the conceptual foundation for the following section, which explores hypnotherapy not merely as a motivational aid but as a regulatory intervention aimed at minimizing internal disruptions and promoting lasting conscious performance.

4. HYPNOTHERAPY AS A SUBCONSCIOUS PERFORMANCE ALIGNMENT INTERVENTION

Importantly, hypnotherapy should not be viewed as just a method to boost motivation or effort. Instead, it acts as a subconscious performance alignment technique, focusing on internal regulatory mechanisms that influence whether a person can reliably demonstrate their conscious skills under professional pressures. Recognizing this difference is crucial to uphold ethical standards and ensure clarity in organizational contexts.

4.1 Neurocognitive Foundations of Hypnotherapy

From a neurocognitive perspective, hypnosis involves focused attention, decreased peripheral awareness, and heightened engagement with internal experiences. Neuroimaging studies show that hypnotic states cause functional changes in brain networks related to executive functions, self-monitoring, and emotional regulation. Notably, altered connectivity between the prefrontal cortex, anterior cingulate cortex, and limbic areas helps modulate automatic emotional reactions (Landry et al., 2017).

These neural mechanisms enable individuals to participate in performance-critical situations—like evaluations, leadership tasks, or high-pressure decisions—without facing overwhelming stress responses. In workplaces, where performance problems often stem from emotional overarousal instead of skill deficits, this ability is especially important. By reducing threat-related brain activity, hypnotherapy helps recover the executive functions necessary for consistent professional success.

Empirical evidence confirms that hypnotherapy effectively reduces stress, anxiety, and psychosomatic symptoms, all of which can disrupt workplace performance (Lynn et al., 2000b). Importantly, these results are obtained without additional cognitive strain, which makes hypnotherapy particularly ideal for professionals dealing with ongoing mental and emotional demands.

4.2 The Subconscious Performance Alignment Model

This chapter presents the Subconscious Performance Alignment Model (SPAM) to illustrate hypnotherapy's role in business contexts. The model is deliberately simple, focusing on achieving alignment rather than boosting performance by exerting more effort.

The model consists of three interconnected parts:

1. External Performance Demands, covering organizational expectations, role complexity, time constraints, and evaluative settings.

2. Subconscious Regulatory Processes, which include automatic stress reactions, implicit beliefs, emotional conditioning, and habitual regulation methods.
3. Conscious Performance Expression, shown through observable behavior, decision-making quality, emotional stability, and task execution.

The model suggests that conscious performance doesn't stem directly from external demands, nor can it be maintained solely through conscious effort. Instead, the quality of performance depends on how well subconscious regulatory processes align with situational demands. When these subconscious processes view demands as manageable rather than threatening, executive functions stay accessible, enabling clear and stable performance.

Hypnotherapy directly influences the subconscious by adjusting threat perceptions, changing implicit beliefs, and decreasing conditioned emotional responses, which lowers internal interference. As a result, conscious performance improves indirectly without increasing pressure on the already strained executive systems.

This framework based on alignment sets hypnotherapy apart from performance coaching, cognitive skills training, or motivational methods, which mainly focus on conscious behavior. Hypnotherapy isn't about increasing performance directly; it aims to eliminate internal barriers that restrict how performance is expressed.

4.3 Application in Organizational Contexts

In business environments, hypnotherapy works best when combined with a wider approach that emphasizes psychological safety and professional growth. Typical uses involve managing stress, enhancing leadership presence, reducing performance anxiety, boosting decision-making confidence, improving communication skills, and aiding recovery from burnout exhaustion.

Hypnotherapeutic interventions usually aim to identify subconscious triggers linked to work-related stress. Using structured hypnotic techniques, individuals are guided to reframe these triggers, separate performance pressures from fear-based emotional reactions, and strengthen positive internal states like calmness, confidence, and mental clarity. These shifts happen through experiential rebalancing rather than just direct suggestion.

Ethical considerations are fundamental to using hypnotherapy in organizations. Participation should be voluntary, informed, and distinctly separate from management assessments or performance pressure. When conducted within accepted ethical standards, hypnotherapy supports modern occupational health principles that emphasize autonomy, well-being, and sustainable productivity (Sonnentag & Fritz, 2015).

4.4 Implications for Sustainable Performance

Hypnotherapy directly targets subconscious regulatory mechanisms, providing a route to lasting professional performance that differs from effort-based models. Instead of depending on conscious self-control, it helps restore access to cognitive and emotional resources suppressed by stress and negative conditioning.

This approach is especially important in modern business settings marked by ongoing pressure rather than single performance issues. As companies become more aware of the limits of traditional performance strategies, initiatives that lighten internal cognitive and emotional burdens become increasingly strategic.

When viewed as a subconscious performance alignment technique, hypnotherapy enhances not only personal effectiveness but also strengthens organizational resilience by fostering long-term psychological sustainability.

5. ETHICAL, PRACTICAL, AND ORGANIZATIONAL IMPLICATIONS OF HYPNOTHERAPY IN BUSINESS SETTINGS

Using hypnotherapy in business settings involves critical ethical, practical, and organizational issues. Although it provides a scientifically supported approach to addressing subconscious factors influencing performance, its implementation in professional environments requires clear boundaries, ethical guidelines, and organizational protections. Absent these frameworks, applying hypnotherapy may lead to misunderstandings, misuse, or opposition from individuals and organizations.

This section explores the ethical principles essential for responsible use, the practical factors involved in implementing hypnotherapy, and the wider organizational impacts of using it as a performance alignment tool.

5.1 Ethical Considerations in Organizational Hypnotherapy

Ethical practice is essential when applying hypnotherapy in business environments due to the existing power dynamics and organizational evaluation structures. It should be clearly presented as a voluntary and supportive option, not a means of performance enforcement or managerial dominance. Employees' participation must be based on informed consent, with transparent explanation of the intervention's purpose, procedures, and boundaries.

Professional ethical guidelines highlight that hypnosis does not entail loss of control, suggestibility exceeding personal values, or behavioral manipulation against an individual's will (*Ethical Principles of Psychologists and Code of Conduct*, n.d.-a). However, misconceptions still exist, especially outside clinical settings.

Practitioners need to offer clear psychoeducation to help participants see hypnosis as a collaborative and self-directed process.

Confidentiality is a vital ethical concern. In organizational settings, personal disclosures might be seen as relevant to performance reviews or career progress. Ethical hypnotherapy demands a clear distinction between therapeutic content and organizational reporting. While aggregate results can be shared for program assessment, individual psychological data must stay confidential (Barnett, 2019).

Furthermore, hypnotherapy must be administered solely by properly trained and credentialed professionals who possess expertise in both clinical practice and organizational dynamics. When unqualified practitioners or casual wellness programs use hypnotherapy, it damages its credibility and raises the likelihood of potential harm.

5.2 Practical Integration Within Business Environments

Practically, hypnotherapy works best when part of a larger organizational well-being or performance sustainability strategy, rather than as an isolated treatment. According to the Subconscious Performance Alignment Model, it should be viewed as a way to minimize internal distractions and improve psychological regulation, rather than as a fix for perceived underperformance.

Implementation can take place via individual sessions, structured programs, or as part of executive coaching and employee assistance programs. Occupational health psychology research indicates that interventions focusing on stress regulation and emotional recovery are most successful when they align with organizational culture and have leadership backing (Sonnentag & Fritz, 2015b).

Clear boundaries around scope are crucial. Hypnotherapy in business should primarily address work-related stress, performance anxiety, emotional regulation, and recovery from cognitive overload. It is not intended to replace clinical mental health treatment for psychiatric disorders, nor should it be viewed as a one-size-fits-all solution for organizational issues challenges.

Time efficiency and accessibility also play key roles in adoption. Hypnotherapy can deliver measurable results without the need for lengthy training or continuous mental effort, making it especially suitable for busy professionals. Nevertheless, it is important to set realistic expectations about outcomes, focusing on gradual progress rather than instant change.

5.3 Organizational Implications and Cultural Impact

At the organizational level, incorporating hypnotherapy signifies a wider shift in how performance is understood and supported. Traditional models focus on output, efficiency, and conscious effort, often neglecting the psychological toll of continuous pressure. Conversely, alignment-based strategies acknowledge that lasting productivity relies on internal regulation and mental resilience.

Organizations integrating hypnotherapy within ethical and evidence-based practices demonstrate a dedication to employee well-being that surpasses superficial wellness programs. This approach can foster greater trust, lower stigma regarding mental health support, and boost retention, especially in high-stress sectors.

Additionally, the alignment perspective redefines performance challenges as systemic issues instead of individual shortcomings. Recognizing the influence of subconscious regulation on performance variability allows organizations to shift from deficit-based stories to more compassionate and supportive approaches. This change aligns with modern models of psychologically healthy workplaces that focus on prevention, recovery, and resilience (Maslach & Leiter, 2016c). However, organizational readiness is essential. Without supportive leadership, clear policies, and ethical oversight, hypnotherapy may be seen as invasive or experimental. Thus, successful implementation depends on aligning organizational values, leadership practices, and psychological interventions.

5.4 Implications for Sustainable Professional Performance

The ethical and practical considerations discussed above support the main idea of this chapter: sustainable professional performance requires more than just conscious effort. When used responsibly, hypnotherapy provides a method to recalibrate subconscious regulatory processes that limit performance under ongoing stress.

Instead of increasing demands on individuals, hypnotherapy helps restore cognitive clarity, emotional stability, and adaptive participation. It enhances existing organizational strategies and tackles the limitations of effort-based performance models.

As business environments grow more complex and intense, interventions focusing on alignment instead of exertion will become more important. Hypnotherapy's role isn't to push performance beyond human limits, but to help professionals perform reliably within those limits.

6. APPLICATION OF THE SUBCONSCIOUS PERFORMANCE ALIGNMENT MODEL IN BUSINESS SETTINGS

The Subconscious Performance Alignment Model allows hypnotherapy to be used in business settings by focusing on internal alignment instead of just surface-level performance issues. Today, many organizational performance problems stem from ongoing stress and subconscious threat reactions, rather than a lack of skills or motivation.

6.1 Executive Stress Regulation and Decision-Making

Executive decision-making is very vulnerable to cognitive disruptions caused by stress. Chronic stress hampers the functioning of the prefrontal cortex, leading to decreased cognitive flexibility and less accurate judgment (Arnsten, 2009c). Hypnotherapy in this model focuses on reconditioning subconscious stress, aiding emotional regulation and improving decision-making clarity under pressure.

6.2 Burnout Prevention and Performance Sustainability

Burnout occurs when there is a persistent disconnect between subconscious coping strategies and job requirements. Studies highlight emotional exhaustion and cognitive disengagement as essential aspects of burnout (Maslach & Leiter, 2016d). By recalibrating subconscious stress responses, the model promotes resilience and sustainable performance over the long term, focusing on lasting effects rather than immediate symptom relief.

6.3 Integration into Organizational Programs

The model can be ethically incorporated into leadership development and corporate wellness programs as a framework for enhancing performance. When used with informed consent and professional supervision, hypnotherapy can complement existing psychological and organizational strategies (Organización Mundial de la Salud, 2022).

7. HYPNOTHERAPEUTIC STRATEGIES WITHIN THE SUBCONSCIOUS PERFORMANCE ALIGNMENT MODEL

The Subconscious Performance Alignment Model uses specific hypnotherapeutic techniques to ethically access and adjust subconscious processes affecting workplace performance. These methods are not meant as clinical therapy, but as structured psychological interventions that help align internal mental states with external performance requirements.

7.1 Ego-Strengthening for Alignment Reinforcement

Ego-strengthening techniques aim to boost internal stability, self-efficacy, and emotional regulation. In organizational settings, these interventions help professionals sustain psychological balance during stressful situations. Studies show that ego-strengthening enhances stress resilience and adaptive behavior by strengthening positive self-perception and internal resources (Hammond, 1990).

Within the model, ego-strengthening enhances the alignment interface by stabilizing subconscious emotional responses, which helps reduce performance anxiety and emotional volatility.

7.2 Guided Imagery for Emotional Recalibration

Guided imagery helps alter emotional memories and reduce anticipatory stress. By tapping into the subconscious with symbolic and sensory cues, individuals can adjust their emotional reactions related to performance situations. Neurocognitive studies confirm that imagery influences emotional and physiological responses, especially during stressful moments (Kosslyn et al., 2001).

In the alignment model, guided imagery helps reframe stress-related emotional patterns that hinder conscious performance.

7.3 Future Pacing and Performance Integration

Future pacing entails mentally practicing desired performance states within realistic professional situations. This method helps incorporate aligned subconscious responses into expected workplace challenges. Performance psychology research indicates that mental rehearsal improves behavioral consistency and boosts confidence (Driskell et al., 1994).

Within the model, future pacing enhances alignment between conscious goals and subconscious expectations, minimizing internal resistance during actual performance.

7.4 Self-Hypnosis for Sustained Alignment

Self-hypnosis techniques are introduced to help users maintain alignment outside of formal sessions. When taught ethically and supervised properly, self-hypnosis aids in ongoing stress management and emotional balance. Research shows that self-hypnosis can improve self-regulation and the sense of control in demanding situations. (Patterson et al., 2010).

8. CASE ILLUSTRATION: MODEL VALIDATION THROUGH PRACTICE

A representative case example is provided to demonstrate the practical use of the Subconscious Performance Alignment Model. This illustration aims for conceptual validation rather than empirical generalization, aligning with qualitative and clinical reporting standards.

8.1 Initial Subconscious–Conscious Misalignment

The case concerned a mid-level corporate professional experiencing ongoing performance anxiety, indecision, and emotional exhaustion despite possessing sufficient technical skills and organizational backing. Efforts like time management training and cognitive reframing yielded little change. Clinical evaluation indicated underlying subconscious threat conditioning linked to evaluative stress and previous performance failures.

These presentations support research showing that stress-related performance issues usually stem from automatic emotional reactions instead of conscious skill deficiencies (*Choke | Book by Sian Beilock | Official Publisher Page | Simon & Schuster*, n.d.).

8.2 Hypnotherapeutic Intervention

Using the Subconscious Performance Alignment Model as a guiding framework, hypnotherapeutic sessions centered on identifying and reconditioning maladaptive emotional patterns and stress responses. Techniques involved focused attention induction, guided imagery, and future pacing aimed at professional performance goals. All interventions were performed ethically, with informed consent and a clear focus on enhancing performance.

In this context, hypnosis served as a way to access and alter subconscious emotional memories, aligning with established neurocognitive models of hypnotic responsiveness (Oakley & Halligan, 2009).

8.3 Observed Performance Changes

Post-intervention observations showed decreased anticipatory anxiety, better emotional regulation during stressful tasks, and enhanced decisional confidence. The individual also reported more consistent behavior and less cognitive fatigue, suggesting a stronger alignment between subconscious processes and conscious performance goals.

These results highlight insights from performance psychology research that stress the importance of emotional regulation in maintaining optimal job performance (Gross, 2015).

8.4 Clinical Interpretation and Limitations

In the Subconscious Performance Alignment Model, observed improvements are seen as restoring harmony between subconscious and conscious levels. However, since this is based on a single case, the results cannot be widely applied. More empirical studies are needed to assess the model's effectiveness across different organizational settings.

9. EVIDENCE-BASED AND SCHOLARLY INTEGRATION

The Subconscious Performance Alignment Model is based on converging evidence from neuroscience, performance psychology, and stress regulation research. Although the model is conceptual, its key assumptions are supported by well-established empirical findings related to subconscious processing, emotional regulation, and occupational performance.

9.1 Empirical Support for Subconscious Stress Regulation

Research consistently shows that much of human cognition and emotional regulation occurs outside conscious awareness. Automatic stress responses, triggered by limbic system activation, can hinder executive functions and attentional control when under pressure (LeDoux, 2012). These findings bolster the model's claim that performance issues frequently stem from subconscious misalignment rather than deliberate incompetence.

Hypnosis has been demonstrated to influence attention, perception, and emotional processing, allowing access to subconscious mechanisms that help regulate stress (Landry et al., 2017). This establishes a neuropsychological foundation for using hypnotherapy as an alignment intervention in professional settings.

9.2 Parallels with Performance Psychology

The model is aligned with performance psychology frameworks that highlight emotional regulation, attentional control, and mental flexibility as key factors for sustained performance. Research in high-performance areas shows that having internal coherence between emotional states and task demands is essential for consistent execution (Gucciardi et al., 2015).

By presenting hypnotherapy as a way to improve internal harmony, the model broadens performance psychology from just conscious skill development to also encompass subconscious adjustment.

9.3 Justification of Originality and Relevance

Existing workplace interventions mainly focus on cognitive-behavioral techniques and skills development. The Subconscious Performance Alignment Model adds innovation by explicitly incorporating subconscious processes into business performance strategies, without treating employees as having issues or viewing hypnotherapy solely as clinical therapy.

This perspective centered on alignment provides a new way to view organizational psychology, leadership growth, and workplace well-being.

9.4 Directions for Empirical Validation

Future research ought to concentrate on defining alignment constructs clearly, creating reliable measurement tools, and assessing results via controlled organizational studies. Longitudinal studies would be especially useful for examining long-term performance sustainability and the effectiveness of burnout prevention.

10. ETHICAL, CULTURAL, AND ORGANIZATIONAL CONSIDERATIONS

Implementing hypnotherapy in business settings demands careful attention to ethical, cultural, and organizational safeguards. The Subconscious Performance Alignment Model highlights the importance of responsible application to protect psychological safety, maintain autonomy, and uphold professional integrity.

10.1 Informed Consent and Voluntary Participation

In workplace settings, it is essential to obtain clear informed consent due to the risk of perceived coercion. Participation in hypnotherapy should always be voluntary, with explicit communication that these programs are optional and not connected to job performance or career progression. Ethical standards in applied psychology emphasize the need for autonomy and transparency in non-clinical interventions (*Ethical Principles of Psychologists and Code of Conduct*, n.d.-b).

10.2 Cultural Perceptions of Hypnosis

Cultural beliefs greatly affect how people respond to hypnosis. In certain settings, hypnosis might be linked to stigma, feelings of losing control, or misconceptions stemming from media portrayals. Practitioners should use culturally appropriate language, describing hypnotherapy as focused attention and self-regulation instead of suggestibility or control. Cross-cultural studies emphasize the importance of tailoring psychological interventions to fit different cultural norms and beliefs (Bernal et al., 2009).

10.3 Safeguards Against Coercive or Misuse

Organizations should ensure hypnotherapy is not misused to silence genuine workplace issues or push conformity. The model clearly opposes coercive uses and highlights alignment as a way to support personal well-being and genuine performance. Ethically implementing this requires setting clear limits to distinguish between improving performance and maintaining organizational control.

10.4 Practitioner Competence and Professional Standards

Interventions in organizational settings should only be carried out by qualified professionals trained in hypnotherapy and psychological ethics. Following established professional standards is crucial for safeguarding participants and preserving credibility (Organizaci6n Mundial de la Salud, 2022).

11. STRATEGIC IMPLICATIONS FOR ORGANIZATIONS

The Subconscious Performance Alignment Model reinterprets hypnotherapy as a strategic asset for organizations instead of just a mental health treatment. By focusing on internal alignment, organizations can improve performance while also promoting psychological well-being.

11.1 Hypnotherapy as Performance Infrastructure

Traditional workplace mental health programs often concentrate on managing symptoms. However, this approach treats hypnotherapy as a foundational component for performance—helping with sustained focus, emotional control, and resilience. Studies show that proactive psychological strategies lead to higher productivity and lower absenteeism (Cooper & Cartwright, 1994) .

11.2 Human Capital Optimization Through Alignment

Aligned subconscious and conscious processes help employees perform efficiently without overburdening their cognition or emotions. This approach, based on alignment, promotes talent retention, enhances leadership effectiveness, and fosters long-term engagement. Increasingly, human capital research acknowledges psychological resources as vital to maintaining organizational competitiveness (Luthans et al., 2020).

11.3 Implications for HR Policy and Leadership Development

Human resource policies and leadership training programs can incorporate alignment-based interventions within comprehensive development frameworks. When carried out ethically, these initiatives complement coaching, resilience training, and organizational psychology, fostering a psychologically sustainable work environment.

12. FUTURE DIRECTIONS

The Subconscious Performance Alignment Model offers multiple opportunities for both theoretical advancement and empirical exploration. As organizations place greater emphasis on mental sustainability, future research should aim to broaden the model's applicability, improve measurement methods, and enhance its integration within organizational psychology.

12.1 Digital and Hybrid Delivery Formats

Advances in digital mental health platforms provide opportunities to adapt alignment-based hypnotherapeutic interventions for virtual and hybrid work settings. Guided audio programs, app-supported self hypnosis, and blended coaching models can improve accessibility while ensuring ethical safeguards. Emerging evidence indicates that digitally delivered psychological interventions are feasible for stress management and performance enhancement (Andersson et al., 2019).

12.2 Measurement of Alignment Outcomes

A key research focus is to operationalize and measure the alignment between subconscious and conscious processes. Future research should create psychometrically reliable tools to evaluate constructs related to this alignment, including emotional congruence, stress reactivity, and performance sustainability. Incorporating both objective and self-report measures will enhance the empirical support for the model.

12.3 Cross-Cultural Applicability

Considering cultural differences in views of hypnosis and mental health treatments, it is crucial to validate approaches across cultures. Studies should explore how alignment methods appear in various organizational and socio-cultural settings, while maintaining ethical standards and sensitivity to context (Hofstede, 2010).

12.4 Integration with Organizational Psychology Research

Further integrating established organizational psychology frameworks—like job demands–resources theory and psychological capital—could improve the model's theoretical consistency and cross-disciplinary significance. This approach might also promote wider acceptance in both business and academic circles.

13. CONCLUSION: THEORETICAL AND PRACTICAL CONTRIBUTION

This chapter argues that conscious performance in business is mainly limited by subconscious alignment. Even with sufficient skills, motivation, and resources, professionals can see their performance decline due to unresolved subconscious stress and emotional mismatches.

The chapter introduced the Subconscious Performance Alignment Model, offering a new conceptual framework that incorporates hypnotherapy into business psychology while avoiding medicalizing ordinary occupational stress. This model positions hypnotherapy as an ethical, structured method for aligning internal psychological states with external performance requirements.

The model broadens performance psychology by explicitly including subconscious mechanisms into organizational performance discussions. In practice, it provides organizations with a sustainable alternative to interventions that target symptoms, focusing instead on resilience, consistency, and psychological efficiency.

When used responsibly and professionally, hypnotherapy can be a useful tool for improving human resources and fostering workplace well-being. The Subconscious Performance Alignment Model provides a fresh outlook on maintaining performance, highlighting subconscious alignment as an essential element of contemporary organizational success.

REFERENCES

Andersson, G., Carlbring, P., Titov, N., & Lindefors, N. (2019). Internet Interventions for Adults with Anxiety and Mood Disorders: A Narrative Umbrella Review of Recent Meta-Analyses. *Canadian Journal of Psychiatry*, *64*(7), 465–470. DOI: 10.1177/0706743719839381;ISSUE:ISSUE:DOI PMID: 31096757

Arnsten, A. F. T. (2009a). Stress signalling pathways that impair prefrontal cortex structure and function. *Nature Reviews. Neuroscience*, *10*(6), 410. DOI: 10.1038/NRN2648 PMID: 19455173

Arnsten, A. F. T. (2009b). Stress signalling pathways that impair prefrontal cortex structure and function. *Nature Reviews. Neuroscience*, *10*(6), 410. DOI: 10.1038/NRN2648 PMID: 19455173

Arnsten, A. F. T. (2009c). Stress signalling pathways that impair prefrontal cortex structure and function. *Nature Reviews. Neuroscience*, *10*(6), 410. DOI: 10.1038/NRN2648 PMID: 19455173

Bargh, J. A., & Chartrand, T. L. (1999). The unbearable automaticity of being. *The American Psychologist*, *54*(7), 462–479. DOI: 10.1037/0003-066X.54.7.462

Barnett, J. E. (2019). The ethical practice of psychotherapy: Clearly within our reach. *Psychotherapy (Chicago, Ill.)*, *56*(4), 431–440. DOI: 10.1037/PST0000272 PMID: 31815506

Baumeister, R. F., Vohs, K. D., & Tice, D. M. (2007). The Strength Model of Self-Control. *Current Directions in Psychological Science*, *16*(6), 351–355. DOI: 10.1111/J.1467-8721.2007.00534.X

Beilock, S. L., & Carr, T. H. (2001). On the fragility of skilled performance: What governs choking under pressure? *Journal of Experimental Psychology. General*, *130*(4), 701–725. DOI: 10.1037/0096-3445.130.4.701 PMID: 11757876

Bernal, G., Jiménez-Chafey, M. I., & Domenech Rodríguez, M. M. (2009). Cultural Adaptation of Treatments: A Resource for Considering Culture in Evidence-Based Practice. *Professional Psychology, Research and Practice*, *40*(4), 361–368. DOI: 10.1037/A0016401

Burn-out an "occupational phenomenon": International Classification of Diseases. (n.d.). Retrieved December 18, 2025, from https://www.who.int/news/item/28-05-2019-burn-out-an-occupational-phenomenon-international-classification-of-diseases

Choke | Book by Sian Beilock | Official Publisher Page | Simon & Schuster. (n.d.). Retrieved December 18, 2025, from https://www.simonandschuster.com/books/Choke/Sian-Beilock/9781416596189

Cooper, C. L., & Cartwright, S. (1994). Healthy Mind; Healthy Organization—A Proactive Approach to Occupational Stress. *Human Relations*, *47*(4), 455–471. DOI: 10.1177/001872679404700405;SUBPAGE:STRING:ABSTRACT;WEBSITE:WEBSITE:SAGE;REQUESTEDJOURNAL:JOURNAL:HUMA;WGROUP:STRING:PUBLICATION

Diamond, A. (2012). Executive Functions. *Annual Review of Psychology*, *64*, 135. DOI: 10.1146/ANNUREV-PSYCH-113011-143750 PMID: 23020641

Driskell, J. E., Copper, C., & Moran, A. (1994). Does Mental Practice Enhance Performance? *The Journal of Applied Psychology*, *79*(4), 481–492. DOI: 10.1037/0021-9010.79.4.481

Dweck, C. S. (2006). *Mindset: The new psychology of success*. https://psycnet.apa.org/record/2006-08575-000

Ethical principles of psychologists and code of conduct. (n.d.-a). Retrieved December 18, 2025, from https://www.apa.org/ethics/code

Ethical principles of psychologists and code of conduct. (n.d.-b). Retrieved December 18, 2025, from https://www.apa.org/ethics/code

Evans, J. S. B. T., & Stanovich, K. E. (2013). Dual-Process Theories of Higher Cognition: Advancing the Debate. *Perspectives on Psychological Science*, *8*(3), 223–241. DOI: 10.1177/1745691612460685;WGROUP:STRING:PUBLICATION PMID: 26172965

Gross, J. J. (2015). Emotion Regulation: Current Status and Future Prospects. *Psychological Inquiry*, *26*(1), 1–26. DOI: 10.1080/1047840X.2014.940781;ISSUE:ISSUE:DOI

Gross, J. J., & John, O. P. (2003). Individual differences in two emotion regulation processes: Implications for affect, relationships, and well-being. *Journal of Personality and Social Psychology*, *85*(2), 348–362. DOI: 10.1037/0022-3514.85.2.348 PMID: 12916575

Gucciardi, D. F., Hanton, S., Gordon, S., Mallett, C. J., & Temby, P. (2015). The Concept of Mental Toughness: Tests of Dimensionality, Nomological Network, and Traitness. *Journal of Personality*, *83*(1), 26–44. DOI: 10.1111/JOPY.12079;JOURNAL:JOURNAL:14676494;WGROUP:STRING:PUBLICATION PMID: 24428736

Hammond, D. Corydon. (1990). *Handbook of hypnotic suggestions and metaphors*. 602. https://wwnorton.com/books/Handbook-of-Hypnotic-Suggestions-and-Metaphors

Hockey, R. (2014). *The psychology of fatigue : work, effort and control*. 272. https://books.google.com/books/about/The_Psychology_of_Fatigue.html?id=oQBeAwAAQBAJ

Hofstede, G. (2010). *Cultures and organizations: Software of the mind*. https://e-edu.nbu.bg/pluginfile.php/900222/mod_resource/content/1/G.Hofstede_G.J.Hofstede_M.Minkov%20-%20Cultures%20and%20Organizations%20-%20Software%20of%20the%20Mind%203rd_edition%202010.pdf

Kosslyn, S. M., Ganis, G., & Thompson, W. L. (2001). Neural foundations of imagery. *Nature Reviews Neuroscience 2001 2:9, 2*(9), 635–642. https://doi.org/DOI: 10.1038/35090055

Landry, M., Lifshitz, M., & Raz, A. (2017a). Brain correlates of hypnosis: A systematic review and meta-analytic exploration. *Neuroscience and Biobehavioral Reviews, 81*(Pt A), 75–98. https://doi.org/DOI: 10.1016/j.neubiorev.2017.02.020

Landry, M., Lifshitz, M., & Raz, A. (2017b). Brain correlates of hypnosis: A systematic review and meta-analytic exploration. *Neuroscience and Biobehavioral Reviews, 81*(Pt A), 75–98. https://doi.org/DOI: 10.1016/j.neubiorev.2017.02.020

Landry, M., Lifshitz, M., & Raz, A. (2017c). Brain correlates of hypnosis: A systematic review and meta-analytic exploration. *Neuroscience and Biobehavioral Reviews, 81*(Pt A), 75–98. https://doi.org/DOI: 10.1016/j.neubiorev.2017.02.020

LeDoux, J. (2012). Rethinking the Emotional Brain. *Neuron, 73*(4), 653–676. DOI: 10.1016/j.neuron.2012.02.004 PMID: 22365542

LeDoux, J. E., & Pine, D. S. (2016). Using Neuroscience to Help Understand Fear and Anxiety: A Two-System Framework. *The American Journal of Psychiatry, 173*(11), 1083–1093. DOI: 10.1176/APPI.AJP.2016.16030353 PMID: 27609244

Luthans, F., Youssef, C., & Avolio, B. (2020). *Psychological capital and beyond - Liberty University*. 2024. https://global.oup.com/academic/product/psychological-capital-and-beyond-9780199316472

Lynn, S. J., Kirsch, I., Barabasz, A., Cardeña, E., & Patterson, D. (2000a). Hypnosis as an empirically supported clinical intervention: The state of the evidence and a look to the future. *The International Journal of Clinical and Experimental Hypnosis, 48*(2), 239–259. DOI: 10.1080/00207140008410050 PMID: 10769986

Lynn, S. J., Kirsch, I., Barabasz, A., Cardeña, E., & Patterson, D. (2000b). Hypnosis as an empirically supported clinical intervention: The state of the evidence and a look to the future. *The International Journal of Clinical and Experimental Hypnosis*, *48*(2), 239–259. DOI: 10.1080/00207140008410050 PMID: 10769986

Maslach, C., & Leiter, M. P. (2016a). Understanding the burnout experience: Recent research and its implications for psychiatry. *World Psychiatry; Official Journal of the World Psychiatric Association (WPA)*, *15*(2), 103–111. DOI: 10.1002/WPS.20311;REQUESTEDJOURNAL:JOURNAL:20515545;JOURNAL:JOURNAL:20515545;WGROUP:STRING:PUBLICATION PMID: 27265691

Maslach, C., & Leiter, M. P. (2016b). Understanding the burnout experience: Recent research and its implications for psychiatry. *World Psychiatry; Official Journal of the World Psychiatric Association (WPA)*, *15*(2), 103. DOI: 10.1002/WPS.20311 PMID: 27265691

Maslach, C., & Leiter, M. P. (2016c). Understanding the burnout experience: Recent research and its implications for psychiatry. *World Psychiatry; Official Journal of the World Psychiatric Association (WPA)*, *15*(2), 103. DOI: 10.1002/WPS.20311 PMID: 27265691

Maslach, C., & Leiter, M. P. (2016d). Understanding the burnout experience: Recent research and its implications for psychiatry. *World Psychiatry; Official Journal of the World Psychiatric Association (WPA)*, *15*(2), 103–111. DOI: 10.1002/WPS.20311;REQUESTEDJOURNAL:JOURNAL:20515545;JOURNAL:JOURNAL:20515545;WGROUP:STRING:PUBLICATION PMID: 27265691

McEwen, B. S., & Morrison, J. H. (2013a). The Brain on Stress: Vulnerability and Plasticity of the Prefrontal Cortex over the Life Course. *Neuron*, *79*(1), 16–29. DOI: 10.1016/J.NEURON.2013.06.028 PMID: 23849196

McEwen, B. S., & Morrison, J. H. (2013b). The Brain on Stress: Vulnerability and Plasticity of the Prefrontal Cortex over the Life Course. *Neuron*, *79*(1), 16–29. DOI: 10.1016/J.NEURON.2013.06.028 PMID: 23849196

Oakley, D. A., & Halligan, P. W. (2009). Hypnotic suggestion and cognitive neuroscience. *Trends in Cognitive Sciences*, *13*(6), 264–270. DOI: 10.1016/j.tics.2009.03.004 PMID: 19428287

Oakley, D. A., & Halligan, P. W. (2013). Hypnotic suggestion: opportunities for cognitive neuroscience. *Nature Reviews Neuroscience 2013 14:8*, *14*(8), 565–576. https://doi.org/DOI: 10.1038/nrn3538

Organización Mundial de la Salud. (2022a). Directrices de la OMS sobre salud mental en el trabajo. *World Health Organization Guidelines on Mental Health at Work*, 1–143. https://www.who.int/publications/i/item/9789240053052

Organización Mundial de la Salud. (2022b). Directrices de la OMS sobre salud mental en el trabajo. *World Health Organization Guidelines on Mental Health at Work*, 1–143. https://www.who.int/publications/i/item/9789240053052

Patterson, D. R., Jensen, M. P., Wiechman, S. A., & Sharar, S. R. (2010). Virtual reality hypnosis for pain associated with recovery from physical trauma. *The International Journal of Clinical and Experimental Hypnosis*, *58*(3), 288–300. DOI: 10.1080/00207141003760595;JOURNAL:JOURNAL:NHYP19;PAGE:STRING:ARTICLE/CHAPTER PMID: 20509069

Phelps, E. A., & LeDoux, J. E. (2005). Contributions of the amygdala to emotion processing: From animal models to human behavior. *Neuron*, *48*(2), 175–187. DOI: 10.1016/j.neuron.2005.09.025 PMID: 16242399

Sonnentag, S., & Fritz, C. (2015a). Recovery from job stress: The stressor-detachment model as an integrative framework. *Journal of Organizational Behavior*, *36*(S1), S72–S103. DOI: 10.1002/JOB.1924

Sonnentag, S., & Fritz, C. (2015b). Recovery from job stress: The stressor-detachment model as an integrative framework. *Journal of Organizational Behavior*, *36*(S1), S72–S103. DOI: 10.1002/JOB.1924

Chapter 7
Subconscious Leadership Conditioning and Executive Decision-Making Through Hypnotherapy

Jeni Kakadiya
https://orcid.org/0009-0002-8143-1859
Shoolini University, India

Sangeeta Kakkar
https://orcid.org/0009-0007-9139-8040
Shoolini University, India

ABSTRACT

This chapter explores how subconscious cognitive and emotional processes influence executive judgment and leadership effectiveness, especially in complex and uncertain conditions. It applies dual-process models of cognition and draws on research from cognitive psychology, neuroscience, and leadership studies. The chapter highlights hypnotherapy as a scientifically supported method for engaging and influencing subconscious processes that affect leadership performance. It covers the neurocognitive basis of hypnotherapy, reviews evidence on attention control, emotional regulation, stress management, and cognitive flexibility, and discusses its use in executive coaching and leadership development. Ethical and professional standards are also considered to ensure responsible application within organizations. Overall, hypnotherapy is presented as a credible, evidence-based tool for improving decision-making and leadership skills.

DOI: 10.4018/979-8-3373-2317-6.ch007

1. INTRODUCTION

Executive leaders today operate in complex, rapidly changing environments with high cognitive demands. They must process vast amounts of information, balance competing priorities, manage organizational stakeholders, and make strategic decisions amid uncertainty. Traditional leadership models focus on conscious, rational decision-making, assuming leaders rely on logical reasoning. However, increasing psychological and neuroscientific evidence indicates that only part of decision-making is conscious. Subconscious processes—working below awareness—are crucial in how leaders interpret situations, control emotions, assess risks, and decide (Kahneman, 2011).

The idea of the subconscious mind has been a central topic in psychology for a long time, with early theorists acknowledging that some mental processes are not available to conscious reflection (Freud, 1915). In modern cognitive psychology, dual-process models differentiate between a quick, automatic system—typically linked to subconscious processing—and a slower, analytical system used consciously during decision-making (Evans & Stanovich, 2013). Leaders, especially when stressed or pressed for time, tend to depend on heuristics, emotional signals, and automatic response patterns that stem from the subconsciLeaders, especially when stressed or pressed for time, tend to depend on heuristics, emotional signals, and automatic response patterns that stem from the subconscious (Kahneman, 2011). Relying heavily on this can be helpful in everyday situations but might also lead to cognitive biases, emotional responses, and poor strategic choices in high-stakes settings.

In this context, psychological interventions that deliberately target the subconscious are important for leadership growth and improving performance. Hypnotherapy—defined as guiding suggestions to reach altered states of focused attention and increased responsiveness—serves as one such approach. Unlike coaching or cognitive training that mainly involve conscious reasoning, hypnotherapy aims to influence subconscious processes to bring about changes in automatic thoughts, emotional reactions, and implicit beliefs (Heap & Aravind, 2002). Research in clinical psychology shows that hypnotherapeutic techniques can impact behavior, perception, and emotional states, with evidence supporting their effect on neural mechanisms involved in attention and cognitive control (Halligan & Oakley, 2013).

Despite the widespread use of hypnotherapy in clinical areas such as pain management, anxiety reduction, and habit change. (Hammond, 2010; Montgomery et al., 2000), The use of hypnotherapeutic interventions in executive leadership is still underexplored in organizational research. This chapter proposes that these interventions could offer a novel way to condition leadership subconsciously—through structured hypnotic suggestions and imagery to influence core cognitive and emotional patterns. The goal is to improve decision-making, emotional regulation, and resilience in leadership contexts.

This chapter serves three main purposes. It first places executive decision-making within relevant psychological and neuroscientific frameworks, highlighting the interaction between conscious and subconscious processes. Next, it explains the fundamental concepts of hypnotherapy, including how hypnotic states may impact cognition and behaviour. Finally, it develops a conceptual framework for using hypnotherapy as a conditioning tool for leaders, supported by theoretical reasons and examples from research. Overall, it aims to expand leadership development discussions beyond traditional conscious-focused approaches, providing an integrated view of how subconscious conditioning can enhance executive performance.

The following sections will examine evidence supporting the influence of subconscious processing on leadership decision-making, explain the scientific principles behind hypnotherapeutic methods, and discuss practical uses in organizational contexts. By combining psychological theories with leadership application, this chapter seeks to offer scholars and practitioners a solid foundation for viewing hypnotherapy as a credible and innovative element of leadership development programs.

2. EXECUTIVE DECISION-MAKING: A PSYCHOLOGICAL PERSPECTIVE

Executive decision-making involves a complex interaction of cognitive, emotional, and contextual factors. Unlike everyday operational choices, executive decisions typically entail long-term consequences, high uncertainty, ethical issues, and large organizational effects. Psychological research increasingly acknowledges that these decisions cannot be fully explained by rational choice models alone; they are influenced by both conscious thinking and subconscious cognitive processes (Moore & Bazerman, 2012).

From a cognitive psychology perspective, executive decision-making is limited by bounded rationality. Leaders function with incomplete information, limited time, and cognitive overload, leading them to depend on mental shortcuts or heuristics (Simon, 1957). Heuristics enable quick decision-making but can lead to systematic errors like confirmation bias, overconfidence, and availability bias—well-documented in managerial settings (Kahneman, 2011). These biases often influence individuals unconsciously, highlighting how subconscious thinking affects leadership actions.

Emotional processes add complexity to executive decision-making. Affective neuroscience research shows that emotions are not just disruptive but fundamental to judgment and decision-making (Damasio, 1994). However, during intense emotional situations—like crises, organizational conflicts, or high-stakes negotiations—

executives may find their cognitive flexibility diminished and judgment compromised. Chronic stress, often present in senior leadership roles, worsens this by affecting working memory and executive control functions managed by the prefrontal cortex (Arnsten, 2009a). As a result, leaders under ongoing stress might rely on instinctive, emotion-based reactions instead of thoughtful analysis.

Dual-process theories provide a helpful framework for understanding these dynamics. In this model, System 1 is quick, intuitive, and mostly subconscious, while System 2 is slower, effortful, and under conscious control. (Evans & Stanovich, 2013). Executive leaders often switch between these systems, but high cognitive load and emotional stress lead to greater dependence on System 1 thinking. While intuitive decisions can work well in familiar situations, they pose risks when subconscious biases or unhealthy emotional patterns influence strategic decisions.

Importantly, leadership experience influences subconscious decision-making patterns. Past successes, failures, and organizational cultures help form implicit leadership schemas—mental models that unconsciously guide perception and actions (Lord et al., 1984). Over time, these schemas can become fixed mental frameworks that shape risk tolerance, attitudes towards authority, and how people interact with others. Although experience is typically seen as a valuable asset in leadership, hidden subconscious patterns that are not examined might hinder adaptability and innovation, especially in fast-changing business settings.

In this psychological landscape, conventional leadership development—like skills training, mentoring, and coaching—mainly focus on conscious awareness and behavior change. Although these methods provide clear benefits, they might not fully address the underlying subconscious drivers of decision-making. This highlights the importance of interventions that directly target subconscious cognitive and emotional processes. Hypnotherapy, by promoting focused attention and suggestibility, provides a structured approach to influence automatic responses and implicit beliefs that influence executive decisions (Oakley & Halligan, 2013).

Understanding executive decision-making as a layered psychological process underpins the exploration of hypnotherapy as a leadership tool. By engaging both conscious thought and subconscious patterns, organizations can better assist leaders in gaining clarity, managing emotions, and maintaining ethical standards in their decisions. The following sections will delve into how hypnotherapeutic principles and methods can be incorporated into leadership development to navigate these psychological complexities.

3. THE SUBCONSCIOUS MIND IN LEADERSHIP BEHAVIOR

Leadership behavior isn't just the result of deliberate thinking or conscious intention. Instead, it is heavily shaped by subconscious cognitive and emotional processes that function automatically and constantly. The subconscious mind significantly affects how leaders perceive their environment, interpret social signals, manage emotions, and exercise authority. Though these processes mostly occur outside of conscious awareness, they strongly impact leadership effectiveness, especially in high-stakes business settings.

Psychologically, the subconscious mind includes implicit memories, conditioned responses, emotional patterns, and core beliefs that influence behavior automatically without conscious thought (Wilson, 2004). In leadership situations, these subconscious factors show up as automatic stress reactions, recurring decision habits, and gut instincts. Although intuition is appreciated in seasoned leaders, it's crucial to understand that such intuitive responses are influenced by previous experiences and emotional conditioning, which might not always match current organizational needs or ethical guidelines.

Leadership schemas offer a helpful framework for understanding subconscious leadership behaviors. These schemas are mental structures that organize previous knowledge and experiences, shaping perception and actions (Fiske & Taylor, 2013). Leaders form mental frameworks about authority, competence, risk, and trust based on their personal backgrounds, organizational norms, and past leadership roles. Once these schemas are formed, they operate automatically, influencing behavior in a way that seems natural or instinctive. For instance, a leader who has succeeded by being assertive and controlling may unconsciously revert to authoritarian behaviors, even when situations call for collaboration and emotional awareness.

Emotional conditioning deepens subconscious leadership patterns. Neuroscience shows that emotionally intense experiences are stored more vividly in memory and tend to shape future actions (LeDoux, 1996). In leadership positions, frequent exposure to stress, conflict, or high responsibility can condition emotional reactions like hypervigilance, defensiveness, or avoidance. Over time, these reactions may become automatic, influencing leadership behavior unconsciously. If not addressed, these patterns can weaken decision-making, interpersonal skills, and the organizational environment.

The subconscious plays a crucial role in leadership decision-making, especially under uncertainty. When information is incomplete or unclear, leaders tend to depend more on subconscious pattern recognition and emotional cues to make their decisions (Dane & Pratt, 2007). Although this process can speed up decision-making, it also makes one more prone to bias and emotional influence. Cognitive biases like overconfidence, loss aversion, and sticking to the status quo are frequently caused by subconscious emotional responses rather than logical reasoning (Kahneman & Tversky, 2018). These biases can greatly impact strategic choices, mergers and acquisitions, risk evaluations, and ethical considerations.

The subconscious mind significantly impacts leadership identity and self-view. Unconscious beliefs regarding competence, authority, and self-esteem influence how leaders express themselves and engage with others (Lord & Hall, 2005a). Leaders who unconsciously link leadership to perfectionism might feel increased anxiety and face decision paralysis, while those who connect authority with dominance may find it hard to show empathy and foster inclusion. These identity-related tendencies are difficult to change with only cognitive approaches because they are rooted in subconscious belief systems.

Given how subconscious processes are fundamental to leadership behavior, interventions targeting these underlying mechanisms are highly valuable. Hypnotherapy provides a structured method for accessing and shaping subconscious thoughts by promoting focused attention and lowering resistance to suggestions (Oakley & Halligan, 2013). By using carefully crafted hypnotic techniques, leaders can increase their awareness of automatic patterns, reframe unhelpful beliefs, and develop more adaptive emotional and cognitive responses. This method does not replace conscious skill-building but enhances it by targeting the underlying psychological factors that influence behavior.

Understanding leadership behavior through subconscious processing offers a key foundation for using hypnotherapy in executive settings. Recognizing the role of implicit beliefs, emotional conditioning, and automatic thoughts allows organizations to go beyond superficial solutions and adopt more in-depth leadership development approaches. The following section will examine the scientific and conceptual bases of hypnotherapy, highlighting its importance and validity as a method for subconscious leadership training.

4. HYPNOTHERAPY: CONCEPTUAL AND SCIENTIFIC FOUNDATIONS

Hypnotherapy is a structured psychological approach that uses hypnosis—a focused state of attention and increased openness to suggestion—to promote changes in thoughts, emotions, and behaviors. Contrary to common myths, hypnosis does not cause unconsciousness or loss of control; instead, it involves focusing attention while individuals stay aware, responsive, and able to think critically (Michael Heap, 2001). Modern scientific views see hypnosis as a dynamic interplay involving attentional control, expectation, and suggestion, rooted in well-known cognitive and neuropsychological mechanisms.

Clinically, hypnotherapy combines hypnotic induction with therapeutic suggestions to target unhealthy thought, emotion, and behavior patterns. The induction methods usually include relaxation, imagery, or focused attention, helping shift attention from external stimuli to internal cognitive processes. This transition correlates with decreased activity in brain areas related to self-monitoring and heightened activity in regions connected to imagination and emotion regulation (Halligan & Oakley, 2013). These neurocognitive changes establish a context where suggestions are more easily incorporated into existing beliefs and automatic responses.

Neuroscientific research continues to strengthen evidence for hypnotic phenomena. Functional neuroimaging shows that hypnotic suggestion can alter activity in brain areas linked to perception, attention, and executive functions, such as the anterior cingulate cortex and prefrontal regions (Raz et al., 2005. These findings question earlier beliefs that hypnosis is just role-playing or compliance, instead supporting its recognition as a genuine psychological state with identifiable neural markers. Notably, the same brain areas are involved in executive decision-making, emotional regulation, and cognitive flexibility—key skills for effective functioning leadership.

Hypnosis is closely connected to neuroplasticity, which is the brain's ability to reorganize itself based on experience. During hypnosis, therapeutic suggestions can strengthen beneficial neural pathways by consistently triggering specific cognitive and emotional states (Hammond, 2010). In practical contexts, this process is known as conditioning, where repeated hypnotic experiences reinforce particular responses like calm focus, confidence, or mental clarity. For leaders, this conditioning can enhance resilience during stress and promote more consistent decision-making.

A fundamental element of hypnotherapy is suggestibility, which refers to how responsive individuals are to verbal or symbolic cues. Although suggestibility levels differ among people, research shows that most individuals can gain advantages from hypnotic techniques when these methods are customized to suit them (Lynn et al., 2008). Among executives, traits like high motivation, goal focus, and cognitive engagement—typical of leadership positions—can increase receptiveness to hypnotherapy, especially when presented as a way to boost performance rather than as a clinical intervention.

Ethical practice is a core element underpinning the scientific credibility of hypnotherapy. Professional guidelines highlight the importance of informed consent, transparency about objectives, and respecting clients' autonomy (American Psychological Association, 2017). In leadership settings, this ethical framework is crucial because interventions need to clearly differentiate between providing therapeutic support and exerting organizational influence. When used correctly, hypnotherapy does not force beliefs or behaviors but instead encourages self-directed change that aligns with the leader's values and goals.

Hypnotherapy, despite proven effectiveness in clinical psychology, is still rarely used in organizational and leadership growth programs. This underuse is partly due to ongoing misconceptions and limited cross-disciplinary communication between clinical psychology and management fields. Nevertheless, as organizations become more aware of the shortcomings of solely cognitive training, interest in holistic interventions that target subconscious processes is increasing. Hypnotherapy, backed by empirical research and ethical standards, provides a scientifically valid approach to accessing the deeper psychological factors influencing leadership behavior.

In summary, hypnotherapy is supported by strong conceptual and scientific bases that align with modern ideas about cognition, emotion, and neuroplasticity. Its ability to affect subconscious processes through focused attention and suggestion makes it a useful addition to leadership development programs. The next section will expand on this by exploring how hypnotherapy can be used specifically for subconscious leadership conditioning, turning theory into targeted strategies for executive decision-making.

5. SUBCONSCIOUS LEADERSHIP CONDITIONING THROUGH HYPNOTHERAPY

Subconscious leadership conditioning involves deliberately altering automatic cognitive, emotional, and behavioral patterns that affect how leaders perform. Unlike skill training aimed at conscious awareness, this method focuses on recalibrating unconscious responses that influence perceptions of challenges, emotional regulation, and authority display. Hypnotherapy provides a structured and ethically sound approach to this process by accessing the subconscious through focused attention, imagery, and therapeutic suggestions.

Hypnotherapeutic conditioning is based on the idea that repeated exposure to certain mental states can reinforce neural pathways, which boosts the chance of adopting positive responses in real-life situations. In leadership, this might mean training oneself to maintain calm focus during stressful decisions, building confidence in uncertain contexts, or handling emotional reactions better during conflicts. Using hypnotic induction helps leaders enter a state where resistance to change diminishes, and subconscious learning becomes easier. This makes it more effective to internalize new, adaptive behaviors than through simply using cognitive efforts (Hammond, 2010).

One of the main focuses of subconscious leadership conditioning is the executive self-concept. Leadership psychology research shows that implicit beliefs regarding competence, authority, and responsibility greatly shape leadership behavior (Lord & Hall, 2005). Hypnotherapeutic techniques like ego-strengthening and guided imagery can help reinforce a stable and adaptive leadership identity. For instance, leaders might be guided to visualize themselves responding effectively to complex decisions, linking leadership challenges to feelings of competence and clarity instead of anxiety or self-doubt. Over time, this conditioning can change automatic self-assessments that affect decision confidence and follow-through.

Reducing cognitive bias is another key use of hypnotherapeutic conditioning. As previously mentioned, biases like overconfidence, loss aversion, and confirmation bias often operate subconsciously and remain despite conscious recognition. Hypnotherapy can help lessen these biases by enhancing metacognitive awareness and shaping alternative responses. For example, hypnotic suggestions might focus on fostering cognitive flexibility, encouraging openness to disconfirming evidence, and prompting a reflective pause before making judgments. While hypnosis may not completely eliminate bias, it can lessen the emotional impact that sustains biased thinking, thus aiding more balanced decision-making (Oakley, 2008).

Emotional regulation is key to effective leadership, especially in uncertain settings with high interpersonal demands. Persistent stress and emotional overload can weaken executive functions and lead to more reliance on unhealthy automatic responses (Arnsten, 2009b). Hypnotherapeutic conditioning methods, such as progressive relaxation and affective imagery, have demonstrated their ability to decrease physiological stress responses and improve emotional regulation (Montgomery et al., 2000). For leaders, training to maintain calm emotional states in simulated high-pressure scenarios can enhance resilience and help prevent emotional escalation during actual organizational crises.

Subconscious conditioning also enhances ethical decision-making, as ethical judgments are shaped not only by deliberate reasoning but also by emotional intuition and implicit moral frameworks (Haidt, 2001). Hypnotherapy can support value-driven leadership by fostering emotional alignment with ethical principles. Using imagery and suggestion, leaders may enhance their connections between ethical behavior and personal integrity, decreasing the chances of making unethical choices under stress. This approach is especially important in organizational settings where ethical lapses can lead to serious reputational and financial damage.

Subconscious leadership conditioning via hypnotherapy needs to be tailored to each individual and the specific context. Leadership challenges differ across industries, cultures, and organizational setups, requiring customized strategies. Successful hypnotherapeutic programs for leaders usually combine assessment, clear goal setting, and repeated conditioning sessions, often alongside executive coaching. This holistic approach helps align subconscious conditioning with conscious leadership objectives and organizational standards.

In summary, hypnotherapy offers a structured approach to conditioning subconscious processes that impact decision-making, emotional control, and ethics. By targeting the underlying psychological factors of leadership performance, hypnotherapy goes beyond standard development methods and provides an additional option for improving executive effectiveness. The following section will explore how to apply these principles practically to boost decision quality in business environments.

6. HYPNOTHERAPY FOR ENHANCING EXECUTIVE DECISION QUALITY

The quality of executive decisions depends not only on access to information and analytical skills but also on the leader's ability to manage attention, emotions, and cognitive flexibility under pressure. High-stakes business decisions are often made in environments with limited time, ambiguity, and emotional intensity. In these situations, subconscious processes can heavily influence judgment and choices. Hypnotherapy provides a structured way to improve decision quality by conditioning subconscious responses that promote clarity, calmness, and thoughtful assessment.

Decision fatigue poses a major risk to decision quality in executive roles, as extended mental effort drains cognitive resources, leading to diminished self-control and a greater dependence on automatic, heuristic-driven judgments (Baumeister et al., 1998). Hypnotherapeutic techniques can reduce decision fatigue by fostering restorative mental states and enhancing attention recovery. Methods like hypnotic relaxation and guided mental rehearsal help leaders achieve calm alertness, thus conserving the cognitive resources needed for making complex decisions.

Focused attention is essential for making good decisions. Executive leaders often face multiple demands that can split their attention and hinder judgment. Research indicates that hypnosis can improve selective attention and decrease vulnerability to distractions by helping individuals narrow their focus of awareness (Raz et al., 2005). In leadership settings, hypnotherapeutic conditioning can enhance sustained attention during activities like strategic planning, negotiations, and crisis management. By boosting attentional control at the subconscious level, leaders may find their decision-making process becomes clearer and more consistent.

Emotional regulation is crucial for sound executive judgment. While emotions offer important insights, unregulated emotions may distort perception and reasoning. Research indicates that stress-induced emotional reactivity can impair prefrontal cortex function, leading to decreased cognitive flexibility and heightened impulsivity (Arnsten, 2009). Hypnotherapy aids emotional regulation by training leaders to develop adaptive emotional responses. This process enables them to recognize emotional cues without feeling overwhelmed. By repeatedly using hypnosis in simulated high-pressure situations, leaders can learn to link stress signals with calm and responsive behavior instead of anxiety or defensiveness.

Hypnotherapy aids emotional regulation by training leaders to develop adaptive emotional responses. This process enables them to recognize emotional cues without feeling overwhelmed. By repeatedly using hypnosis in simulated high-pressure situations, leaders can learn to link stress signals with calm and responsive behavior instead of anxiety or defensiveness also enhances decision quality through subconscious rehearsal and mental simulation. Mental imagery under hypnosis allows leaders to rehearse complex decisions and anticipate potential outcomes in a controlled psychological environment. This process is consistent with research demonstrating that mental simulation can improve performance by strengthening neural pathways associated with planning and execution (Decety, 1996). For executives, such rehearsal may improve preparedness for negotiations, ethical dilemmas, and strategic transitions, reducing uncertainty and enhancing confidence.

Ethical consistency adds to decision quality and can be strengthened through subconscious conditioning. When leaders make ethical mistakes, it is often due not to a lack of moral understanding but to situational pressures and emotional justifications that override ethical goals. Moral intuition, which functions mostly at a subconscious level, significantly influences ethical judgment (Haidt, 2001). Hypnotherapeutic techniques can help align subconscious moral instincts with consciously held values, boosting ethical determination in times of organizational pressure.

Importantly, hypnotherapy does not substitute analytical decision-making frameworks but supplements them by targeting the psychological states that underpin decision processes. When leaders are mentally exhausted, emotionally stable, and fully attentive, they can execute rational analysis more effectively. By strengthening the subconscious roots of decision making, hypnotherapy improves the overall quality of the decision process itself, rather than simply affecting results in isolation.

In summary, hypnotherapy improves decision-making in executives by reducing cognitive fatigue, boosting attentional control, aiding emotional regulation, and promoting ethical consistency. These advantages make hypnotherapy a useful supplement to executive development initiatives, especially in high-pressure and complex environments. The next section will examine how these individual benefits can be applied on an organizational level within business and corporate contexts.

7. PRACTICAL APPLICATIONS IN BUSINESS AND ORGANIZATIONAL SETTINGS

Implementing hypnotherapy in business and organizational settings requires a disciplined, ethical, and outcome-oriented approach. Although traditionally associated with clinical and therapeutic contexts, its application in areas such as executive coaching, leadership development, and corporate wellness is increasing. This trend underscores the expanding awareness that effective leadership relies not only on skills but also on psychological well-being, emotional regulation, and subconscious mental processes.

A common application of hypnotherapy in organizations is in executive coaching. This approach typically focuses on clarifying objectives, modifying behaviors, and enhancing performance through reflective dialogue and feedback. However, many leaders encounter persistent issues such as decision-making anxiety, confidence fluctuations, or stress reactions that are not fully addressed by cognitive strategies alone. Hypnotherapy can complement coaching by targeting subconscious barriers that impede progress. For example, hypnotic methods can bolster confidence in strategic decisions or reduce anticipatory anxiety prior to key presentations and negotiations (Passmore, 2020).

An emerging use case is in leadership development programs. Companies are investing more in building long-term leadership pipelines, focusing on skills like emotional intelligence, resilience, and ethical decision-making. Hypnotherapy can be integrated as a voluntary, personalized tool to help leaders internalize these qualities. Using guided imagery and subconscious practice, participants can develop adaptive responses that reflect organizational values and leadership skills. This method helps learning move beyond classroom teaching to include psychological change, making leadership development outcomes more enduring.

Hypnotherapy is also relevant for corporate wellness programs and stress management efforts. Long-term workplace stress has been associated with reduced cognitive abilities, poorer decision-making, and higher burnout rates among senior leaders (Maslach & Leiter, 2016). Hypnotherapeutic relaxation and stress-reduction methods have proven effective in lowering physiological stress indicators and improving mental well-being (Hammond, 2010). When included in holistic wellness programs, hypnotherapy can help leaders sustain mental clarity and emotional stability, which in turn can enhance organizational performance.

Organizations need to think about how to deliver hypnotherapeutic interventions and their suitability for different contexts. These interventions can be conducted through one-on-one sessions, small-group workshops, or combined with coaching and training in blended formats. For example, individual sessions are ideal for senior executives facing confidential or sensitive decision-making issues, while group formats may work well for stress management or resilience training. It is crucial that participation remains voluntary, with transparent communication about the goals, process, and limits of hypnotherapy to maintain ethical standards.

Measurement and evaluation are essential for organizations adopting new practices. Business contexts emphasize tangible results, requiring suitable indicators to gauge the success of hypnotherapy efforts. Possible metrics include decreases in self-reported stress, better decision-making confidence, improved emotional control, and observable behavioral shifts reported via 360-degree feedback. Although qualitative results are useful, integrating them with quantitative data enhances organizational trust in the intervention's effectiveness (Grant, 2017).

Cultural and organizational readiness play a crucial role in the effective use of hypnotherapy. Attitudes towards psychological interventions differ across industries and cultures, and misconceptions about hypnosis can lead to resistance. To implement hypnotherapy successfully, education, transparency, and alignment with organizational values are necessary. Presenting hypnotherapy as a tool for performance enhancement and self-regulation, rather than as a clinical treatment, may help gain approval from business leaders. Moreover, it is vital that practitioners have the right credentials and follow ethical standards to foster trust within the organization.

In summary, hypnotherapy can be successfully used in business and organizational contexts when integrated carefully into current leadership, coaching, and wellness programs. Its strength is in targeting subconscious psychological mechanisms that impact leadership actions, supplementing conventional development methods. Using evidence-based practices and ethical safeguards, organizations can utilize hypnotherapy as a strategic tool to improve executive performance and decision-making. The following section will explore ethical, cultural, and professional issues more thoroughly, offering guidance for responsible implementation.

8. ETHICAL, CULTURAL, AND PROFESSIONAL CONSIDERATIONS

Implementing hypnotherapy in executive and organizational settings requires careful attention to ethical, cultural, and professional standards. Unlike conventional leadership tools, hypnotherapy targets subconscious thoughts and emotions, which raises concerns about autonomy, consent, power relationships, and responsibility. Explicitly addressing these issues is crucial to ensure that hypnotherapeutic practices are conducted ethically, transparently, and in accordance with psychological best standards.

Informed consent is fundamental to ethical hypnotherapy. Practitioners must be fully aware of hypnosis's nature, the goals of the treatment, potential benefits, and possible risks or limitations. It's important to address misconceptions like loss of control or manipulation to foster informed choices. Ethical standards confirm that hypnosis does not eliminate personal agency; people remain aware and make choices throughout the process (American Psychological Association, 2017). In organizational contexts, consent should be given freely and without coercion, especially when interventions are provided or sponsored by employers.

Closely linked to consent is the matter of autonomy and power dynamics. Executive leaders frequently work within hierarchical systems where organizational influence can subtly affect involvement in developmental activities. Therefore, it is crucial to present hypnotherapy as a voluntary option rather than a compulsory requirement. Practitioners should clearly distinguish between aiding personal leadership growth and pursuing organizational goals, always prioritizing the leader's psychological health and personal values.

Confidentiality is another vital ethical issue. Hypnotherapy sessions can bring up personal insights, emotional experiences, or hidden beliefs that leaders might prefer to keep private within their organizations. Professional guidelines emphasize strict confidentiality and require clear agreements on what, if any, information can be shared with organizations or sponsors (American Psychological Association, 2017). Aggregate or anonymized results can be shared for program evaluation, but individual disclosures must stay protected unless explicitly authorized.

Cultural factors significantly influence the ethical use of hypnotherapy in leadership contexts. Beliefs about mental health, authority, and psychological treatment affect how hypnosis is received and understood. In certain cultures, hypnosis might be stigmatized or mistaken for mystical rituals, while in others, it is more widely accepted. Effective, culturally responsive hypnotherapy involves understanding these beliefs and tailoring language, metaphors, and strategies to fit cultural contexts (Hammond, 2010). Practitioners should steer clear of applying culturally mismatched frameworks and instead work closely with leaders to guarantee cultural alignment.

Professional competence and scope of practice are equally important considerations. Hypnotherapy should only be performed by practitioners with proper training, credentials, and commitment to established professional standards. In leadership situations, practitioners need to differentiate between performance improvement and clinical treatment. Although hypnotherapy can help reduce stress or boost confidence, it is not a replacement for mental health care when clinical conditions exist. Ethical practice necessitates referring individuals to appropriate professionals if leaders show symptoms outside the practitioner's area of expertise (Heap & Aravind, 2002).

Integrating hypnotherapy into organizational systems prompts important questions about ethics and accountability. Organizations using hypnotherapeutic techniques should implement clear policies defining practitioner qualifications, ethical standards, and procedures for handling concerns or complaints. These governance frameworks help build trust and credibility, while also safeguarding both leaders and organizations from ethical violations.

In summary, ethical, cultural, and professional aspects are fundamental to the responsible application of hypnotherapy in executive leadership settings. Emphasizing informed consent, autonomy, confidentiality, cultural awareness, and professional skill, hypnotherapy can be incorporated into organizations with integrity and trust. These factors help ensure that subconscious leadership conditioning remains a supportive, empowering process rather than an invasive or coercive one. The following section will explore the challenges, limitations, and future opportunities, placing hypnotherapy within a broader research and practical framework.

9. CHALLENGES, LIMITATIONS, AND FUTURE DIRECTIONS

9.1 Organizational Misconceptions and Resistance

A major obstacle in using hypnotherapy in business and executive settings is ongoing resistance from organizations, mainly due to common misconceptions. Although extensive research over the years has proven hypnosis to be a valid psychological tool, many corporate leaders still link hypnotherapy to entertainment or pseudoscience. These misconceptions can damage its credibility and discourage executives from participating in hypnotherapy. Studies show that skepticism usually arises from limited understanding of its scientific and practical basis, rather than from scientific evidence contradicting it (Lynn et al., 2000). Overcoming this resistance involves education, clear communication, and integrating hypnotherapy into recognized fields like leadership development, cognitive psychology, and performance enhancement.

9.2 Individual Differences in Hypnotic Responsiveness

Another significant limitation is the variability in hypnotic responsiveness among individuals. Studies consistently show that people's ability to experience hypnotic phenomena varies, influenced by factors like attentional absorption, expectancy, motivation, and cognitive flexibility (Halligan & Oakley, 2013). In executive contexts, this variability indicates that hypnotherapy results can differ among leaders. Some may see significant gains in focus, emotional control, and decision-making confidence, while others might experience more modest effects. This highlights the need for personalized assessments, realistic goal setting, and flexible intervention approaches instead of a one-size-fits-all method.

9.3 Limitations of Existing Research in Business Contexts

Although hypnosis has substantial support in clinical and experimental psychology, there is limited research specifically on its use in executive decision-making and organizational leadership. Most existing studies draw conclusions from related fields like stress management, sports psychology, and clinical performance results (Yapko, 2012). Though informative, these studies do not entirely reflect the complexity of leadership roles, organizational pressures, and strategic decision-making demands. Furthermore, methodological limitations such as small sample sizes, cross-sectional designs, and dependence on self-report measures restrict the broader applicability of the findings. A strong need exists for longitudinal, organization-focused studies that directly measure leadership performance indicators.

9.4 Ethical and Scope-of-Practice Constraints

Ethical boundaries are crucial when using hypnotherapy in leadership contexts. While leadership challenges can sometimes be linked to psychological issues or mental health conditions, hypnotherapy should never replace clinical treatment like psychotherapy or psychiatric care. Professionals must adhere to guidelines that stress practicing within their competence and referring clients to specialists when necessary (American Psychological Association, 2017). Upholding this distinction safeguards both leaders and practitioners, ensuring the ethical integrity of hypnotherapeutic practice.

9.5 Challenges in Organizational Integration

Incorporating hypnotherapy into organizational systems faces practical challenges related to scalability, standardization, and measuring results. Leadership development programs usually focus on clear, short-term outcomes and standardized delivery. However, hypnotherapy is inherently experiential and personalized, which complicates large-scale adoption. Additionally, leadership qualities like decision-making, ethical judgment, and emotional regulation are hard to measure with typical performance metrics. Effective integration must therefore involve adaptable program structures that honor individual differences while fitting organizational evaluation methods (Lynn et al., 2000).

9.6 Future Directions for Research and Practice

Despite these challenges, there are several promising avenues for developing hypnotherapy within business environments. Combining insights from leadership psychology, cognitive neuroscience, and applied hypnosis can lead to a better understanding of how subconscious processes impact executive actions. Additionally, progress in neuroimaging and psychophysiological tools provides new opportunities to objectively assess cognitive and emotional changes linked to hypnotherapeutic treatments (Halligan & Oakley, 2013). Furthermore, creating structured, evidence-based hypnotherapy protocols specifically designed for leadership settings could improve consistency, credibility, and acceptance within organizations.

9.7 Cultural and Global Considerations

As organizations expand across cultural boundaries, hypnotherapy applications in the future need to consider cultural differences in leadership norms, mental health beliefs, and attitudes toward psychological treatments. How hypnosis is perceived culturally can greatly impact engagement and effectiveness. Studies emphasize the importance of culturally responsive practices, such as tailoring language, metaphors, and intervention approaches to fit cultural values and expectations (Hammond, 2010d). Cross-cultural research is vital for the ethical and effective implementation of hypnotherapy in international leadership settings.

9.8 Concluding Perspective on Challenges and Growth Potential

In summary, hypnotherapy shows considerable potential for improving executive decision-making and leadership skills. However, its use must be carefully guided by an awareness of its limitations and organizational challenges. It is important to tackle misconceptions, honour individual differences, expand the empirical research, and uphold ethical standards for responsible use. Ongoing interdisciplinary research, professional training, and organizational education are key to future integration of hypnotherapy into leadership and organizational development frameworks.

10. CONCLUSION

This chapter explores hypnotherapy as a structured and ethical approach to improving executive decision-making and leadership skills in modern business settings. As organizations face growing complexity, uncertainty, and cognitive challenges, traditional leadership models focusing solely on rational and conscious thought seem inadequate. By combining insights from cognitive psychology, neuroscience, and applied hypnosis, the chapter suggests that subconscious processes significantly influence executive behavior, judgment, and performance—yet are often underused.

The discussion emphasized that executive decision-making is shaped not just by analytical reasoning but also by subconscious beliefs, emotional conditioning, past experiences, and automatic thinking patterns. These hidden factors influence how risks are perceived, ethical judgments are made, emotions are regulated, and strategic clarity is maintained. When used responsibly and ethically, hypnotherapy provides a scientifically validated approach to access and modify these subconscious patterns. Techniques like ego strengthening, guided imagery, and subconscious rehearsal can help leaders improve consistency in decisions, boost resilience, and increase confidence in high-pressure situations (Yapko, 2012).

This chapter also highlights that hypnotherapy should not be seen as a standalone solution or replacement for traditional leadership development or mental health treatments. Instead, it works best as a complementary method within executive coaching, leadership training, and organizational wellness programs. When used thoughtfully, hypnotherapy can help leaders handle cognitive load, reduce decision fatigue, and develop adaptive leadership mindsets that support organizational values and ethics (Lynn et al., 2000).

The chapter also emphasized ethical, cultural, and professional factors crucial for responsible use. Core issues include informed consent, autonomy, confidentiality, cultural sensitivity, and scope of practice, which are vital for preserving the integrity of hypnotherapy in business contexts. Leaders should participate voluntarily, practitioners must stay professionally competent, and organizations are advised to implement transparent governance to uphold ethical standards (American Psychological Association, 2017). These safeguards are especially crucial considering the power relations naturally present within organizational hierarchies.

Examining challenges and limitations emphasizes the importance of cautious and critical analysis. Misconceptions within organizations, individual variability in hypnotic response, and gaps in current research highlight the need for continued empirical studies. Future research should focus on long-term, organization-centered investigations that measure leadership results, decision-making quality, and ethical conduct. Collaboration across disciplines, including leadership experts, neuroscientists, and hypnosis researchers, will be essential to deepen theoretical insights and enhance practical applications (Halligan & Oakley, 2013).

In conclusion, hypnotherapy is an emerging and promising method for leadership development that recognizes the importance of the subconscious in executive performance. When used ethically, scientifically, and in appropriate contexts, it provides valuable opportunities to improve conscious performance by conditioning the subconscious. As organizations look for innovative and psychologically informed ways to boost leadership effectiveness, hypnotherapy could become a significant factor in the future of executive decision-making and overall organizational success.

REFERENCES

American Psychological Association. (2017). *Ethical principles of psychologists and code of conduct.* https://www.apa.org/ethics/code

Arnsten, A. F. T. (2009a). Stress signalling pathways that impair prefrontal cortex structure and function. *Nature Reviews Neuroscience 2009 10:6, 10*(6), 410–422. https://doi.org/DOI: 10.1038/nrn2648

Arnsten, A. F. T. (2009b). Stress signalling pathways that impair prefrontal cortex structure and function. *Nature Reviews Neuroscience 2009 10:6, 10*(6), 410–422. https://doi.org/DOI: 10.1038/nrn2648

Arnsten, A. F. T. (2009c). Stress signalling pathways that impair prefrontal cortex structure and function. *Nature Reviews Neuroscience 2009 10:6, 10*(6), 410–422. https://doi.org/DOI: 10.1038/nrn2648

Baumeister, R. F., Bratslavsky, E., Muraven, M., & Tice, D. M. (1998). Ego depletion: Is the active self a limited resource? *Journal of Personality and Social Psychology, 74*(5), 1252–1265. DOI: 10.1037/0022-3514.74.5.1252 PMID: 9599441

Damasio, A. R. (1994). *Descartes' Error: Emotion, Reason, and the Human Brain.* https://philpapers.org/rec/DAMDEE

Dane, E., & Pratt, M. G. (2007). Exploring Intuition and its Role in Managerial Decision Making. Https://Doi.Org/10.5465/Amr.2007.23463682, *32*(1), 33–54. https://doi.org/DOI: 10.5465/AMR.2007.23463682

Decety, J. (1996). The neurophysiological basis of motor imagery. *Behavioural Brain Research, 77*(1–2), 45–52. DOI: 10.1016/0166-4328(95)00225-1 PMID: 8762158

Evans, J. S. B. T., & Stanovich, K. E. (2013a). Dual-Process Theories of Higher Cognition: Advancing the Debate. *Perspectives on Psychological Science : A Journal of the Association for Psychological Science, 8*(3), 223–241. https://doi.org/DOI: 10.1177/1745691612460685

Evans, J. S. B. T., & Stanovich, K. E. (2013b). Dual-Process Theories of Higher Cognition: Advancing the Debate. *Perspectives on Psychological Science, 8*(3), 223–241. DOI: 10.1177/1745691612460685;WGROUP:STRING:PUBLICATION PMID: 26172965

Fiske, S. T., & Taylor, S. E. (2013). Social Cognition: From Brains to Culture. *Social Cognition: From Brains to Culture.* https://doi.org/DOI: 10.4135/9781529681451

Freud, S. (1915).. . *The Unconscious., 41*, 159–215.

Grant, A. M. (2017). The third 'generation' of workplace coaching: Creating a culture of quality conversations. *Coaching (Abingdon, UK)*, *10*(1), 37–53. DOI: 10.1080/17521882.2016.1266005

Haidt, J. (2001a). The emotional dog and its rational tail: A social intuitionist approach to moral judgment. *Psychological Review*, *108*(4), 814–834. DOI: 10.1037/0033-295X.108.4.814 PMID: 11699120

Haidt, J. (2001b). The emotional dog and its rational tail: A social intuitionist approach to moral judgment. *Psychological Review*, *108*(4), 814–834. DOI: 10.1037/0033-295X.108.4.814 PMID: 11699120

Halligan, P. W., & Oakley, D. A. (2013a). Hypnosis and cognitive neuroscience: Bridging the gap. *Cortex*, *49*(2), 359–364. DOI: 10.1016/J.CORTEX.2012.12.002 PMID: 23375442

Halligan, P. W., & Oakley, D. A. (2013b). Hypnosis and cognitive neuroscience: Bridging the gap. *Cortex*, *49*(2), 359–364. DOI: 10.1016/j.cortex.2012.12.002 PMID: 23375442

Hammond, D. C. (2010a). Hypnosis in the treatment of anxiety- and stress-related disorders. *Expert Review of Neurotherapeutics*, *10*(2), 263–273. DOI: 10.1586/ERN.09.140 PMID: 20136382

Hammond, D. C. (2010b). Hypnosis in the treatment of anxiety- and stress-related disorders. *Expert Review of Neurotherapeutics*, *10*(2), 263–273. DOI: 10.1586/ERN.09.140;JOURNAL:JOURNAL:IERN20;CTYPE:STRING:JOURNAL PMID: 20136382

Hammond, D. C. (2010c). Hypnosis in the treatment of anxiety- and stress-related disorders. *Expert Review of Neurotherapeutics*, *10*(2), 263–273. DOI: 10.1586/ERN.09.140 PMID: 20136382

Hammond, D. C. (2010d). Hypnosis in the treatment of anxiety- and stress-related disorders. *Expert Review of Neurotherapeutics*, *10*(2), 263–273. DOI: 10.1586/ERN.09.140 PMID: 20136382

Heap & Aravind. (2002). *Hartland's Medical and Dental Hypnosis - 4th Edition | Elsevier Shop*. https://shop.elsevier.com/books/hartlands-medical-and-dental-hypnosis/heap/978-0-443-07217-8

Kahneman, D. (2011). *Thinking, fast and slow*. https://psycnet.apa.org/record/2011-26535-000

Kahneman, D., & Tversky, A. (2018). Prospect theory: An analysis of decision under risk. *Experiments in Environmental Economics*, *1*, 143–172. DOI: 10.2307/1914185

LeDoux, J. E. (1996). *The emotional brain: The mysterious underpinnings of emotional life.* https://psycnet.apa.org/record/1996-98824-000

Lord, R. G., Foti, R. J., & De Vader, C. L. (1984). A test of leadership categorization theory: Internal structure, information processing, and leadership perceptions. *Organizational Behavior and Human Performance*, *34*(3), 343–378. DOI: 10.1016/0030-5073(84)90043-6

Lord, R. G., & Hall, R. J. (2005a). Identity, deep structure and the development of leadership skill. *The Leadership Quarterly*, *16*(4), 591–615. DOI: 10.1016/J.LEAQUA.2005.06.003

Lord, R. G., & Hall, R. J. (2005b). Identity, deep structure and the development of leadership skill. *The Leadership Quarterly*, *16*(4), 591–615. DOI: 10.1016/J.LEAQUA.2005.06.003

Lynn, S. J., Kirsch, I., Barabasz, A., Cardeña, E., & Patterson, D. (2000). Hypnosis as an empirically supported clinical intervention: The state of the evidence and a look to the future. *The International Journal of Clinical and Experimental Hypnosis*, *48*(2), 239–259. DOI: 10.1080/00207140008410050 PMID: 10769986

Lynn, S. J., Kirsch, I., & Hallquist, M. N. (2008). *Social cognitive theories of hypnosis.* https://psycnet.apa.org/record/2007-19668-005

Maslach, C., & Leiter, M. P. (2016). Understanding the burnout experience: Recent research and its implications for psychiatry. *World Psychiatry; Official Journal of the World Psychiatric Association (WPA)*, *15*(2), 103. DOI: 10.1002/WPS.20311 PMID: 27265691

Michael Heap, K. K. A. (2001). *Hartland's Medical and Dental Hypnosis - 4th Edition | Elsevier Shop.* https://shop.elsevier.com/books/hartlands-medical-and-dental-hypnosis/heap/978-0-443-07217-8

Montgomery, G. H., Duhamel, K. N., & Redd, W. H. (2000a). A meta-analysis of hypnotically induced analgesia: How effective is hypnosis? *The International Journal of Clinical and Experimental Hypnosis*, *48*(2), 138–153. DOI: 10.1080/00207140008410045 PMID: 10769981

Montgomery, G. H., Duhamel, K. N., & Redd, W. H. (2000b). A meta-analysis of hypnotically induced analgesia: How effective is hypnosis? *The International Journal of Clinical and Experimental Hypnosis*, *48*(2), 138–153. DOI: 10.1080/00207140008410045 PMID: 10769981

Moore, D. A., & Bazerman, M. H. (2012). Introduction. *Judgment in Managerial Decision Making*. https://www.wiley.com/en-us/Judgment+in+Managerial+Decision+Making%2C+8th+Edition-p-9781118065709

Oakley, D. A. (2008). *Hypnosis, trance and suggestion: Evidence from neuroimaging*. https://awspntest.apa.org/record/2007-19668-014

Oakley, D. A., & Halligan, P. W. (2013). Hypnotic suggestion: Opportunities for cognitive neuroscience. *Nature Reviews. Neuroscience, 14*(8), 565–576. DOI: 10.1038/NRN3538 PMID: 23860312

Passmore, J. (2020). The Coaches' Handbook. *The Coaches' Handbook*. https://doi.org/DOI: 10.4324/9781003089889/COACHES-HANDBOOK-JONATHAN-PASSMORE

Raz, A., Fan, J., & Posner, M. I. (2005a). Hypnotic suggestion reduces conflict in the human brain. *Proceedings of the National Academy of Sciences of the United States of America, 102*(28), 9978–9983. DOI: 10.1073/PNAS.0503064102 PMID: 15994228

Raz, A., Fan, J., & Posner, M. I. (2005b). Hypnotic suggestion reduces conflict in the human brain. *Proceedings of the National Academy of Sciences of the United States of America, 102*(28), 9978–9983. DOI: 10.1073/PNAS.0503064102 PMID: 15994228

Simon, H. A. (1957). *Models of man; social and rational.* https://psycnet.apa.org/record/1958-00363-000

Wilson, T. D. (2004). *Strangers to Ourselves : Discovering the Adaptive Unconscious By Timothy D. Wilson Read Ebooks Book details Language : English*. https://www.hup.harvard.edu/books/9780674013827

Yapko, M. D. (2012). Trancework: An introduction to the practice of clinical hypnosis, Fourth edition. *Trancework: An Introduction to the Practice of Clinical Hypnosis, Fourth Edition*, 1–638. https://doi.org/DOI: 10.4324/9780203126271

Chapter 8
Being Self-aware:
Integrating Hypnotherapy in Corporate Wellness Program

Bhagyashree Kulkarni
https://orcid.org/0009-0009-6996-4020
Independent Researcher, India

U. Pratibha
https://orcid.org/0000-0002-8047-8236
Ali Yavar Jung National Institute of Speech and Hearing Disabilities, India

ABSTRACT

The purpose of this chapter is to explore, identify and explain various strategies that can be integrated into corporate wellness programs using self-hypnosis or hypnotherapy interventions. Also, how these strategies will take the organization as well as employees to the path of transformation by 'Being Self-aware', to resolve psychological and physiological issues and also act as preventive care. How self-awareness via practices of self-hypnosis or hypnotherapy can help evolve individuals as well as organizations to a better today and tomorrow.

TODAY'S CORPORATE CHALLENGE

In today's world Corporates are facing challenges with employee engagement, productivity, commitment, ineffective communication, lack of innovation/creativity, recruiting people as well as retaining them.

For Employees, they need fast appreciation, fast growth, fast promotions, fast money – everything with 'supersonic speed'. And if that does not happen, they de-

DOI: 10.4018/979-8-3373-2317-6.ch008

cide to jump to the next organization without giving themselves a chance or without understanding how the organization works.

For Employers they 'need everything yesterday', meaning employees joining the organization need to get going faster than they can, proving themselves highly productive from Day 0.

It's like any other relationship in life that leads to disappointment when expectations are not met. That's where all problem starts, both physical and mental health.

Any relationships we look at within an organization - management and employees, team lead and team members, within team members, within peers there are always expectations from both sides. Even if expectations are fulfilled most of the time and not fulfilled once or twice, issues develop resulting in conflict within (inner conflict) and conflict outside. It gradually leads to misunderstandings, miscommunication, emotional imbalance, frustration, stress, burnout, anxiety, blame game, not being able to take decisions, losing interest, reduced productivity and eventually losing a resource. It's a vicious circle!

Please see *Figure 1* to understand the cause-effect diagram, causes that can result into mental or physical health issues at workplace.

Figure 1.

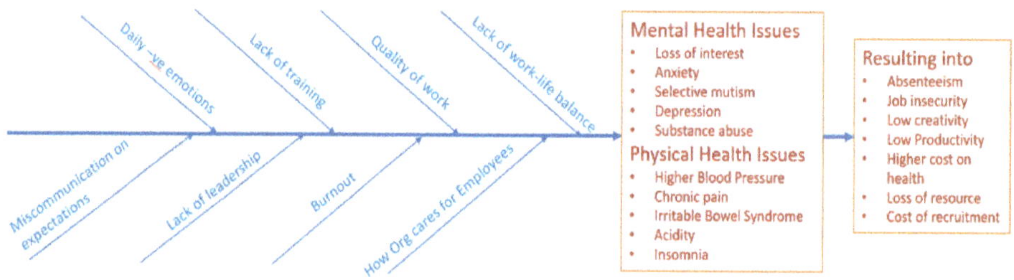

Ishikawa – Cause & Effect diagram

Examples of causes that can result into Mental or physical health issues at Workplace

Patience is the virtue, although that seems to have been lost on either side!

As per the report by WHO (World Health Organization) mental health issues affecting employees at work cost around US$1 trillion per year (N.A., Mental health at work, 2024). Similarly, the CDC (Centers for Disease Control and Prevention) has also published a document on stress management at the worksite with an overview of Occupational stress and health along with case studies proving the impact of stress on physical and mental health (Murphy & Schoenborn, 1987). As per the Gallup

Employee Wellbeing indicator, 58% are struggling with key well-being measures like life evaluation, daily negative emotions, burnout and how strongly employees believe that their organization cares about their well-being. (N.A., Gallup Employee Wellbeing Indicator, 2023)

With the aforementioned its most critical to find ways to become more aware and call for an action.

WHAT CAN HELP? 'KNOWING THYSELF"

'Being Self-aware' be it individual employee or an organization is most important. That's where self-hypnosis or hypnotherapy intervention can help. It can be a catalyst for corporate wellness – for management as well as employees!

'Knowing thyself' - to understand self, to identify disempowering beliefs, to identify trigger points, to reflect, to identify self-potentials as well as accept the weaknesses, to become self-reliant, clear mind, confident, to communicate effectively, to be empathetic, to bounce back from failures, to have healthy relationships across – in all these aspects of corporate life Hypnotherapy can help!

Communication with yourself or outside, it is the key to a successful endeavour!

KEY THINGS ON ORGANIZATIONAL SIDE

For organizations to know their long-term vision and where they want to take the organization in future, where to take the citizens of organization along with them, setting the expectations right up front when employees are hired is probably the first step to a successful relationship. It should be clear, honest communication and clear directions to employees which will help them to know what to expect and what is expected from them.

Also, there are few key things that organization should take into consideration for having healthy, prosperous and long-term relationship with employees.

Please see below Figure *2* to understand these key items from organizational side.

Figure 2. Key areas for organization to take care

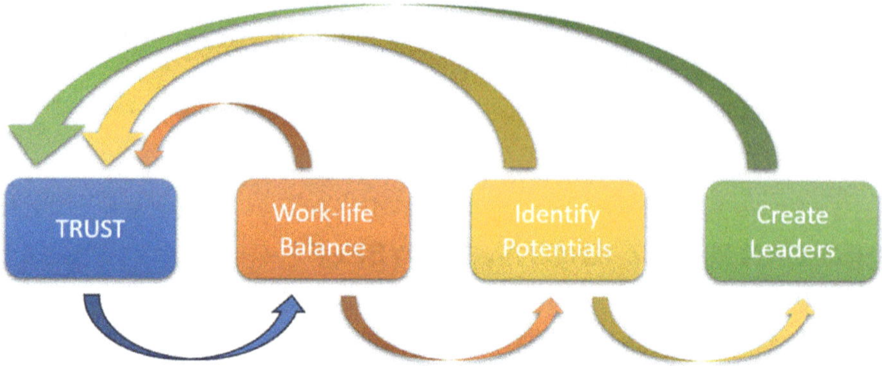

- Trust is very basic and important attribute. Once trust is established within employees that can help go long way in relationship of employees and organization.
- With trust employees can express freely, have an open dialogue. Their areas of interest and where they want to grow along with alignment of the same with objectives of organization. Be satisfied at work as you are doing what you like and which intern help having positive impact on personal life, can bring work-life balance for employees. This can have positive impact on trust even more.
- Happy employee at work, can lead to being high performer and potentials being recognized. More responsibility, personal growth in terms of experience as well as monetary gain can boost the career path for employees. Again, this will have a positive impact of trust within the organization.
- And with that experience, and loving the work that one is doing along with the value that they are adding to the organization success as well as their own – new leaders can be created / born. Again, this helps making the trusting relationship last longer.

Now let's go through them one by one to understand in more details.

1. **Promote healthy culture & values within** – of trust, respect, support, patience, acceptance, open dialogue, creativity, innovation, diversity and inclusion.

All aligning to the leadership qualities, trust is a very important attribute. Instilling trust in individuals is the key thing for leaders. Please see Figure 3 below.

Figure 3. Building trust

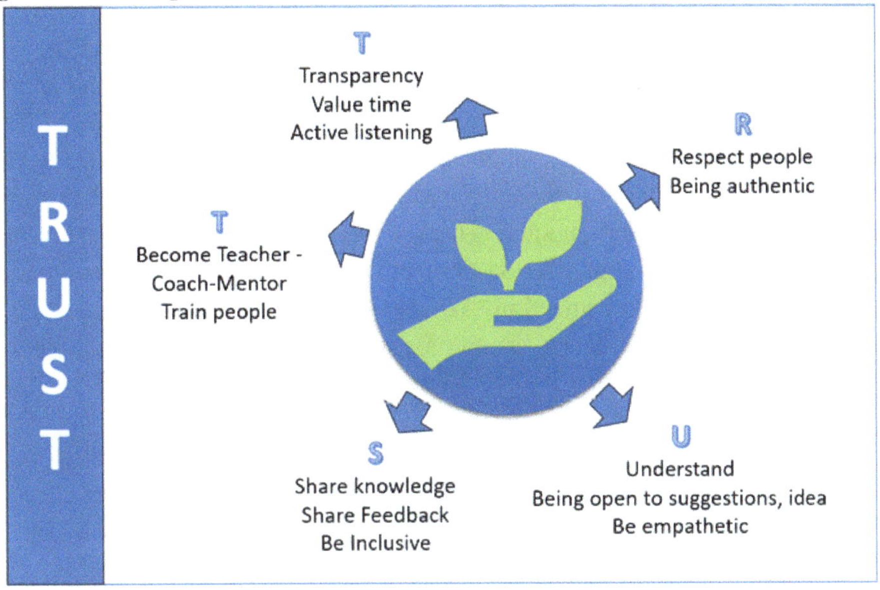

To inbuilt culture of trust within the employees of organization -

- Respect individual by active listening, value everybody's time, be open to ideas, encourage calculated risk taking & innovation.
- Maintain transparency, be inclusive so employees feel being part of one team, share knowledge, share vision, share feedback and be honest.
- Encourage open communication, cultivating empathy and lead by example.
- Inspire better thinking and evaluating situation/scenario by seeking information to have expected outcome.

2. **Maintain work-life balance** – move away from the madness of 24x7. Certain sanity checks like work hours to be mandated, time with family, flexible working hours and help support the well-being of an individual mentally and physically by providing avenues either at the campus or some support outside.

It's important that leadership follows the same balance in their work-life, which is adapted vicariously by employees. The fact that our own leaders can follow it, so can we – brings the confidence in employees to manage their work-life balance as well.

Work-life balance is related to how an individual is able to perform all the roles in his/her life with enjoyment, satisfaction and with quality of life (N.A., 2018). It's been known to people from 1930, although came into practice probably from 1980 onwards. Key factors being global markets, competition and so with that overloaded work schedules as well as impacted quality of work playing role in the same.

With global markets and competition, lot of times quality of work and area of liking is lost. That can prolong work completion and also deplete quality of task. With open dialogue and trusting relationship, employees can help express themselves without hesitation. With no autocracy, if every employee's input is valued, they will come forward sharing ideas and also what are their area of interest which eventually can be aligned with organization's objectives. That will be win-win situation for both employees and organization. As employee will be happy and satisfied at work, then they will find a way to spend time with family and friends, maintaining work-life balance.

Figure 4. Work – Family – Friends balance

Organization leaders should be able to insist on realistic schedule having clear vision, knowing their teams and broader picture. They should encourage open dialogue by which people are able to set realistic goals, timelines for the same and be able to say 'No'. Or otherwise say 'Yes' to work that they love and take more responsibility by which they can achieve work satisfaction. Regular time-offs to spend time with family and for individual hobbies is key to maintaining work-life balance. Certain activities like sports, participation in the running programs, yoga is something that can be participated by leaders and so the employees will follow.

3. **Identify the true potentials of employees** and enable them to upskill in the area of future requirements. Make them responsible and accountable so that they can use their problem-solving skills independently. Cultivate innovation, create conducive environment for individual to recognize, understand and showcase their true potentials by showing trust in them. Understand and separate high performers vs potential leaders. Both are equally important for the organization to grow. Let them learn from their failures. This can help organization to create an asset for the long term.

Figure 5. True potential

- Self starter, can work solo as well as within team
- Quick learner, competitive, driven by success
- Master in the area of work
- Always top of their game

4. **Create new leaders** – give opportunities to talents within the organization and create a trail of good leadership. Allow homegrown talent to be the next successors – nurture them, coach & train them. By giving opportunity to your existing people to grow as leader, that helps in building trust, employees see that they have future within the organization.

Figure 6. Create new leaders

- Opportunity for home grown talent
- Identify people with
    - greater Emotional Intelligence
    - who can understand self & other's emotions
    - Take calculated risk and better thinker
    - Take people along with them & grow together

Organization is known by employees, the true asset of the organization. Although, leadership carries the torch forward for organization – of culture, values and belief system. Looking up to leadership, employees assimilate the culture, values and belief system increasing organizational citizenship (Singh, 2016), (Thiruvenkadam, 2017).

Below Figure 7[REMOVED REF FIELD] is the representation of what is expected out of leadership while gaining the trust (Castrillon, 2023), creating a work-life balance within by 'walking the talk' not just provide but follow the work-life-balance (Pham, 2023), identify individual potentials (N.A., Identifying High-Potential Employees: Everything You Should Know, N.A.) and develop new leaders within – home grown talent.

Figure 7. Mind map

Mind map representing what are key items expected from Organizational "Leadership" side

And now if you see, all the above leadership qualities can be worked on by leader "being self-aware", one with strong integrity, mindful, having empathy, excellent communication and resilient. One who is taking the employees forward along with him/her in this path of growth within organization. All these attributes can be worked on by "being self-aware" and with the help of hypnosis.

KEY THINGS ON EMPLOYEE SIDE

1. Understand, accept and adopt the culture of the organization.

When one talks about how employees adapt to the organisation, they would have to actively learn about the organisation's values, behaviours and norms and embrace them, thus, becoming one with it and try to becoming an active contributing member of the organisation. It will involve understanding the culture of the organisation, knowing their mission statement, accepting it the culture and finally adopting it. Understand the core principles of the organization, its working style and expectations. Characteristics of organization culture may include mutual respect, respect of time, what matters most – people within the organization, innovation & creativity, open to change, transparency across the board, inclusivity, collaboration and recognition. To know more is possible by asking questions, observing behaviour and participating in organisational events.

At the time of on-boarding HR can also arrange the session to let new comers understand culture of organization as well as value & belief system. Such kind of sessions also can be arranged during the year for reaffirming across the population for better employee engagement. Vicarious learning can also help in understanding by watching peers, seniors and management. Last but not the least, the employee can seek feedback from his/her mentor in the organisation as how to align his/her behaviour with organisational culture as well as internalize it.

2. Understand and follow the organization's vision and how it is aligned with yours for mutual growth, win-win situations for both.

Understanding organization's vision is very important as that's how individual can align their own vision with organizations. The way it's important to understand the culture, equally important is vision – which way is the future for the organization. Creating a win-win situation is important because it will help both the employer and employee. Employees need to grasp the organisation's drive, know its long-term goals and aspirations and work towards them in such a way that it supports the employee's career growth also. If goals are aligned then employee is also motivated and can be creative towards his/her own goal achievement which in-turn will benefit organization as well.

This is possible only when employees will build a clear understanding of the organisation's vision, self-reflect on their personal goals and find common ground amidst all this. Proactive engagement and open communication will further enhance this process. Individual needs to understand the current market needs, how best organization can project itself within the competitors, what is missing and what can make a great impact - all this will help. Contributing his/her expertise, taking initiative and collaborating effectively with colleagues across teams, departments, divisions, locations at different levels will pave way further for a creating win-win situation for employee as well as employer. This will eventually help in improving employee engagement.

3. Ease of working within a team or working independently as a self-starter.

By understanding the culture and vision of the organization, when it comes to implementing or executing or contributing to this vision – working with people is the key. That's where collaboration comes into picture. Team collaboration and also at the same time to work independently is indeed an asset one could possess. Being an active listener, having a clear communication, effective time management along with setting clear goals will help in this process.

Setting the expectations from others as well as from self can help reduce any conflict situations. Setting the prioritization and clear communication of the same can help keep the clarity. Asking questions if anything is unclear or answering some questions if the team member isn't clear can help do the job right the first time.

Being flexible and trying to adjust the employer's approach based on the situation in the organisation and alternating between team work and independent work may prove to be helpful in the process. Self-assessment and seeking feedback and also holding a positive attitude adds to the entire process of team collaboration and independent work.

All the above will help in creating a positive impact and putting self in a better position eventually to progress in career path.

4. Clear communication in terms of what is working and what is not.

Communication is an important skill and factor that surely does have its impact on employer-employee relationship. Establishing open communication channels, encouraging feedback, and ensuring that all messages are clear, concise and timely. This will help creating trusting relationship between the organization and employee. Also, with the standard & clear communication, it helps employee create trust within themselves as well.

This is possible only if regular meetings at office take place and also if they have open door policy where they can approach their employers with their question and concerns. In addition to this, employees must share their perspective, thus creating a climate of empathy around in the office.

Similarly, it's important for an organization to encourage employees to communicate what is working for them and what is not. Lot of times a certain task or responsibility is given to an individual and if individual is not interested in doing that, they should be able to say "No" or ask for more responsibility with "Yes". If employee is not inclined to do that type of task, then the work will not be done efficiently and of good quality resulting into disappointment for employee as well as employer. Similarly, if employee is seeking higher responsibility but unable to say "Yes- I am ready", then disappointment on his/her side which can affect performance, productivity and eventually being dissatisfied. To avoid such situations, clear communication is extremely important.

It's also important that employee understand the role and responsibility and if any doubt, get it clarified by their seniors or managers. Lot of time, ambiguity in the role and responsibility can add into frustration and dissatisfaction.

Same way, communication between team members is equally important to avoid mis-understandings as well as getting the work done right the first time, as will be discussed in the next point.

5. Interest in making it right the first time, learn from failures and commitment.

As aforementioned, clear communication is the key for effective collaboration and getting things done efficiently, same way doing it right the first time is also key. The collaborative approach between employees and employers, centered on the importance of achieving accuracy from the outset, learning from setbacks, and demonstrating commitment, is crucial for cultivating a productive and positive workplace. When both parties emphasize the significance of getting things right the first time, it minimizes the risk of expensive errors and promotes high-quality outcomes.

Employers who foster a culture that values learning from mistakes establish an environment where employees feel secure in taking risks and innovating, as errors are perceived as opportunities for development rather than failures. This shared dedication to excellence, along with the recognition that improvement is a continuous journey, builds trust and accountability. Ultimately, when employees and employers align their focus on learning, growth, and initial accuracy, it results in a collaborative atmosphere that enhances satisfaction, performance, and long-term success for both parties.

Attitude of doing it right the first time shows the commitment of an employee. It also shows how much employee cares for the quality of the job and impact that will create for others. Saving cost and time is another aspect that is shown, if job is not done right the first time. This is a very key attribute that every employee should acquire and internalize for the benefit of self and organization.

6. Being open to change

In today's situations, things change very fast and so is the requirement from organization to work in fast paced market. It's important that every employee is adaptable and open to change. Scenarios and situations can change although one should be willing to accept the change, make suggestions and ready to accommodate. Every situation individual should be able to look at it from different perspective as why is that change required from either client side or organization side. And also try to understand what does that mean to him/her.

Change may mean upskilling oneself, change also may mean that certain process has changed or some changes in the management etc. Ask questions instead of assumptions, to understand what it is that has resulted into making this change. Employees can also be proactive and come up with suggestions by which they can request to be involved in implementing that change organization wide, be integral part of it. This can also help in understanding the way organization works and how it makes decision of certain changes. Shows the flexibility of an employee that they are open to change and willing to participate for the betterment of organization.

Please see Figure 8, by making it easy to understand & adapt organization culture, overall vision, clear communication, autonomy with authority, inclusion in decision making and believing in employees even in times of failures to make them learn from it and become resilient, trust can be built between employees and organization. Once trust is built, working within the team as one, knows he/she has the strong support, growing with team as well as being able to express themselves assertively, setting clear expectations and managing time - can create a better work-life balance for employees. With trust and work-life balance productivity and performance will increase producing win-win situations for both employees and organization. Reward and recognition will help create motivation in new learning and upskilling. Individuals will be able to see their future in the organization creating a strong bond and long-term relationship.

Figure 8. Achievning long-term relationship

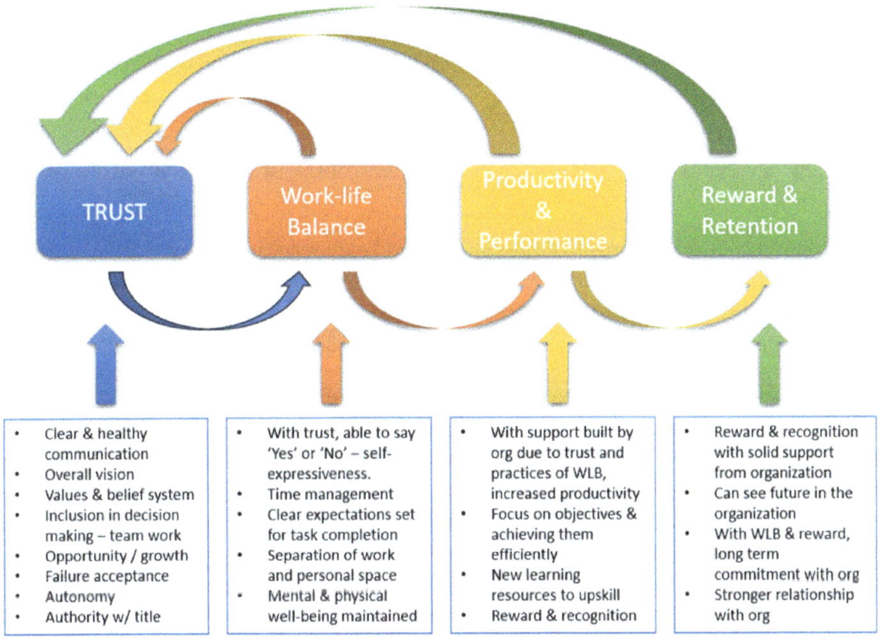

PURPOSE

What is Hypnosis & Hypnotherapy

Hypnosis is psychophysiological state with reduced peripheral awareness and focused attention characterized by an enhanced capacity for response to suggestions (N.A., Society of Psychological Hypnosis, 2014).

As per Milton H. Erickson, founding president of American Society of Clinical Hypnosis, Hypnotherapy is essentially communication of ideas and understandings to an individual in such a way that he/she will be most receptive to the presented idea and there by motivated to explore his/her own body potentials for the control of his/her psychological and physiological responses and behaviour (Erickson, 1967).

Hypnotherapy is a modality of psychotherapy using process of hypnosis, similar to other modalities like Behaviour therapy, Cognitive therapy, Humanistic therapy, Integrative or holistic therapy (combination of multiple therapies) (N.A., Different approaches to psychotherapy, 2009).

Importance and usage of Hypnotherapy in today's world

There are various books, articles, research papers written on the effective usage of hypnotherapy or hypnosis in various aspect of work life across the lifespan, physiological or psychological.

Please see below in Table 1 some of the examples of the same with a reference to literature reviewed.

Table 1. Examples of hypnotherapy usage

Area of work	Literature
Psychological Well-being	Increasing Psychological well-being Through Hypnosis (Guse, 2014)
Stress management	Group hypnosis for stress reduction and improved stress coping: a multicentre randomized controlled trial (Fisch, et al., 2020)
Performance	Impact of hypnotherapy on examination anxiety and scholastic performance among school children (Mathur, 2011)
Self-Regulation	Clinical Hypnosis with Children and Adolescents—What? Why? How? Origins, Applications, and Efficacy (Kohen, 2014)
Sleep Issues	Improving sleep and cognition by hypnotic suggestion in the elderly (Cordi, 2015)
Pain Management	Hypnotherapy for the management of chronic pain (Elkins, 2007)
Obesity	The Use of Self-Help Strategies in Obesity Treatment. A Narrative Review Focused on Hypnosis and Mindfulness (Pellegrini, 2021)
IBS	Long term benefits of hypnotherapy for irritable bowel syndrome (Gonsalkorale, 2003)
Acid reflux	Observation Of Reducing Heartburn Pain In Gastroesophageal Reflux Disease (Gerd) With Hypnotherapy (Hutomo, 2024)
High Blood Pressure	Pilot study of a brief hypnotic induction: Effects on blood pressure, heart rate, and subjective distress in patients diagnosed with hypertension (Upoyo, 2022)
Headache	Evaluation of the effect of hypnotherapy on the headache (Ahmadi, 2018)

It's not limited to the aforementioned areas, but can be extended to various other areas like depression, habits like smoking etc. It's been researched across the continents, countries and across life span in a various different aspect of life.

Myths about Hypnosis

Even though there are so many research papers, books, articles on the usage of hypnotherapy as indicated in Table 1, still there are lot of myths about hypnosis.

1. Hypnosis is sleep and losing control – hypnosis is not a sleep; it's an increased focal attention. Client is relaxed, alert and conscious.
2. Therapist takes control over, its projected upon client– Hypnotherapist projects nothing on client, in fact he/she taps natural trance capacity inherent in client.
3. Only weak-minded people can be hypnotized – Mentally healthy people can be hypnotized as it requires a focused attention to enter into trance. Schizophrenics, people with severe character disorder, with neurological deficit who will have difficulty in concentrating will have challenge.
4. Once hypnotized one cannot resist– hypnosis can be used by therapist only when client co-operates. If client decided not to go into hypnosis, then he or she will not.
5. One can be hypnotized to do things against their will- this is not specific to hypnosis, capacity to influence is there even outside of hypnotic trance.
6. Hypnotherapist must be charismatic person – not at all, although it's very important that hypnotherapist is professionally trained.
7. Women are more hypnotizable than men – 70% of men and women are hypnotizable to a degree, it does not differ with sex.
8. Creates dependency- in a way we all are dependent on others someway. Although therapist knows that ultimate goal is to make client self-reliant and independent by teaching self-hypnosis. Teaching them strategies for problem solving along with self-hypnosis can regain their confidence having control over their own life.
9. Person can get stuck in hypnotic trance- It's a focused attention, which client can end anytime. So, there is no possibility of getting stuck in trance state.
10. May be used to recall memory – No, hypnosis cannot help in recall of memory accurately. People can remember selectively out of an experience or can remember things that did not happen.
11. Hypnosis is dangerous – Hypnosis itself is not dangerous, but trance state can be used mischievously. Hypnotic state is neutral state of concentration and if unethically exploited then harm may result.

And so on. Literatures, books like (Spiegel, 1981), (Yapko, 2003) have clarified above concerns effectively.

With that said now we can go to the purpose of this chapter, knowing that Self-hypnosis & Hypnotherapy can be helpful in "Being Self-aware".

Purpose of this chapter

The purpose of this chapter is to explore, identify and explain various strategies that can be integrated into corporate wellness programs using self-hypnosis or hypnotherapy interventions. Also, how these strategies will take the organization as well as employees to the path of transformation by 'Being Self-aware', to resolve psychological and physiological issues and also act as preventive care. How self-awareness via practices of self-hypnosis or hypnotherapy can help evolve individuals as well as organizations to a better today and tomorrow.

HOW? SELF-AWARENESS AS A PATH TO TRANSFORMATION

There are different approaches to a path of transformation by integrating Hypnotherapy or self-hypnosis at various levels in an organization's wellness program. It can be a combination of individual sessions or group sessions depending on which area to be worked on. In organizations, a gap analysis can be done to identify the areas where hypnotherapy can be used as an intervention.

Since we are talking about hypnotherapy as an intervention, only trained hypnotherapist or any other medical professional with training of hypnosis should be imparting the sessions of hypnosis whether it's a group session or individual session.

Top-Down approach

Top-down approach should include top management (C-Suite) level then rolling it to senior management as well as middle-level management. It can be in the area of self-development in terms of leadership qualities as well as managing physical/mental health issues. Being at such a high-level stress management is a very common challenge and impact of the same on the physical health. Demand of managing stressful situations, individuals at the higher-level may face issues like high blood pressure, acidity, irritable bowel syndrome, obesity, insomnia and so on.

Below are the key areas where hypnotherapy as an intervention can be applied to tackle these issues.

1. To enhance ways of managing stress effectively, and healthy working habits.
2. To see both sides of the coin and make the right decision which helps both organizations and clients. Being able to see alternate reality – see the other side of the coin. To be able to create opportunity in adversity, by cultivating growth mindset.

3. Believing is seeing – so enhance the ability of a leader to become an effective leader by working on empowering beliefs. To believe in the organization, self and the employees to make it happen. To replace disempowering beliefs for developing more enhanced leadership qualities – empathy, resilience, courage etc.
4. To be able to 'walk the talk' – healthy and effective communication so they become an example for all the upcoming leaders and inspire the entire population. It can also work on conversational improvement as to what influence/impact one can have on their clients/counterparts to convince them.

Leadership along with HR of the organization can perform gap analysis and identify where they think development of leadership qualities is required or where it can enhance to make it more effective. Mental health workshops organized during the year on specific intervals to help educate everyone as well as online sessions for groups to train them in self-hypnosis for identified purposes or availability of hypnotherapist at the mental health clinic on the campus can help.

Figure 9. Categorization of proposed type of sessions

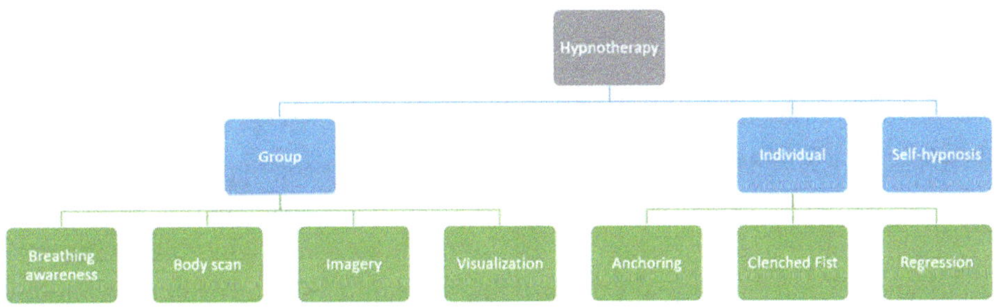

Now let's go through areas one by one as what can help in workplace mental health program for C-Suite, senior & mid-level managers.

Stress management

Stress is important aspect of life. Stress can be due to family issues/pressure, work related, interpersonal relationships, financial issues, physical issues or environmental issues. Stress can be helpful in self-development by pushing an individual beyond its comfortable boundaries, if handled effectively. Although if not handled well and if persisted for long time, can create psychosomatic issues.

For any leadership level, stress management is the most important aspect for surviving and thriving. With demands of current global world, stress is imminent.

To manage stress, important aspect is to become self-aware, understand your own belief system and own trigger points. It's a key to understand self, become self-aware, become aware of own thoughts and feelings, become self-reliant, being focused and to be able to cope stress in a positive way creating positive impact on self and others.

Figure 10. Impact of stress

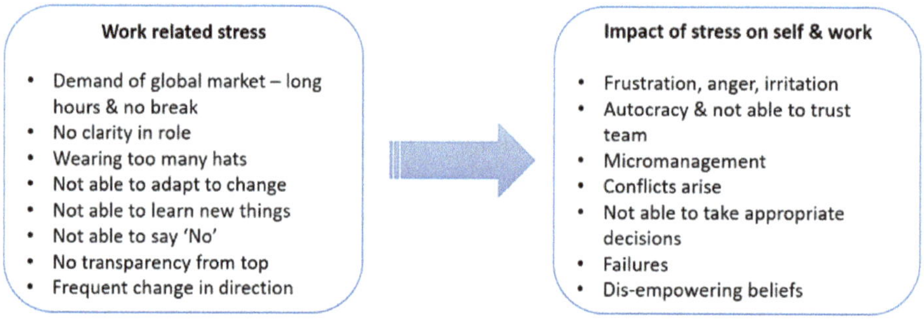

Hypnotherapy can help in stress management using group hypnosis or individual therapies (Patra, 2021), (Fisch, et al., 2020), (Murphy & Schoenborn, 1987).

Within group hypnosis certain generic suggestions can be given using imagery, visualization & metaphors. Teaching body relaxation with breathing awareness & progressive muscular relaxation can help relax body, and mind will follow automatically. Similarly, body scan can help in quick grounding of body and mind. In addition to these, ego strengthening / enhancement can help in becoming more self-reliant, having positive change and able to adjust to the environment (Lavertue, 2002), (Patra, 2021), (Facco, 2020), (Stafrace, 2004). Below areas that can be worked on by practicing self-hypnosis or hypnotherapy.

- To calm body and mind – the more one learns to remain calm, better understanding of situation one can have and then take informed decision or action.
- To be aware of self – strengths and weaknesses.
- To be in the present, have clear mind, so one can think clearly and take better decisions.

- Improving concentration to get better prioritization of work and clear communication. Communication is the key – setting expectations for self and others.
- To be assertive and influential with confidence.
- Being more creative and able to see alternate reality, see other side of the coin.
- To be empathetic, able to understand other's emotions.
- Become pro-active and learn from failures. Become resilient.
- To bring work-life balance
- Positive suggestions with empowering beliefs to go from "What?" to "So what".

If there are unique challenges faced by individuals with high intensity of stress, individual sessions can be taken to make them self-aware, understand their belief system and replacing dis-empowering beliefs with empowering beliefs.

Common or customized recordings of the same can be provided to participants so they can practice affirmations on regular basis. The more practice they do and persistent they are, it will become a handy tool for them to face any stressful situation in life professionally or personally.

Being at the top

As a leader, individual go through different situations in life - facing failures and achieving successes. Being at the top is not easy. As the time goes by if individuals who have been up at the top leadership level for long and are unable to adapt or to change or be agile, they may get lonely. It's also possible that in an event of previous failures, being human - autocracy, micromanagement, unrealistic expectations may creep in to make it a success at any cost. In these cases, issues may arise between leaders and the employees. In situations like this hypnotherapy can help.

Also, it doesn't have to be any specific situation, getting to the higher-level journey can be completely different than sustaining at the that level. To be at that position performing at your optimum level also needs realization, reflection and mind training. For those cases also hypnotherapy can help.

- Body relaxation is the foundation to any further work. With calm body, mind will become calm and able to think clearly.
- To realize and reflect on situations & scenarios in past and learn from them.
- To practice being in the present.

- To identify trigger points, any anger / fear / frustration situations and go to the root cause of it. It may be due to previous failure or unsupportive environment etc.
- To identify disempowering beliefs and replace them with positive empowering beliefs.
- To understand relationship with self and others. To relate to others and able to practice active listening.
- To be more transparent and trust others. Work as a team.
- To understand the alternate reality and achieve win-win situation.

Please refer to Figure 8. In cases where specific situation that needs to be worked on, visualization with multisensory experience can be used by hypnotherapist in individual session. Otherwise, imagery can be also used to relax along with positive affirmations.

For issues related to anger, fear, worry – anchoring techniques can be used. One -on- one session with hypnotherapist to get to the deep-rooted issues behind these emotions can be worked on to have better coping mechanisms.

Cognitive behaviour hypnotherapy (CBH) – cognitive reframing can be used to change the way how event or situation as its perceived to more positive and realistic perspective (Teimouri, 2024).

In cases where past events impacting the present, regression can be used in hypnotherapy. In the session of hypnosis, individual can revisit these events and resolve these issues which probably are deep in his/her subconscious.

Similarly clenched fist technique can help in replacing current negative feelings by tapping on past positive feelings.

For positive affirmations, self-hypnosis recordings can be provided. So, individuals can practice them on regular basis.

To build bridges

For mid-level managers it's a tough task to balance between top leadership and the leaders who are reporting to them. Stakeholder management is key. Being able to research all the information and have multiple options or solutions ready is the key while working with two parties. One should know the problems and along with that able to propose multiple solutions. Does not matter if its higher management or the junior level managers reporting to self. To chieve win-win situation, complete in-depth analysis along with problems and possible solutions can help. To be able to reach to that outcome, knowing self along with calm mind and clear head is needed. Hypnosis can help in achieving the same.

Lot of times, mid-level managers may have issues with unclear job description, feeling powerless and so unable to perform at their fullest extent. In that case also hypnosis can help. Starting with breathing awareness, muscle relaxation and then to ego strengthening. Identify issues can help to clarify what is going wrong.

- Body scan, calm body and calm mind.
- Being able to understand self and others equally well so any stressful situation can be handled.
- Better team work – healthy perception of each other.
- Improved cooperation and acceptance – cognitive reframing.
- Conflict resolution with availability of alternatives - to achieve win-win situation.
- Being able to ask the right questions and clear responsibilities.
- Being assertive in the communication and come to conclusion.

All the above ways can help C-suite, senior level and mid-level managers to know themselves better as well as knowing others. And in this process hypnotherapy can help.

Summary of Top-down approach

With practice of Self-hypnosis and hypnotherapy individual leader can become Self-aware. 'Being Self-aware' will help him/her to lead effectively, connect with people and manage situations coming their way efficiently. Leading the way for themselves, organization as well as others.

Figure 11. Being Self-aware

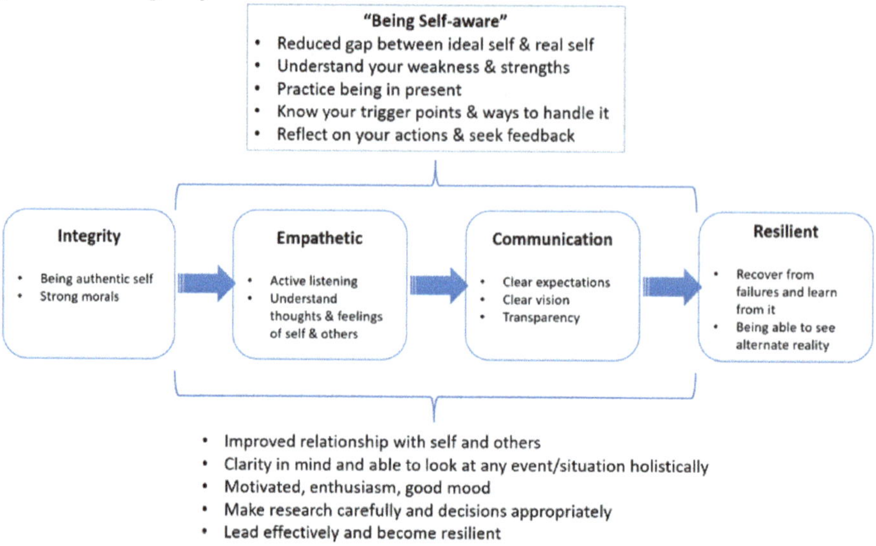

Once the Top-Down approaches are implemented where leadership is going through transformative change, everyone else in the organization can notice that change easily.

After all, a lot of vicarious learning happens in the organizational space and everyone is watching how their leaders behave. Hypnotherapy intervention can help to create a conducive environment for others to follow their leaders. So, working on the top level is the key and it automatically flows down to below levels by following leaders.

Bottom-Up approach

Bottom-up approach should include entry level - fresh from college graduates, few years' experience individuals and team lead or junior level managers. To start with entry-level employees and then roll upward. It can be in the area of self-discipline, performance improvement, understanding self, being able to express themselves, being able to say "Yes" or "No" to the work that you like or not, being able to work with others, being adaptable, growing together as a team and motivation to learn new things.

Hypnotherapy is a scientific method that helps to enhance focal awareness and reduces peripheral awareness, enabling an individual to access their subconscious mind and tap higher resources like hope, courage, confidence as well as comfort in the process of healing along with growth. Of course, there are reservations about hypnotherapy or hypnosis, although by clarifying misconceptions can be alleviated as well as sharing current-day research articles about the usage of hypnotherapy in various mental and physical health.

Again, in the bottom-up approach also physical/mental health issues like chronic stress, burnout, loss of interest, acidity, irritable bowel syndrome, obesity etc can be worked on using various techniques of hypnotherapy.

Studies/books/research papers like (Coelho & Silva, 2024), (Coventry, 2022), (Patra, 2021) have concluded that integrating hypnotherapy intervention into workplace wellness programs is an innovative approach towards achieving the well-being of employees as well as organizations with increased productivity.

Stress management

Stress is given, be it high level management or entry level employees. Coming to the corporate world from college, one can feel stress as you need to be a self-starter, inquisitive, managing timelines, keeping up with the deliverables, learning new things, being creative to come up with different solutions, trying to be ahead of the game to succeed. All this can create stress and if not handled wisely can impact mental and physical health. Today's workplace demands are very high due to competition in the market place which is unavoidable. Individuals at this level may face issues in physical health like acidity, irritable bowel syndrome, obesity, insomnia, habits like smoking and so on.

It is known that hypnotherapy can help young employees manage their stress. It helps in creating a deep state of relaxation which in turn helps in lowering the stress hormone Cortisol thereby calming the nervous system. Simple techniques like breathing awareness, progressive muscular relaxation come handy for the same. This could be introduced as part of the orientation program in the beginning upon recruitment. In addition to this, it is important that new recruits hold a positive mindset as they are taking first steps towards career. Hypnosis can play important role in helping these young minds in replacing self-limiting beliefs with positive and empowering ones. Ego strengthening or enhancement are techniques of Hypnosis that could be included in employee wellness programs so as to facilitate employee growth and productivity, both personal and professional.

Entry level

For entry level employees, it can start from induction training which teaches habits of self-care, self-discipline, self-awareness, being honest, quick learning with a focused mind, respect, being able to collaborate, clearly communicating, presenting at the meetings etc can be instilled in fresh graduates, entry-level employees or managers. Being more assertive than aggressive, being able to reach across the isles and influence the decision makers all can be worked on. This will help in asking the right questions, in terms of understanding the culture, vision, mission of the organization as well as individual's role and responsibility and being able to communicate well. Communication is the key to work collaboratively.

Workshops and group therapy can help build teams, creating an open culture where individuals within the team are tolerant of each other as well as open to dialogues – agreement or disagreement. Group sessions can also help to increase concentration, productivity and creativity.

Team leads or junior managers

Team leads or junior managers with few years of experience, they are either new to world of work or new to the current work setting. So, working with a team or getting work done from a new team is a challenge. Hence HR driven corporate wellness program can incorporate ego strengthening techniques to help employees cope with the new role and also in working with team. It can help deal with initial anxiety and adjust to new environment. HR department can think of orientation program where in new recruits are trained through technique of ego strengthening and develop clarity of thought, clear communication, respect for co-workers etc.

Conflict management is another key area. If there are conflicts within the team, here in again hypnosis can help in accessing a relaxed suggestible state where they can explore underlying emotions, and check if there is any negative perceptions or thoughts and try to develop more constructive responses to conflict. Hypnosis can further facilitate deeper self-awareness, reduce emotional reactivity and enhance empathy among team members. These are key elements in resolving any conflicts within a team.

Keeping employees engaged

Keeping employees engaged is key aspect of healthy organization and healthy employee relationship. There are various models for employee engagement as per the literature review (Padhi, 2015). Employee engagement refers to the energy, commitment of an individual towards his/her job. It's not limited to only that but also indicates if employee has the belongingness and do they think about organization's benefit, betterment and impact that it can bring.

It's important that employees feel that the work they are doing has a positive impact for the organization, their contribution matters, they feel the safety and security. Reward and recognition programs will definitely help although feeling of valued, security and safety is where hypnosis can help. Group hypnosis to emphasize and re-emphasize as how every individual working for the organization matters can help strengthening the feeling of being valued. How programs provided by organization are supporting individuals in terms of upskilling, work-life balance can be indicated. Of course, as mentioned earlier, group session or individualized sessions can also help in developing confidence, feeling of security and self-awareness.

It can also help in providing the emotional support when needed giving safety and security to the employee by providing access to personalized sessions by professional hypnotherapist.

Summary of Bottom-up approach

With hypnotherapy and self-hypnosis entry-level, team leads or junior level managers can become "Self-aware". 'Being Self-aware' will help him/her in self-discipline, self-care, conflict management, performance improvement, time management, creativity, motivation to learn new things etc so they have an excellent career progression in their life.

Managing stress is a key aspect of any wellness program. Including hypnosis in corporate wellness programs can aid in stress management, thereby enhancing work performance and overall well-being. It enables individuals to gain insight and perspective on dealing with stress, improving their coping abilities. Additionally, it can enhance sleep quality, leading to increased energy levels and better focus during office hours. By managing stress and promoting well-being, hypnosis helps employees perform better at work and achieve their goals. Ultimately, hypnosis—by boosting work performance, reducing stress, and enhancing confidence and motivation—contributes to effective time management and equips employees to cope with workplace competition.

In addition to managing stress, hypnosis can also help new employees build confidence in situations where they might face challenges. For instance, it can assist them when they are required to give a presentation, speak up during a meeting, or even express their opinions on simple matters. These challenges can be addressed and improved upon individually.

Hypnosis can also help in boosting employee engagement. Group sessions to emphasize on how every individual working for the organization matters can help strengthening the feeling of being valued. Emphasizing on how programs provided by organization are supporting individuals in terms of being fair, new learnings, work-life balance etc can be indicated with the help of HR.

HYPNOTHERAPY FOR PHYSIOLOGICAL ISSUES

As discussed previously, there can be various physical health issues that can be faced by individuals in workplace handling day to day challenges. It does not matter if one is from board, management, senior manager or entry level employee. Issues can be faced by anybody across the working life-span. And if these issues are not addressed on timely basis they can result into various physical issues. Few of them shown in the Table 2 below.

Table 2. Physiological issues

Physiological issues	Hypnotherapy	References
Acid reflux	Oesophageal-directed hypnotherapy 7 weekly sessions along with recording of 16 minutes.	(Riehl, 2016), (Hutomo, 2024)
IBS – irritable bowel syndrome	Gut directed hypnotherapy up to 12 weekly 1 hr sessions. Ego strengthening was also used. Plus, recommended home practice.	(Gonsalkorale, 2003)
Obesity	By audio or video track.	(Pellegrini, 2021)
Blood pressure	Audio recording of 15 minutes	(Upoyo, 2022)
Sleep issues	Audio of 13 minutes	(Cordi, 2015)
Chronic pain	Cognitive hypnotherapy along with self-hypnosis – twelve 60 minutes sessions alternately every week. After that Self-hypnosis individually every day for 10-15 minutes.	(Elkins, 2007), (Roja, 2013)
Headache	5 sessions of 30 minutes and then Self-hypnosis recordings to practice at home.	(Ahmadi, 2018)
Habits – like smoking	Reducing smoking at workplace. Smoking-ban policy along with hypnotherapy session.	(Sorensen, Beder, Prible, & Pinney, 1995)

All aforementioned can be worked on using hypnotherapy. As indicated in the literature also individuals were provided self-hypnosis recording so that they can practice at home in many cases. Once the individual sessions are conducted by trained hypnotherapist, he/she can suggest possible self-hypnosis for ongoing purpose. In certain scenarios, along with hypnotherapy, life style change, diet, routine and bringing in some discipline may also be required.

PREVENTIVE CARE

Hypnotherapy can also be introduced in the wellness program as a preventive care. Knowing the pattern of work, competition within and outside, and demands from the competitive markets, programs can be designed more as prevention of any physical or mental health issues and enhance the capability of individuals to sustain such situations and become more resilient.

There are various literature indicating use of hypnosis as preventive care like cardiovascular diseases (CVD) (Leo, 2024), used in burnout (Ruysschaert, 2009), habits like smoking relapse (Carmody, 2017) as well as making individuals self-reliant (Facco, 2020) etc. In addition to the aforementioned, having good sleep is the key criteria for optimum functioning of an individual. Hypnosis can help in achieving that and also act as preventive care reducing risk of all those health conditions which may cause eventually due to sleep deprivation (Chamine, 2018).

Preventive care has become a big focus in today's healthcare world. We're all familiar with traditional methods like vaccinations, regular check-ups, making healthy choices, and catching issues early. But now, some less conventional approaches—like hypnosis—are starting to turn heads. Hypnosis often gets a bad rap as something mysterious or just for entertainment, but it actually has solid psychological and therapeutic roots.

Recent research shows it could play a surprisingly useful role in preventive care, helping people tackle stress, lower risk factors, and make healthier choices before problems arise. In a thorough review of 49 meta-analyses by (Rosendahl, 2024), they found strong evidence that hypnosis can make a real difference for both mental and physical health. The biggest benefits showed up in areas like pain management, medical procedures, and treatments tailored for kids and teens. Furthermore, another study by (Elkins G. R., 2025), it was found that Hypnosis has proven to be a helpful tool for managing stress, anxiety, and even physical symptoms like hot flashes. One powerful example comes from a case study where hypnosis helped a breast cancer survivor reduce hot flashes by more than 70%. In a review carried out by (Jensen, 2017), it was highlighted that studies have looked into how hypnosis influences brain activity, especially in regions like the anterior cingulate and prefrontal cortex. The results suggest that hypnosis could be customized to improve strategies for preventive care.

There are many advantages of using hypnosis as a preventive care. It scores high as a non-pharmacological approach which is cost effective. It can reduce long term costs by addressing risk factors before they actually turn into any serious health problems. One cannot deny the fact that patient empowerment is another advantage. The patient is empowered to work on himself or herself, whereby the patient actively engages on their health management. This fosters a sense of control and responsibility on their well-being. Finally, by addressing both body and mind, hypnosis is considered as a holistic healing approach.

The growing acceptance of holistic and mind body approaches in healthcare has further opened the door for hypnosis to play a more central role. As research into hypnotherapy continues to expand, more evidence supports its efficacy in diverse areas. This application of hypnosis in diverse areas highlights it not just as a treatment, but as a proactive tool to equip individuals with greater psychological flexibility and control over their health behaviours. Hypnosis has the potential to be a valuable component of preventive care by addressing the psychological roots of physical illness, encouraging healthier habits, and enhancing mental resilience. As society shifts towards more proactive and personalised healthcare models, it offers a promising, science backed method to support long term wellness and disease prevention

Also, Self-hypnosis can be a part of everyday life like yoga. Practice of ego-strengthening can help individuals become self-reliance and resilient. Ego strengthening scripts can be general as per gaps identified by HR and top management. It also can be customized on the basis of what one thinks a weakness and want to improve or enhance their capabilities.

Thus, introducing hypnotherapy and self-hypnosis in wellness program will help organizations prevent physiological issues as well as psychological for employees. It will also help organization reduce overall cost across different areas including healthcare.

KEY TAKEAWAYS - HYPNOTHERAPY & SELF-HYPNOSIS AS AN INTERVENTION IN WORKPLACE WELLNESS PROGRAM

Based on the gap analysis by the HR and management, below in Table 3 are some of the strategies that can be integrated in corporate wellness program. This will help organization to become more effective, efficient and understand themselves as who they are and how they need to proceed for the time ahead. Similarly, they can help the employees also to become "Self-aware" moving towards path of transformation.

Table 3. Strategies for integration

1. Workshops– Workshops held by certified hypnotherapist few times in a year based on requirement. They can be for the various purposes like self-awareness, stress management, performance improvement, being assertive etc. Separate workshops can be created for upper management and remaining workforce so specific topics can be covered.
2. Group Sessions – for purposes of stress management, replacing dis-empowering belief by empowering belief to restore healthy relationship between the teams or across the departments, improving confidence, understanding alternate reality so problem solving becomes effective. These sessions should be held by certified hypnotherapist. They can be in regular frequency.
3. Self-hypnosis training – in workshops and group sessions on specific areas self-hypnosis audio recordings can be given to participants for regular practices. They can be generic on the area of common issues that needs to be handled within the organization.
4. Hypnotherapy one-one – for any issues faced by individuals be it mental or physical, on-site hypnotherapist can help by having personalized one on one sessions. Lot of times individuals are faced with situations in life like loss of loved ones or some event that has made a huge impact on individual due to which they are unable to work to their optimum levels – in these cases hypnotherapy sessions can help.
5. Integration with existing wellness program – create it as a change in life-style, as Yoga or mindfulness is been included in the corporate wellness programs same way self-hypnosis also can be integrated in existing program.

HR along with hypnotherapist can define a plan for understanding the impact/outcome of hypnotherapy by using certain scales/questionnaires before and after the use of hypnotherapy and/or use of self-hypnosis e.g. Maslach Burnout Inventory.

Workshops and group sessions can be aligned with World Health Day or Mental health day etc. They can help in spreading awareness about how important "Knowing thyself" is and how hypnotherapy and self-hypnosis can help.

CONCLUSION

Integrating hypnotherapy intervention offers a transformative opportunity for an organization. In the complexities of today's world, 'Being Self-aware' at the employees as well as organisational level will help organizations build strong organizational citizenship behaviour as well as increase perceived organizational support (Eisenberger, 1986) with a sustainable workforce. This will help in reducing absenteeism, burnout and turnover, increasing productivity, increasing employee engagement, job satisfaction and retaining the assets for organization making it healthy and sustainable. Hypnosis is gaining recognition globally as a tool to reduce stress, change behaviours, and improve performance (Coelho & Silva, 2024) (Patra, 2021).

Hypnosis is safe, cost-effective, non-addictive, non-pharmacological technique which can be self-administered and will help becoming self-aware and self-reliant. It can be used as preventive care as well, eventually saving costs for the organization over the long term.

Even though hypnotherapy is becoming popular as a complementary therapy, used by medical professionals in various fields still it's not very openly accepted or adopted by institutions be it medical or non-medical. Lack of information as well as mis concepts about the therapy have been the main barriers (Coventry, Occupational health and safety receptivity towards clinical innovations that can benefit workplace mental health programs: anxiety and hypnotherapy trends., 2022). Many people still view hypnosis with scepticism, associating it with pseudoscience or entertainment rather than as a legitimate therapeutic approach.

There are references about using hypnosis in work context based on literature review, although it's not used to the extent, to its potential that it should be - knowing its benefits. On top of that, HR professionals and corporate leaders often lack awareness and understanding of its benefits, which makes it harder to accept as a viable wellness option. Cultural norms and conservative workplace attitudes may also make it difficult to have open conversations about mental health tools like hypnosis. So, introducing it into corporate wellness programs isn't without its challenges. Another key hurdle is the shortage of certified practitioners and standardized protocols, which raises concerns about credibility and effectiveness, making companies hesitant to invest in such programs.

Scientific evidences and success stories from around the world showcase how clinical hypnosis can help lower stress, boost focus, self-awareness and encourage positive behaviour changes—this could help challenge misconceptions and build trust in effectiveness of hypnosis. With mental health and employee well-being becoming bigger priorities in the workplace, especially after the pandemic, companies are starting to show interest in exploring new, holistic ways to support their employees. Progressive workplace cultures, driven by startups and multinational companies, are opening up room for innovative wellness strategies, including introducing hypnosis by trained professionals.

Partnerships between psychologists, hypnotherapists, and HR teams can also help create safe and structured approaches for using hypnosis in companies. On top of that, media and influencers sharing positive stories about hypnosis could play a role in changing perceptions.

We have to remove the mis concepts, educate people via various media and get hypnotherapy and self-hypnosis in to regular practice within the workplace. Also, for getting trained therapist it's important to have hypnotherapy included in the curriculum for psychologist and medical professionals. This will eventually lead to hypnosis finding its place in corporate wellness programs.

Collectively, the wellness of an employee will eventually make the organization's well-being better, prospering and functioning at its best!

REFERENCES

Ahmadi, A. M. (2018). Evaluation of the effect of hypnotherapy on the headache. *Sleep and Hypnosis (Online)*, *20*(2), 114–119.

Carmody, T. P. (2017). Hypnosis for smoking relapse prevention: A randomized trial. *The American Journal of Clinical Hypnosis*, *60*(2), 159–171. PMID: 28891777

Castrillon, C. (2023, Dec 17). *5 Powerful Strategies to build Trust in the Workplace*. Retrieved from Forbes: https://www.forbes.com/sites/carolinecastrillon/2023/12/17/5-powerful-ways-to-build-trust-in-the-workplace/

Chamine, I. A. (2018). Hypnosis intervention effects on sleep outcomes: A systematic review. *Journal of Clinical Sleep Medicine : JCSM : Official Publication of the American Academy of Sleep Medicine*, *14*(2), 271–283. PMID: 29198290

Coelho, A., & Silva, A. (2024, September). *THE ROLE OF HYPNOSIS IN THE WORK CONTEXT.* Retrieved from Google Scholar: https://estudogeral.uc.pt/retrieve/276354/Toma%CC%81s%20Pereira-%20Dissertac%CC%A7a%CC%83o%20Versa%CC%83o%20Final%20.pdf

Cordi, M. J. (2015). Improving sleep and cognition by hypnotic suggestion in the elderly. *Neuropsychologia*, *69*, 176–182. PMID: 25660206

Coventry, P. (2022). Anxiety: A Subconscious Workplace Mental Health Challenge: Develooments in Subsconscious Solusion. *Scholarly Journal of Psychology and Behavioral Sciences*, https://lupinepublishers. com/psychology-behavioral-science-journal/pdf/SJPBS

Coventry, P. (2022). Occupational health and safety receptivity towards clinical innovations that can benefit workplace mental health programs: Anxiety and hypnotherapy trends. *International Journal of Environmental Research and Public Health*, *19*(13), 7735. PMID: 35805401

Eisenberger, R. H. (1986). Perceived organizational support. *The Journal of Applied Psychology*, *71*(3), 555.

Elkins, G. J. (2007). Hypnotherapy for the management of chronic pain. *The International Journal of Clinical and Experimental Hypnosis*, *55*(3), 275–287. PMID: 17558718

Elkins, G. R. (2025). Clinical Hypnosis: A Contemporary, Evidence-Based Perspective. *Journal of Health Service Psychology*, •••, 1–13.

Erickson, M. H. (1967). *An Introduction to the Study and Application of Hypnosis for Pain Control.* Springer Berlin Heidelberg.

Facco, E. (2020). Hypnosis for resilience. *OBM Integrative and Complimentary Medicine*, *5*(3), 1–20.

Fisch, S., Trivaković-Thiel, S., Roll, S., Keller, T., Binting, S., Cree, M., & Teut, M. (2020). Group hypnosis for stress reduction and improved stress coping: A multicenter randomized controlled trial. *BMC Complementary Medicine and Therapies*, •••, 1–14. PMID: 33187503

Gonsalkorale, W. M. (2003). Long term benefits of hypnotherapy for irritable bowel syndrome. *BMJ Journal Gut*, *52*(11), 1623–1629. PMID: 14570733

Guse, T. (2014). Increasing psychological well-being through hypnosis. In *Increasing psychological well-being in clinical and educational settings: Interventions and cultural contexts* (pp. 91–102). Springer.

Hutomo, Y. (2024). Case Study: Observation of Reducing Heartburn Pain in Gastroesophageal Reflux Disease (Gerd) With Hypnotherapy. *Jurnal Health Sains*, *5*(10), 767–773.

Jensen, M. P. (2017). New directions in hypnosis research: Strategies for advancing the cognitive and clinical neuroscience of hypnosis. *Neuroscience of Consciousness*, *2017*(1), nix004. PMID: 29034102

Kohen, D. P. (2014). Clinical Hypnosis with Children and Adolescents—What? Why? How?: Origins, Applications, and Efficacy. *Children (Basel, Switzerland)*, *1*(2), 74–98. PMID: 27417468

Lavertue, N. E. (2002). The effectiveness of a hypnotic ego-strengthening procedure for improving self-esteem and depression. *Australian Journal of Clinical & Experimental Hypnosis*, *30*(1), 1–23.

Leo, D. G. (2024). "Close your eyes and relax": The role of hypnosis in reducing anxiety, and its implications for the prevention of cardiovascular diseases. *Frontiers in Psychology*, *15*, 1411835. PMID: 39035095

Mathur, S. (2011). Impact of hypnotherapy on examination anxiety and scholastic performance among school children. *Delhi Psychiatry Journal*, *14*(2), 337–342.

Murphy, L. R., & Schoenborn, T. F. (1987). *Stress management in work settings.*

N.A. (2009). *Different approaches to psychotherapy.* Retrieved from American Psychological Association: https://www.apa.org/topics/psychotherapy/approaches

N.A. (2014). *Society of Psychological Hypnosis.* Retrieved from https://www.apadivisions.org/division-30/about/#:~:text=In%202014%2C%20the%20Div.%2030%20Executive%20Committee%20prepared,by%20an%20enhanced%20capacity%20for%20response%20to%20suggestion

N.A. (2018). *Work-life balance.* Retrieved from APA Dictionary of Psychology: https://dictionary.apa.org/work-life-balance

N.A. (2023). *Gallup Employee Wellbeing Indicator.* Retrieved from https://www.gallup.com/394424/indicator-employee-wellbeing.aspx

N.A. (2024, September 2). *Mental health at work.* Retrieved from https://www.who.int/news-room/fact-sheets/detail/mental-health-at-work

N.A. (N.A.). *Identifying High-Potential Employees: Everything You Should Know.* Retrieved from Envisia Learning: https://www.envisialearning.com/blog/leadership-development/identifying-high-potential-employees/

Padhi, B. (2015). A Study on Employee Engagement Models for Sustainability of Organisation. [IJRDMR]. *International Journal of Research and Development-A Management Review*, *4*(4), 79–85.

Patra, D. (2021). *The Role of Hypnosis in Addressing Stress at the Workplace due to Psychosocial Issues.* Lincoln Research and Publications Limited.

Pellegrini, M. C. (2021). The use of self-help strategies in obesity treatment. A narrative review focused on hypnosis and mindfulness. *Current Obesity Reports*, *10*(3), 351–364. PMID: 34050891

Pham, E. (2023, Feb 27). *Forbes.* Retrieved from Five Strategies for Improving Work-Life Balance: https://www.forbes.com/councils/forbesbusinesscouncil/2023/02/27/five-strategies-for-improving-work-life-balance/

Riehl, M. E. (2016). Feasibility and acceptability of esophageal-directed hypnotherapy for functional heartburn. *Diseases of the Esophagus*, *29*(5), 490–496. PMID: 25824436

Roja, Z. K. (2013). The effects of a medical hypnotherapy on clothing industry employees suffering from chronic pain. *Journal of Occupational Medicine and Toxicology (London, England)*, *8*, 1–15. PMID: 24066847

Rosendahl, J. A. (2024). Meta-analytic evidence on the efficacy of hypnosis for mental and somatic health issues: A 20-year perspective. *Frontiers in Psychology*, *14*, 1330238. PMID: 38268815

Ruysschaert, N. (2009). (Self) hypnosis in the prevention of burnout and compassion fatigue for caregivers: Theory and induction. *Contemporary Hypnosis*, *26*(3), 159–172.

Singh, U. (2016). Organizational trust and organizational citizenship behaviour. *Global Business Review*, *17*(3), 594–609.

Sorensen, G. P., Beder, B. M., Prible, C. R., & Pinney, J. B. (1995). Reducing Smoking at the Workplace: Implementing a Smoking Ban and Hypnotherapy. *Journal of Occupational and Environmental Medicine*, *37*(4), 453–460. PMID: 7670901

Spiegel, H. (1981). Hypnosis: Myth and reality. *Psychiatric Annals*, *11*(9), 16–23.

Stafrace, S. P. (2004). SELF-ESTEEM, HYPNOSIS AND EGO-ENHANCEMENT. *Australian Journal of Clinical & Experimental Hypnosis*, *32*(1), 1–35.

Teimouri, L. S. (2024). Comparing the effectiveness of mindfulness-based stress relief group therapy and cognitive-behavioral hypnotherapy on work-family conflict. *Research in Clinical Psychology and Counseling*, *13*(2), 127–142.

Thiruvenkadam, T. (2017). Organizational citizenship behavior: Its definitions and dimensions. *GE-International Journal of Management Research*, *5*(5), 46–55.

Upoyo, A. S. (2022). Pilot study of a brief hypnotic induction: Effects on blood pressure, heart rate, and subjective distress in patients diagnosed with hypertension. *The International Journal of Clinical and Experimental Hypnosis*, *70*(1), 83–90. PMID: 34875965

Yapko, M. D. (2003). *Trancework: An introduction to the practice of clinical hypnosis* (3rd ed.). Brunner-Routledge.

KEY TERMS AND DEFINITIONS

Alternate reality: Being able to see the other side of the coin, trying to find the positive aspect in situation, getting a different perspective.

Body scan: Focusing on each body part and notice the feeling. It's about being aware, grounded and connected to your body.

Breathing awareness: Mindful breathing where one is being aware of breath in and out happening all by itself. And as the body gets relaxed, mind also follows.

Cognitive reframing: Being able to look at the situation from different perspective, which may change the meaning of situation and along with that thinking and behaviour as well.

Ego Strengthening: To develop strong and resilient ego.

Employee engagement: Feeling of employee to be valued within the organization as well as belongingness. How much involved they are in thinking about organization's benefit.

Guided Imagery: Imagination of pleasant place to reduce stress in body & mind.

Organizational citizenship behaviour: Anything positive that employee do by themselves to benefit organization.

Perceived organizational support: Individual's perception with regards how much organization cares for their well-being and their contribution.

Progressing muscular relaxation: Systematic tensing and releasing muscles from top to bottom. Helps in reducing stress and relaxing body as well as mind.

Self-hypnosis: Process of getting into a trance like state using hypnosis script or autosuggestions.

Visualization: Visualization involves imagination and emotions.

Chapter 9
Beyond Bell Curve:
Reimagining Gifted and High-Functioning Education

Suchitra S. Sakpal
https://orcid.org/0000-0002-8293-7328
Shoolini University, India

Sunil Kumar
https://orcid.org/0000-0002-2362-1972
Shoolini University, India

ABSTRACT

This chapter aims to reframe gifted education not as identification and extraction but as ecological design. Instead of retrofitting rigid structures through differentiation or enrichment, we propose an alternative architecture that operates in parallel to traditional schooling. This architecture is fluid, permeable, and responsive to developmental variation. It builds environments. This chapter argues that the persistent challenges in educating gifted and twice-exceptional learners arise not from deficiencies in everyday instructional practice but from a fundamental misalignment embedded in the structure and design of educational systems.

INTRODUCTION

Education stands at a threshold where the limits of its industrial era architecture are increasingly visible. The age graded classroom, standardized curriculum, and norm referenced assessment systems still structure most contemporary schooling. These designs assume developmental uniformity: that intellect, emotion, and social maturity progress in synchrony. Yet the lived experience of many gifted and

DOI: 10.4018/979-8-3373-2317-6.ch009

high functioning learners contradicts this assumption. Neurodiversity scholarship, beginning with Armstrong's (2010) articulation of neurological variation as natural, challenges the notion that a single developmental rhythm can or should define the school experience. Emotional intelligence research (Salovey & Mayer, 1990), studies of creative cognition, and the expansion of digital and artificial intelligence discourse further underscore that human development encompasses cognitive, affective, existential, and creative dimensions.

Within these conversations, one group of learners makes the inadequacy of traditional design unmistakable. Their thinking accelerates ahead of emotional consolidation. Their curiosity widens faster than their regulatory systems can contain. They ask questions that stretch the boundaries of curricular time. Silverman (2013) captures this developmental pattern under the term asynchronous development, describing learners whose cognitive, emotional, imaginative, and existential growth unfolds at uneven tempos. Asynchronous development is not a minor variation but a defining structure of high potential (Silverman, 1997). To view such learners only through academic potential is to miss their essence. They perceive the world in heightened resolution, feeling deeply, thinking rapidly, and often struggling to reconcile their internal intensities with the pace of the external environment.

Affective neuroscience helps explain why this mismatch has consequences. Immordino Yang and Damasio (2007) demonstrate that emotion organizes attention, memory, and meaning making. When emotional and cognitive rhythms diverge, learning environments that dismiss or suppress affect become environments that suppress learning itself. The gifted learner who appears bored is often under stimulated. The learner who appears oppositional may be navigating the cognitive emotional dissonance of existential questioning or sensitivity. Without frameworks for interpreting such intensity, systems misdiagnose giftedness as disorder (Webb et al., 2005).

THEORETICAL FRAMEWORK

The framework draws on multiple knowledge domains, each contributing distinct insights. Developmental psychology provides the lens through which asynchronous development is understood (via Dąbrowski's Theory of Positive Disintegration and Vygotsky's sociocultural theory). Gifted education research offers the historical lineage and empirical grounding (Renzulli, 1978; Gardner, 1983; Silverman, 2013; Subotnik et al., 2011) Equity scholarship diagnoses the systemic barriers that perpetuate under identification and underserving of diverse learners (Ford, Grissom & Redding, Steele & Aronson). Global policy innovations illuminate what is structurally possible exemplified by Finland's flexible learning pathways and Norway's modular, competency-based systems. Empirical evidence on curriculum compacting, acceleration outcomes, and affective neuroscience findings on emotion-cognition integration further substantiate the design principles underlying the proposed architecture.

This synthesis integrates foundational theories (Dąbrowski, 1964; Vygotsky, 1978; Renzulli, 1978) with contemporary meta-analyses (Steenbergen-Hu & Moon, 2011; King, 2022) to ground the parallel architecture model in validated scholarship. Literature review prioritised seminal works on asynchronous development (The Columbus Group, 1991) and twice-exceptional education (Ronsley-Pavia et al., 2015), whilst incorporating recent evidence on equity interventions and educational reform (Fullan, 2015). Illustrative vignettes throughout the chapter serve as heuristic devices, bridging abstract theory with relatable scenarios, rendering the architecture's implications more accessible without functioning as empirical evidence. This approach ensures the proposed architecture builds on validated scholarship whilst advancing a novel synthesis for global educational reform.

Three Interconnected Constructs The framework rests on three interconnected constructs that illuminate the challenges of asynchronous development and advocate for systemic redesign. First: Asynchronous Development as a Defining Characteristic[1]symptoms often attributed to the learner rather than the structural incompatibility of rigid systems with neurodivergent development (Roeper, 1990). Second: Programmatic Accommodations versus Architectural. Third: The Parallel Architecture as a Responsive Alternative, in response to this architectural mismatch, this chapter proposes a parallel architecture an integrated, responsive educational model anchored in four interdependent pillars:

Asynchrony as the Conceptual Centre: Giftedness is rarely linear. As Silverman (2013) notes, gifted development is defined not by the accumulation of ability but by the unevenness of its unfolding. Cognitive complexity often outpaces emotional integration. Moral awareness blooms early while self-regulation remains age typical. Curiosity leaps while sensory thresholds remain delicate. Dąbrowski (1964) offers the broadest framework for understanding such intensity. His Theory of Positive Disintegration conceptualizes psychological tension, inner conflict, and heightened emotional response not as pathology but as developmental catalysts. Contemporary work continues to affirm this view. Limont and Piechowski (2024) demonstrate that emotional intensity when scaffolded appropriately predicts growth toward higher levels of autonomy and moral reasoning. Piechowski (2006) emphasizes that intensity is the phenomenological signature of developmental potential.

Dąbrowski's model outlines five levels of psychological development, beginning with primary integration (Level I) and rising toward secondary integration (Level V), characterized by authenticity, autonomous values, and alignment of thought, feeling, and action. Most gifted adolescents operate at Level II, where inner disintegration arises without a clear hierarchy of values (Mendaglio, 2008). Educational environments can support progression only when they provide emotional scaffolding, opportunities for meaning making, and mentorship that normalizes internal conflict. Environmental fit therefore becomes developmental infrastructure. When environments mismatch the learner's internal rhythm, the result is fragmentation or withdrawal. When environments align with the learner's intensity, as Dąbrowski (1972) suggests, tension becomes a wellspring for creativity, ethical clarity, and integrative development.

Twice Exceptional Learners: Complexity Compounded: If asynchronous development strains the limits of traditional schooling, twice exceptional learners expand those limits further. These learners exhibit both high ability and a disability or neurodivergent profile such as ADHD, autism, dyslexia, anxiety, or dyspraxia. Their cognitive strengths and challenges interact dynamically (Olszewski Kubilius et al., 2019). Because strengths mask challenges and challenges mask strengths, many twice exceptional learners become invisible in systems relying on standardized performance or referral-based identification.

The Integrative Learner: Minds That Move Beyond Disciplinary Lines: Some learners display a form of cognition that does not respect disciplinary borders. Mathematics, music, literature, ecology, and ethics arrive not as separate subjects but as interlocking patterns. Gardner (1983) describes this as multi domain synthesis, yet the phenomenon extends beyond multiple intelligences. It reflects an innate capacity to perceive the structural architecture of ideas.

The integrative learner metabolizes knowledge. When reading about neuronal firing, they connect it to the rhythm of storms. When encountering poetic form, they recognize mathematical symmetry. Concepts migrate across domains, seeking coherence. Renzulli's (1978) early work anticipated such minds, noting that creativity emerges when above average ability converges with curiosity and commitment. The integrative learner carries this convergence as default orientation. The phenomenology of asynchronous and twice exceptional development. Although stylized, they align with empirical work documenting cognitive emotional divergence (Silverman, 2013; Daniels & Piechowski, 2009).

The Nineteen-Year-Old Who Thinks in Loops

At nineteen, he reads once and remembers. Arguments, metaphors, tonal shifts: everything settles into a self-turning mechanism. His cognition is recursive, constantly recombining past and present input. This continuous synthesis is exhilarating yet exhausting. Social interaction moves too slowly for his processing speed, and emotional noise depletes him. He is not withdrawn; he is regulating bandwidth. Without emotional anchoring and structured rhythm, such cognition risks burnout.

With mentorship, he becomes a systems thinker capable of integrating complexity into clarity.

The Girl Who Feels Everything at Full Volume

Her emotional responses arrive with immediacy and intensity. Adults misinterpret depth as fragility, passion as instability. Yet her sensitivity signals advanced moral attunement. She reads literature not for analysis but for the emotional architecture of character. In Dąbrowskian terms, she lives in the early stages of multilevel awareness, where emotion becomes the catalyst for values differentiation (Dąbrowski, 1972). This learner infers conclusions before lessons begin. Experience has taught her to hide understanding to avoid disrupting classroom pacing. Containment is misread as detachment, yet internally her cognition is racing. She is not bored; she is protecting coherence. These portraits, supported by empirical findings (Alias et al., 2013; Webb et al., 2005), illustrate that asynchronous and twice exceptional learners experience the world in high resolution.

Patterns in High Functioning and Twice Exceptional Development

High functioning learners demonstrate rapid abstraction, sharp moral intuition, and a persistent search for meaning. Their growth is uneven, shaped by asynchrony between advanced cognition, emotional intensity, and sensory receptivity (Silverman, 2013). This divergence produces friction in environments designed for uniform pacing.

Dąbrowski's overexcitabilities provide a useful interpretive lens. Psychomotor intensities are frequently mistaken for hyperactivity. Intellectual intensities are experienced by adults as argumentative behaviour. Emotional intensities are pathologized as maladjustment. Empirical studies confirm that teachers often misinterpret intensity as misbehaviour (Alias et al., 2013). Without appropriate interpretation frameworks, giftedness is obscured by adult discomfort.[2]

Twice exceptional learners intensify this pattern. Their dual asymmetry rapid cognition coexisting with regulatory difficulty creates discontinuity in performance. As Olszewski Kubilius, Subotnik, and Worrell (2019) argue, talent development for such learners requires integration: challenge and support delivered simultaneously. When either is missing, development collapses into underachievement, internalized inadequacy, or misdiagnosis.

Steenbergen Hu and Moon's (2011) meta-analysis clarifies that acceleration reliably benefits high ability learners, contradicting the myth that advanced pacing harms social development. Yet schools often reject acceleration because it disrupts age based cohorting. This reveals the deeper tension: the logic of schooling prioritizes uniformity over developmental fit.

Why Parallel Architecture Is Necessary?

The system's logic is linear, incremental, and time bound. High functioning and twice exceptional development are nonlinear, recursive, and intensity bound. These logics cannot be reconciled by adding enrichment clusters or pull-out programs. As Fullan (2020) observes, structural inertia restricts the scope of change possible within existing architectures. Tomlinson et al. (2002) propose the Parallel Curriculum Model (PCM), a design that structures learning across four concurrent curricula: Core, Connections, Practice, and Identity. The model assumes that learners must traverse different cognitive terrains as their profile evolves. Identity provides the existential grounding missing from most gifted programs (Kerr, 2009). Parallelism is not an alternative track. It is a conceptual infrastructure enabling movement across domains and levels of complexity.

Asynchrony as Defining Architecture: The Columbus Group defined giftedness as asynchronous development in which advanced cognitive abilities and heightened intensity combine to create inner experiences and awareness that are qualitatively different from what is developmentally typical. Silverman (2013) later emphasized that this definition foregrounds the lived complexity of giftedness rather than the measurable indicators often associated with high ability. It does not reference IQ. It does not depend on achievement. It names asynchrony and intensity as the central conditions that shape the developmental experience. An eight-year-old who grasps algebraic structures intuitively yet struggles to decode the social choreography of the playground also inhabits asynchrony. Silverman (2013) and contemporary guides for families and educators, including the Davidson Academy (2024).

Dąbrowski's Overexcitabilities

The five domains of overexcitability illustrate how this intensity manifests. (table remains as you provided it)

Table 1. Dąbrowski's Overexcitabilities

Domain	Manifestation	Common Misreading
Psychomotor	Restless energy, surplus movement	ADHD, "disruptive"
Sensual	Acute sensory awareness	"Overreactive"
Intellectual	Constant questioning, analysis	"Argumentative"

continued on following page

Table 1. Continued

Domain	Manifestation	Common Misreading
Imaginational	Rich fantasy, vivid recall	"Off task," "dreamy"
Emotional	Intense affect, empathy	"Overly sensitive"

Source: Created by author(s)

Research confirms that high functioning learners are often misinterpreted. Alias, Rahman, Abd Majid and Mohd Yassin (2013) documented that overexcitabilities can be easily mistaken for behavioural concerns. Webb and colleagues (2005) further noted that questioning, empathy, and restlessness are frequently misread as oppositionality, emotional dysregulation, or inattentiveness.

Cognitive and Affective Integration

Neuroscience reinforces the inseparability of thought and emotion. Immordino Yang and Damasio (2007) demonstrated that emotion organizes attention, guides meaning making, shapes moral reasoning, and consolidates memory. For asynchronous learners, this integration is amplified. Cognition and emotion do not operate on separate tracks. They form a reciprocal system. Architecturally, this means emotional development cannot be positioned as peripheral. It becomes structural. Csikszentmihalyi (1990) described flow as a condition in which capacity and challenge are balanced in a way that generates engagement rather than overwhelm

Twice Exceptionality: Discontinuity as Developmental Reality

These profiles challenge traditional school structures because they elude categorical placement.

Table 2. Twice Exceptional Profiles

2e Profile	Manifestation	Common School Response
Gifted + ADHD	Rapid insight, scatter focus	Misdiagnosed as lazy, defiant
Gifted + Autism	Deep specialization, social dissonance	No programming, lost in shuffle
Gifted + Dyslexia	Advanced reasoning, reading gaps	Disqualified by test scores

Source: Created by Author[3]

Why Existing Systems Cannot Hold Nonlinear Development?

The systems approach within gifted education has broadened. Theories of multiple intelligences, talent development, and schoolwide enrichment have expanded the conceptual map (Gardner, 1983; Renzulli, 1978; Renzulli and Reis, 1985). Work on deliberate practice has illuminated expertise development across domains (Ericsson, Krampe, and Tesch Romer, 1993). These contributions expanded possibility yet remained overlays.

Classrooms still follow the clock. Time moves in increments while the learner's mind moves in leaps. Even the most thoughtful differentiation cannot create enough space. Meta analyses consistently show that acceleration benefits high ability learners across academic and psychosocial domains (Steenbergen Hu and Moon, 2011). Bloom (1984) showed that one to one or near individualized instruction can elevate performance dramatically. The issue is not lack of evidence.

Table 3. Distinguishing factors between Gifted Learner, High Functioning Learners Twice Exceptional Learner (2e)

Dimension	Gifted Learner	High Functioning Learner	Twice Exceptional Learner (2e)
Primary Definition	Identified primarily through above average cognitive ability relative to age peers (often measured through IQ or standardized performance) (Renzulli, 1978).	Learner whose cognitive, emotional, imaginative, and existential development unfolds at an accelerated and uneven pace, with intense inner experience and depth seeking thinking (Silverman, 2013).	Learner who demonstrates high ability *and* co-occurring learning disability or neurodivergent profile (ADHD, ASD, dyslexia, dyspraxia, anxiety etc.). Abilities and challenges interact dynamically (Steenbergen Hu and Moon, 2011).
Core Developmental Pattern	Generally advanced cognitive capacity within age appropriate social and emotional development.	Cognitive growth significantly exceeds emotional, regulatory, or social development asynchronous development across internal domains.	Dual asynchrony: intense cognitive strengths plus difficulty in processing, regulation, motor planning, language, executive functioning, or social integration (Webb et al., 2005).
Typical Classroom Presentation	High achievement when challenged visible academic capability.	Appears bored, withdrawn, or restless when unchallenged highly conceptual questions may seem abstract or "too advanced."	Can appear inconsistent, unpredictable, or "average" because strengths and challenges mask each other misunderstood frequently.

continued on following page

Table 3. Continued

Dimension	Gifted Learner	High Functioning Learner	Twice Exceptional Learner (2e)
Emotional and Sensory Profile	Emotionally attuned but generally regulated within typical developmental range.	High emotional depth, intense empathy, vivid inner world, existential concerns emerging early (Dąbrowski, 1972).	Emotional intensity combined with regulatory difficulty may experience frustration, shame, or confusion regarding internal contradictions.
Common Misinterpretations	"Smart," "high achiever," "advanced."	"Overthinker," "too sensitive," "intense," or "difficult."	"Lazy," "unmotivated," "immature," "defiant," or "not living up to potential."
Primary Educational Need	Enriched curriculum and opportunities for depth and complexity.	Flexible pacing, philosophical inquiry, emotional scaffolding, mentorship, and autonomy in learning.	Integrated supports: cognitive challenge plus structured learning support, sensory accommodations, and psychological grounding (Olszewski Kubilius, Subotnik, and Worrell, 2019).
Risk When Unsupported	Under stimulation and reduced engagement.	Identity fragmentation, depression, existential anxiety, self-withdrawal from learning meaning (Immordino Yang and Damasio, 2007).	Chronic mislabelling, learned helplessness, anxiety, academic underachievement, internalized confusion.

Source: Created by author(s)

Flexible and Fast Track Pathways: Reassembling Time in Education

To redesign structures for asynchronous learners, the first variable that must be reconsidered is time. The conventional school clock, organized by age-based cohorts and fixed progression, assumes development unfolds at a uniform pace. Yet research shows that cognitive acceleration often occurs years ahead of emotional or regulatory development (Silverman, 2013). For some learners, the clock is misaligned from the start; their internal tempo outpaces the system's cycles.

Globally, several systems have begun reconfiguring the temporal architecture of schooling. Finland offers one of the clearest demonstrations of flexible learning pathways in higher education, allowing multiple entry points, cross institutional mobility, and modular credentialing (IIEP UNESCO, 2019). Progression is tied to competence rather than chronological pacing. Norway's modular vocational training pilots advance this principle further: courses break into discrete units, and learners move forward once competence is demonstrated, not once sufficient minutes have elapsed.

The Question of Equity: Who Is Recognized, and Who Is Not?

Any discussion of gifted education must address the stark inequities embedded in identification practices. Research is consistent: students of colour, students from low-income families, multilingual learners, and girls in STEM domains remain significantly underrepresented in gifted programs relative to their population (Peters et al., 2023). The issue is not prevalence but visibility. Universal screening provides one of the strongest correctives to referral-based identification. When all students are assessed, representation of historically marginalized groups increases by as much as 25 to 50 percent (Peters et al., 2023).

Bias infiltrates every stage of the identification process. Grissom and Redding (2016) show that teachers often interpret identical student behaviours differently depending on race and linguistic background. A Black child advocating for their perspective may be labelled disruptive; a white child displaying identical assertiveness is perceived as intellectually engaged. Stereotype threat a psychological response documented by Steele and Aronson (1995) further suppresses performance among students who are aware that their group is stereotyped as less able..

Renzulli's Conception and the Enrichment Triad Model as Curricular Core

Renzulli's contribution offers a curricular foundation that aligns naturally with the developmental and sociocultural theories already embedded in this chapter. In the Three Ring Conception of Giftedness, gifted behaviour emerges from the interaction of above average ability, creativity, and task commitment. Renzulli (1978) framed this not as a fixed trait but as a pattern that becomes visible under conducive conditions. Subsequent empirical refinements affirmed that giftedness is a behavioural phenomenon that depends on context, opportunity, and meaningful engagement rather than strictly measured capacity (Renzulli et al., 1981; Renzulli and Reis, 1997).

The Schoolwide Enrichment Model operationalizes this conception. At its center is the Enrichment Triad Model, an instructional design that organizes student learning through three modes of enrichment. Type I Enrichment introduces broad exploratory experiences. Type II Enrichment builds the process skills and methodological awareness required for deeper inquiry. Type III Enrichment involves sustained engagement with authentic problems that require original methodology and creative productivity. Renzulli (1977) described Type III work as the point at which the learner functions as a first-hand investigator rather than a consumer of content. Renzulli and Reis (1997, 2021) extended this structure across whole school models.

Theoretical Synthesis: Integrating Potential, Instruction, and Curriculum

Table 4. Theoretical Synthesis: Integrating Potential, Instruction, and Curriculum

Theoretical Pillar	Core Concept for PFES Architecture	Architectural Application	Goal for the Learner
Dąbrowski (Theory of Positive Disintegration)	Dąbrowski's view that psychological development advances through cycles of disintegration and reintegration, shaped by overexcitabilities that heighten emotional, cognitive, and sensory responsiveness (Dąbrowski, 1964)	Affective coaching that helps learners interpret intensities as developmental signals rather than deficits, with inquiry structures that require internal commitment and reflective choice.	To transform developmental tension into higher levels of autonomous personality formation and increasingly self-determined action.
Vygotsky (Sociocultural Theory)	The Zone of Proximal Development and the principle that growth occurs through scaffolded collaboration with a more knowledgeable other (Vygotsky, 1978).	Dynamic Assessment for identifying developmental readiness, mastery-based progression, and sustained mentorship models that reflect the relational mechanisms described by Lidster and Williams (2012) and Townsend (2022).	To extend potential by learning within an evolving developmental zone rather than being restricted to fixed instructional levels.
Renzulli (Three Ring Conception and Enrichment Models)	Creative productivity, above average ability, and task commitment as interacting contributors to gifted behaviour (Renzulli, 1978; Renzulli et al., 1981).	Use of the Total Talent Portfolio, curriculum compacting, and authentic Type III investigations that engage students in real problems and creative production (Renzulli, 1977; Iowa Department of Education,).	To cultivate creative contribution through sustained, personalized engagement and the development of disciplined autonomy.

(Created by Author)

The Parallel, Flexible Educational System

The Parallel, Flexible Educational System is designed to replace the static, time bound model with a developmental design organized around readiness, mastery, and demonstrated need. It functions alongside the traditional structure but is not subordinate to it. The PFES organizes learning in domains rather than age cohorts, allowing students to work with intellectual peers rather than chronological peers. Early proposals for ungraded environments and domain specific grouping appear in work by the Davidson Institute (2005) and various state models such as those outlined by the Florida Department of Education (2018). The principle is straightforward: pacing and grouping follow cognition rather than age.

Advancement within the PFES is mastery based. A student moves when they demonstrate competency rather than when they complete a prescribed amount of seat time. Townsend (2022) described this as a shift from scheduling to sequencing, where the sequence is determined by developmental progression rather than the calendar.

Curriculum Compacting becomes an essential mechanism within this architecture. Designed to eliminate redundancy for high ability students, compacting replaces mastered content with advanced coursework or Enrichment Triad activities (Iowa Department of Education, n.d.; Purcell and Renzulli, 1998; Reis et al., 1993). Research continues to affirm that compacting maintains achievement, increases engagement, and frees cognitive space for deeper or more advanced exploration.

One of the most empirically supported interventions for high ability learners is curriculum compacting. Reis and Renzulli (1992) developed the procedure to eliminate content students have already mastered and replace it with enrichment or acceleration. Research shows that compacting 40 to 50 percent of curriculum results in equal or higher achievement than full exposure to grade level material (Reis et al., 1998). In science, compacted learners outperform peers significantly.

The compacting cycle unfolds in three phases:

- Assess prior knowledge through pre assessment;
- Streamline curriculum by removing mastered content;
- Replace the freed time with enrichment, acceleration, or mentorship.

The history of gifted education is marked by oscillation between innovation and constraint. Early psychometric approaches, shaped decisively by Terman's work, positioned IQ as the principal index of potential, slicing the expanse of human capacity into ranked percentiles (Terman, 1925). Later scholarship widened the frame. Gardner introduced a multidimensional view of intelligence, Sternberg emphasized analytic, creative, and practical reasoning, and Renzulli foregrounded the interaction of ability, creativity, and task commitment (Gardner, 1983; Sternberg, 1985; Renzulli, 1978). Even as theory expanded, implementation lagged. Programs grew in number but rarely in inclusiveness. Access remained tied to cultural capital and referral practices, leaving many high potential learners outside the boundaries of opportunity (Ford, 2014).

Across these evolutions, a shared insight has become increasingly clear. Giftedness is context dependent, relational, and shaped by culture, identity, and circumstance. Developmental systems theorists such as Lerner (2018) argue that potential emerges through dynamic interactions between individual and environment. Transformational models within this tradition position giftedness not as possession but as contribution, realized through supportive ecologies rather than fixed traits.

What unifies these perspectives is the recognition that gifted development is rarely linear. Advanced cognition travels with emotional intensity, existential attentiveness, and depth-oriented perception. Daniels and Piechowski (2009) describe this braid as the signature of complex development, one that unravels in uniform environments and coheres in responsive ones.Dąbrowski's theory provides a developmental rationale for these phenomena. Studying individuals with exceptional potential, Dąbrowski (1964) observed heightened reactivity across psychomotor, sensual, intellectual, imaginational, and emotional domains. He termed these intensities overexcitabilities, arguing that they signal developmental potential rather than pathology. Mendaglio (2008) later clarified that these intensities reflect the psyche's readiness for transformation.

Dąbrowski's Five Overexcitabilities and Their Educational Interpretation

Table 5. Dąbrowski's Five Overexcitabilities in Gifted Learners.

Overexcitability	Manifestation	Educational Implication	Common Misinterpretation
Psychomotor	Rapid speech, high energy, need for movement, nervous habits, preference for action	Needs opportunities for physical expression benefits from movement breaks and kinaesthetic learning	Misdiagnosed as ADHD seen as disruptive rather than energetic
Sensual	Heightened response to sensory input textures, sounds, smells, visual stimuli aesthetic appreciation	Requires attention to sensory environment may need accommodations for lighting, noise, fabrics	Dismissed as "picky" or "oversensitive" sensory needs unmet
Intellectual	Deep curiosity, love of problem solving, theoretical thinking, capacity for sustained concentration, questioning	Needs complex problems, access to advanced resources, time for deep investigation	Interrogated as challenging authority questions seen as disrespectful
Imaginational	Rich fantasy life, vivid dreams, creativity, daydreaming, elaborate pretend play	Requires creative outlets benefits from open ended projects and narrative thinking	Accused of lying daydreaming seen as inattention
Emotional	Deep feelings, concern for others, empathy, existential anxiety, sensitivity to criticism	Needs social emotional curriculum benefits from discussion of big questions and moral reasoning	Labelled as "too sensitive" emotional expression pathologized

Source: Created by author) *Adapted from Dąbrowski (1964), Alias et al. (2013), and Medaglia (2008).*

Empirical work affirms these observations. Alias et al. (2013) found that nearly ninety percent of gifted learners show at least one overexcitability at high levels. These characteristics are not ancillary. They are expressions of the same developmental energy that drives advanced cognition. A learner who asks many questions is exhibiting intellectual hunger. One who weeps over a novel's distressing moment is demonstrating emotional depth. One who struggles to sit still may be expressing psychomotor intensity that requires a different physical environment.

The question for educators is whether intensity is interpreted as signal or noise. In systems designed for neurotypical pacing, intensity is often misread as challenge, impulsivity, or insolence. In systems designed for asynchronous development, intensity becomes information. It tells the educator what matters to the learner, how they process the world, and what they require to thrive. International research underscores this point. Universal screening reduces racial and socioeconomic disparities in identification, yet bias persists in interpreting behaviour that deviates from age-based norms (Makel, Peters, and Rambo Hernandez, 2020; Peters and Matthews, 2023).

The Cost of Misfit

Internally, such learners' experience fragmentation. Curiosity contracts to fit the room. The term boredom does not capture the precision of this experience. It is not idleness. It is chronic undernourishment. Neuroscience affirms that emotion is central to attention, memory, and moral thought (Immordino Yang and Damasio, 2007). When curiosity collapses, learning becomes brittle. A child may maintain compliance while losing connection to meaning.

The system responds with lowered expectations. Strengths bury needs. Needs eclipse strengths. The learner slips between diagnostic categories and instructional supports. This is especially true for twice exceptional learners whose cognitive and regulatory patterns amplify discontinuity (Steenbergen Hu and Moon, 2011).

Giftedness rarely unfolds in a linear arc. As Silverman (2013) observes, asynchrony is its defining architecture; cognitive complexity and emotional intensity do not advance in unison but braid together at uneven tempos. Dąbrowski's early formulation of the Theory of Positive Disintegration positioned emotional intensity not as pathology but as developmental potential, a view increasingly supported by contemporary affective neuroscience (Dąbrowski, 1964; Limont & Piechowski, 2024). Within this framework, tension becomes signal. Inner conflict between current self and possible self can catalyse movement toward more integrated levels of personality development, provided the environment offers containment, meaning, and relational clarity. Piechowski (2006) underscores that these surges of emotion are not incidental; they form the scaffolding through which higher integration becomes possible.

Positive Disintegration as Developmental Path

The levels of Dąbrowski's theory illustrate the uneven and often turbulent process through which higher psychological organization develops. Primary integration is marked by external regulation and minimal internal conflict. Unlevel disintegration introduces conflict without a hierarchy of values, a stage where many gifted adolescents reside (Medaglia, 2008). Multilevel disintegration begins the recognition of higher and lower values, and organized multilevel functioning reflects deliberate self-transformation. Secondary integration, the highest level, involves alignment between values and action.

The Masking Effect

The learner internalizes confusion: perhaps they are not smart, perhaps they are lazy, perhaps their mind is unreliable. Research from the Child Mind Institute (2024) documents that many twice exceptional students are misidentified or entirely unrecognized because their profiles defy categorical assessment. The question shifts from "Is this student [4]gifted?" to "How does this student demonstrate capacity under conditions that fit?" Identification becomes not an event but an unfolding profile.

For twice-exceptional learners, masking operates on an even narrower margin, were gifts obscure disabilities and vice versa. Verbal strengths in a gifted dyslexic child might produce sophisticated oral arguments yet yield error-laden written work dismissed as laziness rather than accommodation needs. Similarly, mathematically advanced students with ADHD may demonstrate elegant reasoning in bursts of hyperfocus but struggle with multi-step tasks or assignment completion, leading educators to misinterpret inconsistency as inconsistent effort instead of domain-specific cognitive variance. This dual masking creates a paradox: gifts mask the disabilities that require support, while disabilities mask the gifts that demand acceleration. Consequently, these learners remain unidentified and unsupported, perpetuating cycles of underachievement, emotional strain, and lost potential in systems that prioritize uniformity over individual developmental architecture.

The Question of Equity: Who Gets to Be Gifted?

Any shift toward flexible educational architecture must confront an enduring issue: identification. Students from low-income communities, students of colour, English language learners, and girls in mathematics and science continue to be underrepresented in gifted education (Peters et al., 2023; National Centre for Education Research, 2022). Universal screening provides a corrective. When all students are assessed rather than only those referred, identification of underrepresented students increases between twenty-five and fifty percent (Peters et al., 2023). This increase reflects visibility, not inflation. Talent is revealed when the system looks for it rather than relying on subjective referral.

The Architectural Turn in Educational Design

Education, at its strongest, is not machinery but environment. Architecture mediates the relationship between form and experience. Traditional schooling, shaped by predictable rhythms and standardized pacing, tends to remain structurally immobile despite waves of reform (Fullan, 2020). Novel practices are layered atop rigid foundations, producing oscillation rather than transformation.

A parallel architecture resolves this by building alongside the existing structure rather than attempting forced renovation (Banathy, 1991). It creates a permeable, adjacent ecosystem where new forms of learning emerge without destabilizing the conventional system. Each architecture carries its own logic: one tied to chronological age and uniform progression, the other tied to readiness, intensity, and developmental variation (Pfeiffer, 2015). Parallel architecture is not elitist; it is developmental necessity. It recognizes that some learners' internal tempos cannot be reconciled with fixed external pacing.

The Four Guiding Principles

The parallel model is anchored in four interdependent principles.

- Personalization, which honours individual rhythms.
- Mastery, which prioritizes depth and recursive understanding over speed.
- Inquiry, which situates learning in living questions.
- Mentorship, which provides relational grounding and reflective scaffolding.

These principles operate across curriculum, assessment, mentorship networks, and affective support. Every intersection becomes an active site where pedagogy, psychology, and governance meet.

Parallel Pathways and the PCM Framework

The Parallel Curriculum Model (PCM) offers one operational structure. It maintains four concurrent curricula Core, Connections, Practice, and Identity, each serving a distinct developmental purpose (Tomlinson et al., 2002). A learner may accelerate through Core mathematics, explore interdisciplinary links in literature, apply disciplinary practice in the arts, and examine values and identity within social studies. Giftedness is not global. Parallel pathways reflect this truth by allowing learners to move fluidly across domains rather than be fixed to a single trajectory. Movement, not sorting, is the heart of parallel design.

Flexible and fast track learning pathways require rethinking one of the most taken for granted assumptions in schooling: time. Standard progression nine years of school, followed by secondary education, followed by university functions as invisible architecture. It regulates who may advance, when, and at what pace. Yet the assumption that time must be fixed is historically contingent rather than developmentally grounded. When a learner's pace exceeds or diverges from age-based expectations, the clock becomes constraint rather than scaffold.

International models already demonstrate that pacing can be flexible without undermining academic integrity. In Finland, Flexible Learning Pathways allow students to enter, pause, and reenter programs at multiple points, with cross institution mobility and recognition of prior learning built directly into policy (IIEP UNESCO, 2019). At the secondary level, Finland's vocational and training system relies on modular qualification units tied to demonstrated competence rather than seat time, enabling learners to progress rapidly or consolidate when necessary (OECD, 2020). Norway's modular adult learning pilots work similarly: modules are completed upon mastery, not attendance, enabling learners to advance or redirect based on competence acquisition rather than time spent. These systems share two architectural principles. The first is flexibility, in which structure adapts to the learner rather than the learner contorting to the structure. The second is velocity, in which pace aligns with readiness. High functioning learners often experience a time mismatch. Their cognition runs ahead of instructional tempo, creating boredom, withdrawal, or internal retreat. When systems allow pace to bend, cognitive energy is conserved rather than depleted. The learner remains aligned rather than constrained. Rigid progression, by contrast, is maintained through funding structures, staffing models, age-based cohorts, and assessment tied to seat time. Flexibility requires modular curricula, competency-based credentials, recognition of prior learning, and funding mechanisms tied to outcomes rather than attendance. Finland's open study credit system demonstrates how policy alignment makes flexibility not only possible but structurally sustainable.

Universal Design for Learning: Reducing the Need for Retrofitted Accommodation

Universal Design for Learning (UDL) anticipates variability at the design stage rather than correcting for it after the fact. CAST (2018) describes UDL as providing multiple means of engagement, representation, and expression, shifting responsibility from the learner to the environment. UDL benefits gifted learners in two fundamental ways. First, it opens pathways for accessing advanced content without artificial gatekeeping. Second, it legitimizes diverse modes of demonstrating understanding. Cholach (2011) shows that when UDL is implemented at scale, gifted learners experience significant gains in depth and autonomy.

Social Emotional Architecture: Designing for Stability and Integration

For asynchronous learners, emotional intensity is not an accessory to cognition; it is part of its architecture. Immordino Yang and Damasio (2007) demonstrate that emotion shapes attention, memory, reasoning, and moral judgment. For high functioning learners, these processes are magnified. Without emotional support, cognitive acceleration becomes fragile.

Perfectionism illustrates this dynamic. Hamachek (1978) distinguishes between adaptive perfectionism, which is paired with resilience, and maladaptive perfectionism, which is fuelled by shame and avoidance. Gifted children who excel early without encountering challenge are particularly vulnerable to maladaptive patterns because they lack experience with productive struggle. When difficulty finally emerges, they misinterpret it as evidence that their ability has evaporated. Dweck's (2006) work on fixed and growth mindsets strengthens this argument. . Normalizing confusion, modelling error correction, and recognizing strategic approaches even when answers are incorrect help students internalize challenge as inherent to learning. These practices cannot be reduced to scripts. They emerge through relationships and classroom cultures that prioritize process over performance.

Dweck, (2006) further highlighted Praise directed toward intelligence encourages fragility; praise directed toward effort cultivates resilience. Educators must therefore normalize confusion and treat mistakes as information rather than failure. This is especially important for twice exceptional learners, whose internal contradictions produce heightened vulnerability.

The social emotional architecture of the parallel system treats emotional development as curricular core. Mentorship is not an optional relationship but structural necessity. Neihart and Pfeiffer (2021) show that mentorship-based models significantly increase engagement and self-efficacy among twice exceptional learners. Mentors help learners metabolize intensity, name contradictions, and build coherence. In traditional settings, gifted learners are often expected to be self-regulating. In parallel systems, self-regulation is guided, not presumed.

This dynamic increases vulnerability to maladaptive perfectionism, which is characterized by rigid self-criticism and catastrophic thinking when standards are not met (Hamachek, 1978). Conversely, adaptive perfectionism pairs high standards with self-compassion and realistic expectations.

Cultural Epistemologies and Decolonizing Gifted Education

Gifted education has long been shaped by Eurocentric definitions of ability, privileging analytical and linguistic reasoning while marginalizing collectivist, relational, artistic, or moral forms of intelligence. Ford, Grantham, and Whiting (2021) argue that giftedness must be reframed as culturally situated rather than universally defined. Without such reframing, identification structures continue to privilege learners whose cognitive expressions match dominant cultural codes. UNESCO's "Futures of Education" initiative highlights the importance of culturally embedded pedagogies in designing equitable systems (UNESCO, 2021). A parallel architecture benefits from this global lens by acknowledging that giftedness manifests differently across epistemic traditions.

For example:

- Indigenous knowledge systems emphasize stewardship, relational reasoning, and ecological intelligence.
- Many African epistemologies prioritize moral discernment, communal responsibility, and narrative sophistication.
- East Asian traditions value perseverance, humility, and depth of mastery.

It creates structures where diverse forms of complexity can be recognized, nurtured, and advanced. The question becomes not "Who fits the model?" but "How do we expand the model so the learner can be seen?"

Evidence from South Korea illustrates how culturally contextualized AI supported personalization can improve differentiation outcomes when educator voice guides algorithmic interpretation (Kim et al., 2022). Technology.

Bias and the Limits of Traditional Identification

Bias persists in referral-based identification systems. Teachers often interpret identical behaviours differently depending on student demographics (Grissom & Redding, 2016). Standardized testing privileges students with cultural or linguistic backgrounds and disadvantages those with processing challenges or test anxiety. Stereotype threat depresses performance among groups who expect negative evaluation (Steele & Aronson, 1995). These mechanisms collectively suppress visibility of giftedness in underserved populations.

Implementation: From Theory to Design

Translating this architecture into practice requires specific structures at the school level. Flexible grouping replaces tracking with dynamic, domain specific configurations. Time is allocated for compacting processes, including pre assessment and planning for replacement activities. Investment in universal screening and portfolio systems forms the structural backbone of equitable identification. Gifted education specialists act as instructional consultants rather than pull out providers, enabling capacity building across the system.

Table 6. Parallel Curriculum Model Four Dimensions of Learning

Parallel	Focus	Purpose	Gifted Learner Benefit
Core Curriculum	Essential knowledge, concepts, principles, skills	Ensure fundamental disciplinary understanding	Accelerates through foundational content when mastery is rapid avoids unnecessary repetition
Curriculum of Connections	Links across concepts, disciplines, time, contexts	Develop interdisciplinary thinking and transfer	Satisfies characteristic need to see patterns, make unusual connections, understand systems
Curriculum of Practice	Discipline based performance, application, expertise	Build authentic competence through real world application	Provides challenge through complexity develops identity as practitioner rather than student
Curriculum of Identity	Personal reflection, values, growth	Foster self awareness and integration of learning with self concept	Addresses existential questions supports integration of intensity with identity

Source: Adapted from Tomlinson et al. (2002) Kerr (2009) Table created by Authors

Living Architecture: The Framework

Figure 1. The 4×4 Framework for Gifted Education Reimagined, with four principles on one axis and four components on the other. Each cell represents an intersection where principle and structure interact for example, "Personalization × Curriculum" or "Inquiry × Assessment.")

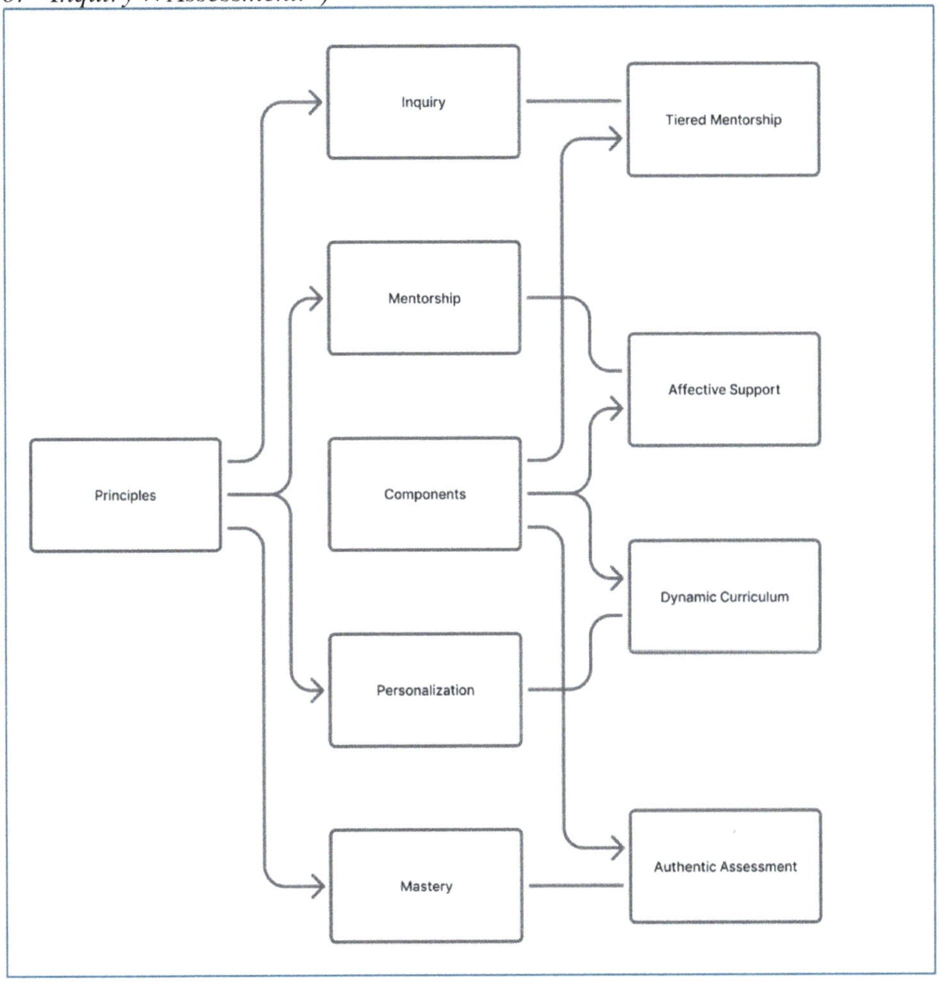

The notion of a four-by-four architecture rests on a simple but profound premise: learning environments are ecological systems. They are shaped not only by what is taught, but by how developmental rhythms, emotional realities, cultural identities, and structural affordances coproduce the conditions for growth. In this model, four developmental principles Personalization, Mastery, Inquiry, and Mentorship intersect with four structural domains Curriculum, Assessment, Mentorship Networks, and Affective Support. Their intersections are not descriptive categories but active developmental arenas where theory, design, and practice converge.

A Four-by-Four Architecture: A Proposed Theoretical Foundation

From a developmental standpoint, systems theorists argue that human growth is nonlinear, recursive, and contingent on environmental fit (Lerner, 2018). Gifted learners, particularly those with asynchronous or twice exceptional profiles, experience this contingency with heightened intensity. Their development cannot be reduced to isolated domains; cognition, emotion, motivation, and identity interact continuously. A system that separates these elements through fragmented programming cannot support coherent development.

Sociocultural theorists, beginning with Vygotsky (1978), emphasize that learning is relational. Growth occurs when individuals participate in guided activity within culturally meaningful contexts. The parallel system extends this idea by positioning mentorship networks and affective support not as peripheral services but as structural components that shape developmental trajectories.

Gifted education scholarship provides a third pillar. Renzulli's focus on creativity, task commitment, and above average ability established that talent emerges through interaction among traits, opportunities, and environments (Renzulli, 1978). Subotnik, Olszewski Kubilius, and Worrell (2011) later reframed giftedness as talent development over time rather than a fixed trait. Their work implies that environments must be adaptable, sustained, and developmental if high potential is to mature into expertise and contribution. The four-by-four architecture operationalizes this developmental orientation.

Finally, the learning sciences reinforce that challenge, autonomy, feedback, and affective safety act synergistically to support deep learning (Bruner, 1996; Csikszentmihalyi, 1990). When any of these conditions is absent, learning becomes brittle. When integrated, learning becomes robust. The four-by-four framework is built on this theoretical lineage.

The Four Structural Domains

Curriculum: Curriculum is reconceived as modular, permeable, and multipath way. It supports vertical acceleration, horizontal expansion, interdisciplinary investigation, and identity work. This aligns with Renzulli's Triad Model and the Parallel

Curriculum Model, which emphasize that young people require different types of curriculums at different moments (Renzulli & Reis, 1997; Tomlinson et al., 2002).

For twice exceptional learners, the tension produced by rapid cognition, uneven regulation, and heightened affect is not an anomaly. It reflects a developmental pattern in which cognitive and emotional systems mature at different tempos, creating a profile that can either catalyse adaptive intelligence or become a source of chronic misfit depending on environmental conditions (Medaglia, 2008).

Curriculum Compacting as Mechanism of Fit: Curriculum compacting translates mastery into time for depth. It is a direct expression of an educational system that treats time as variable rather than fixed (Reis & Renzulli, 1992). When students demonstrate advanced understanding, unnecessary repetition is removed, instruction is condensed, and the gained time is redirected toward enrichment, acceleration, independent inquiry, or creative production. Empirical evidence shows that students whose curriculum is compacted achieve at equal or higher levels in core subjects and demonstrate significant gains in science achievement (Reis et al., 1998). The mechanism is straightforward: eliminating redundancy sustains engagement, expanded depth nurtures expertise, authentic inquiry fuels motivation, and calibrated challenge builds resilience. Compacting shifts learning from procedural compliance to meaningful exploration.

The Three Phase Process: Curriculum Compacting: Curriculum compacting is the operational mechanism that transforms recognition of mastery into time for depth. The procedure is straightforward. The implications are profound. *Implementation considerations:*

- Curriculum design must permit vertical depth (going faster) and horizontal breadth (moving across domains).
- Assessment must shift from "time spent" to "competency demonstrated."
- Mentorship, not clock, becomes pacing guide.
- Funding models must reward outcomes, not attendance.
- Student wellbeing metrics must track pace + coherence, not just completion.

Curriculum compacting is the systematic procedure for eliminating content students have already mastered, replacing that time with enrichment or acceleration (Reis & Renzulli, 1992). Research demonstrates that when teachers compact 40 50% of grade level curriculum for high ability students, those students achieve at the same level or higher on standardized assessments than peers who received 100% of standard instruction (Reis et al., 1998). In science, students whose curriculum was compacted outperformed control groups significantly. This is counterintuitive only if we assume more exposure equals more learning. For students who grasp concepts rapidly, repetition produces disengagement rather than mastery. Compacting creates time. That time becomes space for depth.

Figure 2. Curriculum Compacting Cycle

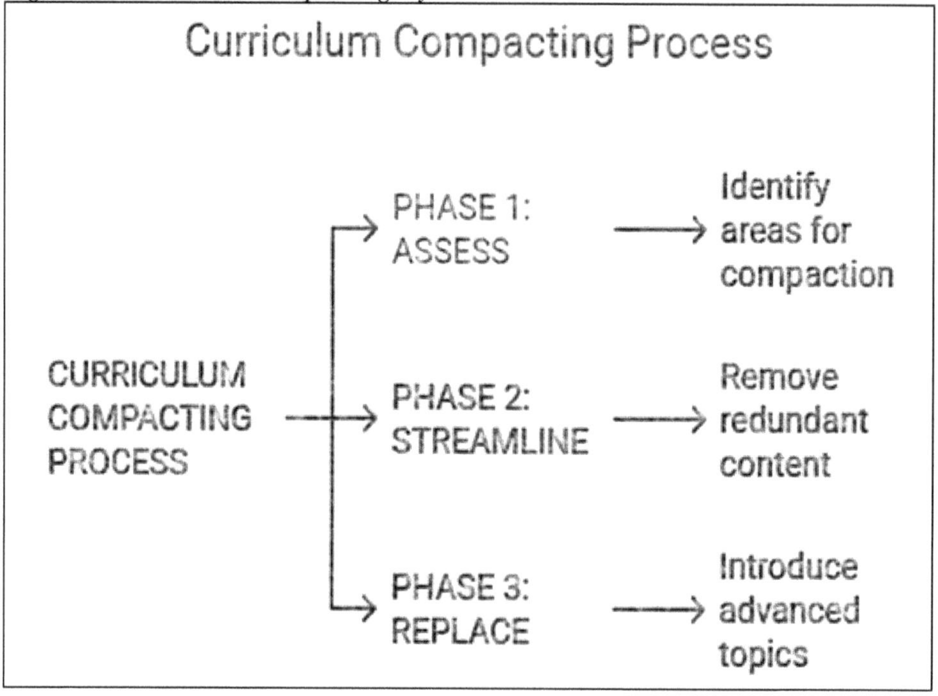

PHASE 1: ASSESS

- Pre assess learning objectives
- Identify what student already knows
- Document mastery level (>80% typically)
- Determine content that can be eliminated

PHASE 2: STREAMLINE

- Remove redundant practice
- Eliminate material already mastered
- Condense instruction on remaining content
- Create time for replacement activities

PHASE 3: REPLACE

- Enrichment: Depth within discipline
- Acceleration: Move to advanced content
- Independent study: Self-selected investigation

- Mentorship: Work with expert
- Creative production: Original work

Source: Adapted from Reis & Renzulli (1992) Reis et al. (1998)

Research documents outcomes when teachers compact 40 50% of curriculum for high ability students (Reis et al., 1998):

- No decrease in achievement on standardized assessments across mathematics, social studies, and spelling
- Significant increases in science achievement for compacted groups
- Higher engagement reported by students in replacement activities
- No negative effects on noncompacted students in same classrooms

This is the more for less phenomenon. Less time on repetition. More achievement. The mechanisms are straightforward:

- Elimination of boredom increases engagement
- Time for depth rather than breadth develops expertise
- Opportunity to pursue interest fuels intrinsic motivation
- Experience with challenge builds resilience

Mentorship as Architectural Structure

Growth demands presence. Parallel systems embed mentorship as a structural element rather than a supplemental resource. The mentor functions not as authority but as co-traveller in complexity. Learners often encounter a constellation of mentors: disciplinary guides, reflective interlocutors, and models of creative risk. Empirical work shows that mentorship-based programming increases engagement and self-efficacy for twice exceptional learners more effectively than pullout or acceleration only models (Neihart & Pfeiffer, 2021). Mentorship holds contradiction: capability and struggle, confidence and overwhelm. The developmental journey becomes lattice rather than ladder.

Affective Support

Affective support sits at the intersection of neuroscience and developmental psychology. The evidence is unequivocal: emotion organizes cognition and guides learning (Immordino Yang & Damasio, 2007). In traditional systems, affective support is auxiliary. In the parallel system, it becomes structural. It includes sensory modulation, emotional literacy, narrative reflection, and environments designed for psychological safety.

Cognitive–Affective Integration as Architectural Principle

Cognition and emotion operate as a single ecological system. Neuroscience shows that emotion influences attention, learning, reasoning, and moral judgment (ImmordinoYang & Damasio, 2007). This relationship is intensified in asynchronous learners whose cognitive acceleration often coexists with heightened sensitivity. Within the parallel architecture, emotional development is not supplementary. It is structural. Mentorship provides grounding. Inquiry provides direction. Mastery provides calibration. When these conditions align, they generate flow a state in which challenge, skill, and meaning converge (Csikszentmihalyi, 1990).

This integration is the developmental heartbeat of the system.

Figure 3. Cognitive–Affective Integration

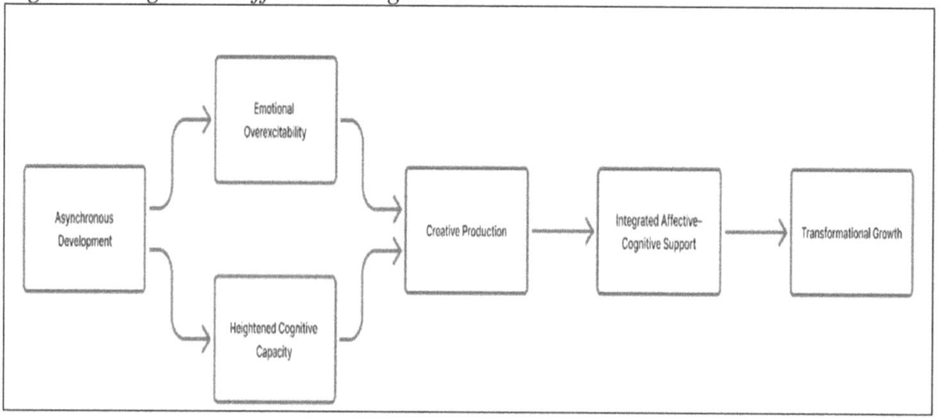

Leveraging Technology Responsibly: AI as Augmentation, Not Determinant

Artificial intelligence now sits at an inflection point in educational design. As Luckin (2018) argues, AI can serve as a powerful augmentation tool, supporting personalized trajectories, early detection of mismatch, and continuous formative feedback. Properly used, machine learning systems can identify when a learner is under challenged, track growth across domains, and propose next steps aligned with mastery rather than age. But the ethics of implementation matter. Williamson and Eynon (2020) caution that educational AI is not neutral; it reflects the assumptions and data structures from which it is built. Algorithmic systems trained on biased samples risk reproducing inequity at scale. For gifted learners, whose profiles already defy normative patterns, algorithms can misread outlier data as error rather than signal.

Responsible AI in the parallel system therefore follows three non-negotiable:

- Transparency in how recommendations are generated;
- Human in the loop design, where educators remain interpretive authorities;
- Bias auditing, ensuring demographic parity in recommendations and assessment.

When AI is conceptualized as accountability rather than automation, it becomes a tool for structural equity. It can help monitor who is being under challenged, who is being overlooked, and which interventions sustain long term engagement. But it cannot replace the pedagogical judgment necessary for supporting complex, nonlinear development.

From Identification Event to Continuous Process

A continuous identification model mitigates these limitations. At a structural level, several policy mechanisms support equity. Universal screening increases identification among underserved populations (Peters et al., 2023). Sustained professional development enables teachers to recognize diverse presentations of giftedness. Transparent accountability structures track representation across demographic groups. Teacher certification requirements that include gifted education reduce the mismatch between expectations and training.

Assessment as Information System: Beyond Gatekeeping

Assessment in this context cannot remain a gatekeeping mechanism. It must function as a continuous information system. When teachers engage as designers rather than implementers, the assessment environment becomes part of the developmental architecture (Hargreaves & Fullan, 2012). Professional learning communities and digital mentorship networks allow educators to share expertise, analyse learner trajectories, and refine instructional decisions in real time. When educators experience personalized learning structures themselves, their capacity for pedagogical empathy strengthens. A modern assessment system captures both academic and affective outcomes. Multimodal portfolios, learner narratives, mentor documentation, and community feedback provide a textured evidence base. Integrating qualitative patterns with quantitative indicators acknowledges that cognitive development is inseparable from emotional and motivational states (Csikszentmihalyi, 1990).

A modern assessment system captures both academic and affective outcomes. Multimodal portfolios, learner narratives, mentor documentation, and community feedback provide a textured evidence base. Integrating qualitative patterns with quantitative indicators acknowledges that cognitive development is inseparable from emotional and motivational states (Csikszentmihalyi, 1990). Periodic ecosystem audits can track diversity, accessibility, wellbeing, and pedagogical alignment. To support such an ecosystem, assessment must shift from event to process. Rather than determining who "qualifies," assessment in the parallel system answers a different set of questions:

- What does this learner need now?
- Under what conditions do their strengths emerge?
- Where does challenge align with developmental readiness?
- What forms of expression best reveal their thinking?

Wiliam (2011) notes that formative assessment is the most powerful driver of learning when feedback is specific, actionable, and embedded. In a parallel architecture, assessment becomes a continuous conversation. Multi modal portfolios, mentor logs, student narratives, and community feedback form a rich evidence base that values qualitative insight alongside quantitative progress. For twice exceptional learners, assessment highlights the interplay between capability and support needs. A student who performs poorly on timed writing tasks but excels in oral analysis is not inconsistent; they are multidimensional. Assessment ceases to be a gate. It becomes a map.

Figure 4. Educational Design

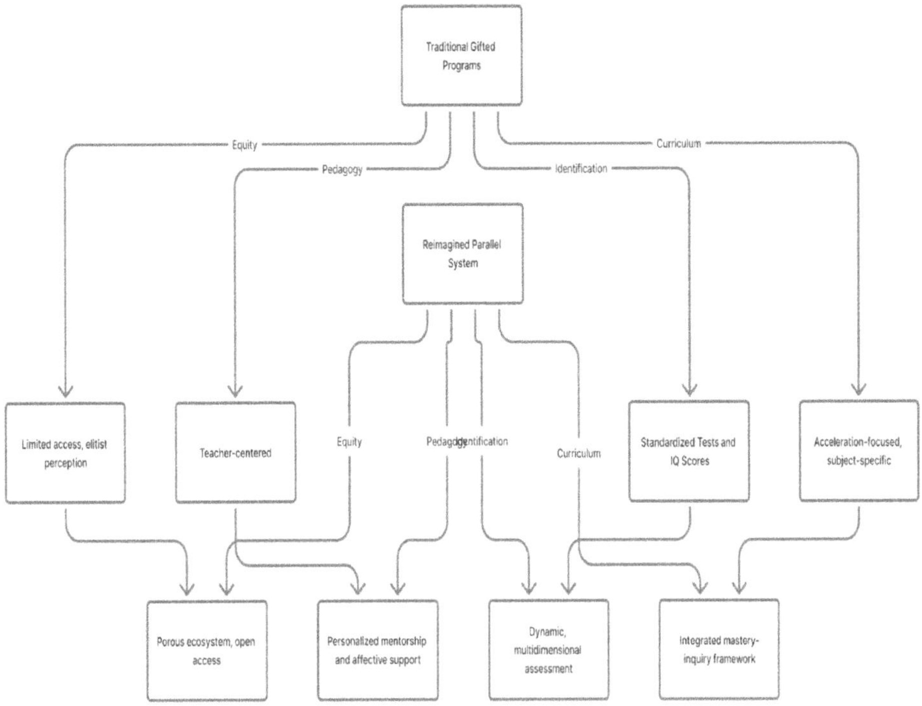

CONCLUSION

From a Problem of Practice to a Challenge of Educational Design: This chapter advances the premise that the enduring difficulties in serving gifted and twice-exceptional learners do not stem from shortcomings in day-to-day practice, but rather from a deeper misalignment in the design of educational systems themselves. Linear, standardized frameworks remain fundamentally incompatible with the diverse, nonlinear developmental trajectories inherent in neurodivergent learners. Addressing these mismatches calls for more than incremental or programmatic fixes; it demands a shift toward architectural innovation as exemplified by the proposed parallel framework, grounded in Personalization, Mastery, Inquiry, and Mentorship. Central to this argument is the conviction that efforts to merely accommodate developmental variance within a rigid infrastructure are inherently limited. The parallel architecture reframes intensity, asynchrony, and exceptionality as organizing principles for educational ecosystems, warranting systemic redesign rather than temporary adjustment. The intent of this theoretical model is to catalyse a movement from retrofitting solutions to fundamentally re-envisioning the environments in which learners grow. The complexity of redesigning educational systems cannot be overstated. Nevertheless, sustainable transformation is possible and necessary, echoing the broader educational reform literature that underscores the futility of isolated interventions in the face of systemic misalignment (Fullan, 2015; Tyack & Cuban, 1995). Realigning educational design for high-functioning and twice-exceptional learners is not a peripheral task, but a recognition of developmental diversity as the prevailing norm (Silverman, 2013).

A Glimpse into a Day Inside the four-by-four Parallel System: Morning begins without bells. Students arrive in staggered rhythms, some drawn to tables, others to the garden, others to studios or laboratories. The atmosphere is quiet but concentrated. Curiosity sets the pace. A student analysing the ethics of artificial intelligence pauses and stares into space, reworking the problem internally. Other sketches a visual model of symmetry, integrating geometry with aesthetic form. Nearby, a group debates a moral dilemma in a classic text, their conversation unhurried and exploratory. Mentors circulate. They do not stand at the front but move alongside learners. One kneels beside a student and asks, "What are you noticing here that you did not see yesterday?" Dialogue, not direction, fosters progression. Difficulty arises, but it is held rather than dismissed. Confusion becomes a site of inquiry. The room's sensory design softens emotional turbulence: natural light, quiet corners, movement spaces. For twice exceptional learners, the classroom responds rather than resists.

REFERENCES

Alias, A., Rahman, S., Abd Majid, R., & Mohd Yassin, S. F. (2013). Dąbrowski's overexcitabilities profile among gifted students. *Asian Social Science*, *9*(16), 120–126. DOI: 10.5539/ass.v9n16p120

Armstrong, T. (2010). *Neurodiversity: Discovering the extraordinary gifts of autism, ADHD, dyslexia, and other brain differences*. Da Capo Press.

Banathy, B. H. (1991). *Systems design of education: A journey to create the future*. Educational Technology Publications.

CAST. (2018). *Universal Design for Learning Guidelines* (Version 2.2). http://udlguidelines.cast.org

Child Mind Institute. (2024). *Twice-exceptional kids: Both gifted and challenged*. https://childmind.org/article/twice-exceptional-kids/

Cholach, J. (2011). *Universal Design for Learning and gifted students in the 21st century classroom* (Master's thesis). University of Lethbridge.

Columbus Group. (1991). *Definition of giftedness* [Unpublished transcript]. https://www.gifteddevelopment.com/definitions-giftedness

Csikszentmihalyi, M. (1990). *Flow: The psychology of optimal experience*. Harper and Row.

Dąbrowski, K. (1964). *Positive disintegration*. Little, Brown.

Dąbrowski, K., Kawczak, A., & Piechowski, M. M. (1972). *Mental growth through positive disintegration*. Gryf.

Daniels, S., & Piechowski, M. M. (Eds.). (2009). *Living with intensity*. Great Potential Press.

Davidson Academy. (2024). *Understanding asynchronous development in gifted children*. https://davidsonacademy.unr.edu/blog/asynchronous-development/

Davidson Institute. (2005). *Social and emotional needs of gifted children*. https://www.davidsongifted.org/gifted-blog/social-and-emotional-needs-of-gifted-children/

Dweck, C. S. (2006). *Mindset*. Random House.

Ericsson, K. A., Krampe, R. T., & Tesch-Römer, C. (1993). Deliberate practice in expert performance. *Psychological Review*, *100*(3), 363–406. DOI: 10.1037/0033-295X.100.3.363

Florida Department of Education. (2018). *Best practices in gifted education*. https://www.fldoe.org/core/fileparse.php/7676/urlt/BestPracticesGifted.pdf

Ford, D. Y. (2014). *Recruiting and retaining culturally different students in gifted education*. Prufrock Press.

Ford, D. Y., Grantham, T. C., & Whiting, G. W. (2021). Equity in gifted education. *Gifted Child Today*, *44*(1), 4–18. DOI: 10.1177/1076217520975531

Gardner, H. (1983). *Frames of mind: The theory of multiple intelligences*. Basic Books.

Grissom, J. A., & Redding, C. (2016). Discretion and disproportionality. *AERA Open*, *2*(1), 1–25. DOI: 10.1177/2332858415622175 PMID: 26942210

Hamachek, D. E. (1978). Psychodynamics of perfectionism. *Psychology: A Journal of Human Behavior, 15*(1), 27–33.

Hargreaves, A., & Fullan, M. (2012). *Professional capital*. Teachers College Press.

IIEP UNESCO. (2019). *Flexible learning pathways in higher education*. UNESCO. https://unesdoc.unesco.org/ark:/48223/pf0000367761

Immordino-Yang, M. H., & Damasio, A. (2007). We feel, therefore we learn. *Mind, Brain and Education : the Official Journal of the International Mind, Brain, and Education Society*, *1*(1), 3–10. DOI: 10.1111/j.1751-228X.2007.00004.x

Iowa Department of Education. (n.d.). *Curriculum compacting*. https://educateiowa.gov/pk-12/learner-supports/talented-gifted/curriculum-compacting

Kim, J., Lee, H., & Cho, Y. H. (2022). Learning design for AI collaboration. *Education and Information Technologies*, *27*, 6069–6104. DOI: 10.1007/s10639-021-10831-6

King, E. V. (2022). Twice-exceptional learners and SEL. *Journal for the Education of the Gifted*, *45*(2), 112–135. DOI: 10.1177/10762175221078945

Lerner, R. M. (2018). *Developmental science*. Routledge., DOI: 10.4324/9781315156123

Lidster, T., & Williams, M. (2012). Dynamic assessment. *Language and Sociocultural Theory*, *1*(1).

Luckin, R. (2018). *Machine learning and human intelligence*. UCL Press.

Medaglia, S. (2008). Gifted adolescents and disintegration. In Mendaglio, S. (Ed.), *Dąbrowski's theory of positive disintegration* (pp. 13–40). Great Potential Press.

Mendaglio, S. (2008). Positive disintegration as developmental. In Mendaglio, S. (Ed.), *Dąbrowski's theory* (pp. 1–12). Great Potential Press.

Ministry of Education. (2020). *National education policy 2020*. Government of India.

National Association for Gifted Children. (2019). *The excellence gap*. https://www.nagc.org/resources-publications/resources-parents/excellence-gap

National Center for Education Research. (2022). Do underrepresented students benefit from gifted programs? https://ies.ed.gov/ncee/rel/regions/northeast/blogs/blog39_underrepresented_gifted.asp

Neihart, M., Reis, S. M., Robinson, N. M., & Moon, S. M. (2021). *The social and emotional development of gifted children*. Prufrock Press.

OECD. (2020). *PISA 2018 results*. OECD Publishing., DOI: 10.1787/5f07c754-

Peters, S. J., Gentry, M., Whiting, G. W., & McBee, M. T. (2023). Who gets served? *Journal of Advanced Academics*, *34*(1), 7–33. DOI: 10.1177/1932202X221124958

Pfeiffer, S. I. (2015). *Essentials of gifted assessment*. Wiley.

Piechowski, M. M. (2006). *Mellow out, they say. If I only could*. Yunasa Books.

Purcell, J. H., & Renzulli, J. S. (1998). *Total talent portfolio*. Creative Learning Press.

Reis, S. M., & Renzulli, J. S. (1992). Using curriculum compacting to challenge the above-average. *Educational Leadership*, *50*, 51–51.

Reis, S. M., Westberg, K. L., Kulikowich, J. M., & Purcell, J. H. (1998). Curriculum compacting outcomes. *Gifted Child Quarterly*, *42*(2), 123–129. DOI: 10.1177/001698629804200206

Renzulli, J. S. (1977). *The enrichment triad model*. Creative Learning Press.

Renzulli, J. S. (1978). What makes giftedness? *Phi Delta Kappan*, *60*(3), 180–184.

Renzulli, J. S., Reis, S. M., & Smith, L. H. (1981). *The revolving door identification model*. Creative Learning Press.

Renzulli, J. S., & Reis, S. M. (1997). The schoolwide enrichment model: New directions for developing high-end learning. Handbook of gifted education, 2, 136-154.

Salovey, P., & Mayer, J. D. (1990). Emotional intelligence. *Imagination, Cognition and Personality*, *9*(3), 185–211.

Silverman, L. K. (2013). *Giftedness 101*. Springer.

Steele, C. M., & Aronson, J. (1995). Stereotype threat. *Journal of Personality and Social Psychology*, *69*(5), 797–811. DOI: 10.1037/0022-3514.69.5.797 PMID: 7473032

Steenbergen-Hu, S., & Moon, S. M. (2011). The effects of acceleration on high-ability learners: A meta-analysis. *Gifted Child Quarterly*, *55*(1), 39–53.

Subotnik, R. F., Olszewski-Kubilius, P., & Worrell, F. C. (2011). Rethinking giftedness. *Psychological Science in the Public Interest*, *12*(1), 3–54. DOI: 10.1177/1529100611418056 PMID: 26168418

Subotnik, R. F., Olszewski-Kubilius, P. E., & Worrell, F. C. (2019). High performance: The central psychological mechanism for talent development.

Tyack, D., & Cuban, L. (1995). *Tinkering with utopia: A century of public school reform*.

Tomlinson, C. A., Kaplan, S. N., Renzulli, J. S., Purcell, J. H., Leppien, J. H., Burns, D. E., Strickland, C. A., & Imbeau, M. B. (2002). *The parallel curriculum*. Corwin Press.

Townsend, C. (2022). *What is mastery-based learning?* Mastery Collaborative. https://mastery.org/what-is-mastery-based-learning/

UNESCO. (2021). *Reimagining our futures together*. UNESCO.

Vygotsky, L. S. (1978). *Mind in society: The development of higher psychological processes*. Harvard University Press.

Webb, J. T., Amend, E. R., Webb, N. E., Goerss, J., Beljan, P., & Olenchak, F. R. (2005). *Misdiagnosis and dual diagnoses of gifted children and adults*. Great Potential Press.

Wiliam, D. (2011). *Embedded formative assessment* (2nd ed.). Solution Tree Press.

Williamson, B., & Eynon, R. (2020). Historical threads of AI in education. *Learning, Media and Technology*, *45*(3), 223–235. DOI: 10.1080/17439884.2020.1798995

KEY TERMS AND DEFINITIONS

Asynchronous Development: The phenomenon where a child's cognitive, emotional, and physical maturation diverge significantly.

Overexcitabilities (OEs): A core concept in TPD referring to innate, heightened responses to stimuli across five dimensions: intellectual, emotional, imaginational, psychomotor, and sensual.

Twice Exceptional (2e): A term describing students who exhibit both high ability (giftedness) and a co-occurring learning disability or difference, such as ADHD, dyslexia, or autism spectrum disorder (ASD).

Chapter 10
From Spiritual Resilience to Professional Achievement:
Mapping the Inner Architecture of Excellence

Sunil Kumar
https://orcid.org/0000-0002-2362-1972
Shoolini University, India

Suchitra S. Sakpal
https://orcid.org/0000-0002-8293-7328
Shoolini University, India

Manjunath B. R.
Shoolini University, India

ABSTRACT

This chapter examines the spiritual resilience and professional achievement, arguing that sustained performance in demanding environments depends on factors beyond effort, skills, and measurable outcomes. In high-pressure contexts marked by constant evaluation and emotional strain, stability often arises from intangible factors such as meaning, belonging, and intrinsic motivation. Spiritual resilience is thus conceptualized at the intersection of workplace spirituality and social belongingness. Grounded in existential theory and resilience research, the model draws on Frankl's view that meaning renders adversity bearable and Bandura's emphasis on agency rooted in self-belief. Self-efficacy is central, translating meaning and

DOI: 10.4018/979-8-3373-2317-6.ch010

connection into action while shaping how effectively support is utilized. High inner trust enables individuals to convert limited support into momentum, whereas low trust can diminish the impact of even substantial support.

INTRODUCTION

Achievement is often measured by promotions or external recognition; however, in practice, it originates from deeper, more intrinsic factors. It encompasses the perseverance that sustains individuals in challenging roles, the moral clarity that informs difficult decisions, and the capacity to approach work with ongoing integrity. When individuals perceive alignment between their labor and personal values, they demonstrate greater engagement and authenticity. Empirical research supports this perspective: employees who experience spiritual congruence in the workplace report higher levels of engagement, ethical sensitivity, and resilience (Obregon et al., 2024).

However, meaning in isolation can become burdensome, potentially manifesting as internal pressure (Walsham et al., 2023). Belonging is therefore essential, as it enables individuals to uphold their values without apprehension. This sense of belonging fosters an environment where meaning is generative rather than depleting. Evidence from educational and healthcare settings illustrates this dynamic: teachers grounded in shared values exhibit higher self-efficacy and stronger connections with students, while nurses in spiritually supportive environments manage stress with greater stability. Thus, belief is not an isolated phenomenon but is reinforced within a community context (Marshall, 2002).

Frankl (2006) posited that pain becomes bearable when reframed through the lens of purpose, emphasizing a realistic rather than romantic perspective. While suffering is an inherent aspect of human experience, individuals are more likely to endure it when it is integrated into a coherent framework of meaning. Existential anxiety as the sense of disconnection that arises when life lacks depth; however, when individuals act in accordance with their core values, this anxiety can be transformed into motivation and purposeful action (Davidov & Russo-Netzer, 2022). Existential theory does not eliminate difficulty but instead reconfigures it, suggesting that engagement, particularly deep, value-aligned, and authentic engagement, is more critical than ease. Furthermore, the theory asserts that genuine belonging accommodates difference. Neff (2003) highlights that self-compassion is cultivated not through comparison but through recognition. When individuals are accepted unconditionally, they develop resilience to persist, even amid uncertainty.

Workplace spirituality extends beyond formal belief systems; it centers on coherence, or the alignment between external roles and internal identity. Organizations that foster such coherence benefit not only from increased productivity but also from enhanced care, innovation, and resilience. Self-efficacy operationalizes this coherence by bridging the gap between values and behaviors. Individuals with strong self-efficacy demonstrate greater persistence, adaptability, and leadership. Additionally, self-efficacy moderates the impact of supportive environments, explaining why some individuals thrive while others do not, despite similar external conditions. This variation is attributed to differences in inner trust (Bandura, 2013). The proposed model does not seek to oversimplify these dynamics; rather, it conceptualizes spirituality as providing direction, belonging as offering safety, and self-efficacy as enabling action. Collectively, these elements constitute the arc of spiritual resilience, representing not a prescriptive formula but a nuanced perspective on human functioning.

Resilience is not a trait one either has or lacks. It is a way of being with difficulty, a way that bends without breaking. As (2014) called it "ordinary magic," and that phrase holds. Resilience is not rare. But it is easily overlooked, especially in high-pressure environments where struggle is hidden behind achievement. This model understands resilience not as a solo act but as something quietly upheld by both inner belief and outer belonging. Spirituality gives direction. Belonging gives ballast. Together, they steady self-efficacy, the belief that one's efforts can shape outcomes.

Bandura (2013) framed self-efficacy as the confidence to act. But confidence is not built in isolation. It is fed by coherence. When students or workers see their efforts as meaningful, they are more likely to persist. When they feel seen by others while persisting, their hope becomes sustainable. This is why spirituality and belonging both matter. Spirituality offers a compass. It turns adversity into purpose. Belonging offers refuge. It keeps that purpose from unravelling in loneliness. Baumeister and Leary (2017) showed that the need to belong is fundamental. Brewer (1991) added that we seek not just connection, but connection that honours difference. Classrooms and workplaces that allow people to be whole, that ask not for perfection but for presence, become places where resilience takes root.

Neuroscience confirms what the psyche already knows: exclusion hurts as much as physical pain (Eisenberger, 2012). Inclusion, then, is not a bonus. It is a buffer. Psychologically safe environments restore energy. They protect the cognitive and emotional bandwidth required for learning, adaptation, and growth. The interplay is subtle but strong. Meaning makes hardship bearable. Belonging makes it shareable. Self-efficacy makes it actionable. Resilience lives in integration.

Empirical research continues to affirm this. Spiritual coping and optimism mediate the link between stress and satisfaction in students. Arslan and Coşkun (2023) showed that school belonging supports academic success through the path of resilience. Baş (2025) noted that learners grounded in meaning withstand pressure better. Each study, in its own way, reflects the same pattern: when people feel purpose and connection, they rise.

Connor and Davidson (2003) resilience scale includes faith, support, and competence. These are not traits but conditions. When they met, they activate what Frankl (2006) called the will to meaning. It is not just the "why" that gets people through the "how." It is also the knowing that the "how" is held by others. This model is a response to that knowledge. It extends the literature by showing how self-efficacy mediates and moderates the impact of spiritual and social anchors. It uses Hayes' conditional process approach not as a technical flourish, but to trace the subtle contours of internal life made visible through action.

THE EXISTENTIAL AND RESILIENCE CONTEXT: AN INTEGRATIVE REFLECTION

Resilience without meaning becomes survival. Meaning without resilience becomes fragility. The integration of the two yields something deeper: sustainable engagement. Frankl (1985) wrote that humans can endure almost any "how" if they have a "why." Masten showed that the "how" is not heroic but habitual. Hope, support, coherence, these are not lofty ideals. They are everyday conditions that keep people in motion. When work or learning environments support meaning, belonging, and agency, they do more than boost performance. They restore humanity to effort. They remind us that thriving is not an individual accomplishment but a relational and existential act.

Belongingness, Social Environment, and Excellence: Belonging is not the same as fitting in. It is the experience of being welcomed without needing to edit oneself. In learning and work settings, this kind of acceptance lays the groundwork for self-efficacy to grow. Payne and Whitworth (2022) found that when classrooms encouraged autonomy, students developed more creative self-efficacy and performed better. Vatou (2025) showed that students who felt connected to their schools showed higher resilience. Edmondson (1999) emphasized that psychological safety, not conformity, predicts persistence.

These studies converge on a single point: excellence does not come from pressure. It comes from presence. When people feel safe to be themselves, they try harder not because they must, but because they can. Social support goes beyond kindness. It lowers stress, which in turn frees up cognitive and emotional capacity for growth. Afzal et al. (2019) found that support increased efficacy, which in turn increased performance. Beddoe et al. (2014) added that supervisor trust bolsters resilience. Again, the pattern repeats: when people are held well, they hold themselves with greater strength. This section traces that arc from safety to effort, from meaning to mastery. Not as isolated phenomena, but as a system of human functioning. A system that does not start with strategy, but with trust.

Payne and Whitworth (2022) showed that something simple had been forgotten. When a learning space welcomes people as they are, without asking them to blend in or hide parts of themselves, students begin to relax into their own strength. Their shoulders drop. Their attention steadies. In that kind of atmosphere, self-efficacy grows almost quietly, the way confidence usually does when no one is forcing it. The old rhythm of the Gurukul carried the same truth. A child learned not only from a teacher but from a community that held them with care and spiritual guidance. That sense of being carried became the ground from which persistence and courage rose. Much of the recent research is simply giving language to what earlier traditions understood through lived experience: when a student feels rooted, their abilities unfold.

A setting that protects authenticity works like a catalyst. It allows self-efficacy to do the work it naturally wants to do, to take support, meaning, encouragement, and turn it into action. It is a gentle form of alchemy that happens only when a person does not feel the need to shrink themselves. Kahu et al. (2020) add another layer to this. Their study suggests that when students feel supported, engagement grows, but the path is not direct. Self-efficacy sits in the middle, shaping how support is absorbed. Students who trust their own abilities feel support more vividly and respond with more energy. It becomes a conversation between the environment and the student's inner world. Other studies echo this. Engagement is the movement that self-efficacy sets in motion, and that movement eventually becomes achievement.

Belonging, too, remains central. The feeling of being accepted and held by a group is not a small factor. It shapes well-being, motivation, and persistence in powerful ways (Jetten et al., 2014). It goes deeper than being welcomed. It has to do with being recognized identity and context meeting without friction (Vaccaro et al., 2024). When learning spaces create this kind of safety, students tend to show up with more of themselves, and their work reflects that wholeness. The same rhythm appears in workplaces. Employees who feel they belong contribute more stability and stay longer. A wide range of studies across cultures confirm this. Environments shaped by shared values, which some describe as workplace spirituality, tend to make belonging feel natural (Barrett, 2010). People work differently when they feel connected to a purpose and to each other.

Belonging is not only emotional. It also helps people understand their place in a larger system. It clarifies how their work fits into the whole. Studies across cultures show that belonging strengthens the impact of spiritual climates, especially where collective identity is valued (Ramesh and Sinnu, 2024). When belonging is thin, even meaningful work can feel heavy. Enthusiasm fades. People begin to detach. Belonging, then, becomes the bridge that carries inner meaning into shared motivation.

Social Belonging and Self-Efficacy: Belonging goes hand in hand with spirituality. It answers a basic human need: to feel held, to feel valued. When that need is met, self-efficacy expands easily (Baumeister and Leary, 2017). Brewer (1991) reminds us that belonging is strongest when individuality is not sacrificed. A person's uniqueness becomes part of the community rather than a threat to it. This is why inclusive, non-conformist environments work so well. Payne and Whitworth (2022) saw that students in such spaces tend to believe more deeply in their ability to act. Connection without pressure builds motivation. Wang and Chen (2025) showed that social support elevates self-efficacy, which, in turn, drives engagement toward achievement. Eisenberger (2012) research explains the weight of this. Social exclusion activates the same neural pathways as physical pain. Belonging is not a soft idea. It protects the mind. It preserves emotional and cognitive clarity, the very things learning demands.

Resilience, Spirituality, and Self-Efficacy: Resilience is the capacity to adapt and continue without losing the thread of oneself. It grows quietly. Spirituality keeps hope from thinning out when life becomes uncertain. Masten called resilience ordinary magic; for this reason, it arises from everyday practices and relationships rather than dramatic acts. Self-efficacy strengthens resilience by steadying the belief that one can act even when the path feels narrow. And resilience supports self-efficacy in return. When a person survives difficulty, they begin to trust their own capacity more deeply (Wall, 2005). Neff (2003) work brings these elements together. Authenticity feeds belonging. Belonging anchors resilience. Resilience returns strength to self-efficacy. Yalom (1980) spoke of the courage to face one's own isolation without losing oneself. That courage is the soil from which these qualities grow together. They do not move in a straight line. They form a living system in which each element feeds and steadies the others. When they are present together, spirituality, belonging, resilience, and self-efficacy performance become more than an outcome. It becomes a humane way of navigating difficulty, with meaning and connection intact.

Resilience and Self-Efficacy: Resilience is described as the ability to return to oneself after uncertainty. It is less a rebound than a quiet re-gathering. In students, this capacity is deeply connected to their sense of self-efficacy. When a learner believes in their own ability, challenges stop feeling like verdicts. They become temporary conditions. Cassidy's work with undergraduates reflected this pattern. Students who carried a stronger sense of academic self-efficacy were steadier in the face of difficulty. They approached setbacks with a kind of inner permission that allowed them to continue. The relationship moves in both ways. Resilience can strengthen the effect of self-efficacy just as self-efficacy supports resilience. Cassidy (2015) found that when graduate students had higher resilience, the protective influence of self-efficacy against stress grew more pronounced. Confidence arrives as one strand. Resilience holds the strand in place when pressure rises. Wang and Chen (2025) observed a similar movement: resilience intensified the way social support shaped self-efficacy by reducing stress. What emerges across these studies is a loop of mutual nourishment. Self-efficacy lifts resilience, and resilience deepens self-efficacy. It echoes an older understanding found in Vedic thought, where inner strength, tapas, is not separate from the belief that one is capable. Together, they help a student return to effort with steadiness and hope.

Belonging and Resilience: Belonging sits at the core of human motivation. It shapes not only emotion but the very conditions under which learning becomes possible (Baumeister and Leary, 2017). Brewer (1991) principle of optimal distinctiveness reminds us that people long for connection without losing themselves in the process. When academic environments honor this tension, students hold both their individuality and their membership. Neuroscience confirms how deeply embodied this need is. Eisenberger (2012) showed that social exclusion activates neural pathways like those activated by physical pain. It explains why belonging feels like oxygen and why its absence narrows a student's capacity to think, create, or persist. Spiritual communities and classrooms that cultivate psychological safety act as buffers. They protect the cognitive resources on which resilience depends. Resilience theory places spirituality and belonging side by side. Connor and Davidson (2003) identified faith, social support, and personal competence as central predictors of positive adjustment. Spirituality nourishes meaning. Belonging stabilizes emotion. Together, they turn stress into mastery and allow long-term effort to feel less isolating.

ORGANIZATIONAL IMPERATIVES: STRUCTURAL CHANGE, SPIRITUAL INTEGRATION, AND MEANING

Workplaces are living through a period of profound change. Globalization, climate pressures, rapid technological acceleration, and the blurring of the boundary between personal and professional life have reshaped how people work and what they expect from work (Nayak, et al., 2025). In this shifting landscape, spirituality is emerging not as an ornament but as a stabilizing force. A growing body of research describes workplace spirituality as a developing paradigm that encourages ethical behavior, creativity, empowerment, and a sense of meaning within everyday tasks (Fry, 2008).

At its core, workplace spirituality reflects the alignment between personal values, meaningful work, and a sense of community (Petchsawang and Duchon, 2012). Studies continue to show its relevance. It predicts well-being, eases emotional labor, and supports resilience, decision making, and balance between work and life. In India, findings echo these conclusions. WPS correlates strongly with emotional, social, psychological, and spiritual well-being and continues to predict commitment and satisfaction even when other variables are controlled (Sharma & Garg, 2024). Scholars caution against turning spirituality into doctrine. It must not impose belief or exclude those who differ. As organizations navigate disruption, the invitation is not to manage spirituality but to make space for meaning, coherence, and inner life. These are the conditions that protect individuals from fragmentation during times of change.

The Evolving Need for Holistic Performance Models: Professional and academic environments now operate in an unrelenting state of complexity. Speed, competition, and uncertainty have become common ground. Traditional models that treat motivation as a linear additive force fall short in explaining how people sustain performance in such conditions. Workplace studies show that the turbulence shaped by global shifts and artificial intelligence demands something more integrative, something that recognizes the inner world as part of professional functioning. Spirituality becomes a stabilizing axis in this landscape. When people experience their work as meaningful or value-aligned, their motivation becomes sustainable. Engagement rises. Commitment deepens. These outcomes are well documented. They reinforce the need for models that capture the dynamic interplay between the forces of meaning, belonging, resilience, and self-efficacy, which do not operate in separate channels but in quiet relation with one another.

Identification of the Research Gap and Theoretical Contribution: The existing literature is rich in evidence connecting spiritual well-being, self-efficacy, and performance. Studies show that spiritually supportive environments increase teachers' self-efficacy and improve both academic and professional outcomes. Other studies show that self-efficacy fully mediates the relationship between spiritual well-being and work-family satisfaction.

However, most research stops at correlation or simple mediation. What remains missing is a conditional model, one that acknowledges that the benefits of spirituality depend on a person’s existing confidence and adaptive capacity. Meaning may inspire, but its impact varies depending on how safe, supported, or capable the individual feels. Without capturing these conditional effects, the inner logic behind sustained performance remains partially hidden.

The central contribution of this paper is to offer a Conditional Process Model that recognizes the dual movement of self-efficacy. It acts as a mediator, carrying the effects of spirituality and belonging toward achievement. It also acts as a moderator, shaping the strength of those effects based on a person's level of grounding or resilience. This moderated mediation framework provides the conceptual clarity needed to advance psychological capital research and makes a case for the analytic precision of conditional process modelling (Hayes, 2013).

METHODOLOGY

This study adopts a conceptual approach. It does not generate primary data or test hypotheses. Its purpose is to clarify a psychological process that emerges across multiple bodies of scholarship but is rarely examined as an integrated whole. The framework was developed through close engagement with established literature in psychology, organizational studies, resilience research, and existential theory. Sources were selected for conceptual relevance rather than breadth. Studies on meaning, agency, belonging, and sustained functioning under pressure were read alongside contemporary research to identify recurring patterns and unresolved tensions. Analysis focused on synthesis rather than comparison. Concepts were treated as dynamic processes operating within individuals, rather than as isolated constructs. Attention was given to how meaning, social connection, and perceived agency interact under demanding conditions. Across this literature, self-efficacy repeatedly appeared as a decisive point of variation. In some contexts, it enabled individuals to translate inner conviction and social support into action. In others, it constrained that translation. This dual function informed the conditional structure of the proposed model. No human participants or primary data were involved. Formal ethical approval was therefore not required.

REVIEW OF FOUNDATIONAL CONSTRUCTS

Professional Achievement: Beyond Material Success

Professional achievement is more than advancement or recognition. It is the alignment between personal values and an organization's larger aims. When individuals feel this coherence, their work becomes an expression of who they are rather than an external demand. Research shows that such alignment predicts satisfaction, engagement, and long-term commitment. These qualities precede achievement more reliably than technical competence alone. Spiritually oriented professionals carry certain strengths into their roles. They tend to lead with clarity, solve conflicts with empathy, and inspire through presence as much as through skill. These qualities grow from meaning, not from ambition. They reflect the deeper dividends of workplace spirituality: a sense of purpose that supports both personal flourishing and organizational life.

Workplace Spirituality: Meaning, Community, and Values

Workplace Spirituality has been described in many academic ways; its essence is simple. It is the feeling that one's work and one's inner life are not strangers to each other. It rests on three strands. Work must carry meaning. There must be a sense of community. And the values of the individual must align with those of the institution (Petchsawang and Duchon, 2012; Milliman et al., 2003). When these pieces fall into place, work stops feeling like a performance and becomes participation in something coherent. In such environments, ethical clarity grows almost naturally. When personal values and organizational values align, people do not spend their inner energy negotiating contradictions. The day feels less divided. This alignment protects self-efficacy and resilience because the mind is no longer occupied with hiding or adjusting itself. It can engage fully. The spiritual needs of employees are not ornamentation. They are part of what enables a person to work steadily and with integrity.

Self-Efficacy: The Quiet Engine of Effort

Self-efficacy, shaped by Bandura's long body of work, is the simple belief that one can act and that one's action will matter. It is a powerful predictor of performance, satisfaction, and persistence. In both clinical and organizational settings, people with stronger self-efficacy tend to stay engaged longer and trust their own problem-solving. Spirituality supports this belief from underneath. It gives people a way to see their struggles as part of a meaningful path rather than as indictments of their character. For many, religious or spiritual practices strengthen self-control and conviction. They create a stable inner place from which effort becomes possible. When meaning holds a difficult moment, the moment does not collapse into inadequacy. It becomes part of a larger arc.

Table 1. Key Constructs and Foundational Definitions

Construct	Definition	Literature Reference(s)
Professional Achievement	The attainment of career-related goals, recognition, and advancement driven by intrinsic engagement and value alignment.	Milliman et al. (2003)
Workplace Spirituality (WPS)	The alignment of personal core values, the experience of meaningful work, and a sense of community within the organizational context.	Milliman et al. (2003); Petchsawang & Duchon (2012)
Self-Efficacy	An individual's belief in their capacity to execute behavior is necessary to produce specific performance attainments.	Bandura (2013)

continued on following page

Table 1. Continued

Construct	Definition	Literature Reference(s)
Belongingness	The fundamental human motive to feel accepted, valued, and connected in a group while preserving individuality	Baumeister & Leary (2017); Brewer (1991)
Resilience	The adaptive capacity to rebound from adversity or stress through protective processes such as hope, optimism, and social connection.	Connor & Davidson (2003)

Source: Compiled by author(s)

The conceptual model is synthesized using three complementary theoretical perspectives: Existential theory, the Relational need for Belonging, and Resilience theory.

The Existential Context: Purpose and the Will to Meaning

Frankl wrote that the human spirit finds its strength in purpose. His logotherapy rests on the idea that people can endure almost anything when they believe their struggle serves a real purpose. In academic or organizational life, this translates into an important truth. When individuals feel their tasks are meaningful, motivation rises from within rather than from pressure.

Yalom added that existential anxiety can either paralyze or move a person. When work aligns with inner values, anxiety becomes movement. When work contradicts values, it becomes depletion. Workplace Spirituality offers a way for ordinary tasks to carry existential coherence. The individual does not give more of themselves because they are forced to. They give more because the work resonates with something internal.

The Relational Context: Optimal Belongingness

Alongside spirituality sits belonging. Humans ache for connection. They want to feel part of something without losing themselves in the process. Baumeister and Leary (2017) wrote with clarity about this need. Brewer (1991) extended the idea, reminding us that belonging without individuality is suffocation, and individuality without belonging is loneliness. The body itself confirms this. Eisenberger (2012) showed that social exclusion activates the same pathways as physical pain. Belonging protects not only emotion but cognition. In inclusive environments, students and employees preserve the mental energy needed for learning and work. Spiritual climates naturally nurture belonging because shared meaning becomes a common language. Spirituality stops being a private belief and becomes a shared strength.

The Adaptive Context: Resilience and Spiritual Resilience

Resilience is the capacity to recover, to adapt, to continue with hope. Masten called it ordinary magic because it arises from everyday sources like connection, meaning, and inner steadiness. Spirituality nurtures these forces by offering continuity during uncertainty. It keeps a person anchored. When meaning and resilience come together, they form what this paper calls Spiritual Resilience. Meaning provides direction. Resilience provides duration. One without the other is incomplete. Meaning without resilience becomes fragile. Resilience without meaning becomes mechanical endurance. Connor and Davidson (2003) showed that faith, social support, and competence reinforce each other. Together, they turn stress into mastery and open the path for long-term growth.

The Proposed Conditional Process Framework

The model proposed here rests on a simple layered insight. Spiritual Resilience is the unified force that shapes achievement. It grows from the existential coherence of Workplace Spirituality and the relational grounding of Belongingness. These two together give a person both their direction and their capacity to continue.

- ***Self-Efficacy as Mediator:*** Self-efficacy becomes the bridge through which meaning and belonging turn into action. Work carries a way through spirituality. Belonging protects the mind and reduces distress. Self-efficacy takes these inner conditions and moves them into behavior: persistence, attention, and motivation. Studies already show this pathway. When people feel spiritually grounded, self-efficacy lifts, and outcomes follow.
- ***Self-Efficacy as Moderator:*** Self-efficacy also shapes the strength of these relationships. When confidence is high, support and belonging have a stronger impact. Students who trust their abilities feel teacher support as encouragement rather than pressure. Resilient individuals with strong self-belief experience the greatest buffering against stress. Without self-efficacy, belonging cannot fully do its work. Without confidence, resilience cannot reach its full effect. This makes self-efficacy a conditional force rather than a simple linear factor.

Why is a Conditional Process Model Needed?

These movements cannot be captured by single-path models. The relationships shift depending on how much confidence a person carries. Standard regression cannot hold these conditions. A moderated mediation model, like those described by

Hayes, allows the complexity to be honored rather than flattened. It gives statistical shape to what human experience already shows: meaning, belonging, resilience, and confidence do not act in isolation but in constant quiet conversation.

Figure 1. Conceptual Structure of the Conditional Process Model (Created by author using AI) Note: The flow of the full model integrates WPS and Belonging as inputs to Spiritual Resilience, with Self-Efficacy mediating the main path (X Y) and moderating the relational path (Z M2), requiring advanced statistical analysis.

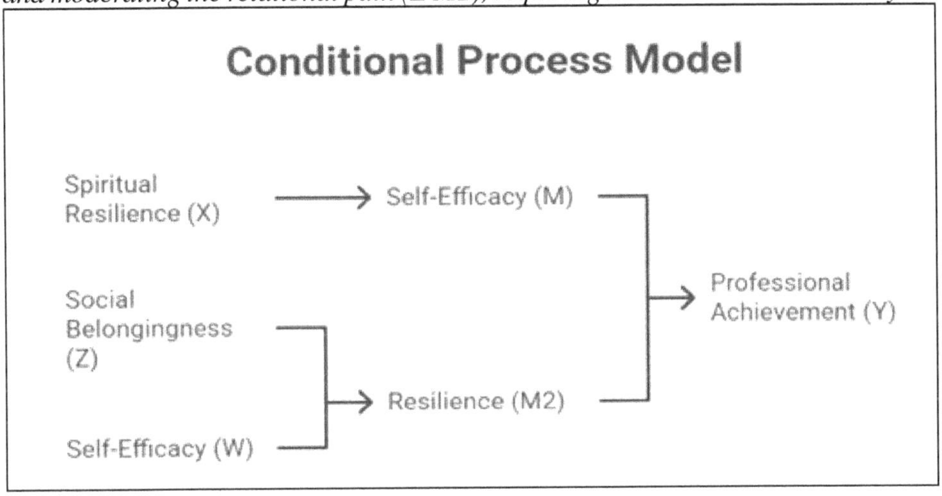

- **Main Independent Variables (Antecedents):** Spiritual Resilience (WPS/Meaning) and Social Belongingness (Relational Safety).
- **Dual Role Variable (Mediator/Moderator):** Self-Efficacy.
- **Outcome Variable:** Professional Achievement.

Figure 2. Flowchart of the dual-function conditional process model

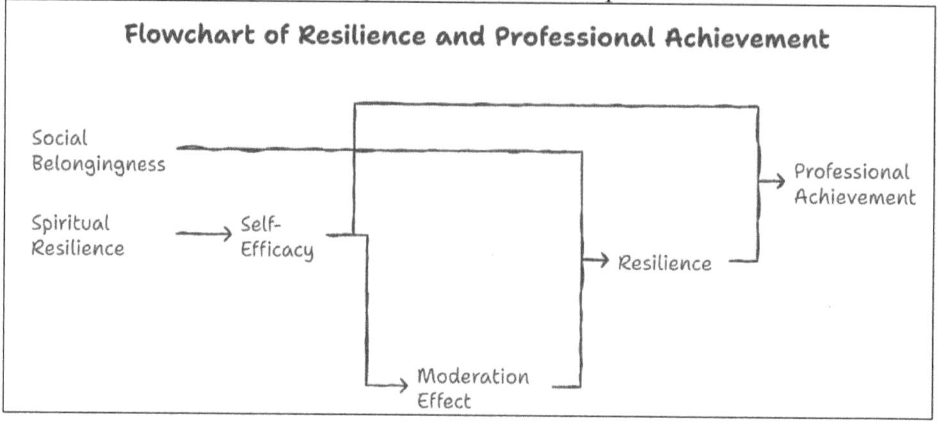

The flowchart structure illustrates:

Path 1 (Mediation): Spiritual Resilience (WPS/Meaning) right arrow Self-Efficacy right arrow Professional Achievement.
Path 2 (Relational/Resilience): Social Belongingness right arrow Resilience right arrow Professional Achievement.
Path 3 (Moderation/Catalysis): An arrow from Self-Efficacy points to the arrow connecting Social Belongingness right arrow Resilience, indicating that high Self-Efficacy strengthens or amplifies the protective effect of belonging on adaptive capacity. This is the crucial conditional effect (Moderated Mediation) that the paper is proposing.

Figure 3. Theoretical propositions for empirical testing

Based on the preceding conceptual analysis, the following theoretical propositions are advanced for future empirical validation:

Table 2. Theoretical Propositions factors

Proposition Number	Proposition Statement	Causal Mechanism & Core Reference
P1	Spiritual Resilience (WPS and Existential Meaning) is positively related to Professional Achievement.	Intrinsic motivation derived from meaning pursuit (Frankl, 2006).
P2 (Mediation of Meaning)	Self-Efficacy fully or partially mediates the positive relationship between Spiritual Resilience and Professional Achievement.	Self-Efficacy acts as the psychological bridge converting purpose into persistent motivation (Bandura, 2013).
P3 (Relational Antecedent)	Social Belongingness is positively related to both Self-Efficacy and Resilience.	Relational safety buffers stress, preserving cognitive resources necessary for high efficacy (Eisenberger, 2012).
P4 (Resilience Pathway)	Resilience significantly mediates the link between Social Belongingness and sustained Professional Achievement.	Belonging provides the social support component of adaptive functioning.
P5 (Reinforcement)	Self-Efficacy and Resilience positively reinforce each other in a self-sustaining loop.	Confidence fosters persistence; successful adaptation strengthens confidence (An et al., 2025).
P6 (Moderated Pathway - The Catalytic Effect)	The positive relationship between Social Belongingness and Resilience is significantly strengthened when Self-Efficacy is high, demonstrating a positive efficacy $\times$ environment interaction.	High efficacy enables individuals to actively leverage environmental support and protective factors (Zhu & Tingting, 2025).
P7 (Conditional Process)	The indirect effect of Social Belongingness on Professional Achievement via Resilience is conditional upon the level of Self-Efficacy (Moderated Mediation).	This confirms the dynamic, non-linear interaction required for true Spiritual Resilience.

Source: Compiled by author(s)

DISCUSSION AND IMPLICATIONS

This work began with a simple intuition. People do not sustain high performance through effort alone. Something quieter holds them. Something that comes from meaning, from connection, from the small inner steadiness that allows a person to stay with their work when it becomes difficult. Over time, that intuition shaped itself into what this paper calls Spiritual Resilience.

The model brings together ideas that have long lived in separate corners of psychology. Existential writings speak about purpose. Relational theories speak about belonging. Research is about adaptation. When placed next to one another, these strands reveal a pattern. Performance becomes sustainable only when meaning, connection, and resilience move together.

Self-efficacy sits at the centre of this movement. It is the part of the psyche that turns quiet inner strength into action. It is also the part that decides how much support a person can use. Meaning without confidence can feel abstract. Support without confidence can feel distant. Resilience without confidence can feel like a struggle without direction. When these elements come together, they create a fuller picture of how human beings continue.

This is why conditional process modelling is needed. The relationships do not unfold evenly. They depend on the person who carries them. Some people can take a small amount of support and turn it into momentum. Others need more safety before they can act. Confidence shapes the effectiveness of belonging and meaning. Modelling this conditionality makes the complexity visible rather than flattening it.

Managerial and Educational Implications

The ideas here offer guidance for those responsible for workplaces or learning environments.

- *Holding Meaning as a Core Element:* In institutions facing rapid change, people need more than clear instructions. They need to feel that their work has coherence. When organizations invite conversations about values and purpose, individuals find a steadier footing. They spend less energy negotiating internal conflicts and more energy creating, thinking, and relating. Meaning becomes a subtle form of ethical grounding. It supports integrity without enforcement.
- *Creating Belonging Without Demanding Sameness:* Belonging cannot be reduced to team building or surface-level friendliness. It asks for an atmosphere that respects individuality. Brewer's principle, the pull between inclusion and uniqueness, remains a helpful reminder. A person cannot flourish where they must hide. Nor can they flourish in isolation. Environments that maintain this balance allow people to recover more easily from stress and stay engaged in their work or studies.
- *Strengthening Self-Efficacy:* Self-efficacy is what allows meaning and belonging to become movement. Institutions can support this by offering training that builds confidence slowly and steadily, especially during times of transition. Spiritual development practices, reflective sessions, mentoring, and skill-based reinforcement can help individuals trust their own capacity. Because confidence shapes how support is absorbed, investing in self-efficacy increases the effectiveness of all other efforts.

Limitations and Future Directions

This paper offers a conceptual frame. Its strength is in bringing ideas together, not in verifying them. The next steps belong to empirical research. Multi-wave designs, longitudinal studies, and conditional process analyses are needed to capture the repeated loops between self-efficacy, resilience, and engagement. There is also more to learn about how culture shapes these relationships. Early findings show that belonging amplifies spiritual meaning differently across contexts. Some cultures locate meaning within the individual. Others locate it within the community. Understanding these subtleties will help refine the model and make it more responsive to real human variation.

CONCLUSION

This chapter proposes *Spiritual Resilience* as an integrative explanation for how individuals sustain engagement and performance over time, particularly under conditions of uncertainty and strain. By bringing together meaning, belonging, and adaptive resilience, and positioning self-efficacy as the central mechanism that translates these inner resources into sustained action, the model moves beyond effort-based accounts of performance toward a more coherent and humane understanding of continuity at work and in learning. Its key contribution lies in highlighting the conditional nature of these relationships: meaning and belonging do not operate uniformly but gain force through an individual's confidence in their own capacity to act, use support, and persist. Although the framework is conceptual and awaits empirical validation through longitudinal and conditional process research, it offers a valuable lens for organizations and educational institutions seeking to foster not just productivity, but endurance, integrity, and human flourishing, by aligning inner coherence with external demands.

REFERENCES

Afzal, S., Arshad, M., Saleem, S., & Farooq, O. (2019). The impact of perceived supervisor support on employees' turnover intention and task performance: Mediation of self-efficacy. *Journal of Management Development, 38*(5), 369–382.

An, R., Qian, G., Mumtaz, A., Alotaibi, K. A., & Wang, X. (2025). Digital fatigue and academic resilience among university students with grit and flexibility as mediators. *Scientific Reports*.

Arslan, G., & Coşkun, M. (2023). School belongingness in academically at-risk adolescents: Addressing psychosocial functioning and psychological well-being. *Journal of Happiness and Health, 3*(1), 1–13.

As, M. (2014). *Ordinary magic: Resilience in development*. Guilford Press. [Google Scholar]

Bandura, A. (2013). Self-Efficacy: The foundation of agency1. In *Control of human behavior, mental processes, and consciousness* (pp. 16-30). Psychology Press.

Barrett, R. (2010). Culture and consciousness: Measuring spirituality in the workplace by mapping values. In *Handbook of workplace spirituality and organizational performance* (pp. 271–291). Routledge.

Baş, G. (2025). How to improve academic achievement of students? The influence of academic emphasis on academic achievement with the mediating roles of school belonging, student engagement, and academic resilience. *Psychology in the Schools, 62*(1), 313–335.

Baumeister, R. F., & Leary, M. R. (2017). The need to belong: Desire for interpersonal attachments as a fundamental human motivation. *Interpersonal development*, 57-89.

Beddoe, L., Davys, A. M., & Adamson, C. (2014). 'Never trust anybody who says "i don't need supervision"': Practitioners' beliefs about social worker resilience. *Practice, 26*(2), 113–130.

Brewer, M. B. (1991). On being the same and different at the same time. *Personality and Social Psychology Bulletin, 17*(5), 475–482.

Cassidy, S. (2015). Resilience building in students: The role of academic self-efficacy. *Frontiers in Psychology, 6*, 1781.

Connor, K. M., & Davidson, J. R. (2003). Development of a new resilience scale: The Connor-Davidson resilience scale (CD-RISC). *Depression and Anxiety, 18*(2), 76–82.

Davidov, J., & Russo-Netzer, P. (2022). Exploring the phenomenological structure of existential anxiety as lived through transformative life experiences. *Anxiety, Stress, and Coping*, *35*(2), 232–247.

Edmondson, A. (1999). Psychological safety and learning behavior in work teams. *Administrative Science Quarterly*, *44*(2), 350–383.

Eisenberger, N. I. (2012). The pain of social disconnection: Examining the shared neural underpinnings of physical and social pain. *Nature Reviews. Neuroscience*, *13*(6), 421–434.

Frankl, V. E. (1985). *Man's search for meaning*. Simon and Schuster.

Frankl, V. E. (2006). *Man's search for meaning*. Beacon Press. (Original work published 1946)

Fry, L. W. (2008). Spiritual leadership: State-of-the-art and future directions for theory, research, and practice. In *Spirituality in business: Theory, practice, and future directions* (pp. 106–124). Palgrave Macmillan US.

Hayes, A. F. (2013). Mediation, moderation, and conditional process analysis. *Introduction to mediation, moderation, and conditional process analysis: A regression-based approach, 1*(6), 12-20.

Jetten, J., Haslam, C., Haslam, S. A., Dingle, G., & Jones, J. M. (2014). How groups affect our health and well-being: The path from theory to policy. *Social Issues and Policy Review*, *8*(1), 103–130.

Kahu, E. R., Picton, C., & Nelson, K. (2020). Pathways to engagement: A longitudinal study of the first-year student experience in the educational interface. *Higher Education*, *79*(4), 657–673.

Marshall, D. A. (2002). Behavior, belonging, and belief: A theory of ritual practice. *Sociological Theory*, *20*(3), 360–380.

Milliman, J., Czaplewski, A. J., & Ferguson, J. (2003). Workplace spirituality and employee work attitudes: An exploratory empirical assessment. *Journal of Organizational Change Management*, *16*(4), 426–447.

Nayak, S., Budhwar, P., & Malik, A. (2025). Technostress of HR professionals: The darker implication of remote work transformations. *International Journal of Human Resource Management*, •••, 1–46.

Neff, K. (2003). Self-compassion: An alternative conceptualization of a healthy attitude toward oneself. *Self and Identity*, *2*(2), 85–101.

Obregon, S. L., Lopes, L. F. D., Silva, W. V. D., Silva, D. J. C. D., Castro, B. L. G. D., Kuhn, N., & Veiga, C. P. D. (2024). The influence of spirituality in the relationship between religiosity and work engagement: A perspective on social responsibility. *Social Responsibility Journal, 20*(10), 1909–1934.

Payne, S. M., & Whitworth, D. E. (2022). Increasing creative self-efficacy: Developing the confidence of biochemistry undergraduates to innovate. *Biochemistry and Molecular Biology Education, 50*(3), 296–306.

Petchsawang, P., & Duchon, D. (2012). Workplace spirituality, meditation, and work performance. *Journal of Management, Spirituality & Religion, 9*(2), 189–208.

Ramesh, A. B. K., & Sinnu, B. (2024). Enhancing workplace spirituality for higher education academicians through human resource practices. *IIMT Journal of Management, 1*(1), 88–97.

Sharma, N., & Garg, N. (2024). Workplace spirituality and organisational effectiveness in the Indian higher education sector: Exploring the relationship and mediating role of positive organisational scholarship factors. *International Journal of Indian Culture and Business Management, 32*(3), 413–439.

Vaccaro, A., Moore, A., Newman, B. M., & Troiano, P. F. (2024). How Students with Disabilities Cope with Bullying, Stereotypes, Low Expectations and Discouragement. *Journal of Postsecondary Education and Disability, 37*(2), 99–113.

Vatou, A. (2025). Examining Resilience, Self-Efficacy and Environmental Chaos Relationship in Early Childhood Education and Care Teachers. *Psychological Inquiry, 7*(3), 73.

Wall, C. L. (2005). *The courage to trust: A guide to building deep and lasting relationships*. New Harbinger Publications.

Walsham, W., Perlman, T. T., & Sihotang, D. (2023). Unraveling the threads: A comprehensive exploration of the interplay be-tween social isolation and academic stress among students. *Law and Economics, 17*(3), 237–255.

Wang, L., & Chen, C. J. (2025). Factors Affecting Student Academic Performance: A Systematic Review. [IJonSE]. *International Journal on Studies in Education, 7*(1).

Zhu, P., & Tingting, W. (2025). A mixed-methods exploration of social networks, self-efficacy, and life satisfaction in rural Chinese high schools. *Frontiers in Psychology, 16*, 1501328.

Chapter 11
Building Resilience in Zillennial:
Hypnotherapeutic Strategies for Stress Management, Authenticity, and Workplace Relationships

Aditi Kalpeshbhai Nanda
https://orcid.org/0009-0003-0259-317X
Shoolini University, India

ABSTRACT

Today's workplaces create unprecedented challenges for young professionals, particularly Zillennials. This chapter explores how clinical hypnotherapy addresses stress, burnout, identity struggles, and relationship difficulties among business professionals. The author examines how hypnotherapy engages subconscious mechanisms maintaining chronic stress, people-pleasing, impostor syndrome, and digital hyperconnectivity. Unlike surface-level wellness programs, hypnotherapy facilitates experiential change at emotional levels, enabling sustainable resilience. This chapter presents practical applications and offers guidance for clinicians and organizational leaders.

1. INTRODUCTION

The world of work has changed dramatically over the past two decades. What we see today-remote meetings, constant email notifications, performance metrics tracking every keystroke-would have seemed almost dystopian to professionals working in the 1990s. Yet here we are, navigating workplaces that demand not just

DOI: 10.4018/979-8-3373-2317-6.ch011

competence, but constant availability, emotional intelligence, and an ever-evolving skill set.

For young professionals straddling the Millennial and Gen Z divide-the so-called Zillennials (Gabrielsen & Lindström, 2021)-this pressure feels particularly acute. They entered the workforce during or after the 2008 financial crisis, came of age watching their parents struggle with job security, and now face expectations that seem to multiply by the year. Be productive. Be authentic. Build your personal brand. Stay connected. Never stop learning. The list goes on.

The mental health consequences are becoming impossible to ignore. Anxiety isn't just common among business professionals anymore-it's almost expected. Burnout has shifted from being a buzzword to a legitimate health crisis recognized by the World Health Organization (2022). And perhaps most tellingly, younger workers report feeling exhausted not just from their tasks, but from the constant performance of appearing capable, composed, and continuously improving (Deloitte, 2023).

Many organizations have responded by rolling out wellness programs. Free meditation apps, mental health days, yoga sessions during lunch breaks. These initiatives come from a good place, but they often miss the mark. Teaching someone to breathe deeply doesn't address why they feel like they can't say no to unreasonable demands. A mindfulness workshop won't resolve the deep-seated belief that their worth depends entirely on their output.

This is where hypnotherapy enters the conversation-not as some magical cure-all, but as a tool that works at a different level than most workplace interventions. While traditional counseling helps people understand their patterns intellectually, hypnotherapy accesses the subconscious mechanisms that actually drive those patterns (Lynn & Kirsch, 2006). It's the difference between knowing you should set boundaries and actually being able to enforce them without crippling guilt.

This chapter explores how hypnotherapy can support Zillennial business professionals in building genuine resilience. We'll examine the clinical foundations, investigate the specific pressures this generation faces, and discuss practical applications. The goal isn't to turn professionals into productivity machines-quite the opposite.

2. UNDERSTANDING HYPNOTHERAPY IN PROFESSIONAL SETTINGS

2.1 What Hypnotherapy Actually Is (And Isn't)

Let's clear up some misconceptions right away. Clinical hypnotherapy has nothing to do with stage shows where people cluck like chickens or forget their own names. The American Psychological Association defines hypnosis as a state of focused attention with heightened responsiveness to suggestion (Elkins et al., 2015)-something that happens naturally throughout our day when we're deeply absorbed in a task or driving on autopilot.

What makes clinical hypnotherapy different is its intentional use for therapeutic purposes. During a hypnotherapy session, you're not unconscious or controlled by the therapist. You're more like being in that mental space right before you fall asleep-aware but relaxed, focused but not overthinking. In this state, your critical, analytical mind quiets down just enough to work with the emotional and automatic parts of your brain that usually run the show behind the scenes.

Think about it this way: You might intellectually know that making a mistake at work doesn't mean you're incompetent. But when you actually make that mistake, your body floods with anxiety, your thoughts spiral, and you spend hours replaying the scenario in your mind. That's because the rational understanding hasn't reached the deeper levels where your emotional responses are encoded. Hypnotherapy creates a bridge to those deeper levels (Yapko, 2012).

Modern practitioners rarely use hypnotherapy in isolation. Instead, they integrate it with other therapeutic approaches-cognitive behavioral techniques to reshape thought patterns, psychodynamic work to understand early experiences, mindfulness practices to enhance present-moment awareness. This integrative approach, sometimes called cognitive hypnotherapy, addresses issues from multiple angles simultaneously (Alladin, 2008).

2.2 Why Business Professionals Need More Than Time Management Tips

Business professionals often exist in a strange therapeutic gray zone. They're not clinically depressed or experiencing panic attacks severe enough to seek psychiatric care. But they're not thriving either. They're exhausted, anxious about performance reviews, losing sleep over decisions, and feeling increasingly disconnected from the work that once excited them.

Traditional therapy helps, certainly. But many professionals find themselves frustrated by the pace of change. They understand their patterns, can articulate where their stress comes from, and know what they "should" do differently. Yet the automatic responses persist (Lazarus & Folkman, 1984). The anxiety still spikes before presentations. The inability to stop checking email continues. The guilt about taking time off doesn't budge.

This is where hypnotherapy offers something different. First, it tends to work more quickly. While traditional therapy might take months to shift deep-seated patterns, hypnotherapy can often produce noticeable changes within a handful of sessions

(Alladin & Alibhai, 2007). For professionals juggling demanding schedules, this efficiency matters.

Second, it works experientially rather than just intellectually. Instead of talking about setting boundaries, you might practice saying no in a hypnotic state, feeling what it's like in your body, working through the anxiety that arises, and rehearsing until it feels more natural. This embodied learning translates more readily into real-world situations.

Third, many workplace stress reactions are automatic-conditioned responses built up over years. You don't consciously decide to feel anxious before every meeting with your boss; it just happens. Hypnotherapy accesses the subconscious level where these automatic responses are encoded, making it possible to rewire them at their source.

Finally, hypnotherapy aligns well with the performance-oriented mindset many professionals already have. It's goal-directed, practical, and focused on measurable outcomes like better focus, increased confidence, or improved sleep. This resonates with people who might be skeptical of more exploratory therapeutic approaches.

2.3 Keeping It Ethical and Appropriate

Before we go further, it's crucial to establish some boundaries. Hypnotherapy for business professionals is not meant to be a band-aid slapped over toxic work environments. It shouldn't be used to help someone "cope better" with genuinely abusive management or unreasonable expectations that would break anyone.

It's also not a replacement for psychiatric care when that's what's actually needed. Someone experiencing severe depression, trauma-related symptoms, or thoughts of self-harm needs a different level of intervention than hypnotherapy can provide.

Good hypnotherapy practice requires proper training, credentials, and ethical guidelines. Clients must give informed consent, understanding what hypnotherapy involves and what it doesn't. Confidentiality matters, especially in corporate settings where there might be pressure to share information with employers. And practitioners need to be clear about their scope-knowing when to refer someone to additional support.

Within these ethical boundaries, hypnotherapy can legitimately help professionals manage stress, prevent burnout, build emotional resilience, and develop healthier relationships with their work identity. The key word there is "help"-it's one tool among many, not a cure-all that exempts organizations from creating healthier work cultures.

3. THE UNIQUE PRESSURES FACING ZILLENNIAL PROFESSIONALS

3.1 When Your Worth Becomes Your Output

There's a particular flavor of anxiety that comes from believing your value as a person depends entirely on how much you produce. It's not just about working hard or wanting to excel-it's deeper than that. It's the gnawing sense that if you're not constantly achieving, optimizing, or moving forward, you're essentially worthless.

This isn't paranoia. It's a rational response to a work culture that has, over the past few decades, increasingly conflated personal worth with professional productivity (Kalleberg, 2018). Neoliberal economic thinking has seeped so thoroughly into workplace culture that many young professionals can't remember a time when self-improvement wasn't framed as a personal responsibility rather than something employers should support.

For Zillennials specifically, this pressure carries extra weight. They watched their parents' generation lose jobs, pensions, and security. They graduated into recessions or unstable job markets. The message they absorbed was clear: you're on your own, so you'd better be exceptional. Good enough isn't enough anymore-you need to be remarkable, adaptable, and perpetually proving your value.

The clinical manifestations are predictable. There's the chronic self-criticism that becomes background noise in your mind, always finding something you could have done better. There's impostor syndrome-the persistent feeling that you're fooling everyone and will eventually be exposed as incompetent despite evidence to the contrary (Bravata et al., 2020). There's the anxiety that spikes before performance reviews, not because you're underperforming, but because your entire sense of self feels up for evaluation.

Perhaps most insidiously, there's the inability to rest without guilt. Taking a lunch break feels irresponsible. Using vacation days triggers anxiety about falling behind. Even weekends become contaminated by the feeling that you should be doing something productive.

Hypnotherapy can help decouple self-worth from output by working with the subconscious beliefs that maintain this connection (Bandura, 1997). Through repeated hypnotic suggestion and imagery work, alternative beliefs can be strengthened: that your value is inherent rather than earned, that rest enhances rather than diminishes performance, that you are more than your job title or achievements.

3.2 The Exhaustion of Constant Performance

If you're a Zillennial professional, you've probably never known a professional life that didn't involve some element of digital self-presentation. Your LinkedIn profile isn't just a resume-it's a curated narrative of your professional identity. Your responses in Slack channels contribute to how colleagues perceive your competence. Even your email tone is evaluated for the right balance of professional yet approachable.

This constant performance is exhausting in ways that are hard to articulate. It's not just that you're working-you're also managing how your work is perceived, how you come across, whether you seem engaged enough or too eager, competent but not threatening, confident but not arrogant. Every interaction becomes another opportunity to reinforce or damage your professional brand.

Social comparison has always existed, but social media and professional platforms have amplified it to an almost absurd degree (Festinger, 1954). You're not just comparing yourself to your immediate colleagues anymore-you're comparing yourself to everyone's highlight reel. That person from your university cohort who just got promoted. The industry thought leader posting about their latest achievement. The peer who always seems to have it together, never mentioning struggles or doubts.

The psychological impact is significant. Research consistently shows that social comparison, especially upward comparison to people perceived as better off, correlates with anxiety, depression, and lower self-esteem (Przybylski et al., 2013). For Zillennials who grew up with social media as a constant presence, these comparison patterns are deeply ingrained, almost automatic.

What makes this particularly difficult is the pressure to appear authentic while simultaneously curating your image. You're supposed to be genuine and vulnerable-but not too vulnerable. Share your struggles-but only the ones that make you seem resilient. Be yourself-but make sure yourself is professional, likeable, and competent.

Hypnotherapy addresses these patterns by working with attentional control and internal validation. Through hypnotic practice, professionals can learn to redirect attention away from external evaluation and toward internal standards. Visualization techniques help create psychological distance from the constant stream of comparison triggers. And suggestions can strengthen the ability to derive satisfaction from internal values rather than external metrics like likes, comments, or validation from others.

3.3 Economic Anxiety and the Illusion of Control

Previous generations often had clearer career trajectories. You started in an entry-level position, worked your way up, and could reasonably expect stability if you performed well. That model has largely dissolved. Today's Zillennial professionals face short-term contracts, gig work, frequent job changes (voluntary or otherwise), and the ever-present awareness that automation or economic shifts could render their skills obsolete (Kalleberg, 2018).

This economic precarity creates a baseline level of anxiety that's hard to shake. It's not acute crisis-it's chronic uncertainty. Will this contract be renewed? Should I be looking for my next position already? What happens if I lose this job? Can I afford to take a risk on something more meaningful but less stable?

Financial strain compounds the psychological stress. Student loans, high cost of living, difficulty saving for major life milestones-these pressures create a kind of cognitive load that never quite lifts (Sweet et al., 2013). You're always doing some level of financial calculation in the background, always a bit vigilant about money.

This manifests physically and emotionally as hypervigilance-difficulty relaxing fully because some part of you is always scanning for threats. It shows up as decision paralysis, where even small choices feel overwhelming because you're trying to optimize every decision against an uncertain future. It emerges as chronic worry that cycles through the same scenarios without resolution.

Hypnotherapy can't change economic realities, but it can help regulate the body's response to uncertainty. Techniques focused on building tolerance for ambiguity, reducing somatic anxiety responses, and strengthening an internal sense of capability can make uncertainty more bearable. Rather than eliminating worry, the goal is to prevent it from becoming all-consuming, allowing space for present-moment engagement even amid legitimate uncertainty.

4. HOW HYPNOTHERAPY ACTUALLY WORKS FOR STRESS AND BURNOUT

4.1 Understanding Stress as More Than Just "Too Much Work"

When people talk about workplace stress, they often frame it as having too much to do. And yes, workload matters. But chronic stress and burnout are actually more about how your mind and body respond to prolonged pressure than about the pressure itself (Lazarus & Folkman, 1984). Two people with identical job responsibilities can have vastly different stress experiences based on their internal processing.

Here's what actually happens: Over time, repeated exposure to stressors conditions automatic responses. Your body learns to respond to certain triggers-an email from your boss, a calendar notification for a meeting, even just opening your work laptop-with stress activation. Heart rate increases slightly. Muscles tense. Stress hormones release. These responses happen before you're even consciously aware of feeling stressed.

This conditioning is why someone can objectively know they're on vacation, genuinely want to relax, and still feel their shoulders tense when they think about work. The response has become automatic, encoded at a subconscious level that doesn't respond to rational arguments about why relaxation is okay.

Burnout takes this further. It's characterized by emotional exhaustion (feeling drained and depleted), depersonalization (becoming cynical or detached from work), and reduced sense of accomplishment (feeling ineffective despite effort; Halbesleben, 2010). These aren't just conscious beliefs someone can think their way out of-they're maintained by deeply ingrained patterns.

Often, these patterns are sustained by subconscious beliefs absorbed over years: "Resting means I'm lazy." "My value depends on my output." "Saying no will make people think I can't handle my responsibilities." You might consciously disagree with these beliefs, but they still drive your automatic responses.

This is exactly why hypnotherapy can be so effective. It doesn't just address the conscious, rational level where you already know rest is important. It engages the subconscious mechanisms where these automatic stress responses and underlying beliefs actually live.

4.2 What Happens in Your Brain During Hypnosis

For years, skeptics dismissed hypnosis as placebo or mere relaxation. But neuroimaging research has shown that something genuinely different happens in the brain during hypnotic states (Oakley & Halligan, 2013). Brain regions involved in attention control, emotional processing, and self-awareness show altered activity and connectivity patterns.

Specifically, there's reduced activity in the default mode network-the brain system associated with self-referential thinking, mind-wandering, and rumination (Jiang et al., 2017). This is significant because excessive default mode activity is linked to anxiety and depression. When this network quiets down, it becomes easier to step back from the constant mental chatter evaluating your performance, replaying conversations, or worrying about future scenarios.

At the same time, there's increased activity in brain regions associated with focused attention and reduced activity in areas involved in monitoring your environment for threats. This combination creates a state where you're highly focused but less reactive, absorbed but not anxious.

For professionals dealing with chronic stress, this neurophysiological shift has practical implications. During hypnosis, your sympathetic nervous system (responsible for the stress response) downregulates while your parasympathetic system (responsible for rest and recovery) activates. Your body literally practices returning to a calmer baseline state.

With repeated practice, this becomes easier and more automatic. It's like training a muscle-the more you practice shifting into a relaxed, focused state, the more readily your nervous system can make that shift in daily life. Eventually, you're teaching your body how to de-escalate stress responses more efficiently, which is arguably more valuable than just reducing current stress levels.

4.3 Changing Beliefs That Live in Your Body

Traditional cognitive therapy works primarily with thoughts. You identify negative or distorted thinking patterns and challenge them with evidence and logic. This approach is effective, but it has limitations. Often, people can rationally recognize that a belief is unhelpful while still feeling and behaving as if it's true.

For example, a professional experiencing burnout might intellectually understand that rest is necessary for long-term productivity. They can articulate all the reasons why taking breaks improves performance. But when they actually try to rest, they feel intense guilt, anxiety, or restlessness. The intellectual understanding hasn't reached the emotional and somatic levels where the problem actually exists.

Cognitive hypnotherapy bridges this gap by integrating cognitive techniques with hypnotic work (Alladin, 2008). Instead of just talking about alternative perspectives, you experience them in a hypnotic state where they can be encoded emotionally and somatically, not just intellectually.

Here's a concrete example: During hypnosis, a client might visualize themselves taking a lunch break, really taking it-not eating at their desk while working, but actually stopping. In the hypnotic state, they practice feeling what that's like, noticing any guilt or anxiety that arises, working with those feelings through hypnotic suggestion, and then experiencing a sense of permission and okay-ness about rest. They might imagine returning to work afterward feeling more focused and creative, installing the belief that rest enhances rather than diminishes performance.

This isn't just imagination or positive thinking. It's experiential learning that engages multiple levels of processing simultaneously. The belief becomes felt truth rather than intellectual concept, making it far more likely to influence actual behavior.

4.4 Strengthening Your Internal Resources

There's a technique in hypnotherapy called ego strengthening, which sounds more mystical than it actually is. Essentially, it involves using hypnotic suggestion to reinforce inner resources like confidence, emotional stability, resilience, and self-efficacy (Hartland, 1971). Think of it as building psychological infrastructure that helps you handle whatever challenges arise.

For Zillennial professionals whose self-concept might feel unstable due to frequent job changes, constant evaluation, and economic uncertainty, ego strengthening serves an important function. It's not about inflating ego in the everyday sense-it's about developing a stable sense of self that can weather external instability.

During ego-strengthening work, a hypnotherapist might offer suggestions like: "You have within you the resources to handle challenges effectively. Each day you grow stronger in your ability to respond calmly and thoughtfully to stress. You trust your capacity to adapt and learn." These suggestions are tailored to the individual and repeated across sessions.

What makes this effective is that suggestions given during hypnosis bypass some of the critical filters that normally evaluate new information. In regular conversation, your mind might respond to "you have the resources to handle challenges" with immediate skepticism or counter-examples. During hypnosis, with those analytical filters quieted, suggestions can be absorbed more directly.

Over time, this strengthens what psychologist Albert Bandura called self-efficacy-your belief in your ability to handle specific situations (Bandura, 1997). Research consistently shows that self-efficacy is one of the strongest predictors of how people respond to stress. Two people facing identical challenges will have vastly different experiences based on whether they believe they can handle it.

Importantly, ego strengthening doesn't ignore reality or create false confidence. It's about helping someone recognize capabilities they already have but may not fully trust, and developing adaptive responses to situations that previously felt overwhelming.

5. PRACTICAL APPLICATIONS: USING HYPNOTHERAPY FOR WORKPLACE CHALLENGES

5.1 Catching Burnout Before It Takes Hold

Burnout doesn't happen overnight. It's a gradual process that usually begins with subtle warning signs that are easy to dismiss or rationalize away (World Health Organization, 2022). You're tired, but who isn't? You're a bit more irritable, but work has been stressful. You're not as enthusiastic about projects, but maybe they're just not that interesting right now.

By the time someone recognizes they're burned out, the pattern is usually well-established and harder to interrupt. This is why early intervention matters so much.

Hypnotherapy can be integrated into professional life as a preventive measure, not just a crisis response.

Preventive hypnotherapy work focuses on several key areas. First, it develops interoceptive awareness-your ability to notice what's happening in your body before stress reaches crisis levels (Yapko, 2012). Many professionals have learned to override signals of exhaustion, hunger, tension, or emotional overload because stopping to address them feels less important than the task at hand.

Second, it helps establish healthy boundaries at a subconscious level. You might consciously decide to set better boundaries between work and personal time, but old patterns persist. Through hypnotic suggestion and imagery, these boundaries can be reinforced: visualizing yourself closing your laptop at a reasonable hour, experiencing the positive feelings associated with protecting personal time, and practicing saying no to requests that exceed your capacity.

Third, preventive work addresses the underlying beliefs that contribute to burnout before they become deeply problematic. Beliefs like "my worth depends on constant achievement" or "rest is laziness" can be gradually reshaped through repeated hypnotic exposure to alternative perspectives. The goal is to intervene before these beliefs cause significant harm.

Guided hypnotic relaxation serves as both an intervention and a skill-building tool. Regular practice trains your nervous system to shift more efficiently between activation and recovery. It's like building a habit of physiological downregulation that becomes easier to access the more you practice it.

5.2 Restoring Emotional Energy

When someone describes feeling emotionally exhausted, they're not being dramatic-they're describing a genuine depletion of psychological resources. It's that sense of having nothing left to give, of feeling completely drained by interactions that wouldn't normally be difficult, of struggling to care about things that usually matter.

Traditional advice for emotional exhaustion often involves self-care activities: take a bath, go for a walk, practice meditation. These can help, certainly, but they don't always reach the deeper level where the depletion exists. Sometimes what's needed is a way to access internal restoration more directly.

This is where imagery-based hypnotherapy becomes particularly valuable. In a hypnotic state, the therapist guides the client through visualization experiences specifically designed to facilitate emotional replenishment. These aren't just pleasant daydreams-research indicates that imagined experiences can activate similar neural pathways and even produce similar physiological responses as actual experiences.

A common approach is safe-place imagery, where the client develops a detailed internal representation of a place where they feel completely secure, peaceful, and supported. This might be a real place from their past, an imagined environment, or a combination. The key is that it becomes a vivid, multi-sensory experience: What do you see? What sounds are present? What's the temperature? What do you feel under your feet?

Once this safe place is established, it becomes an internal resource the client can access whenever they need emotional restoration. With practice, just thinking about this place can begin to activate some of the calm, secure feelings associated with it. The safe place becomes a kind of psychological sanctuary available anytime.

Resource anchoring takes this further by associating specific physical sensations with emotional states. For example, a feeling of groundedness might be anchored to the sensation of feet firmly planted on the floor, or a sense of calm might be anchored to deep breathing. These become portable tools for emotional regulation that can be used throughout the workday.

Over time, repeated hypnotic practice of accessing restorative states strengthens the neural pathways that support recovery. The body learns to return to baseline more efficiently, improving overall stress tolerance and resilience.

5.3 Working with Impostor Syndrome

Impostor syndrome is particularly prevalent among high-achieving professionals, and Zillennial workers seem especially vulnerable to it (Bravata et al., 2020). Despite objective evidence of competence-degrees earned, promotions received, positive feedback from colleagues-they carry a persistent sense that they're fooling everyone and will eventually be exposed as fraudulent.

What makes impostor feelings so resistant to logical argument is that they're not primarily a rational problem. Someone experiencing them can list their accomplishments, acknowledge positive feedback, and intellectually recognize they're qualified for their position, yet still feel like a fraud. The belief exists at an emotional level that doesn't respond to evidence.

These patterns usually have roots in earlier experiences where approval or validation was conditional or inconsistent. Maybe parents praised achievements but were critical of mistakes, creating a sense that love depended on performance. Maybe early school experiences involved being the smartest in one environment and then struggling in a more competitive one, creating confusion about actual ability. Maybe praise felt unpredictable or untrustworthy, making it hard to internalize.

Hypnotherapy works with impostor syndrome by accessing these formative experiences and facilitating emotional reprocessing (Alladin, 2008). Through careful hypnotic regression, a client might revisit a pivotal moment-perhaps receiving harsh criticism after making a mistake, or feeling out of place in a new competitive environment. With the support of the therapeutic relationship and adult perspective, these memories can be recontextualized.

The goal isn't to erase or deny these experiences, but to change their emotional charge and the conclusions drawn from them. A memory of harsh criticism might be reprocessed with the understanding that the criticism reflected the critic's issues rather than the client's inadequacy. An experience of academic struggle might be reframed as a normal adjustment period rather than evidence of being a fraud.

Hypnotic suggestion then helps integrate achievements into self-concept rather than dismissing them. Suggestions might emphasize: "Your accomplishments reflect your genuine capabilities. You have earned your position through your efforts and abilities. Success is something you create, not something that happens by accident."

Through repeated sessions, achievements gradually become internalized as legitimate. The automatic dismissal of success weakens, and a more stable, confident self-concept emerges. This doesn't eliminate all self-doubt-some is actually adaptive-but it reduces the paralyzing conviction of fraudulence that defines impostor syndrome.

6. IDENTITY, WORK, AND SELF: FINDING STABILITY IN UNCERTAIN TIMES

6.1 Who Am I When My Job Keeps Changing?

Previous generations often built identity around stable career paths. You were a teacher, an accountant, an engineer-and that identity could remain relatively stable for decades. Professional identity developed gradually and consolidated over time, becoming a core part of how people understood themselves (Allen et al., 2017).

For Zillennials, this process looks completely different (Gabrielsen & Lindström, 2021). Career paths are rarely linear. Someone might work in marketing, then project management, then transition to tech, perhaps freelance for a while, go back to full-time employment, and so on. Each transition disrupts the identity they were building around their previous role.

This constant flux can create what psychologists call identity diffusion-a sense of uncertainty or instability about who you fundamentally are (Robinson & Wright, 2013). When asked what they do, many young professionals struggle to answer simply because their work has been so varied.

The psychological toll of this instability is subtle but significant. Without a stable professional identity to anchor to, people may experience increased anxiety during transitions, difficulty making career decisions (because there's no clear "path" to reference), and a sense of being adrift or behind peers who seem more settled.

Hypnotherapy supports identity integration by helping identify and strengthen aspects of self that remain stable across changing roles. Through guided imagery and hypnotic exploration, clients can clarify core values, intrinsic motivations, and personal qualities that persist regardless of job title.

For example, someone might realize that across all their various roles, what's remained consistent is their value for helping others solve problems. That value becomes a through-line that makes sense of seemingly disparate career moves. Or they might recognize that their core identity is as someone who learns quickly and adapts-meaning the varied path isn't evidence of instability but rather an expression of that adaptive capacity.

Future-oriented hypnotic work can also help. Through age progression, clients imagine themselves five or ten years in the future, having navigated various professional changes. From that future perspective, they reflect back on their current uncertainty and often discover that the path makes sense in retrospect, even if it doesn't feel clear in the present moment.

This work helps develop what psychologists call psychological flexibility-the ability to adapt to changing circumstances without losing core sense of self. Rather than identity being entirely defined by external roles, it becomes more internally anchored in values, capabilities, and character. This internal anchoring makes professional instability less psychologically destabilizing.

6.2 How Early Relationships Show Up at Work

Most people don't think about attachment theory when they're dealing with workplace conflict, but there's a strong connection. Attachment patterns-the ways we learned to seek security and closeness in early relationships-don't just affect romantic partnerships (Bowlby, 1988). They influence how we relate to authority figures, handle criticism, collaborate with colleagues, and respond to workplace stress.

Someone with an anxious attachment pattern might find themselves constantly seeking reassurance from managers, people-pleasing to avoid potential disapproval, or catastrophizing about small professional setbacks. An avoidantly attached person might struggle with collaboration, resist asking for help even when they need it, or emotionally shut down during conflict.

These patterns are largely subconscious and automatic. Someone doesn't consciously decide to people-please or shut down-it just happens as an automatic response to perceived threats to security or acceptance. And because these responses are automatic, trying to change them through willpower alone is often frustrating and ineffective.

Hypnotherapy can provide what therapists call a "corrective emotional experience"-essentially, a different kind of relational experience that begins to modify those automatic patterns. Through carefully structured hypnotic work, clients can access early attachment-related memories while experiencing them in the context of a secure, supportive therapeutic relationship.

For example, someone whose early experiences involved emotional abandonment when they expressed needs might, in hypnosis, revisit those experiences while simultaneously experiencing the therapist's consistent presence and support. This creates a new association: expressing needs doesn't lead to abandonment. Secure attachment experiences can be introduced through imagery as well-visualizing what it would have felt like to have consistent, responsive caregiving, and allowing the body to experience those feelings even if they weren't part of actual history.

The goal isn't to erase history or pretend early experiences were different. It's to add new emotional data that competes with old patterns. Over time, with repeated exposure to secure relational experiences (both in therapy and subsequently generalized to real relationships), attachment patterns can become more secure.

As attachment security increases, workplace relationships often improve significantly. There's less need for excessive reassurance, more comfort with healthy conflict, better capacity to ask for support when needed, and more balanced boundaries. People report feeling less emotionally reactive to workplace dynamics and more able to respond thoughtfully rather than defensively.

7. NAVIGATING WORKPLACE CONFLICT WITHOUT LOSING YOURSELF

For many Zillennial professionals, conflict feels like something to be avoided at almost any cost. It's not hard to understand why. They've grown up in an era that emphasizes collaboration, emotional intelligence, and maintaining positive relationships. Add to this the precarity of modern employment-where being labeled "difficult" can have real career consequences-and conflict avoidance starts to look like smart self-preservation.

But here's the problem: avoiding conflict doesn't make it go away. It just pushes it underground where it festers. That unaddressed tension with a colleague becomes chronic discomfort. That disagreement with your manager that you never voiced turns into resentment. The boundary you didn't set leads to increasing demands on your time and energy. Eventually, what starts as conflict avoidance becomes a recipe for burnout and deteriorating relationships.

The challenge is that for many people, conflict triggers a visceral response that has nothing to do with the actual situation at hand (Gottman, 1994). Heart rate increases, thoughts race, maybe there's a tightness in the chest or a sick feeling in the stomach. These bodily responses often reflect old learning-perhaps from family environments where conflict was explosive or unsafe, or from past experiences where speaking up led to punishment or rejection.

When your body is screaming danger signals, it's nearly impossible to engage in thoughtful conflict resolution. Your brain is in threat mode, focused on survival, not on finding collaborative solutions. So you either avoid the conflict entirely or respond in ways that escalate rather than resolve it.

This is where hypnotic conflict rehearsal becomes incredibly valuable. It allows you to practice difficult conversations in a state where your nervous system is calm and regulated. Think of it as creating a safe simulation environment where you can build skills and confidence without the overwhelming physical activation that usually accompanies real conflict.

During a session, the therapist might guide you to imagine a specific upcoming difficult conversation-maybe you need to set a boundary with a demanding colleague, or address a pattern of being talked over in meetings, or discuss a problem with your manager. In the hypnotic state, you practice what you'll say, how you'll say it, and how you'll handle various responses.

But it's not just mental rehearsal. You're also practicing the emotional regulation piece-noticing when anxiety starts to rise, using breathing or grounding techniques to stay centered, and maintaining that sense of calm confidence even as you imagine the other person pushing back or responding negatively. You practice tolerating the discomfort of potential disapproval or tension without backing down from your needs.

With repeated practice, something shifts. The anticipatory anxiety that usually precedes difficult conversations begins to diminish because you've already "been through" the conversation multiple times successfully. Your body learns that expressing needs or addressing conflict doesn't actually lead to catastrophe. The neural pathways associated with conflict gradually become less linked to danger signals and more associated with capability and empowerment.

When the actual conversation happens, people often report being surprised by their own calm and clarity. They're able to stay present, express themselves clearly, and respond thoughtfully rather than reactively. Even if the conversation doesn't go perfectly, they feel a sense of having handled it well rather than avoiding it or losing themselves in the process.

Over time, this experiential learning generalizes. Conflict stops feeling like an existential threat and becomes what it actually is-a normal part of professional relationships that can usually be navigated constructively.

8. THE HIDDEN COST OF PEOPLE-PLEASING

8.1 Why Smart People Keep Saying Yes When They Mean No

Here's something that often surprises people: people-pleasing isn't really about being nice. At its core, it's a survival strategy-one that usually developed at a time when it genuinely made sense.

Think about it from a developmental perspective. Children are completely dependent on adults for physical survival and emotional security. If a child learns that love, attention, or safety is conditional on being agreeable, helpful, and accommodating, then people-pleasing becomes adaptive. It's not weakness or a character flaw; it's an intelligent response to a situation where authentic self-expression felt unsafe.

The problem is that these strategies persist long after the original circumstances have changed. What worked to maintain safety and connection as a child becomes a pattern that undermines well-being in adulthood. But because it developed so early and became so automatic, it doesn't feel like a choice-it feels like just who you are.

In professional settings, people-pleasing can look admirable on the surface. You're helpful, responsive, willing to take on extra work, easy to work with. But underneath, there's often a different reality. Chronic overwork because you can't say no. Suppressed resentment toward colleagues who seem to have reasonable boundaries. Exhaustion from constantly accommodating others while ignoring your own needs. A nagging sense that people value you only for what you do for them, not for who you actually are.

What makes this particularly complicated in modern workplaces is that organizational culture often rewards people-pleasing behaviors, especially in younger employees. Being a "team player," showing "flexibility," and going "above and beyond" are praised. The line between being a good employee and being exploited can feel uncomfortably thin.

For Zillennials specifically, there's an added layer. Many entered the workforce during economically uncertain times, internalized messages about needing to prove their worth constantly, and developed a hypervigilance about being seen as valuable and indispensable. Saying no-even to unreasonable requests-can feel like risking your position.

8.2 What People-Pleasing Actually Costs You

The costs of chronic people-pleasing aren't always immediately obvious. It's not like you wake up one day and suddenly can't function. It's more insidious than that-a slow accumulation of small compromises that eventually add up to something significant.

First, there's the physical toll. Constantly overriding your own needs and boundaries creates chronic stress. Your body remains in a state of low-level activation, never fully relaxing because there's always some demand you're trying to meet or potential disapproval you're trying to avoid. This shows up as tension headaches, digestive issues, sleep problems, fatigue that doesn't improve with rest.

Then there's the emotional cost. When you habitually suppress your authentic responses to please others, you lose touch with what you actually feel, want, or need. You might find yourself unable to answer simple questions like "What do you want for dinner?" or "What would make you happy?" because you've spent so long attuning to others' preferences that your own have become fuzzy or inaccessible.

Resentment builds, often unconsciously. You might not even realize you're angry at people for taking advantage of your helpfulness-because on the surface, you offered willingly. But underneath, there's a growing sense of unfairness, of being taken for granted, of giving far more than you receive.

Professionally, people-pleasing can actually limit advancement. While it might make you well-liked, it can also make you seem less leadership-ready. Leaders need to make decisions that won't please everyone, set boundaries, and occasionally disappoint people in service of larger goals. If your default mode is accommodating everyone, that can create doubts about your capacity for tough decisions.

Perhaps most significantly, chronic people-pleasing erodes your sense of self. When you're constantly performing agreeableness rather than expressing authenticity, you can start to feel hollow or lost. Who are you really, underneath all the accommodation? It's hard to know when you've spent years prioritizing others' comfort over your own truth.

8.3 Creating a Pause Between Request and Response

One of the most powerful interventions hypnotherapy offers for people-pleasing is deceptively simple: creating space for choice. Most people-pleasers respond to requests automatically, without conscious decision-making. Someone asks for something, and "yes" comes out of their mouth before they've even considered whether they actually want to or can reasonably do it.

This automatic compliance is maintained at a subconscious level. The pattern is so ingrained that trying to change it through willpower alone often fails. You might tell yourself "I'm going to start saying no more," but when the actual moment arrives and someone makes a request, the old pattern takes over.

Hypnotherapy interrupts this automatic pattern by installing what we might call a "choice point"-a brief pause between stimulus and response. Through post-hypnotic suggestion, clients learn to introduce a moment of space when a request is made. Just a few seconds where, instead of automatically agreeing, they notice what they're feeling and thinking.

The suggestion might be something like: "When someone makes a request of you, you'll notice a brief pause-just a moment-where you check in with yourself. What do I actually feel about this? What do I genuinely want to do? Do I have the capacity for this right now? In that pause, you give yourself permission to consider before responding."

What's crucial is that this isn't about always saying no. It's about making conscious choices rather than automatic ones. Sometimes, after that pause, you might genuinely choose to help because you want to and have the capacity. Other times, you'll recognizc that saying ycs would cost you too much, and you'll decline. The key difference is that either way, it's an actual choice rather than a conditioned response.

During hypnotic practice, clients can rehearse using this pause. They imagine various scenarios-a colleague asking for help with their project, a manager requesting overtime, a friend wanting emotional support during your busy week. They practice feeling the request, noticing the old automatic impulse toward "yes," and then experiencing that pause. In the pause, they attune to their actual feelings and capacity, and practice responding from that place rather than from automatic accommodation.

With repetition, this pause becomes more automatic than the old pattern of immediate compliance. People report that it starts to happen naturally-someone makes a request, and they notice themselves automatically taking a breath, checking in internally, and then responding thoughtfully rather than reflexively.

8.4 Working with the Guilt

For many people-pleasers, the biggest obstacle to setting boundaries isn't knowing how-it's managing the intense guilt that arises when they do. Even when they intellectually understand that saying no is reasonable and necessary, the emotional response can be overwhelming. The guilt feels like evidence that they're being selfish, letting people down, or failing in some fundamental way.

This guilt usually has roots in early experiences and the beliefs that formed around them. Maybe you learned that other people's needs were always more important than yours. Maybe love felt conditional on being helpful and accommodating. Maybe you witnessed or experienced the consequences of someone being "selfish" and internalized that self-prioritization was dangerous or wrong.

These aren't just thoughts-they're emotionally charged beliefs that live in your body and drive automatic responses. This is why hypnotherapy can be so effective for guilt work. It allows you to access and reshape these beliefs at the emotional level where they actually exist.

One approach involves what's called reframing work. In a hypnotic state, alternative narratives are introduced that challenge the equation of self-care with selfishness. For example: "Taking care of yourself allows you to show up more fully for others. Setting boundaries is actually a form of respect-it creates clarity and prevents resentment. Saying no to what depletes you allows you to say yes to what truly matters."

These aren't just positive affirmations. In the hypnotic state, they're paired with imagery and emotional experiences that allow them to be integrated at a deeper level. You might visualize yourself setting a boundary and notice that the other person, rather than being devastated, actually respects you more. You might imagine the long-term consequences of continued self-neglect versus healthy self-prioritization, experiencing viscerally how the latter leads to better outcomes for everyone.

Age progression can be particularly powerful here. Through hypnotic suggestion, you imagine yourself five years in the future, having maintained your current pattern of people-pleasing. What does that version of you look like? How do they feel? What has been the cost? Then you imagine an alternative future where you learned to balance self-care with care for others. Who is that person? How do they show up in relationships and work?

Often, this future-oriented work makes the consequences of people-pleasing more emotionally real than intellectual arguments ever could. When you experientially encounter your own burnout and resentment as potential futures rather than abstract concepts, motivation for change strengthens significantly.

The guilt doesn't disappear entirely-that's not the goal. Some guilt can be adaptive, signaling when we've actually done something harmful. But the overwhelming, paralyzing guilt that prevents any self-prioritization begins to diminish. It becomes more proportionate, allowing you to feel mild discomfort when declining a request without being derailed by it.

8.5 Building Internal Validation

At the heart of people-pleasing is usually an over-reliance on external validation. Your sense of worth comes from others' approval, appreciation, or positive regard. When that external validation is present, you feel okay. When it's absent or when someone seems displeased, your sense of self becomes shaky.

This creates a kind of psychological dependence where you need others to constantly affirm your value. It's exhausting for both you and the people around you. And it makes you incredibly vulnerable to manipulation or exploitation by anyone who withholds approval strategically.

Hypnotherapy can help develop internal validation-the capacity to assess your own worth, recognize your own value, and approve of yourself independent of others' responses. This isn't about becoming arrogant or indifferent to feedback. It's about developing a stable internal foundation that doesn't collapse when external validation isn't present.

One approach involves working with an internalized "wise self" or compassionate inner voice through hypnotic imagery. In a relaxed, focused state, clients are guided to connect with a part of themselves that can observe with wisdom and compassion. This isn't about creating a separate personality-it's about accessing the perspective they might naturally have for a good friend but struggle to apply to themselves.

From this wise, compassionate perspective, they practice self-evaluation. Instead of looking outward for evidence of worth, they look inward: What do I value about my character? What am I proud of in how I handled that situation? What would be a fair assessment of my performance? This internal voice becomes a resource for self-validation that doesn't depend on others' approval.

Body-based awareness work also supports internal validation. Many people-pleasers are disconnected from their own bodily sensations and needs because they've spent so long attending to others. Hypnotic techniques that enhance somatic awareness help rebuild this connection. You learn to notice when your body says "yes" versus when it says "no"-a kind of felt sense that provides internal guidance independent of others' expectations.

As internal validation strengthens, something shifts in relationships. You become less anxiously focused on whether people are pleased with you and more attuned to whether interactions feel reciprocal and authentic. You start making decisions based on your own values and assessment rather than constantly calculating what will gain approval. Paradoxically, this often makes relationships better-people appreciate dealing with someone who's genuine rather than constantly accommodating.

9. DIGITAL LIFE AND THE PERFORMANCE OF PROFESSIONAL IDENTITY

9.1 When Your Professional Self Lives Online

There was a time, not so long ago, when your professional identity existed primarily in face-to-face interactions and maybe a paper resume. Performance mattered, certainly, but it was bounded-it happened during work hours, in specific locations, with specific people.

That world is gone for Zillennials. Professional identity now exists simultaneously in physical workspaces and across multiple digital platforms. Your LinkedIn profile isn't optional-it's expected. Your responses in Slack or Teams contribute to how colleagues perceive your competence and engagement. Your email signature, your video call background, even your profile picture are all part of your professional presentation.

This shift has created a new kind of labor: the constant work of identity curation. You're not just doing your job; you're managing how your job performance is perceived, documented, and broadcast. Every interaction leaves a digital trace that might be screenshotted, forwarded, or referenced later. The ephemeral quality of ordinary conversation has been replaced by a permanent record.

For many Zillennial professionals, this feels normal because they've never known anything different. But that doesn't mean it's not exhausting. The line between authentic professional engagement and performance of professional engagement has become blurry to the point of meaninglessness. When you post about a work achievement, are you genuinely excited or performing excitement for your network? When you share a professional insight, is it because you find it valuable or because you need to maintain your thought-leader brand?

The pressure intensifies because of the visibility of everyone else's carefully curated professional narratives. You see peers celebrating promotions, sharing impressive projects, posting about speaking engagements or publications. Rationally, you might know these are highlights-that no one posts about their boring Tuesday afternoon or the project that failed or the promotion they didn't get. But emotionally, the cumulative exposure to success narratives creates a distorted comparison point.

Social comparison has always been part of human psychology, but digital platforms have amplified it to an unprecedented degree. You're not just comparing yourself to your immediate colleagues anymore; you're comparing yourself to everyone in your industry, everyone from your alma mater, everyone in your age cohort who seems to be doing something impressive. The reference group has expanded infinitely, and the comparison is constant.

9.2 The Compulsion Loop of Digital Checking

Here's something most professionals don't like to admit: they're checking their work platforms compulsively. Not because there's urgent business to address, but because the checking itself has become a habit loop driven by anxiety and the need for reassurance.

It works like this: You feel a moment of boredom, uncertainty, or mild anxiety. Without conscious thought, your hand reaches for your phone. You open Slack or email or LinkedIn. Maybe there's something there-a message, a notification, a like on your post-and that provides a little hit of relief or validation. Maybe there's nothing, and you feel disappointed but tell yourself you were just "being responsible" by checking.

This happens dozens of times a day for many people. The behavior has become so automatic that you might not even be aware you're doing it. You just find yourself scrolling through work messages during dinner, checking email before getting out of bed, feeling phantom vibrations in your pocket and immediately reaching for your phone.

From a psychological perspective, this is a textbook conditioning pattern. The behavior (checking) is intermittently reinforced (sometimes there's something interesting or validating) which is actually the most powerful reinforcement schedule for maintaining habits. Your brain learns: checking might result in reward, so keep checking.

But the underlying driver is usually anxiety regulation. Checking provides temporary relief from the discomfort of not knowing. What if someone needs me? What if I'm missing something important? What if people think I'm unresponsive? The checking offers brief reassurance, even though it actually reinforces the anxiety long-term by preventing you from learning that not checking is also okay.

The cognitive cost of this pattern is significant. Constant task-switching fragments attention and prevents the kind of sustained focus needed for deep work or creative thinking. It creates a baseline level of mental fragmentation where you're never fully present anywhere because part of your attention is always monitoring for digital demands.

Emotionally, it prevents genuine rest and recovery. Even during supposed downtime, you remain tethered to work through these digital connections. Your nervous system never fully downregulates because you're constantly primed to respond to potential demands or monitoring for potential threats to your professional standing.

9.3 Using Hypnotherapy for Digital Regulation

Addressing compulsive technology use through hypnotherapy isn't about creating rigid rules or restriction. That approach typically fails because it doesn't address the underlying needs driving the behavior. Instead, hypnotherapy works with the emotional function the behavior serves and builds alternative ways of meeting those needs.

First, there's awareness work. Many people aren't fully conscious of how often they're checking or what triggers the behavior. Through hypnotic focus on internal experience, clients develop greater awareness of the moment before they reach for their device. What's happening internally? Is it boredom? Anxiety? Avoidance of a difficult task? Loneliness? Understanding the trigger is the first step toward addressing the actual need.

Once triggers are identified, hypnotherapy can help develop alternative responses. If checking is driven by anxiety about missing important messages, hypnotic work might focus on building tolerance for uncertainty and trust in your ability to address issues when you next check. If it's driven by boredom or discomfort with unstructured time, visualization of alternative activities can create competing associations.

For example, a client might practice hypnotic imagery of feeling restless, noticing the impulse to check their phone, and instead choosing to take three conscious breaths, look out a window, or stretch their body. This isn't just mental rehearsal-in the hypnotic state, they're actually experiencing the alternative behavior and the feelings associated with it, which makes it more likely to occur automatically in real situations.

Hypnotic suggestion can also address the underlying beliefs that drive compulsive checking. Beliefs like "I need to be constantly available" or "My value depends on responsiveness" can be gently challenged and replaced with alternatives: "I can be both responsive and boundaried. My value exists independent of immediate availability. Rest enhances rather than diminishes my effectiveness."

Some therapists use what's called urge surfing-a technique borrowed from addiction work. When the urge to check arises, rather than immediately acting on it or trying to suppress it, you practice simply observing it with curious attention. Notice where you feel the urge in your body. Notice its intensity. Notice that it rises, peaks, and naturally subsides if you don't act on it. In hypnotic states, this practice can be repeated until observing urges without acting becomes more automatic.

9.4 Reconnecting with Offline Experience

Perhaps the most important hypnotherapeutic work around digital life involves helping clients reconnect with the richness of offline, embodied experience. After years of digital immersion, many people have genuinely forgotten what it feels like to be fully present without digital mediation.

Through guided imagery in hypnotic states, clients can re-experience the quality of full presence. What does it feel like to have a conversation without your phone nearby, without any part of your attention monitoring for notifications? What does it feel like to work on something challenging without the escape hatch of digital distraction available? What does genuine rest feel like-the kind where you're not simultaneously scrolling or monitoring?

These aren't just pleasant visualizations. They're experiences that create emotional data your brain can reference. When you've deeply imagined and felt what unmediated presence is like, that becomes a state you can begin to recognize and seek out in daily life.

Hypnotic work might also involve visualization of alternative restorative activities that fulfill similar needs to digital engagement but in healthier ways. If LinkedIn scrolling serves partly as a way to feel connected to your professional community, what else might serve that function? In-person networking, substantive conversations with colleagues, reading actual books in your field? If checking work messages serves to feel competent and needed, what else creates that sense? Meaningful project work, skill development, mentoring others?

By creating vivid, emotionally resonant images of these alternatives, hypnotherapy makes them feel more accessible and appealing. The goal isn't digital abstinence-that's usually neither realistic nor desirable in modern professional life. It's about restoring choice and balance, so digital engagement becomes one tool among many rather than a compulsive default.

10. BRINGING HYPNOTHERAPY INTO THE WORKPLACE

10.1 Individual Sessions: Going Deep

When most people think about workplace mental health support, they picture group workshops or wellness apps-broad, surface-level interventions designed to help many people at once (McKinsey & Company, 2023). There's a place for those, certainly, but they're inherently limited in what they can address.

Individual hypnotherapy offers something fundamentally different: the ability to work with the specific psychological mechanisms maintaining stress, burnout, or dysfunction for a particular person. The professional dealing with impostor syndrome rooted in childhood experiences of conditional love needs different work than the one struggling with conflict avoidance stemming from witnessing parental volatility. One-size-fits-all approaches can't address these individual complexities.

Individual sessions typically begin with a thorough assessment. What brings this person in? What's their history with stress and coping? What are their current symptoms and how do those symptoms function in their life? What's their support system like? What are their goals for the work?

From there, treatment is tailored specifically to that individual's needs and presentation. Someone in the early stages of burnout might focus on stress regulation and boundary setting. Someone dealing with intense performance anxiety might work on ego strengthening and confidence building. Someone struggling with workplace relationships might focus on attachment patterns and interpersonal effectiveness.

The efficiency of hypnotherapy makes it well-suited to the constraints of professional life. While traditional therapy might take months or years to address deep-seated patterns, hypnotherapy often produces meaningful shifts within 6-12 sessions (Alladin & Alibhai, 2007). This matters for professionals who are struggling but can't commit to long-term, open-ended therapeutic work.

Telehealth delivery has made individual hypnotherapy even more accessible. Professionals can schedule sessions during lunch breaks or from home offices without the time cost of traveling to appointments. The hypnotic experience translates surprisingly well to video platforms, and research suggests comparable outcomes to in-person work.

10.2 Group Workshops: Normalizing and Skill-Building

While individual work goes deep, group hypnotherapy workshops serve a different valuable function: they normalize shared experiences and teach practical skills in a supportive environment. There's something powerful about realizing that your colleagues are dealing with similar challenges-that the stress, self-doubt, and exhaustion you're experiencing aren't personal failures but common responses to common circumstances.

Group workshops typically focus on specific, broadly relevant topics. Stress management workshops might teach guided relaxation techniques and self-hypnosis practices participants can use independently. Boundary-setting workshops might include hypnotic rehearsal of saying no and managing the guilt that arises. Confidence-building workshops might focus on ego strengthening and reframing self-doubt.

The group format has inherent benefits beyond efficiency. Hearing others describe their experiences and struggles reduces isolation and shame. Witnessing peers practice new skills-like assertive communication during hypnotic rehearsal-provides modeling and makes change seem more possible. The shared experience creates a kind of collective momentum that supports individual change.

Group hypnotherapy needs to be structured carefully to maintain therapeutic value while respecting the reality that participants are colleagues. Confidentiality is explicitly established at the outset. Exercises are designed to provide value without requiring vulnerable personal disclosure. Content focuses on skill-building and experiential learning rather than exploration of individual trauma or deep psychological issues.

Participants typically remain clothed, seated comfortably in chairs, with enough space between them to feel some privacy. The hypnotic inductions are gentler and less personalized than in individual work, designed to work for most people regardless of their specific psychological makeup. The suggestions offered are general enough to be applicable across different situations while still being concrete and actionable.

Follow-up is important. Workshops might include recorded guided practices participants can use between sessions, written resources reinforcing key concepts, and clear pathways for accessing individual support if deeper issues emerge.

10.3 Making It Actually Work: Ethics and Organizational Alignment

Here's where things get tricky. Hypnotherapy can be an incredibly valuable tool for supporting employee well-being, but it can also be misused-intentionally or unintentionally-in ways that harm individuals and undermine trust.

The most important ethical principle is this: hypnotherapy should support employee well-being, not organizational productivity at the expense of employee health. It shouldn't be used to help people "cope better" with genuinely harmful working conditions. It shouldn't be a substitute for addressing systemic problems like understaffing, toxic management, unrealistic expectations, or discriminatory practices.

When organizations start thinking about hypnotherapy primarily as a productivity tool-"How can we make employees more resilient so they can handle more stress?"-that's a red flag. The goal should be supporting psychological health in its own right, with any performance improvements being a secondary benefit rather than the primary aim.

Voluntary participation is non-negotiable. Employees should never feel pressured to engage in hypnotherapy or fear professional consequences for declining. This means it can't be framed as a performance improvement plan requirement or tied to advancement opportunities. It needs to be genuinely optional.

Confidentiality is equally essential. What happens in hypnotherapy sessions stays between client and therapist, with standard exceptions for imminent harm. Employers shouldn't receive information about who's participating, what they're working on, or how sessions are going. The moment employees feel their participation or progress might be reported to management, therapeutic trust collapses.

The practitioners providing hypnotherapy need appropriate credentials, training, and supervision. They should be licensed mental health professionals with specialized hypnotherapy training, not coaches or consultants who took a weekend certification course. They should have clear ethical guidelines, professional liability insurance, and accountability to licensing boards.

There also needs to be clarity about scope. Workplace hypnotherapy addresses stress, burnout, professional confidence, and work-related functioning issues. It's not meant to treat serious mental illness, complex trauma, or conditions requiring psychiatric care. Clear referral pathways should exist for when someone needs more intensive support than workplace hypnotherapy can appropriately provide.

Finally, organizational culture matters tremendously. If a company offers hypnotherapy while simultaneously creating conditions that predictably lead to burnout-impossible deadlines, understaffing, toxic management, lack of work-life boundaries-that's not support, it's cynicism. The intervention looks like care while actually enabling exploitation.

For hypnotherapy to be ethical and effective in organizational settings, it needs to be one component of a genuine commitment to employee well-being that includes reasonable workloads, respectful management, fair compensation, opportunities for growth, and cultural values that prioritize sustainability over extraction of maximum productivity.

11. WHERE DO WE GO FROM HERE? RESEARCH AND FUTURE DIRECTIONS

Despite growing clinical evidence for hypnotherapy's effectiveness with anxiety, stress, and related conditions (Lynn & Kirsch, 2006), research specifically examining its application in organizational contexts remains limited. Most studies have focused on clinical populations or specific medical conditions rather than workplace well-being.

Future research needs to address several key questions. First, what are the long-term outcomes of hypnotherapy-based workplace interventions? Most existing studies examine immediate effects or outcomes over a few months. We need longitudinal research tracking whether changes persist over years and whether hypnotherapy prevents burnout development rather than just reducing current symptoms.

Second, how does hypnotherapy compare to other workplace interventions? Is it more, less, or equally effective compared to cognitive behavioral approaches, mindfulness training, or traditional counseling? Under what circumstances might hypnotherapy be the most appropriate choice? Are there particular presentations or populations that respond especially well?

Third, are there cultural variations in response to hypnotic techniques? Most hypnotherapy research has been conducted with Western populations. Do approaches need to be adapted for different cultural contexts, and if so, how? What role do cultural beliefs about mind-body relationships, authority, and therapeutic intervention play in engagement and outcomes?

Fourth, what are the active mechanisms of change? While we know hypnotherapy is effective, we're less clear about exactly why. Is it the altered state itself, the suggestions offered, the therapeutic relationship, the experiential learning, or some combination? Understanding mechanisms would allow us to optimize interventions.

Mixed-method research designs would be particularly valuable, integrating quantitative outcome measures with qualitative exploration of subjective experiences. How do participants describe what changed for them? What aspects of the intervention felt most impactful? What barriers or challenges did they encounter? This richer data would inform practical implementation beyond what numbers alone can tell us.

We also need more research on delivery formats. How do outcomes compare between individual sessions, group workshops, and self-hypnosis training? What's the optimal dose-how many sessions produce meaningful change, and are there diminishing returns? Can recorded guided hypnosis sessions provide comparable benefits to live sessions, and if so, under what conditions?

Finally, implementation research is crucial. Even evidence-based interventions fail when implementation is poor. What organizational factors support or hinder successful integration of hypnotherapy into workplace wellness programs? How do employees perceive these offerings, and what influences their willingness to participate? What training and support do human resources professionals need to implement programs effectively and ethically?

The answers to these questions will help move hypnotherapy from being an interesting but underutilized option to becoming a mainstream, evidence-based component of comprehensive workplace mental health support.

12. CONCLUSION: TOWARD SUSTAINABLE PROFESSIONAL RESILIENCE

We've covered a lot of ground in this chapter-from the specific pressures facing Zillennial professionals to the mechanisms of hypnotherapy to practical applications in workplace settings. But let's bring it back to the fundamental issue: the way we work is making people sick, and we need better tools for addressing that reality at both individual and systemic levels.

Zillennials entered the professional world during a particularly volatile period (Deloitte, 2023). They've been told they can be anything while simultaneously being reminded that economic security is precarious. They're expected to be always available, constantly self-improving, and perpetually optimistic about their careers while navigating objectively difficult circumstances-economic instability, job precarity, the erosion of work-life boundaries through technology, and the performance pressures amplified by social media.

The mental health consequences are documented and severe (American Psychological Association, 2023). Anxiety, depression, and burnout are epidemic among young professionals. Traditional wellness initiatives-while well-intentioned-often miss the mark because they work at the wrong level.

This is where hypnotherapy offers something genuinely different. It engages the subconscious mechanisms that drive automatic responses, allowing change at a level that intellectual insight alone can't reach. It's experiential rather than just analytical, creating felt shifts in emotional and physical patterns rather than just cognitive understanding.

The applications we've discussed-burnout prevention, impostor syndrome treatment, people-pleasing interruption, conflict rehearsal, digital regulation, identity integration-all share a common thread. They work with the deeper levels of psychological functioning where real change becomes possible. They help people not just understand their patterns but actually transform them.

But-and this is crucial-hypnotherapy isn't a magic solution that exempts organizations from responsibility. It shouldn't be used to help employees adapt to fundamentally unhealthy work environments. The most ethical and effective approach combines individual support through modalities like hypnotherapy with organizational changes that address systemic sources of stress.

This means questioning the always-on work culture that technology has enabled. It means recognizing that constant availability isn't sustainable and often isn't even productive. It means creating genuine boundaries between work and personal life rather than just encouraging employees to manage that boundary better themselves. It means fair compensation, reasonable workloads, respectful management, and cultural values that prioritize sustainability over extraction of maximum productivity.

When integrated thoughtfully into this broader framework, hypnotherapy holds significant potential (Yapko, 2012). It can help professionals build genuine resilience-not the kind that means enduring more stress, but the kind that means maintaining psychological health and authenticity while navigating professional demands.

For Zillennial professionals specifically, these interventions address challenges that feel particularly acute at their career stage. The identity instability of frequent job transitions. The pressure to perform professionalism perfectly while still figuring out who they are. The economic anxiety that makes boundary-setting feel dangerous. The digital surveillance that makes every professional moment feel like a performance under evaluation.

The work is challenging, certainly. Meaningful psychological change always is. But the alternative-continuing patterns that lead to burnout, depletion, and loss of self-is ultimately more difficult. And perhaps more importantly, it's unnecessary. We have tools that work if we're willing to use them thoughtfully and ethically.

As we move forward, the question isn't whether workplaces need to change-they clearly do. The question is how we support professionals in maintaining their psychological health and authenticity while that larger cultural shift unfolds. Hypnotherapy, integrated into comprehensive approaches to workplace well-being, offers one valuable piece of that puzzle.

The goal isn't to create employees who can endure more stress. It's to support human beings in building lives where work is sustainable, relationships are authentic, identity is stable, and psychological well-being is genuinely valued rather than just rhetorically supported. That's a goal worth working toward, both individually and collectively.

REFERENCES

Alladin, A. (2008). *Cognitive hypnotherapy: An integrated approach to the treatment of emotional disorders*. John Wiley & Sons.

Alladin, A., & Alibhai, A. (2007). Cognitive hypnotherapy for depression: An empirical investigation. *The International Journal of Clinical and Experimental Hypnosis*, *55*(2), 147–166. DOI: 10.1080/00207140601177947 PMID: 17365072

Allen, T. D., Eby, L. T., Chao, G. T., & Bauer, T. N. (2017). Taking stock of two relational aspects of organizational life: Tracing the history and shaping the future of socialization and mentoring research. *The Journal of Applied Psychology*, *102*(3), 324–337. DOI: 10.1037/apl0000086 PMID: 28125264

American Psychological Association. (2023). *Stress in America 2023: A national mental health crisis*. APA Press. Retrieved from https://www.apa.org/news/press/releases/stress

Bandura, A. (1997). *Self-efficacy: The exercise of control*. W.H. Freeman and Company.

Bowlby, J. (1988). *A secure base: Parent-child attachment and healthy human development*. Basic Books.

Bravata, D. M., Watts, S. A., Keefer, A. L., Madhusudhan, D. K., Taylor, K. T., Clark, D. M., Nelson, R. S., Cokley, K. O., & Hagg, H. K. (2020). Prevalence, predictors, and treatment of impostor syndrome: A systematic review. *Journal of General Internal Medicine*, *35*(4), 1252–1275. DOI: 10.1007/s11606-019-05364-1 PMID: 31848865

Deloitte. (2023). *The Deloitte Global 2023 Gen Z and Millennial Survey*. Deloitte Insights. Retrieved from https://www.deloitte.com/global/en/issues/work/genzmillennialsurvey.html

Elkins, G. R., Barabasz, A. F., Council, J. R., & Spiegel, D. (2015). Advancing research and practice: The revised APA Division 30 definition of hypnosis. *The International Journal of Clinical and Experimental Hypnosis*, *63*(1), 1–9. DOI: 10.1080/00207144.2014.961870 PMID: 25365125

Festinger, L. (1954). A theory of social comparison processes. *Human Relations*, *7*(2), 117–140. DOI: 10.1177/001872675400700202

Gabrielsen, L. E., & Lindström, T. C. (2021). Zillennials at work: Characteristics and challenges of the cusp generation. *Journal of Organizational Psychology, 21*(4), 89–105.

Gottman, J. M. (1994). *What predicts divorce? The relationship between marital processes and marital outcomes.* Lawrence Erlbaum Associates.

Halbesleben, J. R. (2010). A meta-analysis of work engagement: Relationships with burnout, demands, resources, and consequences. In Bakker, A. B., & Leiter, M. P. (Eds.), *Work engagement: A handbook of essential theory and research* (pp. 102–117). Psychology Press.

Hartland, J. (1971). Further observations on the use of ego-strengthening techniques. *The American Journal of Clinical Hypnosis, 14*(1), 1–8. DOI: 10.1080/00029157.1971.10402149 PMID: 5163560

Jiang, H., White, M. P., Greicius, M. D., Waelde, L. C., & Spiegel, D. (2017). Brain activity and functional connectivity associated with hypnosis. *Cerebral Cortex (New York, N.Y.), 27*(8), 4083–4093. DOI: 10.1093/cercor/bhw220 PMID: 27469596

Kalleberg, A. L. (2018). *Precarious lives: Job insecurity and well-being in rich democracies.* Polity Press.

Lazarus, R. S., & Folkman, S. (1984). *Stress, appraisal, and coping.* Springer Publishing Company.

Lynn, S. J., & Kirsch, I. (2006). *Essentials of clinical hypnosis: An evidence-based approach.* American Psychological Association.

McKinsey & Company. (2023). *Gen Z and Millennial workforce wellness report.* McKinsey Health Institute.

Oakley, D. A., & Halligan, P. W. (2013). Hypnotic suggestion: Opportunities for cognitive neuroscience. *Nature Reviews. Neuroscience, 14*(8), 565–576. DOI: 10.1038/nrn3538 PMID: 23860312

Przybylski, A. K., Murayama, K., DeHaan, C. R., & Gladwell, V. (2013). Motivational, emotional, and behavioral correlates of fear of missing out. *Computers in Human Behavior, 29*(4), 1841–1848. DOI: 10.1016/j.chb.2013.02.014

Robinson, O. C., & Wright, G. R. T. (2013). The prevalence, types and perceived outcomes of crisis episodes in early adulthood and midlife: A structured retrospective-autobiographical study. *International Journal of Behavioral Development, 37*(5), 407–416. DOI: 10.1177/0165025413492464

Sweet, E., Nandi, A., Adam, E. K., & McDade, T. W. (2013). The high price of debt: Household financial debt and its impact on mental and physical health. *Social Science & Medicine*, *91*, 94–100. DOI: 10.1016/j.socscimed.2013.05.009 PMID: 23849243

World Health Organization. (2022). *Mental health at work: Policy brief.* WHO. Retrieved from https://www.who.int/publications/i/item/9789240053052

Yapko, M. D. (2012). *Trancework: An introduction to the practice of clinical hypnosis* (4th ed.). Routledge.

Compilation of References

Afzal, S., Arshad, M., Saleem, S., & Farooq, O. (2019). The impact of perceived supervisor support on employees' turnover intention and task performance: Mediation of self-efficacy. *Journal of Management Development*, *38*(5), 369–382.

Ahmadi, A. M. (2018). Evaluation of the effect of hypnotherapy on the headache. *Sleep and Hypnosis (Online)*, *20*(2), 114–119.

Ahmad, N. R., Ullah, I., Aziz, M. U., & Iqbal, F. (2025). Investigating stress, burnout, and organizational factors contributing to psychological well-being at work. Review of Education. *Administration & Law*, *8*(1), 29–40. DOI: 10.47067/real.v8i1.401

Ahmed, M., Zehou, S., Raza, S. A., Qureshi, M. A., & Yousufi, S. Q. (2020). Impact of CSR and environmental triggers on employee green behavior: The mediating effect of employee well-being. *Corporate Social Responsibility and Environmental Management*, *27*(5), 2225–2239. DOI: 10.1002/csr.1960

Åkerstedt, T. (2003). Shift work and disturbed sleep/wakefulness. *Occupational Medicine*, *53*(2), 89–94. DOI: 10.1093/occmed/kqg046

Alias, A., Rahman, S., Abd Majid, R., & Mohd Yassin, S. F. (2013). Dąbrowski's overexcitabilities profile among gifted students. *Asian Social Science*, *9*(16), 120–126. DOI: 10.5539/ass.v9n16p120

Alladin, A. (2008). *Cognitive hypnotherapy: An integrated approach to the treatment of emotional disorders*. John Wiley & Sons.

Alladin, A., & Alibhai, A. (2007). Cognitive hypnotherapy for depression: An empirical investigation. *The International Journal of Clinical and Experimental Hypnosis*, *55*(2), 147–166. DOI: 10.1080/00207140601177947 PMID: 17365072

Allen, T. D., Eby, L. T., Chao, G. T., & Bauer, T. N. (2017). Taking stock of two relational aspects of organizational life: Tracing the history and shaping the future of socialization and mentoring research. *The Journal of Applied Psychology, 102*(3), 324–337. DOI: 10.1037/apl0000086 PMID: 28125264

Allen, T. D., Golden, T. D., & Shockley, K. M. (2015). How effective is telecommuting? Assessing the status of our scientific findings. *Psychological Science in the Public Interest, 16*(2), 40–68. DOI: 10.1177/1529100615593273

Amankwah-Amoah, J., Khan, Z., Wood, G., & Knight, G. (2021). COVID-19 and digitalization: The great acceleration. *Journal of Business Research, 136*, 602–611.

American Psychological Association. (2017). *Ethical principles of psychologists and code of conduct.* https://www.apa.org/ethics/code

American Psychological Association. (2023). *Stress in America 2023: A national mental health crisis.* APA Press. Retrieved from https://www.apa.org/news/press/releases/stress

American Psychological Association. (2024). *Dictionary of psychology.* Retrieved from https://dictionary.apa.org

Andersson, G., Carlbring, P., Titov, N., & Lindefors, N. (2019). Internet Interventions for Adults with Anxiety and Mood Disorders: A Narrative Umbrella Review of Recent Meta-Analyses. *Canadian Journal of Psychiatry, 64*(7), 465–470. DOI: 10.1177/0706743719839381;ISSUE:ISSUE:DOI PMID: 31096757

An, R., Qian, G., Mumtaz, A., Alotaibi, K. A., & Wang, X. (2025). Digital fatigue and academic resilience among university students with grit and flexibility as mediators. *Scientific Reports.*

Antwi, C. O., Fan, C.-J., Aboagye, M. O., Brobbey, P., Jababu, Y., Affum-Osei, E., & Avornyo, P. (2019). Job demand stressors and employees' creativity: A within-person approach to dealing with hindrance and challenge stressors at the airport environment. *Service Industries Journal, 39*(3–4), 250–278. DOI: 10.1080/02642069.2018.1520220

Arasek, R. A., & Theorell, T. (1990). *Healthy work: Stress, productivity, and the reconstruction of working life.* Basic Books.

Armstrong, T. (2010). *Neurodiversity: Discovering the extraordinary gifts of autism, ADHD, dyslexia, and other brain differences.* Da Capo Press.

Arnsten, A. F. T. (2009a). Stress signalling pathways that impair prefrontal cortex structure and function. *Nature Reviews Neuroscience 2009 10:6, 10*(6), 410–422. https://doi.org/DOI: 10.1038/nrn2648

Arnsten, A. F. T. (2009a). Stress signalling pathways that impair prefrontal cortex structure and function. *Nature Reviews. Neuroscience*, *10*(6), 410. DOI: 10.1038/NRN2648 PMID: 19455173

Arslan, G., & Coşkun, M. (2023). School belongingness in academically at-risk adolescents: Addressing psychosocial functioning and psychological well-being. *Journal of Happiness and Health*, *3*(1), 1–13.

Art of Living Foundation. (n.d.). *Breathing techniques and stress management.* Retrieved from https://www.artofliving.org

As, M. (2014). *Ordinary magic: Resilience in development.* Guilford Press. [Google Scholar]

Ayoko, O. B., & Ashkanasy, N. M. (2020). The physical environment of office work: Future open plan offices. *Australian Journal of Management*, *45*(3), 488–506.

Bailey, D. E., & Kurland, N. B. (2002). A review of telework research: Findings, new directions, and lessons for the study of modern work. *Journal of Organizational Behavior*, *23*(4), 383–400. DOI: 10.1002/job.144

Banathy, B. H. (1991). *Systems design of education: A journey to create the future.* Educational Technology Publications.

Bandura, A. (2013). Self-Efficacy: The foundation of agency1. In *Control of human behavior, mental processes, and consciousness* (pp. 16-30). Psychology Press.

Bandura, A. (1997). *Self-efficacy: The exercise of control.* W.H. Freeman and Company.

Barath, M., & Schmidt, D. A. (2022). Offices after the COVID-19 pandemic and changes in perception of flexible office space. *Sustainability*, *14*(18), 11158.

Bargh, J. A., & Chartrand, T. L. (1999). The unbearable automaticity of being. *The American Psychologist*, *54*(7), 462–479. DOI: 10.1037/0003-066X.54.7.462

Barlow, D. H. . (2004). *Anxiety and its disorders : the nature and treatment of anxiety and panic*. 704.

Barnett, J. E. (2019). The ethical practice of psychotherapy: Clearly within our reach. *Psychotherapy (Chicago, Ill.)*, *56*(4), 431–440. DOI: 10.1037/PST0000272 PMID: 31815506

Barrett, R. (2010). Culture and consciousness: Measuring spirituality in the workplace by mapping values. In *Handbook of workplace spirituality and organizational performance* (pp. 271–291). Routledge.

Baş, G. (2025). How to improve academic achievement of students? The influence of academic emphasis on academic achievement with the mediating roles of school belonging, student engagement, and academic resilience. *Psychology in the Schools*, *62*(1), 313–335.

Baumeister, R. F., & Leary, M. R. (2017). The need to belong: Desire for interpersonal attachments as a fundamental human motivation. *Interpersonal development*, 57-89.

Baumeister, R. F., Bratslavsky, E., Muraven, M., & Tice, D. M. (1998). Ego depletion: Is the active self a limited resource? *Journal of Personality and Social Psychology*, *74*(5), 1252–1265. DOI: 10.1037/0022-3514.74.5.1252 PMID: 9599441

Baumeister, R. F., Vohs, K. D., & Tice, D. M. (2007). The Strength Model of Self-Control. *Current Directions in Psychological Science*, *16*(6), 351–355. DOI: 10.1111/J.1467-8721.2007.00534.X

Beck, A. T., & Clark, D. A. (1997). An information processing model of anxiety: Automatic and strategic processes. *Behaviour Research and Therapy*, *35*(1), 49–58. DOI: 10.1016/S0005-7967(96)00069-1 PMID: 9009043

Beddoe, L., Davys, A. M., & Adamson, C. (2014). 'Never trust anybody who says "i don't need supervision"': Practitioners' beliefs about social worker resilience. *Practice*, *26*(2), 113–130.

Beilock, S. L., & Carr, T. H. (2001). On the fragility of skilled performance: What governs choking under pressure? *Journal of Experimental Psychology. General*, *130*(4), 701–725. DOI: 10.1037/0096-3445.130.4.701 PMID: 11757876

Bernal, G., Jiménez-Chafey, M. I., & Domenech Rodríguez, M. M. (2009). Cultural Adaptation of Treatments: A Resource for Considering Culture in Evidence-Based Practice. *Professional Psychology, Research and Practice*, *40*(4), 361–368. DOI: 10.1037/A0016401

Bhattacharyya, S. S., & Thakre, S. (2021). Coronavirus pandemic and economic lockdown; study of strategic initiatives and tactical responses of firms. *The International Journal of Organizational Analysis*, *29*(5), 1240–1268.

Biggs, A., Brough, P., & Drummond, S. (2017). Lazarus and Folkman's psychological stress and coping theory. *The handbook of stress and health: A guide to research and practice*, 349-364.

BIMA. (2019). The voices of our industry: BIMA Tech Inclusion & Diversity Report 2019. Retrieved from https://bima.co.uk/wp-content/uploads/2020/01/BIMA-Tech-Inclusion-and-Diversity-Report-2019

Bowlby, J. (1988). *A secure base: Parent-child attachment and healthy human development*. Basic Books.

Bradley, E. J., & Biedermann, H.-J. (1985). Bandler and Grinder's neurolinguistic programming: Its historical context and contribution. *Psychotherapy (Chicago, Ill.)*, *22*(1), 59–62. DOI: 10.1037/h0088527

Bravata, D. M., Watts, S. A., Keefer, A. L., Madhusudhan, D. K., Taylor, K. T., Clark, D. M., Nelson, R. S., Cokley, K. O., & Hagg, H. K. (2020). Prevalence, predictors, and treatment of impostor syndrome: A systematic review. *Journal of General Internal Medicine*, *35*(4), 1252–1275. DOI: 10.1007/s11606-019-05364-1 PMID: 31848865

Brewer, M. B. (1991). On being the same and different at the same time. *Personality and Social Psychology Bulletin*, *17*(5), 475–482.

Brown, K. W., & Ryan, R. M. (2003). The benefits of being present: Mindfulness and psychological well-being. *Journal of Personality and Social Psychology*, *84*(4), 822–848. DOI: 10.1037/0022-3514.84.4.822 PMID: 12703651

Bundrant, H. (2024, March 4). *NLP and Hypnosis: Similarities, Differences, and Synergies*. iNLP Center. https://inlpcenter.org/whats-the-connection-between-nlp-and-hypnosis/

Burn-out an "occupational phenomenon": International Classification of Diseases. (n.d.). Retrieved December 18, 2025, from https://www.who.int/news/item/28-05-2019-burn-out-an-occupational-phenomenon-international-classification-of-diseases

Cambridge Core. (2019). *Be Well: A systems-based wellness intervention using mindfulness in the workplace: A case study*. Retrieved from https://www.cambridge.org/core/journals/journal-of-management-and-organization/article/

Cardeña, E., Cardeña-Buelna, D., & Spiegel, D. (2017). Hypnosis for the treatment of anxiety, stress-related disorders, and chronic pain. *Current Psychiatry Reports*, *19*(6), 40. DOI: 10.1007/s11920-017-0791-8

Carmichael, S. G. (2015, August 19). The research is clear: Long hours backfire for people and for companies. Harvard Business Review. https://hbr.org

Carmody, T. P. (2017). Hypnosis for smoking relapse prevention: A randomized trial. *The American Journal of Clinical Hypnosis*, *60*(2), 159–171. PMID: 28891777

CAST. (2018). *Universal Design for Learning Guidelines* (Version 2.2). http://udlguidelines.cast.org

Castrillon, C. (2023, Dec 17). *5 Powerful Strategies to build Trust in the Workplace.* Retrieved from Forbes: https://www.forbes.com/sites/carolinecastrillon/2023/12/17/5-powerful-ways-to-build-trust-in-the-workplace/

Chamine, I. A. (2018). Hypnosis intervention effects on sleep outcomes: A systematic review. *Journal of Clinical Sleep Medicine : JCSM : Official Publication of the American Academy of Sleep Medicine*, *14*(2), 271–283. PMID: 29198290

Child Mind Institute. (2024). *Twice-exceptional kids: Both gifted and challenged.* https://childmind.org/article/twice-exceptional-kids/

Choke | Book by Sian Beilock | Official Publisher Page | Simon & Schuster. (n.d.). Retrieved December 18, 2025, from https://www.simonandschuster.com/books/Choke/Sian-Beilock/9781416596189

Cholach, J. (2011). *Universal Design for Learning and gifted students in the 21st century classroom* (Master's thesis). University of Lethbridge.

Climate Sustainability Directory. (2023). *Psychophysiological stress.* Retrieved from https://climate.sustainability-directory.com/term/psychophysiological-stress

Coelho, A., & Silva, A. (2024, September). *THE ROLE OF HYPNOSIS IN THE WORK CONTEXT.* Retrieved from Google Scholar: https://estudogeral.uc.pt/retrieve/276354/Toma%CC%81s%20Pereira-%20Dissertac%CC%A7a%CC%83o%20Versa%CC%83o%20Final%20.pdf

Columbus Group. (1991). *Definition of giftedness* [Unpublished transcript]. https://www.gifteddevelopment.com/definitions-giftedness

Connor, K. M., & Davidson, J. R. (2003). Development of a new resilience scale: The Connor-Davidson resilience scale (CD-RISC). *Depression and Anxiety*, *18*(2), 76–82.

Conroy, D. E., Kaye, M. P., & Fifer, A. M. (2007). Cognitive Links Between Fear Of Failure And Perfectionism. *Journal of Rational-Emotive & Cognitive-Behavior Therapy 2007 25:4*, *25*(4), 237–253. https://doi.org/DOI: 10.1007/S10942-007-0052-7

Cooper, C. L., & Cartwright, S. (1994). Healthy Mind; Healthy Organization—A Proactive Approach to Occupational Stress. *Human Relations*, *47*(4), 455–471. DOI: 10.1177/001872679404700405;SUBPAGE:STRING:ABSTRACT;WEBSITE:WEBSITE:SAGE;REQUESTEDJOURNAL:JOURNAL:HUMA;W-GROUP:STRING:PUBLICATION

Cooper, C. L., & Marshall, J. (1976). Occupational sources of stress: A review of the literature relating to coronary heart disease and mental ill health. *Journal of Occupational Psychology*, *49*(1), 11–28. DOI: 10.1111/j.2044-8325.1976.tb00325.x

Cooper, C. L., & Quick, J. C. (2017). *The handbook of stress and health: A guide to research and practice*. Wiley Blackwell.

Cordi, M. J. (2015). Improving sleep and cognition by hypnotic suggestion in the elderly. *Neuropsychologia*, *69*, 176–182. PMID: 25660206

Coventry, P. (2022). Anxiety: A Subconscious Workplace Mental Health Challenge: Develooments in Subsconscious Solusion. *Scholarly Journal of Psychology and Behavioral Sciences*, https://lupinepublishers. com/psychology-behavioral-science-journal/pdf/SJPBS

Coventry, P. (2022). Occupational health and safety receptivity towards clinical innovations that can benefit workplace mental health programs: Anxiety and hypnotherapy trends. *International Journal of Environmental Research and Public Health*, *19*(13), 7735. PMID: 35805401

Creswell, J. D. (2017). Mindfulness interventions. *Annual Review of Psychology*, *68*, 491–516. DOI: 10.1146/annurev-psych-042716-051139 PMID: 27687118

Csikszentmihalyi, M. (1990). *Flow: The psychology of optimal experience*. Harper and Row.

Dąbrowski, K. (1964). *Positive disintegration*. Little, Brown.

Dąbrowski, K., Kawczak, A., & Piechowski, M. M. (1972). *Mental growth through positive disintegration*. Gryf.

Damasio, A. R. (1994). *Descartes' Error: Emotion, Reason, and the Human Brain*. https://philpapers.org/rec/DAMDEE

Dane, E., & Pratt, M. G. (2007). Exploring Intuition and its Role in Managerial Decision Making. Https://Doi.Org/10.5465/Amr.2007.23463682, *32*(1), 33–54. https://doi.org/DOI: 10.5465/AMR.2007.23463682

Daniels, S., & Piechowski, M. M. (Eds.). (2009). *Living with intensity*. Great Potential Press.

Dash, B. (2023). *Significance of Nonverbal Communication and Paralinguistic Features in Communication: A Critical Analysis*. https://doi.org/DOI: 10.2015/IJIRMF/202204029

Das, R. (2012). Occupational health concerns of software professionals and their coping strategies. *International Journal of Management Research and Business Strategy*, *1*, 81–85.

Davidov, J., & Russo-Netzer, P. (2022). Exploring the phenomenological structure of existential anxiety as lived through transformative life experiences. *Anxiety, Stress, and Coping*, *35*(2), 232–247.

Davidson Academy. (2024). *Understanding asynchronous development in gifted children*. https://davidsonacademy.unr.edu/blog/asynchronous-development/

Davidson Institute. (2005). *Social and emotional needs of gifted children*. https://www.davidsongifted.org/gifted-blog/social-and-emotional-needs-of-gifted-children/

Davis, S. N., & Tuttle, J. D. (2017). Context, opportunity, and demands: Satisfaction with work-life balance in 26 countries. *Journal of Comparative Family Studies*, *48*(4), 329–347. DOI: 10.3138/jcfs.48.4.329

De Benedittis, G. (2024). Hypnotic Modulation of Autonomic Nervous System (ANS) Activity. *Brain Sciences*, *14*(3), 249. DOI: 10.3390/brainsci14030249 PMID: 38539637

De Benedittis, G. (2025). Brain Mechanisms of Hypnosis. *Brain Sciences*, *15*(2), 142. DOI: 10.3390/BRAINSCI15020142 PMID: 40002475

Decety, J. (1996). The neurophysiological basis of motor imagery. *Behavioural Brain Research*, *77*(1–2), 45–52. DOI: 10.1016/0166-4328(95)00225-1 PMID: 8762158

Deloitte. (2023). *The Deloitte Global 2023 Gen Z and Millennial Survey*. Deloitte Insights. Retrieved from https://www.deloitte.com/global/en/issues/work/genzmillennialsurvey.html

Dexter, Á. (2024). The Impact of Remote Work on Interdisciplinary Collaboration in Game Development Projects.

dgoldenconlin. (2023, August 15). *Writing Across Ancient History and Civilizations*. Mysite. https://www.dgoldenconlin.com/post/writing-across-ancient-history-and-civilizations

Diamond, A. (2012). Executive Functions. *Annual Review of Psychology*, *64*, 135. DOI: 10.1146/ANNUREV-PSYCH-113011-143750 PMID: 23020641

Dillworth, T., Mendoza, M. E., & Jensen, M. P. (2012). Neurophysiology of pain and hypnosis for chronic pain. *Translational Behavioral Medicine*, *2*(1), 65–72. DOI: 10.1007/s13142-011-0084-5 PMID: 24073099

Dilts, R. B. (1983). *Roots of neuro-linguistic programming*. Meta Publications.

Driskell, J. E., Copper, C., & Moran, A. (1994). Does Mental Practice Enhance Performance? *The Journal of Applied Psychology*, *79*(4), 481–492. DOI: 10.1037/0021-9010.79.4.481

Dweck, C. S. (2006). *Mindset: The new psychology of success*. https://psycnet.apa.org/record/2006-08575-000

Dweck, C. S. (2006). *Mindset*. Random House.

Edmondson, A. C. (2018). *The Fearless Orginization*. 21–22. https://learning.oreilly.com/library/view/the-fearless-organization/9781119477242/c04.xhtml

Edmondson, A. (1999). Psychological safety and learning behavior in work teams. *Administrative Science Quarterly*, *44*(2), 350–383.

Einarsen, S., Hoel, H., Zapf, D., & Cooper, C. L. (2003). *Bullying and emotional abuse in the workplace: International perspectives in research and practice*. CRC Press.

Eisenberger, N. I. (2012). The pain of social disconnection: Examining the shared neural underpinnings of physical and social pain. *Nature Reviews. Neuroscience*, *13*(6), 421–434.

Eisenberger, R. H. (1986). Perceived organizational support. *The Journal of Applied Psychology*, *71*(3), 555.

El Kadiri, S., Grabot, B., Thoben, K. D., Hribernik, K., Emmanouilidis, C., Von Cieminski, G., & Kiritsis, D. (2016). Current trends on ICT technologies for enterprise information systems. *Computers in Industry*, *79*, 14–33. DOI: 10.1016/j.compind.2015.06.008

Elkins, G. J. (2007). Hypnotherapy for the management of chronic pain. *The International Journal of Clinical and Experimental Hypnosis*, *55*(3), 275–287. PMID: 17558718

Elkins, G. R. (2025). Clinical Hypnosis: A Contemporary, Evidence-Based Perspective. *Journal of Health Service Psychology*, •••, 1–13.

Elkins, G. R., Barabasz, A. F., Council, J. R., & Spiegel, D. (2015). Advancing research and practice: The revised APA Division 30 definition of hypnosis. *The American Journal of Clinical Hypnosis, 57*(4), 378–385. DOI: 10.1080/00029157.2015.1011465 PMID: 25928776

Elkins, G. R., Barabasz, A. F., Council, J. R., & Spiegel, D. (2015a). Advancing research and practice: The revised APA division 30 definition of hypnosis. *The International Journal of Clinical and Experimental Hypnosis, 63*(1), 1–9. DOI: 10.1080/00207144.2014.961870 PMID: 25365125

Ericksonian Hypnosis: What it is and How it is Used in Therapy | 2025. (2024, March 15). https://psychologyfor.com/ericksonian-hypnosis-what-it-is-and-how-it-is-used-in-therapy/

Erickson, M. H. (1967). *An Introduction to the Study and Application of Hypnosis for Pain Control.* Springer Berlin Heidelberg.

Ericsson, K. A., Krampe, R. T., & Tesch-Römer, C. (1993). Deliberate practice in expert performance. *Psychological Review, 100*(3), 363–406. DOI: 10.1037/0033-295X.100.3.363

Esch, T., Stefano, G. B., Fricchione, G. L., & Benson, H. (2002). Stress in cardiovascular diseases. *Signature (Ramsey, N.J.), 8*(5), 101.

Ethical principles of psychologists and code of conduct. (n.d.-a). Retrieved December 18, 2025, from https://www.apa.org/ethics/code

Ethical principles of psychologists and code of conduct. (n.d.-b). Retrieved December 18, 2025, from https://www.apa.org/ethics/code

European Foundation for the Improvement of Living and Working Conditions. (2016). European Quality of Life Survey. Retrieved October 24, 2022, from https://www.eurofound.europa.eu/data/european-quality-of-life-survey

Evans, J. S. B. T., & Stanovich, K. E. (2013a). Dual-Process Theories of Higher Cognition: Advancing the Debate. *Perspectives on Psychological Science : A Journal of the Association for Psychological Science, 8*(3), 223–241. https://doi.org/DOI: 10.1177/1745691612460685

Evans, J. S. B. T., & Stanovich, K. E. (2013). Dual-Process Theories of Higher Cognition: Advancing the Debate. *Perspectives on Psychological Science, 8*(3), 223–241. DOI: 10.1177/1745691612460685;WGROUP:STRING:PUBLICATION PMID: 26172965

Explorable. (2012). *Three different kinds of stress*. Retrieved from https://explorable.com/three-different-kinds-of-stress

Facco, E. (2020). Hypnosis for resilience. *OBM Integrative and Complimentary Medicine*, *5*(3), 1–20.

Festinger, L. (1954). A theory of social comparison processes. *Human Relations*, *7*(2), 117–140. DOI: 10.1177/001872675400700202

Fisch, S., Brinkhaus, B., & Teut, M. (2017). Hypnosis in patients with perceived stress – A systematic review. *BMC Complementary and Alternative Medicine*, *17*, 323. DOI: 10.1186/s12906-017-1806-0 PMID: 28629342

Fisch, S., Trivaković-Thiel, S., Roll, S., Keller, T., Binting, S., Cree, M., & Teut, M. (2020). Group hypnosis for stress reduction and improved stress coping: A multicenter randomized controlled trial. *BMC Complementary Medicine and Therapies*, •••, 1–14. PMID: 33187503

Fiske, S. T., & Taylor, S. E. (2013). Social Cognition: From Brains to Culture. *Social Cognition: From Brains to Culture*. https://doi.org/DOI: 10.4135/9781529681451

Fitzpatrick, K. K., Darcy, A., & Vierhile, M. (2017). Delivering Cognitive Behavior Therapy to Young Adults With Symptoms of Depression and Anxiety Using a Fully Automated Conversational Agent (Woebot): A Randomized Controlled Trial. *JMIR Mental Health*, *4*(2), e19. DOI: 10.2196/mental.7785 PMID: 28588005

Florida Department of Education. (2018). *Best practices in gifted education*. https://www.fldoe.org/core/fileparse.php/7676/urlt/BestPracticesGifted.pdf

Ford, D. Y. (2014). *Recruiting and retaining culturally different students in gifted education*. Prufrock Press.

Ford, D. Y., Grantham, T. C., & Whiting, G. W. (2021). Equity in gifted education. *Gifted Child Today*, *44*(1), 4–18. DOI: 10.1177/1076217520975531

Franken, E., Bentley, T., Shafaei, A., Farr-Wharton, B., Onnis, L., & Omari, M. (2021). Forced flexibility and remote working: Opportunities and challenges in the new normal. *Journal of Management & Organization*, *27*(6), 1131–1149. DOI: 10.1017/jmo.2021.40

Frankl, V. E. (1985). *Man's search for meaning*. Simon and Schuster.

Freud, S. (1915).. . *The Unconscious.*, *41*, 159–215.

Fromme, D. K. (2011). Humanism: Experiential Approaches. In D. K. Fromme, *Systems of Psychotherapy* (pp. 223–261). Springer New York. https://doi.org/DOI: 10.1007/978-1-4419-7308-5_8

Frost, R. O., Marten, P., Lahart, C., & Rosenblate, R. (1990). The dimensions of perfectionism. *Cognitive Therapy and Research, 14*(5), 449–468. DOI: 10.1007/BF01172967

Gabrielsen, L. E., & Lindström, T. C. (2021). Zillennials at work: Characteristics and challenges of the cusp generation. *Journal of Organizational Psychology, 21*(4), 89–105.

Gardner, H. (1983). *Frames of mind: The theory of multiple intelligences.* Basic Books.

Golden, T. D., & Veiga, J. F. (2005). The impact of extent of telecommuting on job satisfaction: Resolving inconsistent findings. *Journal of Management, 31*(2), 301–318. DOI: 10.1177/0149206304271768

Gonsalkorale, W. M. (2003). Long term benefits of hypnotherapy for irritable bowel syndrome. *BMJ Journal Gut, 52*(11), 1623–1629. PMID: 14570733

González-Ramírez, E., Carrillo-Montoya, T., García-Vega, M. L., Hart, C. E., Zavala-Norzagaray, A. A., & Ley-Quiñónez, C. P. (2017). Effectiveness of hypnosis therapy and Gestalt therapy as depression treatments. *Clinica y Salud, 28*(1), 33–37. DOI: 10.1016/j.clysa.2016.11.001

Gottman, J. M. (1994). *What predicts divorce? The relationship between marital processes and marital outcomes.* Lawrence Erlbaum Associates.

Grant, S. (2023, November 15). NLP Hypnosis Reading vs. Traditional Hypnosis: What Sets Them Apart? *Medium.* https://medium.com/@samanthagrant2024/nlp-hypnosis-reading-vs-traditional-hypnosis-what-sets-them-apart-5b57e3ab6e04

Grant, A. M. (2017). The third 'generation' of workplace coaching: Creating a culture of quality conversations. *Coaching (Abingdon, UK), 10*(1), 37–53. DOI: 10.1080/17521882.2016.1266005

Greenhalgh, L., & Rosenblatt, Z. (1984). Job insecurity: Toward conceptual clarity. *Academy of Management Review, 9*(3), 438–448. DOI: 10.5465/amr.1984.4279673

Grinder, J., & Bandler, R. (with Internet Archive). (1976). *The structure of magic.* Palo Alto, Ca.: Science and Behavior Books. http://archive.org/details/structureofmagic00grin

Grissom, J. A., & Redding, C. (2016). Discretion and disproportionality. *AERA Open, 2*(1), 1–25. DOI: 10.1177/2332858415622175 PMID: 26942210

Gross, J. J. (2015). Emotion Regulation: Current Status and Future Prospects. *Psychological Inquiry*, *26*(1), 1–26. DOI: 10.1080/1047840X.2014.940781;ISSUE:ISSUE:DOI

Gross, J. J., & John, O. P. (2003). Individual differences in two emotion regulation processes: Implications for affect, relationships, and well-being. *Journal of Personality and Social Psychology*, *85*(2), 348–362. DOI: 10.1037/0022-3514.85.2.348 PMID: 12916575

Gucciardi, D. F., Hanton, S., Gordon, S., Mallett, C. J., & Temby, P. (2015). The Concept of Mental Toughness: Tests of Dimensionality, Nomological Network, and Traitness. *Journal of Personality*, *83*(1), 26–44. DOI: 10.1111/JOPY.12079;JOURNAL:JOURNAL:14676494;WGROUP:STRING:PUBLICATION PMID: 24428736

Guse, T. (2014). Increasing psychological well-being through hypnosis. In *Increasing psychological well-being in clinical and educational settings: Interventions and cultural contexts* (pp. 91–102). Springer.

Haidt, J. (2001a). The emotional dog and its rational tail: A social intuitionist approach to moral judgment. *Psychological Review*, *108*(4), 814–834. DOI: 10.1037/0033-295X.108.4.814 PMID: 11699120

Halbesleben, J. R. (2010). A meta-analysis of work engagement: Relationships with burnout, demands, resources, and consequences. In Bakker, A. B., & Leiter, M. P. (Eds.), *Work engagement: A handbook of essential theory and research* (pp. 102–117). Psychology Press.

Halligan, P. W., & Oakley, D. A. (2013a). Hypnosis and cognitive neuroscience: Bridging the gap. *Cortex*, *49*(2), 359–364. DOI: 10.1016/J.CORTEX.2012.12.002 PMID: 23375442

Hamachek, D. E. (1978). Psychodynamics of perfectionism. *Psychology: A Journal of Human Behavior, 15*(1), 27–33.

Hammond, D. Corydon. (1990). *Handbook of hypnotic suggestions and metaphors*. 602. https://wwnorton.com/books/Handbook-of-Hypnotic-Suggestions-and-Metaphors

Hammond, D. C. (2010a). Hypnosis in the treatment of anxiety- and stress-related disorders. *Expert Review of Neurotherapeutics*, *10*(2), 263–273. DOI: 10.1586/ERN.09.140 PMID: 20136382

Hammond, D. C. (2017). Hypnosis in the treatment of stress-related disorders. *The American Journal of Clinical Hypnosis*, *59*(4), 343–350. DOI: 10.1080/00029157.2016.1223593

Hanisch, S. E., Twomey, C. D., Szeto, A. C., Birner, U. W., Nowak, D., & Sabariego, C. (2016). The effectiveness of interventions targeting the stigma of mental illness at the workplace: A systematic review. *BMC Psychiatry, 16*, 1. DOI: 10.1186/s12888-015-0706-4 PMID: 26739960

Hargreaves, A., & Fullan, M. (2012). *Professional capital*. Teachers College Press.

Hartfiel, N., Hetherington, S. H., Darzi, A., Goodman, N., & Spencer, A. (2011). The effectiveness of yoga for the improvement of well-being and resilience to stress in the workplace. *Scandinavian Journal of Work, Environment & Health, 37*(1), 70–76. DOI: 10.5271/sjweh.3137 PMID: 20369218

Hartland, J. (1971). Further observations on the use of ego-strengthening techniques. *The American Journal of Clinical Hypnosis, 14*(1), 1–8. DOI: 10.1080/00029157.1971.10402149 PMID: 5163560

Hasin, H., Johari, Y. C., Jamil, A., Nordin, E., & Hussein, W. S. (2023). The harmful impact of job stress on mental and physical health. *International Journal of Academic Research in Business & Social Sciences, 13*(4), 1–XX. DOI: 10.6007/IJARBSS/v13-i4/16655

Hayes, A. F. (2013). Mediation, moderation, and conditional process analysis. *Introduction to mediation, moderation, and conditional process analysis: A regression-based approach, 1*(6), 12-20.

Health & Safety Executive. UK. (2020). Mental health conditions, work and the workplace. Retrieved February 25, 2022, from https://www.hse.gov.uk/stress/mental-health.htm

Heap & Aravind. (2002). *Hartland's Medical and Dental Hypnosis - 4th Edition | Elsevier Shop*. https://shop.elsevier.com/books/hartlands-medical-and-dental-hypnosis/heap/978-0-443-07217-8

Heap, M. Heap, M. R. J., & Oakley, D. A. (2004). *The Highly Hypnotizable Person*. https://books.google.com/books/about/The_Highly_Hypnotizable_Person.html?id=vvmOAgAAQBAJ

Herald Open Access. (2018). *Physiology of stress and its management*. https://www.heraldopenaccess.us/openaccess/physiology-of-stress-and-its-management

Hewitt, P. L., Flett, G. L., & York, N. (1991).. . *Perfectionism in the Self and Social Contexts: Conceptualization, Assessment, and Association With Psychopathology., 60*(3), 456–470.

Higson-Sweeney, N., Mikkola, A., Smith, L., Shafique, J., Draper, L., Cooper, K., Dunn, B. D., & Loades, M. E. (2022). Nonpharmacological interventions for treating fatigue in adolescents: A systematic review and narrative synthesis of randomised controlled trials. *Journal of Psychosomatic Research, 163*, 111070. DOI: 10.1016/j.jpsychores.2022.111070 PMID: 36327529

Hockey, R. (2014). *The psychology of fatigue : work, effort and control.* 272. https://books.google.com/books/about/The_Psychology_of_Fatigue.html?id=oQBeAwAAQBAJ

Hofstede, G. (2010). *Cultures and organizations: Software of the mind.* https://e-edu.nbu.bg/pluginfile.php/900222/mod_resource/content/1/G.Hofstede_G.J.Hofstede_M.Minkov%20-%20Cultures%20and%20Organizations%20-%20Software%20of%20the%20Mind%203rd_edition%202010.pdf

Holroyd, J. (2003). The science of meditation and the state of hypnosis. *The American Journal of Clinical Hypnosis, 46*(2), 109–128. DOI: 10.1080/00029157.2003.10403582 PMID: 14609297

Hopkins, J., & Bardoel, A. (2023). The future is hybrid: How organisations are designing and supporting sustainable hybrid work models in post-pandemic Australia. *Sustainability, 15*(4), 3086.

Hutomo, Y. (2024). Case Study: Observation of Reducing Heartburn Pain in Gastroesophageal Reflux Disease (Gerd) With Hypnotherapy. *Jurnal Health Sains, 5*(10), 767–773.

IIEP UNESCO. (2019). *Flexible learning pathways in higher education.* UNESCO. https://unesdoc.unesco.org/ark:/48223/pf0000367761

Immordino-Yang, M. H., & Damasio, A. (2007). We feel, therefore we learn. *Mind, Brain and Education : the Official Journal of the International Mind, Brain, and Education Society, 1*(1), 3–10. DOI: 10.1111/j.1751-228X.2007.00004.x

Investing in treatment for depression and anxiety leads to fourfold return. (n.d.). Retrieved December 21, 2025, from https://www.who.int/news/item/13-04-2016-investing-in-treatment-for-depression-and-anxiety-leads-to-fourfold-return

Iowa Department of Education. (n.d.). *Curriculum compacting.* https://educateiowa.gov/pk-12/learner-supports/talented-gifted/curriculum-compacting

It's a New Era for Mental Health at Work. (n.d.). Retrieved December 21, 2025, from https://hbr.org/2021/10/its-a-new-era-for-mental-health-at-work

Jensen, M. P. (2017). New directions in hypnosis research: Strategies for advancing the cognitive and clinical neuroscience of hypnosis. *Neuroscience of Consciousness, 2017*(1), nix004. PMID: 29034102

Jensen, M. P., & Patterson, D. R. (2014). Hypnotic Approaches for Chronic Pain Management. *The American Psychologist, 69*(2), 167–177. DOI: 10.1037/a0035644 PMID: 24547802

Jetten, J., Haslam, C., Haslam, S. A., Dingle, G., & Jones, J. M. (2014). How groups affect our health and well-being: The path from theory to policy. *Social Issues and Policy Review, 8*(1), 103–130.

Jiang, H., White, M. P., Greicius, M. D., Waelde, L. C., & Spiegel, D. (2017). Brain activity and functional connectivity associated with hypnosis. *Cerebral Cortex (New York, N.Y.), 27*(8), 4083–4093. DOI: 10.1093/cercor/bhw220 PMID: 27469596

Joyce, S., Modini, M., Christensen, H., Mykletun, A., Bryant, R., & Mitchell, P. B. (2016). Workplace interventions for common mental disorders: A systematic meta-review. *Psychological Medicine, 46*, 683–697. DOI: 10.1017/S0033291715002408 PMID: 26620157

Kabat-Zinn, J. (1990). *Full catastrophe living: Using the wisdom of your body and mind to face stress, pain, and illness*. Delta.

Kahneman, D. (2011). *Thinking, fast and slow.* https://psycnet.apa.org/record/2011-26535-000

Kahneman, D., & Tversky, A. (2018). Prospect theory: An analysis of decision under risk. *Experiments in Environmental Economics, 1*, 143–172. DOI: 10.2307/1914185

Kahu, E. R., Picton, C., & Nelson, K. (2020). Pathways to engagement: A longitudinal study of the first-year student experience in the educational interface. *Higher Education, 79*(4), 657–673.

Kalleberg, A. L. (2018). *Precarious lives: Job insecurity and well-being in rich democracies*. Polity Press.

Kallesøe, K. H., Andersen, R. R., & Vinther, M. (2014). Coping with work-related stress through Guided Imagery and Music (GIM). *Journal of Music Therapy, 51*(4), 348–365. DOI: 10.1093/jmt/51.4.348

Kallio, S., & Revonsuo, A. (2003). Hypnotic phenomena and altered states of consciousness: A multilevel framework of description and explanation. *Contemporary Hypnosis, 20*(3), 111–164. DOI: 10.1002/ch.273

Karasek, R. A. (1979). Job demands, job decision latitude, and mental strain: Implications for job redesign. *Administrative Science Quarterly*, *24*(2), 285–308. DOI: 10.2307/2392498

Katz, D., & Kahn, R. L. (1978). *The social psychology of organizations* (2nd ed.). Wiley.

Khusid, M. A., & Vythilingam, M. (2016). The emerging role of mindfulness meditation as an effective self-management strategy, part 1: Clinical implications for depression, anxiety, and stress. *Military Medicine*, *181*(9), 961–968. DOI: 10.7205/MILMED-D-15-00412 PMID: 27612338

Kihlstrom, J. F. (2008). The domain of hypnosis, revisited. In Nash, M. R., & Barnier, A. J. (Eds.), *The Oxford handbook of hypnosis* (pp. 21–52). Oxford University Press.

Kim, J., Lee, H., & Cho, Y. H. (2022). Learning design for AI collaboration. *Education and Information Technologies*, *27*, 6069–6104. DOI: 10.1007/s10639-021-10831-6

King, E. V. (2022). Twice-exceptional learners and SEL. *Journal for the Education of the Gifted*, *45*(2), 112–135. DOI: 10.1177/10762175221078945

Kirsch, I., Montgomery, G., & Sapirstein, G. (2011). Hypnosis as an adjunct to cognitive-behavioral psychotherapy: A meta-analysis. *Journal of Consulting and Clinical Psychology*, *63*(2), 214–220. https://www.ncbi.nlm.nih.gov/books/NBK73898/

Kohen, D. P. (2014). Clinical Hypnosis with Children and Adolescents—What? Why? How?: Origins, Applications, and Efficacy. *Children (Basel, Switzerland)*, *1*(2), 74–98. PMID: 27417468

Kosslyn, S. M., Ganis, G., & Thompson, W. L. (2001). Neural foundations of imagery. *Nature Reviews Neuroscience 2001 2:9, 2*(9), 635–642. https://doi.org/DOI: 10.1038/35090055

Koutra, K., Mouatsou, C., & Psoma, S. (2023). The Influence of Positive and Negative Aspects of Perfectionism on Psychological Distress in Emerging Adulthood: Exploring the Mediating Role of Self-Compassion. *Behavioral Sciences (Basel, Switzerland)*, *13*(11), 932. DOI: 10.3390/BS13110932 PMID: 37998679

Krajčík, M., Schmidt, D. A., & Baráth, M. (2023). Hybrid work model: An approach to work–life flexibility in a changing environment. *Administrative Sciences*, *13*(6), 150.

Landry, M., Lifshitz, M., & Raz, A. (2017a). Brain correlates of hypnosis: A systematic review and meta-analytic exploration. *Neuroscience and Biobehavioral Reviews, 81*(Pt A), 75–98. https://doi.org/DOI: 10.1016/j.neubiorev.2017.02.020

Landry, M., Lifshitz, M., & Raz, A. (2017). Brain correlates of hypnosis: A systematic review and meta-analytic exploration. *Neuroscience and Biobehavioral Reviews, 81*, 75–98. DOI: 10.1016/J.NEUBIOREV.2017.02.020 PMID: 28238944

Lavertue, N. E. (2002). The effectiveness of a hypnotic ego-strengthening procedure for improving self-esteem and depression. *Australian Journal of Clinical & Experimental Hypnosis, 30*(1), 1–23.

Lazarus, R. S., & Folkman, S. (1984). *Stress, appraisal, and coping*. Springer.

Learn how to manage your workplace stress. (n.d.). Retrieved December 21, 2025, from https://www.apa.org/topics/healthy-workplaces/workplace-stress

LeDoux, J. (1996). *Cognitive and emotional interactions in the brain: The mysterious underpinnings of emotional life*. 384. https://books.google.com/books/about/The_Emotional_Brain.html?id=7EJN5I8sk2wC

LeDoux, J. E. (1996). *The emotional brain: The mysterious underpinnings of emotional life*. https://psycnet.apa.org/record/1996-98824-000

LeDoux, J. (2012). Rethinking the Emotional Brain. *Neuron, 73*(4), 653–676. DOI: 10.1016/j.neuron.2012.02.004 PMID: 22365542

LeDoux, J. E., & Pine, D. S. (2016). Using Neuroscience to Help Understand Fear and Anxiety: A Two-System Framework. *The American Journal of Psychiatry, 173*(11), 1083–1093. DOI: 10.1176/APPI.AJP.2016.16030353 PMID: 27609244

Leiter, M. P., & Maslach, C. (1988). The impact of interpersonal environment on burnout and organizational commitment. *Journal of Organizational Behavior, 9*(4), 297–308. DOI: 10.1002/job.4030090402

Leo, D. G. (2024). "Close your eyes and relax": The role of hypnosis in reducing anxiety, and its implications for the prevention of cardiovascular diseases. *Frontiers in Psychology, 15*, 1411835. PMID: 39035095

Lerner,R.M.(2018).*Developmentalscience*.Routledge.,DOI:10.4324/9781315156123

Lidster, T., & Williams, M. (2012). Dynamic assessment. *Language and Sociocultural Theory, 1*(1).

Lord, R. G., Foti, R. J., & De Vader, C. L. (1984). A test of leadership categorization theory: Internal structure, information processing, and leadership perceptions. *Organizational Behavior and Human Performance, 34*(3), 343–378. DOI: 10.1016/0030-5073(84)90043-6

Lord, R. G., & Hall, R. J. (2005a). Identity, deep structure and the development of leadership skill. *The Leadership Quarterly*, *16*(4), 591–615. DOI: 10.1016/J.LEAQUA.2005.06.003

Luckin, R. (2018). *Machine learning and human intelligence*. UCL Press.

Luthans, F., Youssef, C., & Avolio, B. (2020). *Psychological capital and beyond - Liberty University*. 2024. https://global.oup.com/academic/product/psychological-capital-and-beyond-9780199316472

Lynn, S. J., Kirsch, I., & Hallquist, M. N. (2008). *Social cognitive theories of hypnosis*. https://psycnet.apa.org/record/2007-19668-005

Lynn, S. J., & Kirsch, I. (2006). *Essentials of clinical hypnosis: An evidence-based approach*. American Psychological Association.

Lynn, S. J., Kirsch, I., Barabasz, A., Cardeña, E., & Patterson, D. (2000a). Hypnosis as an empirically supported clinical intervention: The state of the evidence and a look to the future. *The International Journal of Clinical and Experimental Hypnosis*, *48*(2), 239–259. DOI: 10.1080/00207140008410050 PMID: 10769986

Marshall, D. A. (2002). Behavior, belonging, and belief: A theory of ritual practice. *Sociological Theory*, *20*(3), 360–380.

Maslach, C., & Jackson, S. E. (1981). The measurement of experienced burnout. *Journal of Occupational Behaviour*, *2*(2), 99–113. DOI: 10.1002/job.4030020205

Maslach, C., Jackson, S. E., & Leiter, M. P. (2001). *Maslach burnout inventory manual* (3rd ed.). Consulting Psychologists Press.

Maslach, C., & Leiter, M. P. (2016). *Burnout: The cost of caring*. Malor Books.

Maslach, C., & Leiter, M. P. (2016a). Understanding the burnout experience: Recent research and its implications for psychiatry. *World Psychiatry; Official Journal of the World Psychiatric Association (WPA)*, *15*(2), 103–111. DOI: 10.1002/WPS.20311;REQUESTEDJOURNAL:JOURNAL:20515545;JOURNAL:JOURNAL:20515545;WGROUP:STRING:PUBLICATION PMID: 27265691

Mathur, S. (2011). Impact of hypnotherapy on examination anxiety and scholastic performance among school children. *Delhi Psychiatry Journal*, *14*(2), 337–342.

Matthews, W. J. (2000). Ericksonian approaches to hypnosis and therapy: Where are we now? *The International Journal of Clinical and Experimental Hypnosis*, *48*(4), 418–426. DOI: 10.1080/00207140008410370 PMID: 11011501

McEwen, B. S. (1998). Protective and damaging effects of stress mediators. *The New England Journal of Medicine*, *338*(3), 171–179. DOI: 10.1056/NEJM199801153380307

McEwen, B. S. (2017). Neurobiological and systemic effects of chronic stress. *Chronic Stress (Thousand Oaks, Calif.)*, *1*, 2470547017692328. DOI: 10.1177/2470547017692328 PMID: 28856337

McEwen, B. S., & Morrison, J. H. (2013a). The Brain on Stress: Vulnerability and Plasticity of the Prefrontal Cortex over the Life Course. *Neuron*, *79*(1), 16–29. DOI: 10.1016/J.NEURON.2013.06.028 PMID: 23849196

McKinsey & Company. (2023). *Gen Z and Millennial workforce wellness report*. McKinsey Health Institute.

Medaglia, S. (2008). Gifted adolescents and disintegration. In Mendaglio, S. (Ed.), *Dąbrowski's theory of positive disintegration* (pp. 13–40). Great Potential Press.

Megha. (2024, February 15). *Gestalt Therapy: The Power of the Present Moment in Healing*. Careme.Health. https://careme.health/blog/gestalt-therapy-the-power-of-the-present-moment-in-healing

Mendaglio, S. (2008). Positive disintegration as developmental. In Mendaglio, S. (Ed.), *Dąbrowski's theory* (pp. 1–12). Great Potential Press.

Michael Heap, K. K. A. (2001). *Hartland's Medical and Dental Hypnosis - 4th Edition | Elsevier Shop*. https://shop.elsevier.com/books/hartlands-medical-and-dental-hypnosis/heap/978-0-443-07217-8

Milliman, J., Czaplewski, A. J., & Ferguson, J. (2003). Workplace spirituality and employee work attitudes: An exploratory empirical assessment. *Journal of Organizational Change Management*, *16*(4), 426–447.

Ministry of Education. (2020). *National education policy 2020*. Government of India.

Montgomery, G. H., Duhamel, K. N., & Redd, W. H. (2000a). A meta-analysis of hypnotically induced analgesia: How effective is hypnosis? *The International Journal of Clinical and Experimental Hypnosis*, *48*(2), 138–153. DOI: 10.1080/00207140008410045 PMID: 10769981

Moore, D. A., & Bazerman, M. H. (2012). Introduction. *Judgment in Managerial Decision Making*. https://www.wiley.com/en-us/Judgment+in+Managerial+Decision+Making%2C+8th+Edition-p-9781118065709

Murphy, L. R., & Schoenborn, T. F. (1987). *Stress management in work settings.*

N.A. (2009). *Different approaches to psychotherapy*. Retrieved from American Psychological Association: https://www.apa.org/topics/psychotherapy/approaches

N.A. (2014). *Society of Psychological Hypnosis*. Retrieved from https://www.apadivisions.org/division-30/about/#:~:text=In%202014%2C%20the%20Div.%2030%20Executive%20Committee%20prepared,by%20an%20enhanced%20capacity%20for%20response%20to%20suggestion

N.A. (2018). *Work-life balance*. Retrieved from APA Dictionary of Psychology: https://dictionary.apa.org/work-life-balance

N.A. (2023). *Gallup Employee Wellbeing Indicator*. Retrieved from https://www.gallup.com/394424/indicator-employee-wellbeing.aspx

N.A. (2024, September 2). *Mental health at work*. Retrieved from https://www.who.int/news-room/fact-sheets/detail/mental-health-at-work

N.A. (N.A.). *Identifying High-Potential Employees: Everything You Should Know*. Retrieved from Envisia Learning: https://www.envisialearning.com/blog/leadership-development/identifying-high-potential-employees/

Nardodkar, R., Pathare, S., Ventriglio, A., Castaldelli-Maia, J., Javate, K. R., & Torales, J.. (2016). Legal protection of the right to work and employment for persons with mental health problems: A review of legislation across the world. *International Review of Psychiatry (Abingdon, England)*, *28*, 375–384. DOI: 10.1080/09540261.2016.1210575 PMID: 27499197

National Association for Gifted Children. (2019). *The excellence gap*. https://www.nagc.org/resources-publications/resources-parents/excellence-gap

National Center for Education Research. (2022). Do underrepresented students benefit from gifted programs? https://ies.ed.gov/ncee/rel/regions/northeast/blogs/blog39_underrepresented_gifted.asp

Neff, K. (2003). Self-compassion: An alternative conceptualization of a healthy attitude toward oneself. *Self and Identity*, *2*(2), 85–101.

Neihart, M., Reis, S. M., Robinson, N. M., & Moon, S. M. (2021). *The social and emotional development of gifted children*. Prufrock Press.

Neuron, U. P. (2020). *Work stress: Definition, types, causes and consequences for health*. Retrieved from https://neuronup.us/psychology/work-stress-definition-types-causes-and-consequences-for-health/

Nevis, E. C. (2009). *Gestalt therapy: Perspectives and applications* (1st paperback ed). Routledge.

Oakley, D. A. (2008). *Hypnosis, trance and suggestion: Evidence from neuroimaging.* https://awspntest.apa.org/record/2007-19668-014

Oakley, D. A., & Halligan, P. W. (2013). Hypnotic suggestion: opportunities for cognitive neuroscience. *Nature Reviews Neuroscience 2013 14:8, 14*(8), 565–576. https://doi.org/DOI: 10.1038/nrn3538

Oakley, D. A., & Halligan, P. W. (2009). Hypnotic suggestion and cognitive neuroscience. *Trends in Cognitive Sciences, 13*(6), 264–270. DOI: 10.1016/j.tics.2009.03.004 PMID: 19428287

Oakley, D. A., & Halligan, P. W. (2013). Hypnotic suggestion: Opportunities for cognitive neuroscience. *Nature Reviews. Neuroscience, 14*(8), 565–576. DOI: 10.1038/NRN3538 PMID: 23860312

Obregon, S. L., Lopes, L. F. D., Silva, W. V. D., Silva, D. J. C. D., Castro, B. L. G. D., Kuhn, N., & Veiga, C. P. D. (2024). The influence of spirituality in the relationship between religiosity and work engagement: A perspective on social responsibility. *Social Responsibility Journal, 20*(10), 1909–1934.

OECD. (2020). *PISA 2018 results.* OECD Publishing., DOI: 10.1787/5f07c754-

Olawade, D. B., Wada, O. Z., Odetayo, A., David-Olawade, A. C., Asaolu, F., & Eberhardt, J. (2024). Enhancing mental health with Artificial Intelligence: Current trends and future prospects. *Journal of Medicine, Surgery, and Public Health, 3*, 100099. DOI: 10.1016/j.glmedi.2024.100099

Om Swami. (n.d.). *Reflections on meditation, awareness, and health.* OS.me. Retrieved from https://www.os.me

Organización Mundial de la Salud. (2022a). Directrices de la OMS sobre salud mental en el trabajo. *World Health Organization Guidelines on Mental Health at Work*, 1–143. https://www.who.int/publications/i/item/9789240053052

Organización Mundial de la Salud. (2022b). Directrices de la OMS sobre salud mental en el trabajo. *World Health Organization Guidelines on Mental Health at Work*, 1–143. https://www.who.int/publications/i/item/9789240053052

Padhi, B. (2015). A Study on Employee Engagement Models for Sustainability of Organisation. [IJRDMR]. *International Journal of Research and Development-A Management Review, 4*(4), 79–85.

Padma, V., Anand, N. N., Gurukul, S. M., Javid, S. M., Prasad, A., & Arun, S. (2015). Health problems and stress in Information Technology and Business Process Outsourcing employees. *Journal of Pharmacy & Bioallied Sciences*, *7*(Suppl 1), S9–S13. DOI: 10.4103/0975-7406.15576 PMID: 26015763

Park University. (2023). *The gig economy: Shaping the future of work and business.* Retrieved from https://www.park.edu/blog/the-gig-economy-shaping-the-future-of-work-and-business/

Pascoe, M. C., Thompson, D. R., & Ski, C. F. (2017). Yoga, mindfulness-based stress reduction and stress-related physiological measures: A meta-analysis. *Psychoneuroendocrinology*, *86*, 152–168. DOI: 10.1016/j.psyneuen.2017.08.008 PMID: 28963884

Passmore, J. (2020). The Coaches' Handbook. *The Coaches' Handbook.* https://doi.org/DOI: 10.4324/9781003089889/COACHES-HANDBOOK-JONATHAN-PASSMORE

Patra, D. (2021). *The Role of Hypnosis in Addressing Stress at the Workplace due to Psychosocial Issues.* Lincoln Research and Publications Limited.

Patterson, D. R., Jensen, M. P., Wiechman, S. A., & Sharar, S. R. (2010). Virtual reality hypnosis for pain associated with recovery from physical trauma. *The International Journal of Clinical and Experimental Hypnosis*, *58*(3), 288–300. DOI: 10.1080/00207141003760595;JOURNAL:JOURNAL:NHYP19;PAGE:STRING:ARTICLE/CHAPTER PMID: 20509069

Payne, S. M., & Whitworth, D. E. (2022). Increasing creative self-efficacy: Developing the confidence of biochemistry undergraduates to innovate. *Biochemistry and Molecular Biology Education*, *50*(3), 296–306.

Pellegrini, M. C. (2021). The use of self-help strategies in obesity treatment. A narrative review focused on hypnosis and mindfulness. *Current Obesity Reports*, *10*(3), 351–364. PMID: 34050891

Petchsawang, P., & Duchon, D. (2012). Workplace spirituality, meditation, and work performance. *Journal of Management, Spirituality & Religion*, *9*(2), 189–208.

Peter, B., Schedlowski, M., Warth, M., & Hölzel, L. P. (2020). Stress reduction through group hypnosis in professional settings: A randomized controlled trial. *The International Journal of Clinical and Experimental Hypnosis*, *68*(4), 485–503. DOI: 10.1080/00207144.2020.1780651

Peters, S. J., Gentry, M., Whiting, G. W., & McBee, M. T. (2023). Who gets served? *Journal of Advanced Academics*, *34*(1), 7–33. DOI: 10.1177/1932202X221124958

Pfeiffer, S. I. (2015). *Essentials of gifted assessment*. Wiley.

Pham, E. (2023, Feb 27). *Forbes*. Retrieved from Five Strategies for Improving Work-Life Balance: https://www.forbes.com/councils/forbesbusinesscouncil/2023/02/27/five-strategies-for-improving-work-life-balance/

Phelps, E. A., & LeDoux, J. E. (2005). Contributions of the amygdala to emotion processing: From animal models to human behavior. *Neuron*, *48*(2), 175–187. DOI: 10.1016/j.neuron.2005.09.025 PMID: 16242399

Philpot, N., & Donachie, T. C. (2025). Perfectionism and psychological distress in university students: The role of mistake rumination. *Personality and Individual Differences*, *246*, 113368. DOI: 10.1016/J.PAID.2025.113368

Piechowski, M. M. (2006). *Mellow out, they say. If I only could*. Yunasa Books.

Poddar, S., Kar, B., Samanta, S., & Bhaumi, A. (Eds.). (2021). *Human resource management and mental health: A psychosocial aspect*. KIIT University., DOI: 10.46977/book.2021.hrmmh

Przybylski, A. K., Murayama, K., DeHaan, C. R., & Gladwell, V. (2013). Motivational, emotional, and behavioral correlates of fear of missing out. *Computers in Human Behavior*, *29*(4), 1841–1848. DOI: 10.1016/j.chb.2013.02.014

Purcell, J. H., & Renzulli, J. S. (1998). *Total talent portfolio*. Creative Learning Press.

Qureshi, D. A. (2024, July 23). *NLP Therapy Explained: Discover the Benefits and Techniques*. Therapy Helpers. https://therapyhelpers.com/therapy-types/what-is-neuro-linguistic-programming-therapy/

Rachmad, Y. E. (2024). *Stress Management Theory*. https://doi.org/DOI: 10.17605/OSF.IO/5UT3K

Ramesh, A. B. K., & Sinnu, B. (2024). Enhancing workplace spirituality for higher education academicians through human resource practices. *IIMT Journal of Management*, *1*(1), 88–97.

Rashidi, Z., & Jalbani, A. A. (2009). Job stress among software professionals in Pakistan: A factor analytic study. [MSSE]. *Journal of Independent Studies and Research*, *7*(1), 1–1.

Raygoza Limón, M. E., & Jiménez Sánchez, R. (2024). Perspectives and challenges for the development of leadership in Latin American women. *Entretextos*, *16*(40), 1–19. DOI: 10.59057/iberoleon.20075316.202440738

Raygoza-L, M. E., Orduño-Osuna, J. H., Jimenez-Sanchez, R., Mercado-Herrera, A., Ling, J. C., & Rico, F. N. M. (2024). Leadership and Coaching Management as a Governance Instrument for Sociocultural Development. In Wefald, A. J. (Ed.), (pp. 37–57). Advances in Logistics, Operations, and Management Science. IGI Global., DOI: 10.4018/979-8-3693-5242-7.ch003

Raz, A., Fan, J., & Posner, M. I. (2005a). Hypnotic suggestion reduces conflict in the human brain. *Proceedings of the National Academy of Sciences of the United States of America*, *102*(28), 9978–9983. DOI: 10.1073/PNAS.0503064102 PMID: 15994228

Reis, S. M., & Renzulli, J. S. (1992). Using curriculum compacting to challenge the above-average. *Educational Leadership*, *50*, 51–51.

Reis, S. M., Westberg, K. L., Kulikowich, J. M., & Purcell, J. H. (1998). Curriculum compacting outcomes. *Gifted Child Quarterly*, *42*(2), 123–129. DOI: 10.1177/001698629804200206

Renzulli, J. S., & Reis, S. M. (1997). The schoolwide enrichment model: New directions for developing high-end learning. Handbook of gifted education, 2, 136-154.

Renzulli, J. S. (1977). *The enrichment triad model*. Creative Learning Press.

Renzulli, J. S. (1978). What makes giftedness? *Phi Delta Kappan*, *60*(3), 180–184.

Renzulli, J. S., Reis, S. M., & Smith, L. H. (1981). *The revolving door identification model*. Creative Learning Press.

Riehl, M. E. (2016). Feasibility and acceptability of esophageal-directed hypnotherapy for functional heartburn. *Diseases of the Esophagus*, *29*(5), 490–496. PMID: 25824436

Robinson, O. C., & Wright, G. R. T. (2013). The prevalence, types and perceived outcomes of crisis episodes in early adulthood and midlife: A structured retrospective-autobiographical study. *International Journal of Behavioral Development*, *37*(5), 407–416. DOI: 10.1177/0165025413492464

Rocha, L. E., & Debert-Ribeiro, M. (2004). Working conditions, visual fatigue, and mental health among systems analysts in São Paulo, Brazil. *Occupational and Environmental Medicine*, *61*(1), 24–32. DOI: 10.1136/oem.61.1.24 PMID: 14691269

Roja, Z. K. (2013). The effects of a medical hypnotherapy on clothing industry employees suffering from chronic pain. *Journal of Occupational Medicine and Toxicology (London, England)*, *8*, 1–15. PMID: 24066847

Rosendahl, J., Alldredge, C. T., & Haddenhorst, A. (2023). Meta-analytic evidence on the efficacy of hypnosis for mental and somatic health issues: A 20-year perspective. *Frontiers in Psychology, 14*, 1330238. DOI: 10.3389/FPSYG.2023.1330238/BIBTEX PMID: 38268815

Rugulies, R., Madsen, I. E., & Hjarsbech, P. U.. (2022). Work-related stress and risk of mental disorders: A prospective cohort study. *Frontiers in Public Health, 10*, 849310. DOI: 10.3389/fpubh.2022.849310

Ruysschaert, N. (2009). (Self) hypnosis in the prevention of burnout and compassion fatigue for caregivers: Theory and induction. *Contemporary Hypnosis, 26*(3), 159–172.

Sagar, S. S., & Stoeber, J. (2009). Perfectionism, fear of failure, and affective responses to success and failure: The central role of fear of experiencing shame and embarrassment. *Journal of Sport & Exercise Psychology, 31*(5), 602–627. DOI: 10.1123/JSEP.31.5.602 PMID: 20016111

Salovey, P., & Mayer, J. D. (1990). Emotional intelligence. *Imagination, Cognition and Personality, 9*(3), 185–211.

Sauter, S. L., Murphy, L. R., & Hurrell, J. J. (1999). Prevention of work-related psychological disorders: A national strategy proposed by the National Institute for Occupational Safety and Health (NIOSH). *The American Psychologist, 45*(10), 1146–1158. DOI: 10.1037/0003-066X.45.10.1146

Schaufeli, W. B., & Bakker, A. B. (2004). Job demands, job resources, and their relationship with burnout and engagement: A multi-sample study. *Journal of Organizational Behavior, 25*(3), 293–315. DOI: 10.1002/job.248

Schaufeli, W. B., Leiter, M. P., & Maslach, C. (2009). Burnout: 35 years of research and practice. *Career Development International, 14*(3), 204–220. DOI: 10.1108/13620430910966406

Schein, E. H. (2010). *Organizational culture and leadership* (4th ed.). Jossey-Bass.

Science Direct. (2024). *Mindfulness and mental health: Contemporary applications.* https://www.sciencedirect.com

Selye, H. (1976). *The stress of life* (Rev. ed.). McGraw-Hill.

Sevoz-Couche, C., & Laborde, S. (2022). Heart rate variability and slow-paced breathing:when coherence meets resonance. *Neuroscience and Biobehavioral Reviews, 135*, 104576. DOI: 10.1016/j.neubiorev.2022.104576 PMID: 35167847

Sharma, N., & Garg, N. (2024). Workplace spirituality and organisational effectiveness in the Indian higher education sector: Exploring the relationship and mediating role of positive organisational scholarship factors. *International Journal of Indian Culture and Business Management*, *32*(3), 413–439.

Siegrist, J. (1996). Adverse health effects of high-effort/low-reward conditions. *Journal of Occupational Health Psychology*, *1*(1), 27–41. DOI: 10.1037/1076-8998.1.1.27 PMID: 9547031

Silverman, L. K. (2013). *Giftedness 101*. Springer.

Simon, H. A. (1957). *Models of man; social and rational.* https://psycnet.apa.org/record/1958-00363-000

Singh, U. (2016). Organizational trust and organizational citizenship behaviour. *Global Business Review*, *17*(3), 594–609.

Soler, L., Wieber, F., Allamel-Raffin, C., Gangloff, J.-L., Dufour, C., & Trizio, E. (2013). Calibration: A Conceptual Framework Applied to Scientific Practices Which Investigate Natural Phenomena by Means of Standardized Instruments. *Journal for General Philosophy of Science*, *44*(2), 263–317. DOI: 10.1007/s10838-013-9231-7

Sonnentag, S., & Fritz, C. (2015a). Recovery from job stress: The stressor-detachment model as an integrative framework. *Journal of Organizational Behavior*, *36*(S1), S72–S103. DOI: 10.1002/JOB.1924

Sorensen, G. P., Beder, B. M., Prible, C. R., & Pinney, J. B. (1995). Reducing Smoking at the Workplace: Implementing a Smoking Ban and Hypnotherapy. *Journal of Occupational and Environmental Medicine*, *37*(4), 453–460. PMID: 7670901

Spiegel, E. B., Baker, E. L., Daitch, C., Diamond, M. J., & Phillips, M. (2020). Hypnosis and The Therapeutic Relationship: Relational Factors of Hypnosis in Psychotherapy. *The American Journal of Clinical Hypnosis*, *62*(1–2), 118–137. DOI: 10.1080/00029157.2019.1599319 PMID: 31265368

Spiegel, H. (1981). Hypnosis: Myth and reality. *Psychiatric Annals*, *11*(9), 16–23.

Spill. (2024). *Mental health and workplace stress statistics*. Retrieved from https://www.spill.chat/mental-health-statistics/workplace-stress-statistics

Stafrace, S. P. (2004). SELF-ESTEEM, HYPNOSIS AND EGO-ENHANCEMENT. *Australian Journal of Clinical & Experimental Hypnosis*, *32*(1), 1–35.

Stanton, H. E. (1993). Research Note: Alleviation of Performance Anxiety through Hypnotherapy. *Psychology of Music*, *21*(1), 78–82. DOI: 10.1177/030573569302100106

StatPearls. (2024). *Physiology, stress*. In StatPearls [Internet]. National Center for Biotechnology Information. https://www.ncbi.nlm.nih.gov/books/NBK541120/

Steele, C. M., & Aronson, J. (1995). Stereotype threat. *Journal of Personality and Social Psychology, 69*(5), 797–811. DOI: 10.1037/0022-3514.69.5.797 PMID: 7473032

Steenbergen-Hu, S., & Moon, S. M. (2011). The effects of acceleration on high-ability learners: A meta-analysis. *Gifted Child Quarterly, 55*(1), 39–53.

Study.com. (2024). *Consequences of stress at work: Physiological, psychological and behavioral symptoms*. Retrieved from https://study.com/academy/lesson/consequences-of-stress-at-work-physiological-psychological-behavioral-symptoms.html

Sturt, J., Ali, S., Robertson, W., Metcalfe, D., Grove, A., Bourne, C., & Bridle, C. (2012). Neurolinguistic programming: A systematic review of the effects on health outcomes. *The British Journal of General Practice, 62*(604), e757–e764. DOI: 10.3399/bjgp12X658287 PMID: 23211179

Subotnik, R. F., Olszewski-Kubilius, P. E., & Worrell, F. C. (2019). High performance: The central psychological mechanism for talent development.

Subotnik, R. F., Olszewski-Kubilius, P., & Worrell, F. C. (2011). Rethinking giftedness. *Psychological Science in the Public Interest, 12*(1), 3–54. DOI: 10.1177/1529100611418056 PMID: 26168418

Sunkarapalli, G., & Agarwal, T. (n.d.)... *Fear of Failure and Perfectionism in Young Adults., 4*. Advance online publication. DOI: 10.25215/0403.131

Sweet, E., Nandi, A., Adam, E. K., & McDade, T. W. (2013). The high price of debt: Household financial debt and its impact on mental and physical health. *Social Science & Medicine, 91*, 94–100. DOI: 10.1016/j.socscimed.2013.05.009 PMID: 23849243

Talkspace. (2022). *What is stress? Types of stress and stress management techniques*. Retrieved from https://www.talkspace.com/blog/types-of-stress/

Teimouri, L. S. (2024). Comparing the effectiveness of mindfulness-based stress relief group therapy and cognitive-behavioral hypnotherapy on work-family conflict. *Research in Clinical Psychology and Counseling, 13*(2), 127–142.

Tepe, J. (2025, January 7). *Unlocking the Power of NLP, Hypnosis, and Applied Neuroscience*. John Tepe. https://www.johntepe.com/post/unlocking-the-power-of-nlp-hypnosis-and-applied-neuroscience

Thiel, K. J., & Dretsch, M. N. (2011). The basics of the stress response: A historical context and introduction. *The handbook of stress: Neuropsychological effects on the brain*, 1-28.

Thiruvenkadam, T. (2017). Organizational citizenship behavior: Its definitions and dimensions. *GE-International Journal of Management Research*, *5*(5), 46–55.

Tomlinson, C. A., Kaplan, S. N., Renzulli, J. S., Purcell, J. H., Leppien, J. H., Burns, D. E., Strickland, C. A., & Imbeau, M. B. (2002). *The parallel curriculum*. Corwin Press.

Townsend, C. (2022). *What is mastery-based learning?* Mastery Collaborative. https://mastery.org/what-is-mastery-based-learning/

Tyack, D., & Cuban, L. (1995). *Tinkering with utopia: A century of public school reform*.

Uchida, M., & Kawakami, N. (2010). Work-related stress and psychosomatic medicine. *Industrial Health*, *48*(6), 503–516. DOI: 10.2486/indhealth.48.503

UNESCO. (2021). *Reimagining our futures together*. UNESCO.

Upoyo, A. S. (2022). Pilot study of a brief hypnotic induction: Effects on blood pressure, heart rate, and subjective distress in patients diagnosed with hypertension. *The International Journal of Clinical and Experimental Hypnosis*, *70*(1), 83–90. PMID: 34875965

Vaccaro, A., Moore, A., Newman, B. M., & Troiano, P. F. (2024). How Students with Disabilities Cope with Bullying, Stereotypes, Low Expectations and Discouragement. *Journal of Postsecondary Education and Disability*, *37*(2), 99–113.

Valentine, K. E., Milling, L. S., Clark, L. J., & Moriarty, C. L. (2019a). THE EFFICACY OF HYPNOSIS AS A TREATMENT FOR ANXIETY: A META-ANALYSIS. *The International Journal of Clinical and Experimental Hypnosis*, *67*(3), 336–363. DOI: 10.1080/00207144.2019.1613863 PMID: 31251710

Vatou, A. (2025). Examining Resilience, Self-Efficacy and Environmental Chaos Relationship in Early Childhood Education and Care Teachers. *Psychological Inquiry*, *7*(3), 73.

Vygotsky, L. S. (1978). *Mind in society: The development of higher psychological processes*. Harvard University Press.

Wall, C. L. (2005). *The courage to trust: A guide to building deep and lasting relationships*. New Harbinger Publications. Cassidy, S. (2015). Resilience building in students: The role of academic self-efficacy. *Frontiers in psychology, 6*, 1781. Nayak, S., Budhwar, P., & Malik, A. (2025). Technostress of HR professionals: the darker implication of remote work transformations. *The International Journal of Human Resource Management*, 1-46. Fry, L. W. (2008). Spiritual leadership: State-of-the-art and future directions for theory, research, and practice. In *Spirituality in business: Theory, practice, and future directions* (pp. 106–124). Palgrave Macmillan US.

Walsham, W., Perlman, T. T., & Sihotang, D. (2023). Unraveling the threads: A comprehensive exploration of the interplay be-tween social isolation and academic stress among students. *Law and Economics*, *17*(3), 237–255.

Wang, L., & Chen, C. J. (2025). Factors Affecting Student Academic Performance: A Systematic Review. [IJonSE]. *International Journal on Studies in Education*, *7*(1).

Watson, J. C., Goldman, R. N., & Greenberg, L. S. (2011). Humanistic and experiential theories of psychotherapy. In *History of psychotherapy: Continuity and change* (2nd ed., pp. 141–172). American Psychological Association., DOI: 10.1037/12353-005

Webb, J. T., Amend, E. R., Webb, N. E., Goerss, J., Beljan, P., & Olenchak, F. R. (2005). *Misdiagnosis and dual diagnoses of gifted children and adults*. Great Potential Press.

Weiner, I. B., Stricker, G., & Widiger, T. A. (2012). *Clinical Psychology*. Handbook of Psychology. John Wiley & Sons.

Weissman, D. G., & Mendes, W. B. (2021). Correlation of sympathetic and parasympathetic nervous system activity during rest and acute stress tasks. *International Journal of Psychophysiology : Official Journal of the International Organization of Psychophysiology*, *162*, 60–68. DOI: 10.1016/j.ijpsycho.2021.01.015 PMID: 33561515

Wibawa, , A. P., Bihari Dash, & Kurniawan, F. (2024). Advancements in natural language processing: Implications, challenges, and future directions. *Telematics and Informatics Reports*, *16*, 100173. DOI: 10.1016/j.teler.2024.100173

Wiliam, D. (2011). *Embedded formative assessment* (2nd ed.). Solution Tree Press.

Williamson, B., & Eynon, R. (2020). Historical threads of AI in education. *Learning, Media and Technology*, *45*(3), 223–235. DOI: 10.1080/17439884.2020.1798995

Wilson, T. D. (2004). *Strangers to Ourselves : Discovering the Adaptive Unconscious By Timothy D. Wilson Read Ebooks Book details Language : English*. https://www.hup.harvard.edu/books/9780674013827

World Health Organization. (2022). *Mental health at work: Policy brief.* WHO. Retrieved from https://www.who.int/publications/i/item/9789240053052

World Health Organization. (2024). *Mental health at work.* https://www.who.int/news-room/fact-sheets/detail/mental-health-at-work

Yapko, M. D. (2012). Trancework: An introduction to the practice of clinical hypnosis, Fourth edition. *Trancework: An Introduction to the Practice of Clinical Hypnosis, Fourth Edition*, 1–638. https://doi.org/DOI: 10.4324/9780203126271

Yapko, M. D. (2003). *Trancework: An introduction to the practice of clinical hypnosis* (3rd ed.). Brunner-Routledge.

Zaharia, C., Reiner, M., & Schütz, P. (2015). Evidence-based Neuro Linguistic Psychotherapy: A meta-analysis. *Psychiatria Danubina, 27*(4), 355–363. PMID: 26609647

Zahm, S. G., & Gold, E. K. (2002). Gestalt Therapy. In Hersen, M., & Sledge, W. (Eds.), *Encyclopedia of Psychotherapy* (pp. 863–872). Academic Press., DOI: 10.1016/B0-12-343010-0/00105-7

Zhang, Y., Yang, X.-X., Luo, J.-Y., Liang, M., Li, N., Tao, Q., Ma, L.-J., & Li, X.-M. (2022). Randomized trial estimating effects of hypnosis versus progressive muscle relaxation on medical students' test anxiety and attentional bias. *World Journal of Psychiatry, 12*(6), 801. DOI: 10.5498/WJP.V12.I6.801 PMID: 35978973

Zhu, P., & Tingting, W. (2025). A mixed methods exploration of social networks, self-efficacy, and life satisfaction in rural Chinese high schools. *Frontiers in Psychology, 16,* 1501328

Zucker, T. L., Samuelson, K. W., Muench, F., Greenberg, M. A., & Gevirtz, R. N. (2020). Mindful hypnotherapy to reduce stress and increase mindfulness: A randomized controlled pilot study. *The International Journal of Clinical and Experimental Hypnosis, 68*(2), 169–186. DOI: 10.1080/00207144.2020.1690494

About the Contributors

Manjunath B. R. possesses a rich professional history spanning 16 years, blending 5 years of corporate expertise in the fields of Investment Banking and Business Analytics with 11 years devoted to academic pursuits. His core specialization lies in Applied Finance, with a keen focus on Applied Finance and Business Analytics. He is an active member of the Board of Studies (BoS) for Visvesvaraya Technological University (VTU), a Public University, India for Online Degree Programmes of UG, PG, and PG Diploma. Currently, Dr. Manjunath is serving as a Professor and Director of Academic Affairs at the Faculty of Management Sciences, School of Business Management at Shoolini University. During his corporate tenure, Dr. Manjunath navigated roles of significance, contributing notably to various renowned organizations. His professional journey included pivotal positions at esteemed entities such as JP Morgan Chase in the Philippines, where he played a pivotal role in the Unit Unlisted Trust (UUT) migration project. Subsequently, he contributed his expertise to Fidelity Business Services Pvt. Ltd., focusing on Analytics and Data Services (ADS). His career also encompassed impactful roles at Wipro-UBS as a Corporate Action Specialist and at Thomson Reuters, where he began as a Research Trainee. His commitment extended to consultancy and advisory capacities. He served as a Technical Consultant in Banking and Financial Services (BFS) for a World Bank Project, conducted under the sponsorship of Ernst & Young (EY). He was actively engaged in the implementation of the Leveraging ICT for Growth, Employment, and Governance Project (LICT), initiated by the Bangladesh Computer Council (BCC) under the umbrella of the Government of Bangladesh. More recently, Dr. Manjunath served as a consultant and Finance Faculty for the Nest Academy of Management Education in Dubai, contributing significantly to curriculum development and knowledge dissemination across various UK Qualifications in new-age careers. As a Finance mentor (Online), he engaged with the Australian Business School and Victoria University in Australia. His commitment to academia is evident through tenures at esteemed educational institutions including Bapuji B-Schools, Vidyavardhaka College of Engineering, International School of Management Excellence, as the Professor and Head at the GM Institute of Technology, Department of Studies in Management, and as a Professor of Finance and Business Analytics at Kirloskar Institute of Management. Dr. Manjunath's academic contributions extend to the presentation and publication of 85 research papers and working papers across national and international conferences and journal publications. An expert facilitator, he has conducted numerous workshops and training sessions on advanced tools such as Microsoft Advanced Excel for Managers, R-Statistical Programming Language, and Tableau – Data Visualization for Data Science, both domestically and on global platforms.

Syed Mohammad Haider Rizvi is a distinguished academician, psychologist, and development professional with over two decades of experience spanning education, governance, research, and program development. Currently serving as Professor and Head of the Centre of Psychology and Behavioural Sciences at Shoolini University, he has previously held key advisory roles, including Senior Advisor at Piramal University and Knowledge Partner for the Government of West Bengal. Dr. Rizvi holds a PhD in Psychology from Jawaharlal Nehru University and a Post-Doctorate in Communication for International Development from Sheffield Hallam University, UK. His expertise lies in designing and implementing large-scale educational and developmental programs, conducting impact assessments, and developing strategic policies. He has led numerous projects in areas such as human development, governance reform, competency-based assessment, and behavioral studies. His contributions extend to capacity building, strategic communication, and knowledge management in collaboration with government agencies, NGOs, and international organizations. A prolific researcher and author, Dr. Rizvi has published extensively in national and international journals, contributed chapters to edited books, and presented papers at global conferences. His research interests include stress and coping mechanisms, psycho-social behavior, governance systems, and ICT for development. He has been honored with prestigious awards, including the Manthan South Asia Award for ICT Innovation, and has been a panelist and resource person at numerous academic and professional forums. Dr. Rizvi's work is driven by his commitment to fostering sustainable development, empowering marginalized communities, and enhancing educational and governance frameworks. With his multidisciplinary approach, he continues to shape policy, inspire innovation, and advance knowledge in psychology and social development.

Jeni Kakadiya is a dedicated psychologist and hypnotherapist based in Rajkot, Gujarat, with expertise in psychological counseling, hypnotherapy, and mental health research. Currently pursuing a PhD in Psychology at Shoolini University, she has a strong academic foundation, including a Master's in Psychology and a PG Diploma in Clinical Hypnosis. Jeni has significant experience in counseling, teaching, and research, with a focus on topics like psychological well-being, life satisfaction, and work-life quality. Known for her empathetic approach and commitment to continuous learning, she actively participates in conferences and contributes to advancements in mental health care.

***

Sunil Kumar, currently an Associate Professor at Faculty of Management Sciences, Shoolini University, possesses extensive academic and research experience. With a background in Business Administration, Sunil's research endeavors span multiple domains, including human resource management, e-training, and the application of artificial intelligence in business. His prolific contributions are evidenced by numerous research papers, book chapters, copyrights, and patents. Dr. Kumar has a knack for teaching with expertise in subjects like HR Analytics, Talent Management, Industrial Psychology, and more. He has also successfully guided PhD students and actively contributes to various academic administrative roles. Dr. Kumar's vast research landscape includes topics like AI-based chatbots in recruitment, e-training impact, and more. His papers have been published in esteemed journals like Journal of Workplace Learning and International Journal of Law and Management. Moreover, he has authored books and edited volumes touching upon themes related to the contemporary business environment. Dr. Sunil has been a dynamic participant in numerous workshops, ranging from data analysis to stress

Fabian N. Murrieta-Rico received B.Eng. and M.Eng. degrees from Instituto Tecnológico de Mexicali (ITM) in 2004 and 2013 respectively. In 2017, he received his PhD in Materials Physics at Centro de Investigación Científica y Educación Superior de Ensenada (CICESE). He has worked as an automation engineer, systems designer, as a university professor, and as postdoctoral researcher at Facultad de Ingeniería, Arquitectura y Diseño from Universidad Autónoma de Baja California (UABC) and at the Centro de Nanociencias y Nanotecnología from Universidad Nacional Autónoma de México (CNyN-UNAM), currently he works as professor at the Universidad Politécnica de Baja California. His research has been published in different journals and presented at international conferences since 2009. He has served as reviewer for different journals, some of them include IEEE Transactions on Industrial Electronics, IEEE Transactions on Instrumentation, Measurement and Sensor Review. His research interests are focused on the field of time and frequency metrology, the design of wireless sensor networks, automated systems and highly sensitive chemical detectors.

Jesús Heriberto Orduño-Osuna obtained a Bachelor's degree in Mechatronics Engineering from the Universidad Politécnica de Baja California (UPBC) and a Master's degree in Computational Sciences and Applied Mathematics from Universidad Internacional de La Rioja, Mexico (UNIR Mexico), where he developed projects in application and research in the area of Machine Learning applied to dynamic systems. He is partially studying a Master's degree in Strategic Administration. He has worked as an engineer in the industry, mainly in the Post-Harvest Automation industry as well as in the manufacturing sector, focusing primarily on automation processes, vision systems, and industrial robotics, among others. Currently, he is a part-time lecturer at the Universidad Politécnica de Baja California and the Universidad del Valle de México, teaching courses in Mechatronics, Manufacturing, Energy, and Computing, contributing to the education of engineers with an innovative and technological focus. His research interests are focused on Machine Learning, Automation, and control of industrial processes, Microcontrollers, and digital signal processing.

Maria E. Raygoza-L holds a Ph.D. in Chemistry and Energy from the Engineering Institute of Universidad Autónoma de Baja California and a Bachelor's degree in Industrial Engineering with a specialization in Manufacturing. She currently serves as a full-time professor and researcher at Universidad Politécnica de Baja California and as a Subject Professor at Universidad Autónoma de Baja California, specializing in Energy Engineering and Renewable Energies. With extensive experience in industry, her research interests encompass renewable energy, energy efficiency, environmental studies, energy management systems, and the integration of public policies for sustainable development. She is currently pursuing a second bachelor's degree in Psychology, further broadening her academic horizons.

U. Pratibha is a Faculty in Psychology at the Ali Yavar Jung National Institute of Speech and Hearing Disabilities (Divyangjan) [AYJNISHD],Mumbai with a strong academic foundation and a passion for working in the field of mental health and developmental psychology. She specializes in childhood developmental disorders, behaviour modification, hypnosis and life skills training, combining academic insight with practical interventions to support diverse populations. Currently pursuing her Ph.D. in Psychology from Amity University, Maharashtra, Pratibha holds an M.Phil in Clinical Psychology from Sri Ramachandra Medical College and Research Institute (SRMC & RI), Chennai, and a Postgraduate Diploma in Clinical Hypnosis from CHARUSAT University, Gujarat. She earned her Master's degree in Psychology, with a specialization in Clinical Psychology, from the University of Delhi. Beyond her academic and professional pursuits, Pratibha enjoys reading, writing, travelling, and photography, which enrich her perspective as both an educator and clinician.

Index

L

M

N

O

P

R

S

T

W

Y

Z

www.ingramcontent.com/pod-product-compliance
Lightning Source LLC
LaVergne TN
LVHW081531300926
849161LV00006B/1381
* 9 7 9 8 3 3 7 3 2 3 1 7 6 *